The Randstad

The Randstad metropolitan region encompassing Amsterdam, The Hague, Rotterdam and Utrecht in the western Netherlands is regarded worldwide as a model of a 'successful' polycentric metropolis. It is widely cited as an example of how a region of interconnected small cities can effectively compete globally by providing complementary functions which together match the power of large monocentric cities. The methods of strategic spatial planning, regional design and strategic projects that are said to underpin this polycentric metropolis are used as models for practitioners and students around the world.

But is this high reputation deserved? Does the Randstad really function as a polycentric metropolis? The operation of the Randstad as a polycentric networked region is controversial both in terms of the actual strength of relations between its component parts, and the value of promoting polycentricity in policy. What are the costs and benefits of a Randstad metropolis? Does polycentricity improve the performance of the region in economic, social and environmental terms? How has the polycentric metropolis evolved and what part is played by its delta location? Has spatial planning made a difference in the form and operation of the region today? How will this spatial configuration fare in the face of the climate crisis and need to create healthy cities and regions? Is there benefit in pursuing the idea of a polycentric metropolis in government policy and action, and how?

These questions are of critical interest within the Netherlands but experience in the Randstad offers valuable insights to many other complex urban regions around the world. This book will provide a critical analysis of the Randstad and lessons for strategic planning in other metropolitan regions.

Wil Zonneveld is Professor of Urban and Regional Planning at Delft University of Technology, the Netherlands, and leader of the Section Spatial Planning and Strategy, Department of Urbanism in the Faculty of Architecture and Built Environment. He published extensively on Dutch and European spatial planning, with a particular emphasis on the conceptualization and design of space and territory. He is co-editor of the *Routledge Handbook of Regional Design*.

Vincent Nadin is Emeritus Professor of Spatial Planning and Strategy and former Head of the Department of Urbanism in the Faculty of Architecture and the Built Environment, TU Delft. He is also Visiting Professor at South China University of Technology School of Architecture. He is joint author with the late Barry Cullingworth of the leading textbook *Town and Country Planning in the UK*, co-author of *European Spatial Planning and Territorial Cooperation* and Editor-in-Chief of the Routledge international peer-reviewed journal *Planning Practice and Research*.

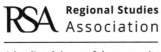 **Regional Studies Association**
A leading & impactful community

 **Routledge**
Taylor & Francis Group

Regions and Cities

Series Editor in Chief
Joan Fitzgerald, *Northeastern University, USA*

Editors
Roberta Capello, *Politecnico di Milano, Italy*
Rob Kitchin, *Maynooth University, Ireland*
Jörg Knieling, *HafenCity University Hamburg, Germany*
Nichola Lowe, *University of North Carolina at Chapel Hill, USA*

In today's globalised, knowledge-driven and networked world, regions and cities have assumed heightened significance as the interconnected nodes of economic, social and cultural production, and as sites of new modes of economic and territorial governance and policy experimentation. This book series brings together incisive and critically engaged international and interdisciplinary research on this resurgence of regions and cities, and should be of interest to geographers, economists, sociologists, political scientists and cultural scholars, as well as to policy-makers involved in regional and urban development.

For more information on the Regional Studies Association, visit www.regionalstudies.org

There is a **30% discount** available to RSA members on books in the *Regions and Cities* series, and other subject-related Taylor and Francis books and e-books including Routledge titles. To order, simply email Luke McNicholas (Luke.McNicholas@tandf.co.uk), or phone on +44 (0)20 701 77545 and declare your RSA membership. You can also visit the series page at www.routledge.com/Regions-and-Cities/book-series/RSA and use the discount code: **RSA225**

For more information about this series, please visit: www.routledge.com/Regions-and-Cities/book-series/RSA

The Randstad

A Polycentric Metropolis

**Edited by
Wil Zonneveld and
Vincent Nadin**

Routledge
Taylor & Francis Group

LONDON AND NEW YORK

First published 2021
by Routledge
2 Park Square, Milton Park, Abingdon, Oxon OX14 4RN

and by Routledge
52 Vanderbilt Avenue, New York, NY 10017

Routledge is an imprint of the Taylor & Francis Group, an informa business

British Library Cataloguing-in-Publication Data
A catalogue record for this book is available from the British Library

Library of Congress Cataloging-in-Publication Data
Names: Zonneveld, Wil, editor. | Nadin, Vincent, editor.
Title: The Randstad : a polycentric metropolis / edited by Wil Zonneveld and Vincent Nadin.
Description: Abingdon, Oxon ; New York, NY : Routledge, 2021. | Series: Regions and cities | Includes bibliographical references and index.
Identifiers: LCCN 2020039904 (print) | LCCN 2020039905 (ebook)
Subjects: LCSH: Regional planning–Netherlands—Randstad. | City planning—Netherlands—Randstad. | Metropolitan areas–Netherlands.
Classification: LCC HT395.N42 R367 2021 (print) | LCC HT395. N42 (ebook) | DDC 307.1/21609492—dc23
LC record available at https://lccn.loc.gov/2020039904
LC ebook record available at https://lccn.loc.gov/2020039905

ISBN: 978-0-415-82609-9 (hbk)
ISBN: 978-0-367-69964-2 (pbk)
ISBN: 978-0-203-38334-6 (ebk)

Typeset in Bembo
by codeMantra

Contents

Figures

Tables

Contributors

Luuk Boelens is full Professor of Spatial Planning at the Centre for Mobility and Spatial Planning of Ghent University. His current research interests deal with the flat ontology and the actor relational approach of spatial planning. Recent research projects focus on a broad area of practical applications: from radical action planning to the governance of mobility, from the coevolutionary differences in planning-history to a cinematic view on planning, from differential mainport policies, towards a tacit focus on the economic geography in major metropolitan delta areas in the world. Future research will focus on an actor relational agenda for Europe and the importance of informal institutional settings in planning.

Nikki Brand is a postdoc researcher in the field of integrated design of infrastructure at Delft University of Technology, specifically the 'Delft Deltas, Infrastructures & Mobility Initiative' (DIMI). She holds Master's Degrees in Human Geography (University of Amsterdam) and Heritage Studies (Free University of Amsterdam). Her 2012 PhD focused on how the allocation of competitive advantages throughout the centuries altered the urban hierarchy within the area currently known as the Randstad.

Martijn Burger is Academic Director at the Erasmus Happiness Economics Research Organisation (EHERO) and Associate professor of Industrial and Regional Economics in the Department of Applied Economics at the Erasmus University Rotterdam. Most of his current research focuses on happiness economics and urban and regional economics.

Rosa Donoso Gomez is the academic advisor of the participation section of the National Research Agenda for Sustainable Urban Development of Ecuador (which is closely connected to the New Urban Agenda signed in Quito at the 2016 UN Habitat III conference), part of the national Sustainable Intermediate Cities Programme. Her research interests include housing and urban planning policies and comparative research focusing on affordable condominium housing in Latin America.

Marja Elsinga is full Professor of Housing Institutions and Governance at Delft University of Technology and Visiting Professor at the College of

Architecture and Urban Planning at Tongji University (Shanghai) where she teaches housing policy for urban planners. She has led several comparative housing research projects for the European Commission. The topics she covers are risks of home ownership, housing as a pension and the future of social housing in Europe. She was associate editor of Elsevier's Encyclopedia of Housing and Home, and holds editorial positions at the journals *Housing and Society* and *Housing Theory and Society.*

David Evers is a senior researcher at the Netherlands Environmental Assessment Agency (PBL), Assistant Professor in planning at the University of Amsterdam and the Netherlands ESPON contact point. He has published on Dutch spatial planning and urbanization, retail development, planning law and policy, new institutionalism and governance and European policy impacts.

Harry van der Heijden is Associate Professor of Housing Systems in the Department of Management in the Built Environment, Faculty of Architecture and the Built Environment, TU Delft. His research interests are housing policies, housing markets and comparative housing research, with a focus on housing production and the position of different tenures within national housing systems.

Carola Hein is full Professor of the History of Architecture and Urban Planning at Delft University of Technology. Her book publications include *The Capital of Europe, Rebuilding Urban Japan after 1945, Port Cities,* the *Routledge Handbook of Planning History,* and *Adaptive Structures for Water Heritage.* Among other major grants, she received a Guggenheim Fellowship to pursue research on the Global Architecture of Oil and an Alexander von Humboldt Fellowship to investigate large-term urban transformation in Hamburg in an international context. She currently works on the transmission of planning ideas among port cities and within landscapes of oil.

Maurits de Hoog is an urbanist, educated at Delft University of Technology (1973–1981). He had his own practice till 1996. From that moment on he has been working in the Planning Department of the City of Amsterdam. From 2008 until 2012 he combined practice in Amsterdam with a Professorship in Metropolitan and Regional Design in the Faculty of Architecture of Delft University of Technology. In 2013 and 2014 he was the startup manager of AMS: the Amsterdam Institute for Advanced Metropolitan Solutions (founded by TU Delft, Wageningen UR and MIT Boston).

Fransje Hooimeijer is Associate Professor at TU Delft and is specialized in system integration of technical conditions in urban design. In her research and teaching she takes a perspective on the city as a technical construction and investigates how these conditions can be utilized better in urban design, and how systems can adapt to new technologies. The focus lies on design and planning processes and how, by representation of the subsurface as engine room of the city, they can be made climate proof, energy neutral, more biodiverse and of better spatial quality.

Wouter Jacobs is Senior Researcher at the Centre for Urban, Port and Transport Economics (UPT) of Erasmus University Rotterdam. His research interests include economic geography and regional development, commodity trade, maritime business services and port city management and evolution. Wouter Jacobs is currently active as Academic Director of the Executive Programme 'Leadership Commodity Trade and Supply Networks' at UPT and as Academic Director 'Study Abroad Programme Maritime Studies', Nanyang Technological University in Singapore.

Evert Meijers is Associate Professor in Economic Geography at the Faculty of Geosciences, Department of Human Geography and Spatial Planning, Utrecht University. He also is a trustee of the Urban Studies Foundation. His research interests include the evolution of the spatial organisation of territories and cities and how this organisation affects social well-being, environmental sustainability and economic competitiveness, the rise of city network externalities next to agglomeration externalities, and the growth and decline of cities and regions more generally.

Han Meyer is Emeritus Professor of Urban Design at Delft University of Technology. His main focus in research and teaching is on the fundamentals of urbanism and on 'delta urbanism', which pays special attention to the search for a new balance between urbanization processes and climate change in vulnerable deltaic territories. Recent books are *Urbanizing Deltas in Transition* (co-edited with Steffen Nijhuis, Techne Press, 2014) and *The State of the Delta. Engineering, urban development and nation building in the Netherlands* (VanTilt, 2017). A new book is *Urbanism: Fundamentals and Prospects* (Boom, 2020).

Vincent Nadin is Emeritus Professor of Spatial Planning and Strategy and former Head of the Department of Urbanism in the Faculty of Architecture and the Built Environment, TU Delft. He is also Visiting Professor at South China University of Technology School of Architecture. He is co-author of *European Spatial Planning and Territorial Cooperation* (2010), joint author with the late Barry Cullingworth of the leading textbook *Town and Country Planning in the UK,* and Editor-in-Chief of the Routledge international peer-reviewed journal *Planning Practice and Research.*

Frank van Oort is Professor of Urban and Regional Economics at the Erasmus School of Economics, Department of Applied Economics. He is also Academic Director of the Institute of Housing and Urban Development Studies (IHS) of Erasmus University Rotterdam, and Fellow at the Tinbergen Institute.

Jan Ritsema van Eck is a human geographer, educated at Utrecht University, now working as a senior researcher at the Netherlands Environmental Assessment Agency (PBL). He has published on mobility, accessibility, functional relations in urban networks, urbanization, land use change, consequences of demographic developments and long-term regional scenarios for the Netherlands.

Joost Schrijnen was Programme Director for the Southwestern Delta in the context of the Dutch Delta Programme (2008–2012), Director Spatial Strategy Almere 2030 (2007–2008), Director Territory and Mobility of the province South Holland (2002–2007) and Board Member of the Rotterdam Urban Design and Housing Agency (1992–2001). He was also Professor of Urban Design of City and Region and Professor of Professional Practice Strategy and Planning at the Faculty of Architecture and the Built Environment of TU Delft (2003–2012). Since 2012 he is an independent spatial management consultant.

Marjolein Spaans is Assistant Professor of Urban Development Management at the Faculty of Architecture and the Built Environment of TU Delft (Department of Management in the Built Environment). She holds a Master's degree in Landscape Planning from Wageningen University and a PhD degree in Urban and Regional Planning from TU Delft. Her research concerns a broad field of work with themes including urban and regional development, spatial governance, international comparison of planning systems, integrated area development and resilience. She has been involved as coordinator or director of a number of inter-faculty and inter-university educational programmes.

Dominic Stead is Professor of Land Use and Transport Planning at Aalto University, Associate Professor of Urban and Regional Development at TU Delft, and Honorary Research Fellow at University College London. His research interests include comparative urban and regional governance and policy transfer. He is an editorial board member of the *European Journal of Transport and Infrastructure Research, European Planning Studies, Journal of Planning Education and Research, Planning Practice and Research,* and *Urban Research and Practice.*

Jan Vogelij is a planning practitioner, active in several European countries. He focuses on the effectiveness of planning for society's future. His 2015 PhD dissertation articulates the importance of sharing ownership for strategic planning's effectiveness through multi-actor/disciplinary co-designing. Jan Vogelij chaired the Dutch association of planners (BNSP) and is a former President of the European Council of Spatial Planners (ECTP).

Ries van der Wouden is Senior Researcher at the Netherlands Environmental Assessment Agency (PBL). He received his MSc and PhD in

Political Science at the University of Amsterdam. His main interest is in the interaction between physical urban structures, urban development and spatial policy. He conducted a number of studies evaluating the effectiveness of spatial planning. He has published on urban development, spatial planning, policy evaluation and political philosophy.

Wil Zonneveld is full Professor of Urban and Regional Planning in the Department of Urbanism, Faculty of Architecture and the Built Environment, TU Delft. The subject of his 1991 PhD thesis was the conceptualisation of space and territory in Dutch regional and national planning. This subject has been addressed many times since then, extending analyses to include transnational and European levels of scale, with a strong emphasis on visualisation and connections with governance capacity.

Acknowledgements

We would like to express our thanks to the authors for their contributions, for readily accepting our recommendations for editing and for their patience in waiting for the full collection to come together. Verena Balz, Dominic Stead and Bas Waterhout were involved in early discussions about this text and provided valuable comments. We are grateful to our editor at Routledge, Chrissy Mandizha, and the series editor, Natalie Tomlinson, for their encouragement and unwavering support. At the start of this project we had very helpful comments from a number of reviewers of the proposal. We hope they are pleased to find that some of their comments have been acted on and trust they will understand where we were not able to follow them up.

Wil Zonneveld and Vincent Nadin

Part I

Introduction

1 Introducing the Randstad

A polycentric metropolis

Vincent Nadin and Wil Zonneveld

Introduction

The Randstad is a cluster of relatively medium–sized and small cities in the western Netherlands that encircles an expanse of largely open land. It is undoubtedly an important urban region, hosting in an area of about 7,000 km^2, Europe's largest seaport, third busiest airport, second largest Internet Exchange, and about 7 million people. But *the Randstad* is much more than this. Since the 1960s, it has acquired distinction as the archetypal polycentric metropolis, an integrated urban ring around a *Green Heart,* with the status of a world-class metropolitan region. There is a presumption too, that government has played an influential role in strengthening the polycentricity of the region, especially through its renowned capability in spatial planning.

But the reality of the polycentric Randstad as opposed to the idea is controversial, as is the role of spatial planning. Do the interconnections between the four main cities – Amsterdam, The Hague, Rotterdam, and Utrecht – and the many smaller settlements in-between function as an integrated polycentric region? Does the economic and social performance of the combined whole of the Randstad add up to more than the sum of its parts? Advocates point to the apparent complementarity of the main cities with a tendency for business and financial functions to be centred in Amsterdam, port and logistics in Rotterdam, governance and international justice in The Hague, and research and development in Utrecht. Critics draw attention to the relatively limited flows of commuters between the cities, and the concentration of the daily urban flows within the individual city-regions, which they argue operate independently.

Naturally, the truth lies somewhere between these opposing views. This book reviews the evidence on both the idea and the reality of the Randstad polycentric metropolis. In this introduction we explain the reasons for producing the book and our questions; elaborate our understanding of the notion of a polycentric metropolis; sketch the key characteristics of the Randstad; and preview its history of spatial development and planning as an orientation for the chapters that follow. But much has been said about the Randstad in the past so why should we take up this task again now?

We know from our work at Delft University of Technology with its highly international community of staff and students that there is a wide and growing interest in the experience of the Netherlands in managing spatial development to resolve competing land use demands in congested and vulnerable environments. Metropolitan planning authorities across the world are exploring the potential of polycentricity to assist in creating more prosperous, environmentally sustainable, and socially just regions. They see the Netherlands, and specifically the Randstad, as a source of inspiration. The Randstad is recognised as an exemplary case – true or not – of effective territorial governance in a polycentric region.

In Europe, the idea of polycentric functional regions is well established at city, region and transnational scales, having first been promoted as a policy option in the late 1990s (CSD, 1999). The aim then was primarily to spatially 'balance' urban development and economic opportunity and to foster better relations between urban and rural areas. About the same time, it became clear that large metropolitan city-regions are the focal point in global international economic competition, and that they tend to be more successful where they have a strong concentration and diversity of skills and services. This condition is delivered by large monocentric cities and their hinterlands, but it might also be delivered by a cluster of cities acting in concert. Thus, regional and local governments took up the polycentricity concept with the primary aim to create an integrated urban cluster with combined weight that would have competitive advantage in international competition, combined with the advantage of accessible metropolitan landscapes due to its spatial structure.

Since the 1990s the importance of polycentricity as a mechanism for creating critical economic and social mass in urban and regional development in European regions has not diminished. Further encouragement and measures to capitalise on the huge potential for strengthening the competitiveness of urban regions through policies for polycentricity will feature in the forthcoming *EU Territorial Reference Framework* (ESPON, 2020) as well as in the draft European *Territorial Agenda 2030* (TA 2030, 2019). Elsewhere in the world, especially in south-east Asia and Latin America, policies for polycentricity have been taken up vigorously, in part where there are clusters of cities, but also as a way forward for huge monocentric agglomerations. In China, strengthening polycentricity within and between cities is a national policy, and an explicit objective of the strategic spatial plans of most cities, including Beijing (Liu and Wang, 2016). It is not surprising therefore that policy makers should continue to look to the Randstad for evidence of the value of polycentricity where it has been promoted in various ways since the 1950s.

However, anecdotally, we find that there is often a misunderstanding about the performance of the polycentric metropolis of the Randstad and the role of spatial planning in creating it. The apparent uniformly good quality of urban development, infrastructure, natural environment and public realm, together with the relatively high level of stability in the governance and economy of the Netherlands, may give a false impression. There is a view in the Netherlands that foreigners see the Randstad through rose-tinted glasses. The views from within the country on the reality and value of a polycentric Randstad tend to be more sceptical. This is not to undermine the achievements over 70 years, but to say that a critical but constructive assessment would be helpful, the ingredients of which this book seeks to provide.

The Randstad and polycentric regions generally are not only vehicles to create critical economic mass. Cooperation among otherwise discrete cities also provides the platform necessary to deal with other pressing challenges. The economic performance criterion is today joined by other goals and priorities on which sustained prosperity depends. This change may be particularly evident in the Netherlands, where the concentration of people, economic output, and social infrastructure lies on land mostly below sea level. Metropolitan regions are in a crucial position to address many other concerns: protecting critical natural capital, strengthening resilience to risks including flooding, mitigating climate change, providing good quality shelter for all, designing environments that are sensitive to the needs of an ageing population, integrating migrants into society, managing urban-rural relations, shaping settlement patterns to avoid unnecessary conversion of open land, and more. And in 2020, the COVID-19 crisis gave to the world a very sharp reminder of the significance of the living environment in cities and regions for the maintenance of the health of their people, and of the importance of building resilient communities, cities and regions that can quickly respond to crises. There is no doubt that the aftermath of COVID-19 will present great tests for territorial governance as city and regional actors reform their objectives and policies in light of changing global and local conditions.

The contributions here provide a platform of understanding that can be employed in weighing the advantages and disadvantages of the spatial form and governance of the Randstad polycentric metropolis for these urgent questions. How government and key players take up these challenges in the future urban development of the Randstad and other metropolitan regions will have critical consequences for their citizens. They should be informed by a review of the origins, performance and likely future of this polycentric metropolis. The chapters in this book update evidence across a number of themes and disciplines to explain the historical conditions giving rise to the Randstad and its later evolution; they review the chequered history of the governance of the Randstad polycentric metropolis as it is has come and gone in national policy; they present competing views of the value of the Randstad as a regional planning concept in the past and for the future; and they review its practical impact on the performance of the region and the Netherlands as a whole while offering a balanced view on the effectiveness of planning. Decision makers around the world will continue to look to the Netherlands for creative examples of regional spatial development and governance, and we hope will benefit from this critical review of the evidence.

In sum, we present this book to provide sources of evidence, but also critical analysis and understanding of a complex global metropolitan region, and through this, possible lessons for strategic planning in other metropolitan regions. We have four main questions that are addressed to varying degrees by the following chapters and to which we return in the conclusion.

- How has the spatial configuration of the Randstad evolved, and what has been the contribution of deliberate societal intervention versus the natural conditions of the delta?
- Does the polycentric Randstad metropolis have real substance in reality in terms of the whole being more than a collection of parts, or is it no more than an idea promoted for professional and political reasons?
- What are the advantages and disadvantages of the Randstad's spatial configuration for meeting economic, environmental and social challenges, for the needs of business, and for the lives of its citizens?
- What is the outlook for the Randstad as a policy concept in the context of the government's competing needs to improve resilience in the vulnerable delta setting, and to meet demands for further urban development and transformation?

Polycentricity and the metropolitan region

What is polycentricity and how would we know if a region is polycentric and if it has delivered the intended benefits? The central notion is that proximate cities share functions, services and labour between them, and combine their complementary strengths in a collaborative way. The cities accrue benefits in terms of their economic standing and opportunities for citizens because they 'borrow size' from the others (Burger *et al.*, 2015; Meijers and Burger, 2017) and that integration between cities in a cohesive urban system improves economic performance of the whole (Meijers *et al.*, 2017). Polycentricity has been a significant concept in European spatial planning since the 1990s, indeed it has been argued that it is central to a 'new European vocabulary' of spatial planning, being 'sufficiently vague to serve as receptacles for the wide range of perspectives' (Gløersen *et al.*, 2007: 418). It may be vague, but the primary purpose has always been clear, to enable regions of dispersed urban centres to compete more effectively in the global economy. Some 'perspectives' may give priority to other objectives too, for example, increased polycentricity may reduce unnecessary duplication of services and inefficient use of land and create more opportunities for citizens in terms of employment, services (including metropolitan landscapes) and social life.

Achieving polycentricity requires capacity in sub-national government to share and enable flows, which, in turn, needs hard and soft infrastructure interventions and shared governance of some functions in the region. Government administrations rarely operate at a scale that enables them to provide the necessary cooperation. Establishing statutory institutions that combine city governments is difficult, and in most cases probably unnecessary, but some platform or platforms for sharing and integrating policy and investment are a prerequisite for pursuing polycentricity. In Europe, since the 1990s there has been a proliferation of special planning areas for functional planning regions, or soft spaces, that cut across formal administrative jurisdictions (Allmendinger *et al.*, 2015a,b). They operate at different scales for many purposes, but include many planning initiatives to strengthen the polycentric attributes of regions. To some extent they provide a 'metagovernance' for the region that overcomes the limitations of fixed territoriality and creates conditions for combining different forms and scales of governance arrangements in smaller units, including their spatial strategy making (Allmendinger and Haughton, 2009).

Spaans and Zonneveld (2015) describe the Randstad and the Green Heart as archetypal 'soft spaces' (although from the mid-1990s the boundaries of the Green Heart were 'hardened' through precise mapping in regulation plans). However, as we explain below, the creation of a governance platform at the Randstad level has eluded its advocates. Nonetheless, there are many other overlapping and intersecting soft spaces within the western Netherlands, where governance platforms have been established and are active, including for the south and north 'wings' of the Randstad (the regions surrounding Amsterdam and Rotterdam-The Hague), inter-municipal cooperation areas, and other ad hoc cooperation arrangements. At the Randstad level, it has not been possible to reach political agreement about the validity of the space and the concept because of the very large number of varied interests and the attitudes of particularly powerful ones. Bounded spaces for government are deeply rooted, not least in the Netherlands where the municipalities are relatively powerful. Local governments can claim legitimacy as the accountable policy maker when it suits them. But even if there is no platform at the Randstad level, the existence and endorsement of the Randstad concept may still play a role in reminding the actors that they are playing on a wider stage than their immediate surroundings.

At the wing level and other sub-spaces within the Randstad, cooperation has proved more workable though still difficult, and a layering of nested planning spaces has emerged with a mix of formal and informal institutions formulating shared policy through varying processes and levels of competence. At this level, cooperation tends to be associated with plainly strong functional relationships with obvious flows of commuters and tangible and intangible goods and services crossing between the constituent jurisdictions. However, the many cooperation arrangements across the Randstad tend to be in the form of networks, with government in control often aligned with business and its agenda over a specified territory, rather than the more fluid bottom–up actor networks that have been advocated (Jauhiainen and Moilanen, 2011).

The lack of deeper cooperation arrangements at the Randstad scale reflects much uncertainty about whether it actually constitutes a functional region, and if the pursuit of polycentricity would bring the benefits claimed. The chapters that follow address these issues thoroughly. Here, we should emphasise that there is very diverse mix of attitudes to the Randstad. There are many advocates. A number of the chapters in this volume refer to the inclusion of the Randstad in Hall's 1966 seminal work, *World Cities*. Hall elevated the Randstad to one of the 'great urban regions of the world' alongside London, Tokyo, New York and others, making up a global network of 'urban concentrations of business, specialised expertise, knowledge and finance' (Pain, 2017: 1). This high ranking in the world urban hierarchy certainly would not be achieved by any one of the main cities alone, indeed, only Amsterdam among the cities of the Randstad figures among the 55 'alpha cities' of the Globalization and World Cities (GaWC) Research Network.[1]

Since then, the Randstad has been celebrated in many publications (especially in other countries). Along with Hamburg, the Randstad is been picked out in a study of soft planning spaces in north-west Europe as a prominent example of a successful initiative that has overcome problems of territorial administrative boundaries 'to accept and include on a pragmatic basis the heterogeneity of actors and consciously avoiding a formal geography and instead promoting flexible or blurred boundaries' (Othengrafen *et al.*, 2015: 227). This perspective is justified only in relation to the cooperation in the sub-spaces of the Randstad. But in practice, too, the Randstad is presented as a model for other regions. In the United Kingdom, the One Powerhouse Consortium (2019: 2) has invoked the example of the Randstad as one of a few global regions that 'have used spatial planning to focus political will, economic activity and social reform to great effect'.

Those who are not enthusiastic (especially in the Netherlands) fall into two camps. There are those that doubt the Randstad's polycentric character but want government to act more forcefully to deliver it, and there are those that refer to the Randstad as a myth, rejecting both its existence or benefits that might accrue from becoming more polycentric. The most notable exponent in the first group is Niek de Boer, former professor at Delft University of Technology from 1969 to 1989, whose 1996 book (in translation) 'The Randstad Does not Exist: the Failure to Pursue a Metropolitan Policy', argued that the government had not addressed but should act at the 'metropolitan scale'. In a similar way, an OECD Territorial Review of the Randstad in 2007 concluded that functional relations in the Randstad operated mostly at the scale of the city-region, but it also strongly advocated national government to intervene to strengthen the functional coherence of the Randstad as a whole to reap benefits from potential agglomeration effects.

A figurehead for the second group is Zef Hemel, a former board member of the Urban Planning Department of Amsterdam who believes the Randstad to be an 'expensive fairy tale', and that it 'bears a striking resemblance to the "Emperor's Clothes"'(2017). Sceptics such as Hemel tend to agree about the importance of networks of cities but argue that such functional connections go well beyond the four core cities of the Randstad within and beyond the Netherlands.

How does these alternative views stand up to the evidence? There is support both for and against, and many commentators end up sitting on the fence. Meijers *et al.* in Chapter 6 and Ritsema van Eck and Van der Wouden in Chapter 7 summarise the different ways that functional relations have been measured. They give a balanced view, explaining that findings on functional coherence depend very much on the indicators used. Whilst the treatment of the Randstad in national policy has been inconsistent, they are in no doubt that spatial planning has made a difference in the Randstad. Meijers *et al.* add that the normative pursuit of polycentricity in the Netherlands has been determined largely by political ideology, rather than the facts, and has been diminished in the face of populism and neoliberalism.

By way of a preview of the dynamics of the Randstad that follows in Part III, the numerous studies of functional relations in the Randstad tend to concentrate on the analysis of commuting flows, but there is also attention to information flows between businesses, residential and business migration, labour market effects, leisure trips, and other measures. The findings are that the bulk of daily urban flows is concentrated in the city regions, but trips by professional and business occupation groups are important at the Randstad scale. Some cities are more connected than others and this is strongest within the north and south wings. Ritsema van Eck and Van der Wouden report in Chapter 7 that flows did not change between the 1990s and early 2000s, but there has been some growth at the Randstad scale of people flows, especially occupations requiring higher level education. Whilst much smaller in absolute terms, these movements may reflect more accurately the metropolitan functions of a global business services that Hall and others refer to. De Hoog explains in Chapter 10 that *metropolitan* functions are not dependent on the daily urban system. Another aspect of this is the increasingly significant role of Amsterdam as a node in the city network, attracting more distant commuting. This relates to its business service function and may also be an indication of the housing shortage and affordability problem highlighted by Elsinga *et al.* in Chapter 9.

On the benefits of polycentricity, an assessment of the Randstad's performance in the early 1990s strongly supports Hall's 1960s assessment by concluding that the collective strengths of the cities together with the sea and air gateways 'propel the Randstad to the top of the European urban hierarchy, making it a world city of the highest level… [but that] In terms of the various advanced producer services and international management activities, the Randstad achieves only a middle-level ranking' (Shachar, 1994: 398). This would support stronger intervention by government on aspects of polycentricity. Since then, the balance of importance of trade and other flows between cities in or beyond their immediate region has changed markedly. Wall (2009) argues that cities of the Randstad now depend more on other international cities than their local neighbours, making the idea of local functional relations and regional polycentricity less, rather than more important. Policy on the Randstad will surely need to keep abreast of these dynamics. The global COVID-19 crisis of 2020 heralds another far-reaching and more swift reform of international business and cultural relations. The performance measure for a polycentric Randstad is perhaps not international economic performance per se, but rather its resilience in recovering from such shocks.

Profile of the Randstad

The term *Randstad* was coined in 1938 by Albert Plesman, a pioneer in aviation and founder of the Dutch airline KLM. He used the term Randstad to express what he saw from his aircraft, a 'rim city' or 'edge city'. The rim is formed by the four main cities as shown in Figure 1.1. (The full story of the genesis of 'Randstad' is given in Chapter 6.) This morphological character of the Randstad will quickly become recognisable to the newcomer. First impressions of the territory of the Randstad are usually that it is flat; that it is clearly urban but interspersed with large stretches of open and intensively used agricultural land; that it is orderly arranged with a clear demarcation of built and unbuilt environment; that if travelling by road or rail it is congested, but if travelling by bike that it is enlightened and open; that citizens are well housed in attractive neighbourhoods; that the historic environment appears to be cared for and well managed; that the urban realm offers a high quality and safe walking environment; and that the people are prosperous and welcoming, if at times a little blunt.

The geography of the Randstad is unmistakably deltaic, with expanses of flat open land crisscrossed by watercourses and historic windmills that remain from a former network of more than 10,000. It is a polder landscape where over eight centuries past generations have reclaimed land from marshes and the sea for agriculture and urban development. The result is a completely artificial landscape of straight lines and intensive agriculture. Water is inescapable, and in the cities too, where canals and dikes form the essential and historic foundations on which the cities were designed and built. The landscape is immediately recognisable as Dutch with its regular, rational, and orderly aesthetic quality. But beneath the surface appearance, urbanisation and intensive agriculture and recreation put huge pressure on the environment. A 2019 EU review (CEC, 2019) noted that progress was being made in improving water and air quality and habitat and biodiversity degradation, but concluded that there is much more to be done if the Netherlands is to meet its national and international commitments.

Estimates of size and significance of the Randstad vary because there is no formal administrative border, no government tier, and therefore no official statistics, as explained below. Reference is often made to figures for the four constituent provinces in which the Randstad sits or their main cities: Flevoland (Almere), North Holland (Amsterdam), Utrecht (province and city) and South Holland (Rotterdam and The Hague). This is a reasonable approximation for many purposes although it does add a large part of mainly agricultural lands in North Holland and Flevoland which are not part of the metropolitan region. But the boundaries of the Randstad are elastic, expanding and contracting depending on the topic and interests pursued. Generally, the geographical meaning of the Randstad has expanded over the decades, notably to take in Almere in Flevoland which was built on land reclaimed

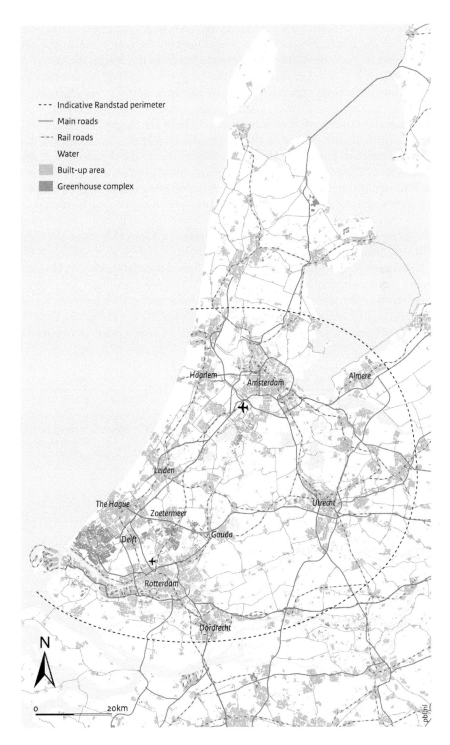

Indicative Randstad perimeter
Main roads
Rail roads
Water
Built-up area
Greenhouse complex

Haarlem
Amsterdam
Almere
Leiden
The Hague
Zoetermeer
Utrecht
Delft
Gouda
Rotterdam
Dordrecht

N

0   20km

Figure 1.1 The Randstad including its wider setting.
Source: Statistics Netherlands (CBS) and NWB, edited by Marnix Breedijk, PBL Netherlands Environmental Assessment Agency.

from the sea from 1974 and formed part of the Amsterdam city-region from the late 1980s. At periods in the history of the Randstad, there has also been an interest in urban corridors that extend beyond the core cities to the east (Germany) in particular, but they are excluded from the discussion here.

To put the Randstad in context, Table 1.1 gives a number of measures for the Randstad in comparison to three 'monocentric world cities'. Bearing in mind the difficulties of international comparison because of varying definitions and administrative structures, the area of the larger Randstad (four provinces) is similar to that of the metropolitan region of Guangzhou, but much larger than Greater London. The four cities of the Randstad and numerous small towns around them have a combined population of about 7 million whilst the four provinces in which the Randstad is based have a joint population of over 8 million, 47% of the total population of the Netherlands. The dependency rate, the proportion of working age population compared to the young and elderly, was around the average for Europe at about 70%, but will be an increasing challenge for government.

As might be expected, the Randstad has a lower population density than the monocentric metropolitan regions. The table gives two estimates for population density, one based on the provinces and the larger figure based only on the constituent city-regions. However, the Netherlands has the highest population density and the highest rate of urbanisation in Europe at 500 persons/km^2

Table 1.1 Comparison of key figures for Randstad and other world cities

	Area, km^2	Population, million[a]	Pop density, pers/km^2	GDP 2019 billion \$[c]	Sustainable cities index ranking[d]	Air traffic capacity million seats[e]
Greater London	1,572	11.6	5,729	851	1	3.9
Guangzhou	7,434	13.3	1,789	382	74	3.5
Los Angeles	4,496	13.2	2,935	1,170	45	3.7
Randstad[b]	8,287/7,000	8.15/7.1	983/1,014	420	12	3.0

Source: Authors.

a Sources: United Nations, Department of Economic and Social Affairs, 2019; Los Angeles-Long Beach-Anaheim, CA Metro Area: US Census Bureau 2019 estimate.

b Randstad: As there is no administrative area for the Randstad, the figures given refer first to the four provinces (Regio Randstad, 2017), and second to our own estimate of the area of the Randstad 7,000 km^2 (the 'extensive Randstad', including Purmerend in the north, Almere and Amersfoort in the east and Dordrecht in the south). The smaller population figure refers to the four city regions.

c Sources: OECD Stat. Available at: https://stats.oecd.org/Index.aspx?DataSetCode=CITIES#, except for Guangzhou: estimated by Asia Times at: https://asiatimes.com/. Randstad figure is sum of the four main cities.

d Source: Arcadis, 2018.

e OAG seat capacity statistics February 2020. Available at: https://www.oag.com/. Later in 2020, capacity was reduced by as much as 95% because of the COVID-19 restrictions on travel.

and 92%, respectively (excluding very small countries)[2], growing from 52% in 1950 (UN Department of Economic and Social Affairs, 2018). These relatively high figures are more pronounced for the Randstad, which has a population density of about 1,000 persons/km^2, although the urban profile is 'low rise'. The population is spread evenly across the region, with only 2.5 million in the four main cities. And it is diverse. In the Netherlands, as a whole for 2019, 27% of the population had a 'migration background', that is, a parent born in another country.[3] The population is also remarkably well-housed in comparison to most other metropolitan regions. Elsinga *et al.* explain in Chapter 9 how post-war governments have intervened strongly to initially solve a housing shortage, and later to improve the conditions of the housing and its urban surroundings. Government-led and subsidised housing has been instrumental in the spatial development of the Randstad, contributing to the conversion of the region from a cluster of self-contained cities to a dense network of urban settlements.

Almost complete urbanisation of the Randstad is reflected in the density of infrastructure. The Netherlands is second only to Belgium among European countries for road density. It has the fifth highest road density in the world, including a very high provision of motorways, some 127 km for each 1,000 km^2 land area, with much of it concentrated in the Randstad and especially around the port of Rotterdam.[4] However, the road network is outshone by the water infrastructure, even though much of that which is keeping the feet of the Dutch dry is invisible. It includes thousands of pumping stations, 22,000 km of dikes and 70,000 km of watercourses. The Randstad has a disproportionate share given that a majority of its surface area is below sea level. Water transport on the other hand is plainly visible. The Randstad has by far the highest density of water transport in Europe save for one region, also in the Netherlands – Zeeland. Railways too are well catered for with South Holland having the seventh most dense network in Europe (133 km/1,000 km^2), behind German and Czech regions. Travellers from most other countries are impressed with the rail service which is a true network with fine stations (part of a national programme of planning projects), and many precise interconnections between lines, and between rail, other public transport, and cycling. Despite its strengths, the public transport network is somewhat weak at the scale of the Randstad. Only the main stations are connected across the Randstad between Rotterdam and Amsterdam, since 2009 with the option of the Netherlands, only high-speed line. This dense infrastructure network also services the ports: Rotterdam Port, the largest port in Europe handling the equivalent of 37,000 '20-foot containers' each day; and Schiphol Amsterdam Airport, the fourth busiest airport in the world for international traffic which provides in the peak period more than 200,000 passenger seats per day.[5]

The development of extensive physical and soft infrastructure has since the seventeenth century gone hand in hand with the growth of the economy and international trade. In 2017 the Randstad (four provinces) was the fourth largest metropolitan economy in Europe, after London, Paris, and the Rhine-Ruhr (also polycentric), and before the COVID-19 crisis was experiencing reasonably good growth throughout the later 2010s of about 2.5% per year. Whilst the Netherlands is probably most well-known for its export of agricultural products, the most important trade for the Randstad is in machinery and transport equipment, manufactured goods and chemical products (Statistics Netherlands, 2019). Petroleum, the import of crude and export of refined and related products, is also important. As Hein explains in Chapter 3, the Randstad, and particularly Rotterdam, forms the hub of the significant 'petroleum landscape' of the Netherlands, though it is not so visible to those not directly involved. In contrast, agriculture is on display in the Randstad, notably the complex of greenhouses in the West- and Eastland between Rotterdam and The Hague which is a major hub of the Dutch intensive, high-tech horticulture industry that has made the Netherlands the second largest exporter of food products in the world after the United States.

Perhaps surprisingly, investment in research and development in the Dutch economy is low at around 2% compared to other European metropolitan areas (only half the rate of Copenhagen for example). The proportion of the labour force with a higher education is also low at 39% compared to London with 49%. In 2007, the OECD warned of a 'brain drain' in the Randstad and the need to do more to attract and retain a highly qualified workforce making effective use of its higher education infrastructure. On the other hand, the Randstad is home to five of the top 75 universities in the world, while Germany has 'only' four.[6]

A dimension of the Randstad that is invisible to the visitor is its (territorial) governance, although aspects can be inferred from the general conditions on view. In Chapters 3 and 4 Meyer and Hooimeijer explain how the challenging water environment gave rise to strong governance and a collaborative culture in the Netherlands from the 1200s that are still prevalent today. Spaans *et al.* bring that up to the present day, presenting the many abandoned attempts to provide for a 'fourth layer' of government for the metropolitan regions and resulting in a convoluted map of contemporary governance arrangements. In sum, there has been little success in providing collaborative governance for the Randstad as a whole, despite calls for administrative reform, for example, in the early 1990s. Dieleman and Musterd (1992) believed that it was time for a metropolitan government with sweeping competences in spatial planning, housing, transport, and more. Such reform is unthinkable now, but there is a serious widening gap in the governance of the metropolitan region beyond the wings as central government retreats from national spatial planning. Collaboration platforms around the two centres of gravity north and south have been more successful. For Schrijnen (Chapter 15) it is a matter of regret that although the Randstad operates and is recognised as metropolis in so many ways, there has been little coordinated policy across the whole metropolis, especially in creating a truly metropolitan transport system.

Episodes in the modern development of the Randstad

The idea of the Randstad as a polycentric metropolis is a consistent feature in the modern history of Dutch spatial development and planning, but there have been many twists and turns. Most of the papers that follow in this volume refer to key stages in this history and explain in more detail the key events and their relevance for the Randstad today. Here, we provide a sketch of the main episodes in the evolution of the Randstad as a general orientation for readers. An elaborate timeline is provided by the *Spatial Planning Calendar: 75 Years of National Spatial Planning in the Netherlands* (Ministry of Infrastructure and Environment, 2013). Also, various chapters in this volume set out a chronology relevant to the topic in question, with varying phases, see in particular, Chapter 11 by Zonneveld and Chapter 13 by Van der Wouden.

We distinguish five key episodes in thinking and practice about the Randstad in Dutch spatial policy from the 1950s to the 2020s. The episodes are, in turn, related to waves of urban growth, wider economic and demographic change, and political priorities. Needless to say, this simple organisation of a 60-year history is in reality not so neat. Layers of detail and the interconnections among these periods are revealed in the following chapters. Over those 60 years the challenge of effectively managing physical urban growth has become more intense as the population of the Netherlands has grown by 70% and GDP per capita has increased six-fold. In meeting that challenge, the controversial notion of the Randstad has usually been present, though in varying form and significance. And it has endured even when eschewed by formal policy. Whilst policies may change abruptly, practices and ways of thinking will change more slowly. The point has been made many times that Dutch planning revolves around a deeply rooted and persistent culture, the doctrine of rule and order. The notions of the Randstad and the Green Heart are so fundamental to this doctrine that 'rescinding these ideas would mean the demise of the doctrine and the institutional arrangements surrounding it' (Faludi and Van der Valk, 1994: 253).

The clustered pattern of cities in what was to become the western Netherlands was fixed from the Middle Ages. In Chapter 2, Brand explains that by 1560 the main cities were pursuing complementary functions and that by 1850 a strengthening national government was beginning to control the expansion of cities and lay the foundations of the polycentric spatial configuration, ensuring that one city, Amsterdam, was not able to dominate. By the beginning of the twentieth century, there was clear recognition in society of an interconnected urban region beyond the individual cities.

1950s and 1960s: containment and the metropolitan network

The priorities in the immediate post-war period were reconstruction and restoring industrial production. Redevelopment in conjunction with rural-urban migration and natural growth meant that the Randstad cities grew quickly. Projections in 1960 forecast that population would almost double by 2000, from 11 to 20 million, though the outcome has been 17.4 million by 2020. The government's willingness and capacity to plan and regulate physical development had also been growing from the 1940s. Stimulated by a new planning agency created in wartime and a 1958 policy advice of a high-level advisory committee, national government created the necessary political, administrative, and research organisations needed to intervene, and so it did.

Experience of the war and occupation reinforced the pre-war view that decentralisation of industrial activity and the containment of a cluster of independent cities were conducive to a more secure, prosperous, and fair society. Later in the 1960s, this was to become the now infamous concept of *gebundelde deconcentratie* or 'concentrated deconcentration'. It was a physical morphological policy but reflecting the strong Christian Democratic culture of the country with its emphasis on small towns and villages, underpinned also by concerns about social and spatial justice, the latter idea known today in Europe as territorial cohesion (Faludi, 2007).

The tools used to promote and implement these ideas began with a 1958 advisory report, *De Ontwikkeling van het Westen des Lands*, the Development of the West of the Country, which called for the continued separation of a ring of distinctive cities around an agricultural heartland, with the anticipated strong urban growth directed to areas beyond the Randstad avoiding suburbanisation or the 'sprawl' of cities. These recommendations were taken up in the ground-breaking first national formal policy statement in 1960, the *Nota Inzake de Ruimtelijke Ordening in Nederlands (*National Spatial Planning Report, or Report on Spatial Organisation of the Netherlands).

It was followed in 1966 by the *Tweede Nota over de Ruimtelijke Ordening* (Second Report on Spatial Planning) which established the principle of concentrated deconcentration and added more specific plans for overspill and new towns. It also took a wider view of the position of the Randstad beyond the Netherlands as part of the western European urban agglomeration (Lambregts, 2009). The assumption underlying both reports was that the cities of the western Netherlands constituted a functional urban region – the Randstad, with two interdependent 'wings', north and south.

The 1950s and 1960s were formative years when government took great strides to lay the foundations of national spatial planning in the Netherlands, of which the Randstad concept was a central element. The three main reports from the 1950s and 1960s drew international attention. The notion of the Randstad was disseminated and popularised first by Burke 1966 who described the Randstad as the 'Greenheart Metropolis', and soon after by Hall as explained above. But the effectiveness of this initial planning, particularly containment policies, is questionable. More successful was the determined policy to meet housing needs leading to peripheral expansion of the cities, and even urban development in the Green Heart.

1970s and 1980s: city regions

In the 1970s the post-war expectation of rapid and sustained economic growth was dashed by the oil crises of 1973 and 1979, leading to economic recession, with high levels of unemployment. This slowed population growth, urban development, and to a degree suburbanisation, although increasing prosperity for many sustained the growing demand for space. The recession and slower growth highlighted the vulnerability of the cities to economic downturns and drew attention to the relatively poor quality of life and residential environments they offered which was contributing to city population decline. Attention shifted to stimulating economic activity, but macro-economic conditions and political ideology favouring a more liberal economic approach meant that by the 1980s retrenchment of government activity was underway across the board in favour of more market-oriented thinking.

The third multi-volume national spatial strategy of 1973 with various updates to 1983 was less ambitious for the Randstad agglomeration overall, concentrating instead on urban renewal and revitalisation of the cities, their commuting zones and growth centres. Urban containment policy pursued urban 'bundling' and 'concentration', primarily through the designation and implementation of urban growth centres and the necessary public transport infrastructure to ensure they were contained in the city-region.

During much of the 1970s and 1980s the Randstad concept was in the doldrums, not forgotten but not a force in planning policy, playing only a secondary role in comparison to the city-regions. Towards the end of the 1980s there was a radical and controversial rethink of the notion, reducing its scope to the three larger city-regions making up a 'West Wing', where there was thought to be most potential to create an internationally competitive economic environment. However, political opposition ensured that this policy, set out formally in a 1988 draft *Vierde Nota over de Ruimtelijke Ordening*, the Fourth Spatial Strategy, was never adopted. The slimmed down city network was roundly criticised for, among other things, undermining the coherence of, and cooperation within, the Randstad and the Green Heart.

1990s: Randstad world city

The essential argument of the late 1980s that the Randstad had significance for the Netherlands international economic competitive position was carried forward to become a major stream of thinking in the 1990s when growth of the cities was re-established. Initially, it was ancillary to traditional concerns with patterns of spatial development, especially housing. The *Vierde Nota over de Ruimtelijke Ordening Extra,* the Fourth National Spatial Planning Report Extra finalised in 1993, became known by the acronym *Vinex,* referring to its major programme of urban expansions around the Netherlands, which were to deliver more than 750,000 homes, a third of which are located in the Randstad.

The 1990s were perhaps the high point of national spatial planning in the Netherlands and for the Randstad. The Vinex programme was orchestrated by central government to deliver largely housing development, with the public sector acting as developer and infrastructure provider. But this planning was not well integrated with other influential sectoral departments, especially Economic Affairs. The role of central government and the leading position of spatial planning were coming into question. The legacy of long recession in the 1980s maintained the government focus on the contribution of spatial policy to economic growth. One important aspect of this was the opportunity to capitalise on the creation of the EU Single Market by cementing the Randstad's position as a world city – a polycentric metropolis of global significance and a gateway for international economic relationships. In this context, government's economic priorities aligned with spatial planning for strengthening the polycentric metropolis of networked cities in the Randstad. It was at this time that Dutch planners were playing a leading role in the formulation of the *European Spatial Development Perspective* (CSD, 1999; Faludi and Waterhout, 2002), which promoted polycentrism and the integration of spatial policy throughout Europe.

Fortuitously, economic growth and growing income from natural gas exploitation provided funding for significant investment in hard and soft infrastructure to strengthen competitive advantage in global gateways, economic clusters and corridors. But during the 1990s, the political 'neoliberal offensive' was also gaining ground, including privatisation and outsourcing of government and dismantling of the welfare state. These changes were to fundamentally reshape Dutch spatial planning in the following decades (De Jong, 2013).

2000s: Rescaling

By the 2000s, free market neoliberal ideology was firmly rooted in Dutch political culture (Waterhout *et al.*, 2013). The very purpose of government came into question and former central government functions were devolved to provinces and municipalities, outsourced to the market, or simply abandoned. National government was less willing to take on a prescriptive position in national spatial development, and the private sector started to take over former government roles reinforced by EU macro-economic policies restraining public spending. There was a 'rescaling' of spatial planning (Roodbol-Mekkes and Van den Brink, 2015) both downwards to local government and upwards to the wider transnational north-west European scale. The approach in spatial policy was less visionary and more pragmatic following the dictum of city-regions as the 'engines' of national economic performance. Emphasis turned away from the Randstad to the engines – the city-regions, and the planning and delivery of key projects to support them, with much less thought to strategic interrelations. Government policy was more sectoral concentrating on improving the competitiveness of clusters of economic activity in the growth areas of knowledge and creative industries (Bontje *et al.*, 2011).

The gap in government policy towards the wider Randstad region was filled by an independent group led by urban design and planning professors of Delft University of Technology and Amsterdam University. The group successively advocated for policy attention to a functionally integrated polycentric metropolis that could compete with other global regions, specifically at the level of the whole international delta of north-west Europe beyond the Randstad. This eventually resulted in a strongly articulated policy statement of the planning aldermen of the four main Randstad cities (Deltametropool, 1998). Thus, spatial strategy and interventions at the scale of the 'Deltametropolis' became a formal part of government policy, taken up in the draft 2001 Fifth Spatial Planning Report (Lambregts and Zonneveld, 2004).

Attention to spatial networks in the wider Delta region was short-lived though as the political colour of government changed which took spatial policy back towards economic priorities. The final 2004 version of the Fifth Report (authorised translation: National Spatial Strategy) was a corporate government plan with a strong lead from the Ministry of Economic Affairs, and for the first time, explicitly recognising the need to deal with the effects of climate change. The Randstad returned as the principal location for the critical drivers of the Dutch economy that would be supported by national government funding: three dominant economic cores (of 13 in the country), nationally significant development projects or zones including Schiphol Airport and the port of Rotterdam (both designated as 'Mainport'), and agricultural complexes or Greenports.

The belated recognition of the need for an integrated strategy also gave rise to the first, and for now, the last, formal planning document that concentrates solely on the Randstad: *Structuurvisie Randstad 2040* (Ministerie van VROM, 2008). Randstad 2040 took its lead from the economic agenda of government and asserted the ambition to strengthen the Randstad as one of Europe's leading urban regions. It demonstrated the connections between policies and investments of various government departments and agencies and set out guiding principles: improving the quality of urban and natural environments, safety and climate resilience, concentrating new urban development in the cities, and improving accessibility, especially around the 'two centres of gravity' in the northern and southern Randstad.

At the end of the 2000s, it seemed that the Randstad idea was restored with government policy taking on the agenda for a polycentric metropolis first established in the 1950s. But *Randstad 2040* did not anticipate and was quickly overtaken by the severe effects of the 2008 banking crisis. Evers and Vogelij in Chapter 14 explain the weaknesses of the process that gave rise to *Randstad 2040* and its core assumptions, not least that high growth would continue. They argue that it failed to address political and economic uncertainties and the lack of wider civil society engagement which fatally undermined the robustness of its approach. After yet another election the document was shelved.

2010s: Randstad backstage

Economic growth in the Netherlands went into reverse following the 2008 global financial crisis, from 3.5% in 2007 to −4.5% in 2009. A fall in global demand and weak domestic conditions created a 'Great Recession', not equalled before or after until the COVID-19 crisis of 2020 (Masselink and Van den Noord, 2009). Naturally, government attention turned to dealing with very high levels of unemployment and slow growth.

A change in the coalition government in 2010 ensured that neoliberal economic ideology remained at the fore. The new national government quickly adopted the *Structuurvisie Infrastructuur en Ruimte* (SVIR), the National Policy Strategy for Infrastructure and Spatial Planning (2012). The Randstad is mentioned in this 'strategy' but it has little content, save for proposals for new road building, a recurring policy goal when liberals and Christian-democrats participate in a government coalition. Here, it draws strongly on the 2007 OECD *Territorial Review of the Randstad Holland* in citing the importance of building roads to ease congestion to support economic growth and the 'business environment'. This and other recommendations in the OECD report such as using the Green Heart to provide housing seemed already outdated when made, and certainly are in 2020. But the report is very clear about the need for the Netherlands to tackle 'the lack of integration of the Randstad to improve its operation as a unified urban area...' (OECD, 2007: 27). It is rather doubtful though whether increasing road capacity could mean anything here.

Economic growth is not everything of course, and other related issues began to figure prominently in the 2010s, not least the risks from climate change, and from that, the need to strengthen resilience in a country where 70% of the wealth generation takes place on land below sea level (Stead, 2014). Despite huge ambitions the Netherlands was lagging behind in some aspects of its climate mitigation and adaptation agenda, for example, in having the lowest share of renewable energy resources of all EU member states.[7]

The limited imagination of central government in addressing these issues through shaping the spatial configuration of the Randstad was confirmed when previously sacrosanct policies, the Green Heart and buffer zones, were formally abandoned. Instead the proposed 'main national spatial structure' is a location map of infrastructure − pipelines, energy, water, nature and other projects, though it does explain the important cross-border connections. Further decentralisation saw that regional planning was taken on by the provinces and the institutions created for the north and south wings as explained above.

The SVIR did not signal the demise of the Randstad idea, but it has been very much backstage in spatial development through the 2010s. Indeed, for much of this time, spatial planning itself has been much less in favour, with its ministry abolished in 2010 and its concerns becoming just one part of the Ministry of Infrastructure and Water Management (in 2017 spatial planning moved again to another ministry). An agenda for simplification of spatial planning as part of a wider transition to 'government as enabler not provider' was adopted in 2012 under the slogan *Eenvoudig Beter*, 'Simply Better'. Its centrepiece proposal is a new *Omgevingswet*, the Environment and Planning Act. The choice of the word 'environment' is not accidental. It marks a step away from 'spatial planning' with the intention to integrate 15 acts completely and about 25 acts partially and all government policies that affect the living environment – and also to integrate the 80 or more related government visions and policy documents in one overarching strategy. The first iteration of that 'simplified' scheme was delivered in 2019 in the *Nationale Omgevingsvisie, Draft National Strategy on Spatial Planning and the Environment* (NOVI).

The NOVI has immense ambitions. The idea that the solution to the urgent need to integrate the impact of sectoral policies on the living environment lies in the creation of one dominant 'environmental' law and strategy is questionable, especially the suggestion that this is a simplification. At the time of writing accession of the Act is proposed for 2022, some ten years after it was conceived. However, in the event, the content of the Draft NOVI is not so different from previous national spatial strategies. The differences are more in the process and specificity. The weakening position of national government means that it has had to engage more with other actors who do have power to deliver, be they, other government departments, local government, agencies, business or civil society. And the draft is very much a general document establishing principles and policies, with few specific designations. Difficult decisions will be left to the provinces, municipalities and agencies, and they will need new tools to balance the many competing interests and priorities set out in the NOVI. The Randstad does figure in the text but rather tangentially, in relation to the challenge of maintaining the open identity of the Green Heart. However, the NOVI still recognises the importance of the maintenance of concentrated development in a polycentric structure of cities 'which function as a single, complementary system' (Ministry of the Interior and Kingdom Relations, 2019: 24) but at the scale of the whole Netherlands rather than the Randstad. In 2020, the claim that the strategy is not a static document but rather a process of constant adaptation will be severely tested if it is to remain significant in the face of the COVID-19 crisis.

2020s post-pandemic Randstad

The crisis from 2020 was a major blow to the Netherlands. From the 1980s city populations were growing and during the 2010s the economy had strengthened, indicated for example, by the declining levels of property vacancy. In the aftermath of the crisis these advances will inevitably be reversed, and some problems that were worsening such as housing affordability, exacerbated. Urban densification in the Randstad in order to deliver a government priority of 1 million new homes by 2030 will certainly be resisted, with changing residential location preferences putting more pressure on open land. The anticipated decline in commuting especially by public transport, and growth in teleworking and online shopping might reduce the demand for commercial space in the Randstad cities, though it will also present opportunities to improve the living environment sought by NOVI.

Despite COVID-19, the Netherlands greatest challenge remains the effects of climate change, and not least in the Randstad where many critical assets are located in the most vulnerable places. NOVI does set the scene for more concerted action on mitigation and adaptation with, for example, a key priority to ensure space for the energy transition, and an emphasis on mixed uses, self-sufficient neighbourhoods, circular cities, and healthy environments. But does the NOVI go far enough in adapting spatial policy to new and possible future conditions? In Chapter 8, Boelens and Jacobs argue that future policy needs to go further with a fundamental rethink of the accepted wisdom around spatial policy and the generation of growth, to new ways of creating prosperity. They cite the example of the shifting objectives of Rotterdam Port from a gateway for goods where profitability is declining, towards business services allied to the port and its international standing. The COVID-19 crisis will strengthen demands for new directions in policy. These may accelerate shifts in economic structure with more attention to the consequences of climate change and the inevitable demands for more attention to healthy environments. We return to these points in the conclusion.

Structure of the book

The following chapters are organised in three sections broadly following the structure of origins, operation, and planning of the Randstad. We begin in Part II with a review of the history of the Randstad and explanation of how no one city evolved to dominate the region. The four chapters explain how the pattern of the Randstad's spatial configuration and distribution of functions arises from the interplay of changing natural environmental conditions especially related to flood risk, waves of technological innovation from windmills to wind turbines, economic and social organisation, and strong government intervention.

Part III examines the contemporary operation of the Randstad as a metropolitan region and asks if the reality of functional relations meets the concept of polycentricity. The five chapters in this section demonstrate the different ways of understanding and measuring functional relationships and complementarity, and outline dominant themes in the discourse of urban development in the Randstad. Part IV reviews changing ideas about how government should organise itself to strengthen and exploit the Randstad, the actual outcomes in governance and policy, and the contribution of spatial planning to shaping its current form and performance. We conclude in the final chapter by returning to, and offering answers to our four main questions.

Notes

1 https://www.lboro.ac.uk/gawc/world2018t.html (accessed 29 June 2020).
2 In Europe, Malta has a higher population density and urbanisation rate, and Iceland a higher urbanisation rate.
3 Source: Statistics Netherlands, see opendata.cbs.nl.
4 Source: Figures for all transport infrastructure are taken from Eurostat Inland Transport Infrastructure at the Regional Level, updated 2020 (accessed 29 June 2020).
5 August 2019: nearly 220.000 on average per day, https://www.schiphol.nl/en/schiphol-group/page/transport-and-traffic-statistics/ (accessed 29 June 2020).
6 Times Higher Education World University Rankings 2020, https://www.timeshighereducation.com/world-university-rankings/2020/ (accessed 29 June 2020).
7 Eurostat renewable energy statistics, January 2020, https://ec.europa.eu/eurostat/statistics-explained/index.php/Renewable_energy_statistics (accessed 29 June 2020).

References

Allmendinger, P. and Haughton, G. (2009). 'Soft spaces, fuzzy boundaries, and metagovernance: The new spatial planning in the Thames Gateway', *Environment and Planning A: Economy and Space*, 41(3), 617–633.

Allmendinger, P., Haughton, G., Knieling, J. and Othengrafen, F (2015a). 'Soft spaces, planning and emerging practices of territorial governance'. In: Allmendinger, P., Haughton, G., Knieling, J. and Othengrafen, F. (Eds) *Soft Spaces in Europe: Re-Negotiating Governance, Boundaries and Borders*. Routledge, London, 3–22.

Allmendinger, P., Haughton, G., Knieling, J. and Othengrafen, F. (2015b). *Soft Spaces in Europe: Re-Negotiating Governance, Boundaries and Borders*. Routledge, London.

Arcadis (2018). *Citizen Centric Cities: The Sustainable Cities Index 2018*. Arcadis, Amsterdam.

Bontje, M., Musterd, S., Kovács, Z. and Murie, A. (2011). 'Pathways toward European creative-knowledge city-regions', *Urban Geography*, 32(1), 80–104.

Burger, M.J., Meijers, E.J., Hoogerbrugge, M.M. and Masip Tresserra, J. (2015). 'Borrowed size, agglomeration shadows and cultural amenities in north-west Europe', *European Planning Studies*, 23(6), 1090–1109.

Burke, G.L. (1966). *Greenheart Metropolis: Planning the Western Netherlands*. MacMillan, London.

CEC, Commission of the European Communities (2019). *The EU Environmental Implementation Review 2019 Country Report: The Netherlands*, Brussels, 4.4.2019 SWD (2019) 133 final.

CSD, Committee on Spatial Development (1999). *European Spatial Development Perspective: Towards Balanced and Sustainable Development of the Territory of the EU*. Luxembourg: Office for Official Publications of the European Communities.

De Boer, N. (1996). *De Randstad bestaat niet [The Randstad Does Not Exist]; De onmacht tot grootstedelijk beleid*. NAi Uitgevers, Rotterdam.

De Jong, A. (2013). 'The Netherlands: Neoliberal dreams in times of austerity', *New Politics*, XIV(2), Web Journal accessed 1 July 2020, newpol.org/.

Deltametropool (1998). *Verklaring van de wethouders ruimtelijke ordening van Amsterdam, Rotterdam, Den Haag en Utrecht over de toekomstige ruimtelijke ontwikkeling in Nederland*

[Declaration of the Spatial Planning Aldermen of Amsterdam, Rotterdam, The Hague and Utrecht on the Future Spatial Development of the Netherlands]. dS+V, Rotterdam.

Dieleman, F.M. and Musterd, S. (1992). 'The restructuring of the Randstad Holland'. In: Dieleman, F.M. and Musterd, S. (Eds) *The Randstad: A Research and Policy Laboratory.* Kluwer Academic Publishers, Dordrecht/Boston/London, 1–16.

ESPON (2020). *ESPON Policy Brief: Polycentric Territorial Structures and Territorial Cooperation.* ESPON EGTC, Luxembourg.

Faludi, A. (2007). 'Territorial cohesion policy and the European model of society', *European Planning Studies*, 15(4), 567–583.

Faludi, A. and Van der Valk, A. (1994). *Rule and Order: Dutch Planning Doctrine in the Twentieth Century.* Kluwer Academic Publishers, Dordrecht/Boston/London.

Faludi, A. and Waterhout, B. (2002). *The Making of the European Spatial Development Perspective; No Masterplan.* Routledge, London.

Gløersen, E., Lähteenmäki-Smith, K. and Dubois, A. (2007). 'Polycentricity in transnational planning initiatives: ESDP applied or ESDP reinvented?' *Planning Practice & Research*, 22(3), 417–438.

Hemel, Z (2017). Free state of Amsterdam Weblog, zefhemel.nl/over/, Accessed 4 February 2020.

Jauhiainen, J.S. and Moilanen, H. (2011). 'Towards fluid territories in European spatial development: Regional development zones in Finland', *Environment and Planning C: Government and Policy*, 29(4), 728–744.

Lambregts, B. (2009). *The Polycentric Metropolis Unpacked: Concepts, Trends and Policy in the Randstad Holland.* PhD University of Amsterdam. Amsterdam Institute for Metropolitan and International Development Studies (AMIDSt), Amsterdam.

Lambregts, B. and Zonneveld, W. (2004). 'From Randstad to Deltametropolis: Changing attitudes towards the scattered metropolis', *European Planning Studies*, 12(3), 299–321.

Liu, X. and Wang, M. (2016). 'How polycentric is urban China and why? A case study of 318 cities', *Landscape and Urban Planning*, 151, 10–20.

Masselink, M. and Van den Noord, P.J. (2009). 'The global financial crisis and its effects on the Netherlands', *ECFIN Country Focus*, 6(10), 1–7. European Commission's Directorate-General for Economic and Financial Affairs, Brussels.

Meijers, E.J. and Burger, M.J. (2017). 'Stretching the concept of "borrowed size"', *Urban Studies*, 54(1), 269–291.

Meijers, E.J., Hoogerbrugge, M.M. and Cardoso, R. (2017). 'Beyond polycentricity: Does stronger integration between cities in polycentric urban regions improve performance?' *TESG: Tijdschrift voor Economische en Sociale Geografie*, 109(1), 1–21.

Ministerie van VROM (Volkshuisvesting, Ruimtelijke Ordening en Milieubeheer) (2008). *Structuurvisie Randstad 2040: Naar een duurzame en concurrerende Europese topregio [Vision Randstad 2040: Towards a Sustainable and Competitive European Top Region].* Ministerie van VROM, The Hague.

Ministry of Infrastructure and Environment (2013). *Spatial Planning Calendar.* Available online: https://www.government.nl/documents/leaflets/2013/07/04/spatial-planning-calendar (accessed 29 June 2020).

Ministry of the Interior and Kingdom Relations (2019). *Draft National Strategy on Spatial Planning and the Environment; A Sustainable Perspective for Our Living Environment.* Ministry of the Interior and Kingdom Relations, The Hague.

OECD (2007). *Territorial Reviews: Randstad Holland, The Netherlands.* OECD Publishing, Paris.

One Powerhouse Consortium (2019). *A Spatial Blueprint for the Midlands*. Barton Willmore, London.

Othengrafen, F., Knieling, J., Haughton, G. and Allmendinger, P. (2015). 'Conclusion – What difference do soft spaces make?' In: Allmendinger, P., Haughton, G., Knieling, J. and Othengrafen, F. (Eds) *Soft Spaces in Europe: Re-Negotiating Governance, Boundaries and Borders*. Routledge, London, 215–235.

Pain, K. (2017). 'World cities'. In: Richardson, D., Castree, N., Goodchild, M.F., Kobayashi, A.L., Liu, W. and Marston, R. (Eds) *International Encyclopedia of Geography: People, the Earth, Environment and Technology*. Wiley Blackwell, Chichester, 1–9 Available online: http://centaur.reading.ac.uk/39142/.

Regio Randstad (2017). *Randstad Monitor: Competitiveness, Business Climate and Quality of Life;* The Randstad Region compared to other metropolitan areas in Europe. Representation of the Randstad Region, Brussel.

Roodbol-Mekkes, P.H. and Van den Brink, A. (2015). 'Rescaling spatial planning: Spatial planning reforms in Denmark, England, and the Netherlands', *Environment and Planning C: Government and Policy*, 33(1), 184–198.

Shachar, A. (1994). 'Randstad Holland: A "World City"?' *Urban Studies*, 31(3), 381–400.

Spaans, M. and Zonneveld, W. (2015). 'Evolving regional spaces: Shifting levels in the southern part of the Randstad'. In: Allmendinger, P., Haughton, G., Knieling, J. and Othengrafen, F. (Eds) *Soft Spaces in Europe: Re-Negotiating Governance, Boundaries and Borders*. Routledge, London, 95–128.

Statistics Netherlands (CBS) (2019). *Dutch Trade in Facts and Figures; Export, Investment and Employment*. Statistics Netherlands, The Hague.

Stead, D. (2014). 'Urban planning, water management and climate change strategies: Adaptation, mitigation and resilience narratives in the Netherlands', *International Journal of Sustainable Development & World Ecology*, 21(1), 15–27.

TA, Territorial Agenda 2030 (2019). *Draft Territorial Agenda 2030 Version December 2019*. Available online: https://www.territorialagenda.eu/renewal-reader/draft-terrtorialagenda.html (accessed 29 June 2020)

United Nations, Department of Economic and Social Affairs (2019). *World Urbanization Prospect*. The 2018 Revision. United Nations, New York.

Wall, R. (2009). 'The relative importance of Randstad cities within comparative worldwide corporate networks', *TESG: Tijdschrift voor Economische en Sociale Geografie*, 100(2), 250–259.

Waterhout, B., Othengrafen, F. and Sykes, O. (2013). 'Neo-liberalization processes and spatial planning in France, Germany, and the Netherlands: An exploration', *Planning Practice & Research*, 28(1), 141–159.

Part II

The origins of the Randstad

2 The making of the urban structure of the Randstad

Nikki Brand

Introduction

This chapter explains when and why the Randstad's contemporary spatial configuration developed. It traces the historical process of spatial transformation from the Middle Ages until the end of the twentieth century with the discernible trends being centre stage. Although many factors influenced change within the urban structure, the chapter is focused on the role of governance, hence the title 'the making of'. Although the Randstad was never a conscious creation, this chapter seeks to demonstrate that governmental action, which can take many different forms, influenced long-term change within the spatial configuration.

This chapter uses a number of concepts which need explanation. When *individual* towns and their spatial features are addressed, the term *urban structure* is used. This is limited to the ground plan of the city and its functions. *Spatial configuration* means the features and character of the Randstad area as a whole in the broadest sense, defining the relations between towns. It includes both the physical appearance of the urban configuration, like connecting infrastructure, relative size of cities and their built-up areas, and the functional division of tasks among the involved settlements.

An important point of departure in the analysis is that every settlement can be characterised by a functional profile that is composed of certain functions like housing, industrial and commercial activities, transport and so on. Through an analysis of long-term change within these functional profiles, the so-called *urban careers* can be defined. Comparing these careers allows insight into functional relationships and the spatial-economic specialities of the cities and towns that form the Randstad. These relationships can be broadly characterised in modern terms as *complementarity* and *competition*. The whole network of functional relationships and urban specialities is called the *urban division of tasks*.

Following Jacobs (1984), this chapter assumes that settlements in general and towns specifically are perpetually locked in competition within their boundaries (Castells, 1996). This competition, shaped by ever-changing boundary conditions, is the driving force behind urban spatial transformation.

A settlement that is systematically successful in the ongoing competition with other settlements boasts an urban career where it eventually transforms into a town, city or even a metropolis. Boundary conditions can be of a natural, technological or governmental nature. They affect the number of competitors and the arena or the rules of conduct in the competition. In the twenty-first century, towns are generally understood as smaller than cities mostly based on population figures, whereas in the Middle Ages, town charters were the key criterion. This chapter predominantly uses the term 'town' to describe a settlement with a broad set of urban features.

An important notion applied in this chapter is *hierarchy*. The uniqueness of the spatial configuration of the contemporary Randstad area is usually defined by its presumed lack of hierarchy between four of its largest towns in terms of functions, inhabitants or built-up area. Much of the current literature about the Randstad stresses the polycentric nature of the configuration, as expressed in the 'complementarity' between the functional profiles of the (present) 'Big Four'. Amsterdam is the financial and cultural centre, Rotterdam has the international harbour, The Hague houses national government and a range of international institutions, and Utrecht is the national distribution hub. Complementarity means that functions that are usually combined in one metropolitan centre are distributed over several towns of more or less comparable size. The term 'complementarity' is extensively applied in this chapter.

Descriptions of the history of the Randstad often start in 1850, as from that moment on the spatial configuration of the Randstad acquired its present polycentric or complementary character (see for example Wagenaar and Van Engelsdorp-Gastelaars, 1986). However, to fully understand how and why the spatial configuration of the Randstad developed, we need to go back to its medieval roots. This is exactly what this chapter seeks to do. It is explicitly focused on nine Randstad towns: Utrecht, Amsterdam, Haarlem, Leiden, Delft, The Hague, Gouda, Dordrecht and Rotterdam (see Figure 1.1 in the preceding chapter for the location of these towns). These are the four largest towns of the contemporary Randstad configuration, plus five others that already enjoyed urban features as early as the Middle Ages (Engel, 2005). The nine towns are located in the current three provinces of Utrecht and North and South Holland. During the Middle Ages the former was known as 't Sticht (bishopric or diocese) while the two Holland provinces were joined together until the 1830s. Utrecht is the only town in its namesake province.

This chapter describes spatial transformation in three consecutive governmental stages: the Middle Ages, the Early Modern age and the threshold to the Modern Era. In these periods, the present Randstad area was successively part of the dynastic heritage of feudal lords (until the 1570s), the Dutch Republic (until 1795) and the Kingdom of the Netherlands (after 1795, although the Kingdom was established in 1815). Within these three main governmental periods, seven successive phases or stages, based on trends within long-term change of the spatial configuration, and especially within the urban hierarchy, are discernible. The analysis of the seventh period, after 1870, is given only brief consideration as many key developments are discussed elsewhere in this volume.

In every governmental period, changes within the division of tasks are described. Explicit attention will be paid to infrastructure and changes in the expansion of the built-up surface. The urban hierarchy is systematically analysed by looking at the dominance of cities vis-à-vis others: does the evolution of some towns run parallel to the relative stagnation of others? The second part of the analysis is focused on the incentives and motives each (type of) government had to influence change within the spatial configuration in general or urban structures specifically. Emphasis is put on the implementation of governmental instruments and strategies in each period. When possible, trends in 'national' and urban policy strategies are identified and compared.

The Middle Ages: from a mosaic of middle-sized towns to a primate city

First phase: foundation based on water infrastructure

As in many urban regions in Europe, the Randstad towns were a medieval creation. In the Randstad territory only Utrecht had evolved into a town in the very early Middle Ages. This city developed from an abandoned Roman fortress and combined the functions of being a religious seat, a bureaucratic center for the Sticht province, a local market and hub of international trade between the German Rhineland, Scandinavia and England. The cultivation of the unattractive peatlands and bogs of Holland resulted in a late but fast urbanisation process compared to other parts of Europe. After the appearance of small, scattered settlements in the twelfth and thirteenth centuries, this low-lying and rather wet area experienced a wave of urbanisation in the fourteenth century. This was the true 'big bang' of Holland's urbanisation pattern, when the foundations for the contemporary spatial configuration of the area were created.

Until the end of the thirteenth century, international transit along the large rivers Rhine and Meuse had been decisive for the spatial configuration of the Randstad area. Therefore, Utrecht (in Sticht province) and Dordrecht (in Holland) were the leading centres. This changed as a result of a shift in the distribution of water discharge over the different river branches within the Dutch delta, and the simultaneous cultivation of the low-lying peatlands. Both towns functioned as hubs for international trade – with Dordrecht developing strongly at the expense of Utrecht in the twelfth and thirteenth centuries. Siltation of the Old Rhine river meant that Utrecht was increasingly avoided by international traffic. Other settlements like Haarlem, Leiden, Delft and Gouda, with The Hague as notable exception, were situated on a network of inland waterways that had been created in the twelfth and thirteeenth centuries as a reaction to the silting-up of the dominant branch of the river Rhine (the *Oude Rijn* or old Rhine, see next chapter) as well. At the end of the twelfth century, the inlet at the North Sea coast near Katwijk was completely closed off. The inland network of water infrastructures redirected excess water to the north and the south, where it could be discharged in, respectively, the *Zuiderzee* (Southern Sea) and the rivers IJssel, Lek (both branches of the Rhine), Merwede and Meuse. At the same time, the inland waterways formed the foundation for a transport network, to which extensions for water traffic were added in the following centuries. Amsterdam was Holland's entrance in the north while Gouda and Schiedam offered this possibility in the south.

The water infrastructure network formed the foundation of the Randstad's later configuration. Without the closure of the Rhine, one could speculate that Leiden or Dordrecht could have become the dominant city of the Dutch delta, capturing the east-west bound traffic of north-west Europe. The closure of the Old Rhine's opening to the North Sea choked off international trade in Utrecht and smothered the pristine urban career of Leiden, Holland's oldest town (Leiden was positioned in the heartland of Holland province and was a stronghold for the local count: coins were also issued there; see De Graaf, 2004). Amongst others, the exchange of wine between German and English traders relocated from Utrecht to Dordrecht in the twelfth century, while beer trade between northern Germany and the urbanised Southern Netherlands moved to Amsterdam. During the Middle Ages, another axis of north-south bound international traffic emerged, for which Amsterdam was conveniently located: near the inland waterways, on the shores of the Southern Sea and close to the town of Utrecht. The trade in German beer brought along other products in its wake.

In general, the settlements positioned on the inland waterways performed a variety of functions like toll collection, military bases, coinage and administration. Possibly they were rural markets too, that derived their right of existence from the cultivation of the peatlands in the Dutch delta. Fisheries played a key role in Amsterdam, and possibly in Rotterdam as well. Everywhere, apart from The Hague, the rise of settlements in the peatlands was accompanied with granting of town charters by the count of Holland to Dordrecht (somewhere between 1200 and 1220), Haarlem (1245), Delft (1246), Leiden (1266), Gouda (1272) and Amsterdam (1275) (Kruisheer, 1988). Rotterdam received its first charter in 1299 during a succession conflict concerning the inheritance of the count's seat. Unfortunately, the charter was immediately removed after the conflict had been settled. Rotterdam finally received its charter as late as 1340 (Van der Schoor, 1999).

In contrast with Sticht province, Holland boasted no religious seats. This was most likely due to the fact that the Sticht was a bishopric, and Holland a county or shire: there was sharp competition between its rulers, the bishop of Utrecht and the Duke of Holland (De Graaf, 2004). The Duke thwarted potential influence from his adversary as much as possible, and for this reason the clergy never became a powerful force in Holland. As a result, the urban careers of Holland settlements boasted comparatively few religious functions.

Utrecht and Dordrecht, compared to the settlements along the coastal dunes and the inland waterways, were both located relatively inland at the banks of large rivers. With their focus on international trade, they formed the urban centre of gravity, both demographically and functionally, of the thirteenth-century spatial configuration. In 1300, Utrecht boasted 5,500 inhabitants, followed closely by Dordrecht with 5,000. Leiden (coinage, ducal fortress) and Haarlem (toll, military support) were both relatively large with 3,000 each; Gouda (toll) and Amsterdam (toll) were small with about 1,000 inhabitants while The Hague (ducal bureaucratic centre) and Rotterdam were even smaller.

Second phase: lowland mosaic without an obvious centre of gravity

This pattern was to change drastically in the fourteenth century when Holland developed from an international transit zone towards an export economy based on trade in indigenous products from urban industry and commercial agriculture, shipbuilding and fisheries (Hoppenbrouwers, 2002). This was related to the increasing importance of the trade axis between the Atlantic coast in the south and the Baltic area, Scandinavia and northern Germany in the north. This axis formed an addition to the traditional trade axis between England and France in the west and southern Germany in the east. Holland was positioned on the intersection of both axes.

This provided new opportunities for livelihoods in the cultivated peatlands in the delta (as explained in Chapter 3): which was a most welcome opportunity as the simultaneous deterioration of agriculture, due to subsidence of peat soils, contributed to the economic shift towards shipping, industry and cattle breeding (Kaptein, 2004). It should be noted here that this leap forward, where Holland towns not merely caught up with but also started to surpass an older generation of medieval settlements on higher ground, was directly related to the initially unprofitable location in the low-lying peatlands. Turning a disadvantage into an advantage (Van Bavel and Van Zanden, 2004), the early positioning of international industry and trade meant that the centre of urban gravity in the Netherlands became located below sea-level.

Depending of the settlements' international orientation, industry took the shape of textile production or brewing, coupled with shipping, shipbuilding and other trade relations. It was only in Dordrecht that urban industry failed to develop. In Utrecht's functional profile, the importance of international trade and shipping declined, parallel to the vigorous growth of most Holland settlements in terms of population and built-up area. Even the village of The Hague with its concentration of administrative functions transformed into a textile-producing centre, after it was hooked up to the inland water network on direct orders of the Count in 1345.

As functional profiles changed, the physical appearance of the settlements altered too. Some grew into towns by expanding their harbours through land reclamation and the creation of workers' housing, often with facilities for textile production (Zweerink, 2011). Apart from the expansion of urban ground plans, the network of water infrastructure was also extended near The Hague, but also near Rotterdam and Delft in the 1340s and 1390s (Brand, 2010). By the beginning of the fourteenth century the result was that Holland could be entered from the south from four different entry points: at Schiedam, Rotterdam, Delfshaven and Gouda. In the north, only the route over Amsterdam and Haarlem provided similar opportunities. Competition between towns in the south was therefore relatively strong compared to the north. This resulted in a decreasing hierarchy between the settlements within the spatial configuration in Holland during a time of continued growth within the region. Apart from distribution of specialities that were more or less comparable across the Holland towns, differences in population size had decreased in a period where urban growth was a common phenomenon. Dordrecht had lost its head start and was, with 7,500 inhabitants, the same size as Haarlem. Delft was third largest in Holland with 6,500, followed by Leiden and Gouda (both 5,000), Amsterdam (4,400), Rotterdam (2,500) and The Hague (1,300). In contrast with the province Sticht, where governmental, religious and industrial functions were concentrated in one major city (Utrecht), in Holland these functions were spread out in a more diffuse manner. Here, a mosaic of activities existed without an obvious centre of gravity. This possibly explains why Utrecht had been able to increase its lead: with 13,000 inhabitants, it was far bigger than any town in Holland.

Third phase: a hierarchy emerges during political setbacks

In a third phase, bundling and concentration of international trade relations on the one hand, and specialisation within industry on the other, resulted in more clarity in the fourteenth-century mosaic of activities distributed over the group of middle-sized and small towns in Holland. In contrast to the two preceding periods, this phenomenon did not appear in tandem with the extension of the water infrastructure network (Brand, 2010; Brand and Van Zanden, 2013) but had mainly political causes. The increase of inequality did not happen overnight but in three 'shocks': the first starting in the 1420s, followed by a second one between the late 1470s and the early sixteenth century and a third one starting in the 1520s (Hoppenbrouwers, 2002).

This was the first heavy setback the young towns in Holland experienced, a process that was for a very large part related to war resulting from the process of state formation (Lesger, 1990, 2001; Van Tielhof, 1995). In the Middle Ages, Europe was governed by competing dynasties of lords and the clergy, who were directed from the holy seat in Rome. As the state formation in Europe entered a particular critical phase after the 1350s, civil strife and outbreaks of violence became common across large parts of Europe. Towns and settlements were required to declare loyalty to one ruler or another, resulting in conflicts among factions with competing interests within towns themselves. This was mostly due to wars of succession and expansionist politics of dynastic lords. In the competition, kings gradually got the upper hand over ecclesiastical power. Provinces were consciously merged into larger territorial units by marital policies, conquest and inheritance. In the second part of the fourteenth century, Holland was added to the reign of the House of Bavaria. After the 1425s, the province was assimilated into an even larger territory, that of the House of Burgundy. At the end of the fifthteenth century, the territory of the House Burgundy merged with that of the House of Habsburg. By the time the Dutch Revolt took off in 1568, both Holland and Sticht (added in the 1520s) were part of the large empire of the Spanish king, who ruled over large parts of Western Europe and the New World.

State formation translated not merely into more versatile boundary conditions for competition among settlements, but also in enlargement of scale and the continual adding of more players to the arena. This was most profound for towns with careers in international industry, trade or administration. As the stakes became higher, sudden shifts in government could lead to changing loyalties between trading towns. In particular, the House of Burgundy was frequently involved in large international conflicts. Blockades of ports and waterways by warfare and embargoes hindered trade, while civil strife disrupted production of key commodities such as beer and clothing, and this at a time when competition from other European beer- and cloth-producing centres on the international market soared. If a town was temporarily blocked off from trade and production, competitors eagerly filled in the open space (Van der Wee, 1987). Temporary absence from the international market was usually heavily punished, especially by competition from cheap cloth-producing towns in England. In the southern Netherlands, the largest consumer market for Holland beer, local brewers discovered how to produce their own quality beers. Holland's urban production was pushed from the market by import substitution from consumer markets, a strategy they had previously performed at the cost of established towns in northern Germany and the Southern Netherlands.

Meanwhile, all over Europe population growth, urbanisation and the damage of warfare inflated demand for cereals, the dominant ingredient for both food and beverage in the medieval diet (Van Tielhof, 1995). Merchants and merchant companies like the Hanseatic League therefore turned away from traditional supply areas in France, to the Baltic area in the north. This brought Amsterdam, a relatively modest centre specialised in Baltic grain trade, into an advantageous position. It was during this period that Amsterdam's Baltic relationships, locally dubbed as 'the mother of all trade', began to cause multiplier effects that would enable the town to jump to the very top of the Randstad hierarchy. Grain was in high demand everywhere, and it enabled Amsterdam merchants widespread access to foreign markets.

By the 1560s, the towns in Holland had developed a complementary division of tasks. The Southern Netherlands, under the lead of Antwerp, took the lead in the international staple market (Israel, 1995). The south concentrated on higher-order products such as finance and international trade.

The north specialised in herring, shipping and shipbuilding, cattle breeding, fuel (peat), grain trade and bulk goods like cloth and linen. Cereals formed the lever to foreign markets: where Amsterdam cereals reached southern Europe, salt and other products to be used in domestic industry returned in the ships' holds (Van Tielhof, 1995). This meant that the economic interests of Holland towns were all in some way related to Amsterdam's Baltic trade, because cloth and linen were traded for grain in the north, and grain was traded for salt in the south. Other Dutch products followed in their wake.

As a result, concentration and bundling appeared in the organisation of trade relations with foreign markets, an economic process from which Amsterdam obviously profited (Lesger, 1990, 2001). Amsterdam became the primary staple market for Baltic cereals in Europe – and via trade with the metropolis of Antwerp, reached the world. In the sector structure of other Holland towns, herring, production and supply of foodstuffs and fuel became more important compared to direct international trade, brewing and textile production (Israel, 1995). These towns developed a less resilient functional profile by specialising on one or two dominant economic activities like cheap cloth (Leiden), beer (Delft and Haarlem), linen (Haarlem), herring (Rotterdam) and ropes, cheese and turf (Gouda). This was often accompanied with a change in the position of towns in the configuration of the nine Randstad towns. For example, Gouda became more or less a regional hub, focused on rural production like brick making, fuels (peat), cheese and cattle. Its international brewery declined.

These changes in urban careers resulted in a fallback in the hierarchy for many towns, both functionally as well as demographically: a disadvantage from which it would prove to be rather hard to recover. The centre of gravity within the configuration obviously shifted to the north: towards Amsterdam. Inequality and hierarchy increased. In the 1560s, Amsterdam with its population of 30,000 was far bigger than Utrecht, that had been surpassed with its impressive 27,500 citizens. Leiden and Dordrecht fell back in the hierarchy with, respectively, 12,500 and 1,000 citizens, with Haarlem (16,000) and Delft (15,000) being larger. Gouda (9,000), Rotterdam (7,000) and The Hague (6,000) were the smallest. The lead taken by Amsterdam manifested itself in an obvious increase of built up area in the fifthteenth and sixteenth centuries. Of the nine towns described here, only Amsterdam had to expand its ground area (Rutte, 2006).

The role of government

Medieval government contributed to the rise of this spatial configuration in several ways – and with various motives. In the hostile political environment of the late Middle Ages, local lords were forced into a continuous quest for ways to survive. In the games of power of the lords and their local gentry, towns were amenities that offered shelter in the midst of battle, allies who supplied military support and enabled them the finance of costly wars and princely grandeur by taxing and lending (Tilly, 1992). For this reason, local and regional lords had a strong incentive to stimulate the rise of towns inside their territories (Rutte, 2002), although not all measures stimulating urban growth were distributed by sovereign government. Towns actively gathered competitive advantages themselves through, among other things, the Hanseatic League. Nevertheless, local lords were able to stimulate the rise and growth of towns using a diverse toolbox. Instruments ranged from exclusive stimuli, like safe conduct for urban merchants, infrastructure concessions, donations of land, property and seigniorial rights, town charters, staple rights and toll exceptions; to measures for the 'benefit of all', for example, international and national trade policy, including trade agreements, staple and minting policy and protectionist measures. This holds particularly true for the thirteenth and fourteenth centuries. Especially in the thirteenth century, the count of Holland seized the opportunity offered by challenges regarding water management and infrastructure of the Dutch delta to stimulate international trade in Dordrecht at the cost of Utrecht. Nevertheless, although Dordrecht enjoyed a privileged position in the thirteenth and fourteenth century, all towns were more or less stimulated with a wide selection of exclusive privileges combined with measures to the benefit of the entire county. In the fifteenth century, though the sovereign lord of the provinces was mostly absent and occupied elsewhere (causing a standstill in policymaking), indirect governmental influence, like heavy taxing and prolonged warfare, was harmful to most towns. Amsterdam alone was relatively spared due to unexpected positive side effects of foreign warfare (Brand, 2012).

The urbanisation of Holland had come at a political price. It turned out that towns were not mere soulless pawns to be played out. The dynastic governmental system was a vulnerable one: the unexpected death of a lord or his heir would frequently lead to eruptions of civil and dynastic expansionist warfare. These bouts of civil unrest created setbacks in the urban economy, but also enabled towns to gather power by bargaining with competing lords (Tilly, 1992). For this reason, from the fourteenth century onward representatives from Dordrecht, Haarlem, Leiden, Delft, Gouda and Amsterdam were added to representative institutions within the government of Holland, where previously local gentry and the clergy had reigned. Such towns eventually acquired a vote within the so-called Estates of Holland. It was particularly during the sixteenth century that the Estates of Holland acquired more power, as the sovereign's court resided far away from the province. Using their tax revenue as leverage, the Estates were able to bargain for collective measures profitable to virtually all towns. The urbanisation of the Randstad area therefore forced the sovereign lord to take the Holland Estates' wishes into account, and through it, the wishes of the so-called voting towns. The growth of jurisdictional units discussed above, however, had unfavourable side-effects. To acquire competitive advantages, Holland now had to compete with other, more established counties that were ruled by the same sovereign.

Usually, such areas were given priority over Holland, especially under the rule of the House of Burgundy, Holland's role was to meet tax requirements and keep quiet (Israel, 1995). This would eventually lead to the Dutch Revolt (1568–1648) and the 80 years'long Dutch War of Independence.

Within Holland, shifts in political power meant that governmental influence on the spatial configuration changed. When dynastic and economic interests collided, the Estates could influence towns' competitive position. This is demonstrated by the many war offensives on behalf of the Estates that were fought to keep the Sound (the straight that kept the Baltic Sea connected with shipping from Amsterdam) free from tolls and trade restrictions (Sicking, 2002, 2006). After the absence of positive measures in the fifteenth century – when Holland was just one of the many provinces ruled by the same sovereign as explained above – in the sixteenth century, stimulating policies resumed. Such policies were mostly aimed at the collective, with one notable exception, Amsterdam received exclusive dispensation for a tax on trade in cereals (Van Tielhof, 1995). This was no coincidence. The voting towns gathered power in the Holland Estates, and their interests were strongly connected to those of Amsterdam. In this way, in the fifthteenth- and sixteenth-century governmental action and/or policy in the broadest sense contributed to the dominance of Amsterdam, and increasing imbalance within the spatial configuration of the nine cities.

Early modern age: the dominance of Amsterdam

Fourth phase: Amsterdam capitalises on its headstart

In the early modern age Amsterdam's dominance within the spatial configuration would increase even further. This happened mainly in two phases, although the first years of the Dutch Revolt – between the early 1560s and the late 1580s – could also be defined as a separate era, where the fate of the towns differed greatly as a result of warfare and trade blockades. For example, trade in Rotterdam profited from the fact that Amsterdam remained loyal to the Spanish king for some time (and was therefore blocked from trade by the revolutionaries). Leiden suffered heavily from the 1573–1574 siege. The Hague was virtually abandoned, because the rebellious government preferred the safety of Delft's nearby city walls. But with the closure of the Scheldt river, the entrance to the Antwerp trade metropolis, a period of unprecedented urban growth started.

With Antwerp cut off from trade, international trade relations concentrated in Amsterdam (Lesger, 2001). This caused multiplier effects in key economic branches and allowed Amsterdam to capitalise on its head start (Musterd and De Pater, 1994). Moreover, due to the war between rebellious provinces and Spain, overseas markets formerly reserved for Spanish and Portuguese merchants were up for the taking. Trade from Amsterdam widened its scope and increased its hold on the international market. The new government of the Dutch Republic supported this development by an active policy of economic warfare, with joint stock monopoly trade companies like the United East India Company (Dutch acronym: VOC: *Verenigde Oost-Indische Compagnie*) and the West Indian Company (WIC: *West-Indische Compagnie*) next to traditional warfare policies in the Sound (Van Tielhof, 2002; 't Hart, 2014). Also helpful was the state of competition within Europe which was at an all-time low because of extensive warfare throughout the continent. War not merely removed competition; it also pushed up demand for all kinds of products like weapons, food and so on (Van der Wee, 1987). The concentration of international trade also made the staple market an attractive place for the elaboration and refinery of intermediates (Lesger, 2004). This phenomenon occurred mostly in the world's staple market. The attraction of Amsterdam was so great that it managed to attract weapon manufacturing from Dordrecht, and part of Dordrecht's river trade with southern Germany. The consequence was that international trade, the stock market, printing and mapmaking expanded fiercely.

Amsterdam's head start resulted in increased specialisation in the other eight towns, creating a more unbalanced spatial configuration. Specialisation of one town in a certain activity often appeared parallel to the disappearance of the same activity in another. Textile, an activity that existed more or less in all towns, concentrated in Leiden while bleaching and elaboration of linen became an exclusive speciality of Haarlem (Van de Ree-Scholtens, 1995). Gouda produced pipes, whilst Delft produced pottery (see Figure 2.1). Delft and Gouda lost the remains of their brewing industry to Haarlem. International trade became the speciality foremost associated with Amsterdam, and

Figure 2.1 Ceiling of the 2015 Delft station showing a 1876 map of the city.
Source: Editors.

to a lesser extent of Rotterdam and Dordrecht. The latter two had their focus primarily on England, France and Germany, whereas Rotterdam dominated open seas and Dordrecht river trade. The two stock monopolist companies, the VOC and the WIC, operated virtually exclusively from Amsterdam and Rotterdam, and to a lesser extent from Delft.

These changes in the functional division of tasks appeared in tandem with the expansion of the inland network of waterways between the 1630s and the 1660s (Brand, 2012). Obstacles in existing passages, which had been hindered by trade restrictions or dams, were released for traffic. Between Amsterdam, Haarlem and Leiden entirely new canals were constructed. Once more, the dominance of Amsterdam in this phase was reflected in differences in the expansion of its built-up area (Rutte, 2006): the town acquired its famous wedge shape form (see Figure 2.2). As a result of the Alteration associated with the Dutch Revolt (when Catholics were no longer allowed to worship in public) many former monastic sites in the towns were confiscated and released for redevelopment. This meant that in many towns change took the shape of redevelopment within the city walls: in Delft, Gouda and Utrecht that was sufficient to accommodate population growth (Van Gramsbergen, 2008). In 1670, Amsterdam's dominance was demonstrated by its astonishing population of 219,000, while Leiden (that at the time resembled a multinational cloth company rather than a town) was a far second with just 67,000. In the south, Rotterdam had also grown swiftly and surpassed Haarlem with 45,000 against 38,000 population. Utrecht had grown very little, reaching just 30,000 inhabitants. Delft 25,000, Dordrecht 2,000, The Hague 2,000 and Gouda 1,500 followed. It was a dynamic phase where many towns changed ranks in the demographic hierarchy.

Figure 2.2 Old warehouses along the Brouwersgracht, part of the 3rd extension of the historic inner city (1613–1625).

Source: Editors.

Fifth phase: stagnation and decay, but less so in Amsterdam

From the second half of the seventeenth century, change in the spatial configuration was increasingly in the shape of change in the functional division of tasks between the towns. No new extensions were added to the existing water infrastructure network: the towns had to make do with the status quo. Change in the urban structure in this fifth phase meant that labour-intensive branches of economic activity in towns were replaced, where feasible, by capital-intensive activities like sugar refinery, tobacco, silk, cotton, spice trade, diamonds, coffee and tea, and distilling of gin and brandy (Van der Schoor, 1999; Van Tielhof, 2002). International harbour towns Amsterdam, Rotterdam and to a lesser extent, Dordrecht, succeeded relatively well in the process of replacement of economic activity. Where no replacement could be found, the penalty was decay both in terms of economy and population. This occurred most dramatically in Leiden, Haarlem, Delft and Gouda. Changes appearing within the spatial configuration were for the largest part a result of the spatial division of tasks developed by the towns during the period of fierce growth in the late sixteenth and early seventeenth centuries. Precisely those cities that had 'profited' from positive multiplier effects of the world staple market, particularly Amsterdam, suffered from economic recession and a shrinking population. Leiden, for example, the second city in the hierarchy, was hit severely after it had so incredibly recovered from the first fallback in the fifteenth century.

Overall, this fifth phase was the second great fallback for towns in the Randstad area, and once more, the hierarchy widened. Towns that produced for international export experienced a rough time in their urban career, and usually, these were also the towns located inland on the infrastructure network.

The decay of Holland towns was for a large part caused (once more) by increasing competition on the international market from states that had previously been absent due to warfare. Most of them re-entered the commercial arena in the second half of the seventeenth century. Armed with protectionist policies and mercantilist strategies, these states, especially France and England, were able to repel Dutch products from their domestic markets. Moreover, the Dutch Republic increasingly lost its grip on its colonial empire, as navies from England and other nations expelled her. This happened first in the West Indies, which affected the WIC and later also in the East, with quite devastating consequences for the VOC (De Vries and Van der Woude, 1997). In contrast to other nations, the Dutch Republic had no massive standing armies and navies and relied on constant bargaining to gather together the necessary military force when needed (Tilly, 1992; Stuurman, 1995). In the long run, this was not sufficient to guarantee access to overseas markets. Worse, the tax requirements needed to finance costly wars were borne precisely by towns: warfare was paid for by increasing taxes inside city walls and by the extension of public debt. This was an inheritance from the Middle Ages, when town governments had used tax revenue as leverage to gain power, which is the other side of the same coin. Therefore, the tax burden was much higher inside the city walls than outside. This was translated into higher costs of labour and therefore expensive urban products, which became less attractive on the international market.

Consequently, industrial towns were hit by decay, which resulted in increasing inequality in the spatial configuration of the Randstad area. Amsterdam managed to increase her lead for some time, although in the late eighteenth century she suffered from shrinkage too. Moreover, in the eighteenth century Amsterdam was joined by some unlikely competitors: first of all, The Hague showed little signs of decay. It housed a relatively wealthy population and needed to expand her built-up surface even in the 'poor' eighteenth century. It was kept alive by tax revenue collected elsewhere in the Republic (Hohenberg and Lees, 1985). Also, Utrecht had profited little from the so-called 'Golden Century', and therefore suffered little from shrinkage, too. Rotterdam manifested itself more and more as a direct competitor in international trade. Due to the relapse of former industrial towns, the demographic hierarchy at the end of the eighteenth century began to resemble the contemporary Randstad: the dominant group of Amsterdam, Rotterdam, The Hague and Utrecht emerged in this period. Change in water discharge of different branches of the Rhine also favoured Amsterdam, at the expense of Dordrecht, that was also bothered by the increase of tolls along the Meuse.

In 1795, the year that the Dutch Republic ceased to exist due to civil war combined with expansionist warfare from France, Amsterdam was more dominant than ever with 221,000 inhabitants against 53,212 in its closest competitor, Rotterdam. In the poor eighteenth century many towns had shifted ranks once more. The Hague was now third with 38,500, followed by Utrecht (32,294), Leiden (30,955), Haarlem (21,227), Dordrecht (18,014), Delft (14,099) and Gouda (11,715).

The role of government

The government of the Dutch Republic had its own incentive to stimulate cities, but their motives were more complex than those of its predecessors. First of all, the Estates of Holland – the dominant party within the Estates General – was composed of representatives of no less than 18 cities (the gentry in total held only one vote; this vote supposedly represented also the interests of the countryside). This meant that, since the Estates of Holland generally put its mark on economic policy in the Republic, from the late sixteenth century onward, 18 squabbling towns needed to reach some sort of agreement on this policy. Therefore, in practice, common economic policy meant urban policy, aimed at the economic interests of voting towns. All urban representatives pursued the welfare of their hometown above all the others, and constantly feared that a competitor might profit disproportionally from a stimulating measure. For this reason, the less powerful village of The Hague was chosen once more to house the government and its institutions. It was a system where jealousy thrived: economic policy had to benefit all, or there was no policy at all.

It was largely for this reason that the government toolbox of the Republic was a rather limited one, compared to its medieval predecessors. It consisted purely of international trade policy, distribution of governmental institutions and the granting of infrastructure concessions. Moreover, the zenith of the distribution of competitive advantage was to be found in the formative period of the Republic between the 1570s and the 1620s, when the survival of the new state was still unsure. Indeed, influential stimuli like the housing of a Chamber of one of the patented companies with a state monopoly, like the VOC and the WIC, were placed in towns where merchants were already active in the patented areas. As with minting and infrastructure concessions, policies of the Republic were mainly concerned with legislating and consolidating urban practices that already existed. The Republic was mostly addressing issues where haste was required, like international economic warfare, but otherwise was not particularly active.

As a result of the Dutch Revolt, competing towns with contrary interests and rivalling urban oligarchies were united against a common enemy: the Spanish Empire. The very few common interests they shared were the suppression of rural industry that could compete with the relatively more expensive urban production, and the protection of Amsterdam's international trade. This resulted in the structural implementation of an a old edict against rural production issued by the sovereign lord, Charles V of the Habsburg Empire, on behalf of the Estates. The edict gave towns not only the possibility to suppress the development of rural industry, but also to block the rise of 'parvenu' settlements that could threaten their economic power base. Being technically a village without city walls like the other Holland towns, The Hague was not allowed to develop industrial activity and was prevented from erecting city walls. Although this rule was not followed to the letter – for example a foundry for cannon production, managed on the orders of the Estates General, was to be found here – the functional profile and long-term career of The Hague was characterised mostly by consumerist activities of the well-to-do inhabitants attracted by the government and the Stadholders court.

Paradoxically, in this sphere of competition, one city profited more than others. Amsterdam was the largest urban centre and a hub within the infrastructure network; it housed the Admiralty (naval base) and the Chambers of both the VOC and the WIC. Also, most of the costly wars fought by the Dutch Republic were in the interest of the Amsterdam international staple market. This was probably because other towns were economically dependent in some way on the staple market. They could not afford Amsterdam's interests to be hurt without hurting themselves. Second, Amsterdam was also the biggest net contributor to the treasury and enjoyed confidence from creditors on the capital market. One could say that the other towns were kept hostage by Amsterdam's economic indispensability. As always, this came at a cost. The Republic's policy was intended to protect international trade; it did not tax income from trade and resisted measures to protect the indigenous market from foreign products. As a consequence, once competition on the international market surged and other countries discovered the effects of protectionist measures, the industrial towns began to wither (Van Tielhof, 2002).

The modern era: the dominance of Amsterdam counterfeited

Sixth phase: Rotterdam, The Hague and Utrecht close in on Amsterdam

Until the 1870s, there was relatively little urban growth in the Randstad. Nonetheless, the spatial configuration altered dramatically towards what would become the twentieth-century polycentric urban pattern. Before the first half of the nineteenth century, only The Hague, Rotterdam and to a lesser extent Utrecht and Haarlem showed some population growth, giving them an advantage over other towns that were still recovering from shrinkage in the first two decades of the nineteenth century. Amsterdam was the most prominent of these towns. In Rotterdam growth was inspired by increasing transit along the Rhine between the two industrialising countries Germany and England, in turn due to the distribution of both national and provincial governmental functions and railway-related activities, mostly metals. Elsewhere, very little happened – although in most towns small steps towards modern industry were taken. Notably in Leiden and Haarlem industry experienced a short-lived revival as a result of subsidies by King William II, related to his monopolist policy in the colonies in the Indonesian archipelago. Once the grants stopped, industrial activity sagged. Delft developed an educational profile, as the town witnessed the establishment in 1842 of what was then known as a Royal Academy of Engineering, next to the existing universities of Leiden and Utrecht. Both latter institutions were created under the rule of the Dutch Republic and acquired national (royal) status. The Academy in Delft was a new, royal creation to compensate for the loss of the training centre for military officers. But these changes in function did not result in substantial population growth in the Randstad, which was in sharp contrast to other parts of the new Kingdom, established in 1815. It was in the second half of the nineteenth century when modern large-scale industry appeared wherever canal and railway met, for example, in Delft, but also in The Hague with consequent effects on growth.

The creation of a large-scale infrastructure network was an important condition for growth. New canals, improving the connection between the Rhine on the one hand and the North Sea on the other, were created on King William I orders between the 1820s and 1840s. Shortly thereafter, towns were connected with railroads, some created by private initiative and some by national state-run companies. However, this infrastructure mostly followed the medieval and early-modern system of waterways, rending it virtually obsolete for passenger traffic. In the second half of the nineteenth century, a liberal administration took over power from the King. Under its rule, two large canals connecting both the vastly growing port of Rotterdam and the stagnant harbour of Amsterdam, with industrialising Germany, were created. The new harbours opened in 1872 and 1876, respectively. Although the administration initially wished to pay exclusively for Rotterdam's connection, a struggle in the Second Chamber of national Parliament over the large international channels that changed the once dominant north-south orientation back to its original shape from east to west, was decided in favour of Amsterdam (Van der Woud, 1987).

Seventh phase: elevation and consolidation of the big four

In the 1870s, a period of unprecedented urban expansion started. Stimulating measures taken earlier finally started to have effect. From the 1870s all towns experienced unimaginable growth built on the functional characteristics they had gathered previously. In 1910, Amsterdam had 597,680 inhabitants with Rotterdam at its heels with 418,000, and The Hague a good third with 287,857. Utrecht had 120,208. The others all remained below 10,000. Strangely, in contrast to the early modern age, virtually no towns changed ranks, although growth was a common phenomenon. Population growth was for a large part caused by industrialisation and higher standards of sanitation that reduced mortality rates. Urban features changed once more, this time dramatically, due to enlargement of scale and specialisation: city walls were removed; upper-class residential areas arose in the vicinity of towns where there were attractive greener pastures; and large-scale industry and workers' housing was developed near canals and railroads. Within the original core of the towns housing gave way to large-scale retail, offices, insurance companies, banks and hotels, a phenomenon dubbed *city formation*. Although the pace at which this happened differed from town to town – Amsterdam, for example, was early while Leiden was late – railroad stations often gave the impulse. These appeared next to traditional local and regional functions like markets, water boards, chambers of commerce, municipal governments, universities and schools, theatres and cafés. Although the urban hierarchy had been consolidated, the ranking of the size of the towns remained constant. What needs to be noted is that the late nineteenth century, and more so the twentieth century, saw the rise of completely new settlements. The group of nine towns that are discussed here were complemented by other new towns, who would pursue their own careers in the boundary conditions offered at the time. Their rise, however, falls out of the scope of this chapter.

The role of government

During the reign of the Republic, the towns themselves had been able to decide on national policy and therefore on each other's competitive position. In so far they were controlled, it was by other towns. Thorbecke, the leader of the liberal political movement, managed to create a central government of unprecedented power in the second half of the nineteenth century. This national state had to negotiate less with its lower tiers of administration, and certainly not with its former adversaries: the urban patriciate. Although the governments of the Dutch kings and the liberal politicians differed greatly, they were faced with comparable challenges and sought possible solutions in comparable directions. The new state was virtually bankrupt and wanted to prove its economic right to existence by developing large-scale industry. The first kings of the Netherlands pursued this aim with an interventionist policy that combined traditional elements like stimulation of the staple market, state monopolies and economic restriction in rural areas with a proactive attitude towards the creation of new infrastructure. The new, liberal administration set about reorganising government in order to create an attractive entrepreneurial climate (Aerts, 1999). In 1840, the province of Holland was split into two separate halves as a means to balance power vis-à-vis the other provinces and national government in general. The provincial administration of the northern part was located in Haarlem instead of in the much larger Amsterdam. The bureaucracy of the south went to accompany national government in The Hague. While government was reorganised, financial responsibilities were altered radically. This happened in tandem with a shift towards an ever more proactive attitude of government on the national level, particularly on infrastructure.

In the second and third quarter of the nineteenth century, the government began a particularly active phase of involvement in the spatial configuration of what was to become the Randstad. Changes in the spatial configuration were mostly the result of a shift to industrial modes of production, the abolition of local taxes and tolls and the construction of (inter)national infrastructure. All this caused a process of enlargement of scale from which 'the West' (the provinces of North- and South-Holland and Utrecht) profited highly (Knippenberg and De Pater, 1988). The city of Utrecht developed into a national infrastructure hub where rail, canal and highways met; it became a national distribution centre. Rotterdam became the leading harbour and for some time was even the world's biggest maritime centre, leaving Amsterdam far behind. Dordrecht lost its role of hub in international (overseas) passages for passengers and bulk goods to Rotterdam; the same happened with Gouda's role as regional hub. Amsterdam was able to maintain its international harbour as a result of the North Sea Channel, but had to acknowledge Rotterdam as superior. The town specialised in financial and cultural services. The Hague, with its ever-increasing national and provincial apparatus, attracted firms and inhabitants and for some time even industry: until the town lost those to Rotterdam's deepwater harbours, too. Leiden and Delft were small industrial centres that both profited from the national universities. The present Randstad configuration with four dominant towns – Amsterdam, Rotterdam, The Hague and Utrecht in this order – had become a fact.

Conclusion

This chapter has summarised a long-term examination of the political economy of the region and the emergence of its urban structure. The functional relations between towns have become increasingly stratified over time. It seems that the hierarchy of the spatial configuration has varied but has generally become ever more established with more levels within which towns of comparable calibre compete. The general pattern is that once a town experienced a setback during an economic crisis it has been virtually impossible to recover, let alone climb up to a higher level. Also, it seems that urbanisation in the Randstad area has generally been a process of urban concentration that has only been varied under extraordinary circumstances.

Looking at the motives and incentives of government over the ages, it can be concluded first that these were always the same: money (tax revenue) and power. Over time, active and less-active phases of governmental involvement with changes in the spatial configuration can be identified. Active phases usually appeared parallel with periods of urban expansion. Only the period of the second and third quarter of the nineteenth century (our sixth phase), when government was very proactive and urban growth marginal, is exempted from this trend.

Second, we can conclude that in regard to the measures taken by government to influence the spatial configuration and urban structure, a distinction can be made between general stimulating measures to the benefit of all towns and exclusive privileges aimed at just one town or several towns. In the Middle Ages the toolkit was mixed, and in the early modern age, common measures were preferred. In the modern era, common policy was so intricate locally that it is almost exclusive.

Third, over time there has been a shift towards a more active approach of central government which constructed and financed infrastructure, a task formerly left to towns themselves. Moreover, we saw a change in financial responsibilities, where central government acquired financial means hitherto belonging to urban government. This has reduced the power of urban government to bargain with central government over policy. Finally, it is remarkable that the reorganisation of governmental responsibilities appear to be in parallel with a change in the implementation and distribution of stimulating measures in policy. After Amsterdam gained power in the Holland Estates, it managed to consolidate its economic power politically by wielding national policy to its advantage during the Dutch Republic's existence. Under the nation state that followed, policy briefly prioritised other economic interests and towns over that of Amsterdam – which facilitated the rise of Rotterdam, The Hague and Utrecht. This suggests that political motives may be a more important driver for the rise of the polycentric Randstad than is often thought.

48   *Nikki Brand*

References

Aerts, R., De Liagre Böhl, H., De Rooy, P. and Te Velde, H. (1999). *Land van kleine gebaren. Een politieke geschiedenis van Nederland 1780–1990 [Land of Small Gestures: A Political History of the Netherlands 1780–1990]*. SUN, Nijmegen.

Brand, N. (2010). 'The rise of the Randstad: An investigation using the rank-size rule (11th – 21st centuries)', *OverHolland*, 9, 55–80.

Brand, N. (2012). *De wortels van de Randstad [The Roots of the Randstad]*; Overheidsin-vloed en stedelijke hiërarchie in het westen van Nederland tussen de 13de en de 20ste eeuw, PhD thesis TU Delft, A+BE 2012 #02. Faculty of Architecture and the Built Environment, Delft.

Brand, N. and Van Zanden, J.L. (2013). 'Infrastructuur in een stedenlandschap. Holland 1200–1850' [Infrastructure in a landscape of cities], *TSEG/Low Countries Journal of Social and Economic History*, 10(3), 3–32.

Castells, M. (1996). *The Rise of the Network Society*. Blackwell, Cambridge, MA.

De Graaf, R. (2004). *Oorlog om Holland, 1000–1375 [War about the Netherlands]*. Ver-loren, Hilversum.

De Vries, J. and Van der Woude, A. (1997). *The First Modern Economy; Success, Failure and Perserverance of the Dutch Economy, 1500–1815*. Cambridge University Press, Cambridge.

Engel, H. (2005). 'Randstad Holland in kaart', [The Randstad in maps], *OverHolland*, 2, 23–45.

Hohenberg, P.M. and Lees, L.H. (1985). *The Making of Urban Europe, 1000–1950*. Harvard University Press, Cambridge, MA.

Hoppenbrouwers, P. (2002). 'Van waterland tot stedenland' [From land of waters to land of cities]. In: De Nijs, T. and Beukers, E. (Eds) *Geschiedenis van Holland [History of Holland]*. Deel 1: tot 1572. Verloren, Hilversum, 103–148.

Israel, J.I. (1995). *The Dutch Republic. Its Rise, Greatness and Fall, 1477–1806*. Oxford University Press, Oxford.

Jacobs, J. (1984). *Cities and the Wealth of Nations*. Random House, New York.

Kaptein, H. (2004). 'Poort van Holland. De economische ontwikkeling 1200-1578' [The Gateway of Holland. Economic Developmen 1200-1578]. In: Carasso-Kok, M. (Ed) *Geschiedenis van Amsterdam 1. Een stad uit het niets: tot 1578 [History of Amsterdam 1: A city appearing from nowhere: until 1578]*. Sun, Amsterdam, 109–174.

Knippenberg, H. and De Pater, B. (1988). *De Eenwording van Nederland [The Unifi-cation of The Netherlands]; Schaalvergroting en integratie sinds 1800*. SUN, Nijmegen.

Kruisheer, J. (1988). 'Stadsrechtbeoorkondiging en stedelijke ontwikkeling' [Decisions on City Charters and Urban Development]. In: Cordfunke, E.H.P., Hugenholtz, F.W.N. and Sierksema, Kl. (Eds) *De Hollandse stad in de dertiende eeuw [The Dutch Town in the Thirteenth Century]*. Walburg Pers, Zutphen, 44–54.

Lesger, C. (1990). *Hoorn als stedelijk knooppunt [Hoorn as Urban Node]; Stedensysteem tijdens de late middeleeuwen en vroegmoderne tijd*. Verloren, Hilversum.

Lesger, C. (2001). *Handel in Amsterdam ten tijde van de Opstand [Trade in Amsterdam during the Uprise]*. Verloren, Hilversum.

Lesger, C. (2004). 'De wereld als horizon [The world as the horizon]; De economie tussen 1578 en 1650'. In: Frijhoff, W. and Prak, M. (Eds) *Geschiedenis van Amster-dam [History of Amsterdam]*. Centrum van de wereld: 1578–1650. SUN, Amsterdam, 103–187.

Musterd, S. and De Pater, B. (1994). *Randstad Holland; Internationaal, regionaal, lokaal*. Van Gorcum, Assen.

Rutte, R. (2002). *Stedenpolitiek en stadsplanning in de Lage Landen (12de-13de eeuw) [City Politics and Town Planning in the Low Countries (12th and 13th Century)]*. Walburg Pers, Zutphen.

Rutte, R. (2006). 'Groei en krimp in de Hollandse stad [Growth and shrinkage of the Holland town]. Stadsuitbreidingen, stedenbouw en ontstedelijking in Holland van de veertiende tot de negentiende eeuw', *OverHolland*, 3, 29–56.

Sicking, L. (2002). 'De integratie van Holland [The integration of Holland]. Politiek en bestuur in de Bourgondisch-Habsburgse tijd'. In: De Nijs, T. and Beukers, E. (Eds) *Geschiedenis van Holland [History of Holland]. Deel 1: tot 1572*. Verloren, Hilversum, 259–290.

Sicking, L. (2006). 'Amphibious warfare in the Baltic: The Hansa, Holland and the Habsburgs'. In: Trim, D.J.B. and Fissel, M.C. (Eds) *Amphibious Warfare 1000–1700*. Brill, Leiden, 69–101.

Stuurman, S. (1995). *Staatsvorming en politieke theorie [State Formation and Political Theory]; Drie essays over politieke en staatkundige ontwikkelingen in Europa vanaf de Vroege Middeleeuwen tot het heden en over het feminisme*. Bert Bakker, Amsterdam.

'T Hart, M. (2014). *The Dutch Wars of Independence: Warfare and Commerce in the Netherlands 1570-1680*. Routledge, London.

Tilly, C. (1992). *Coercion, Capital and European States, AD 990–1992*. Basil Blackwell, Cambridge.

Van Bavel, B.J.P. and Van Zanden, J.L. (2004). 'The jump-start of the Holland Economy during the Late-Medieval crisis, c.1350–c.1500', *Economic History Review*, 75(3), 503–532.

Van de Ree-Scholtens, G. (Ed.) (1995). *Deugd boven geweld [Virtue above Violence]; Een geschiedenis van Haarlem (1245–1995)*. Verloren, Hilversum.

Van der Schoor, A. (1999). *Stad in aanwas: Geschiedenis van Rotterdam tot 1813 [A Growing City: History of Rotterdam until 1813]*. Waanders, Zwolle.

Van der Wee, H. (1987). 'Antwoord op een industriële uitdaging: de Nederlandse steden tijdens de late middeleeuwen en de nieuwe tijd' [Response to an industrial challenge: The Dutch cities during the middle ages and the modern age], *Tijdschrift voor Geschiedenis*, 100(2), 169–184.

Van der Woud, A. (1987). *Het Lege Land [The Empty Land]; De Ruimtelijke Orde van Nederland 1798–1848*. Meulenhoff, Amsterdam.

Van Gramsbergen, E. (2008). 'Verborgen Amsterdam: het Binnengasthuis en de transformatie van de voormalige kloosterterreinen na de Alteratie' [Hidden Amsterdam: The Binnengasthuis and the transformation of former monastery sites after the alteration], *OverHolland*, 6, 21–38.

Van Tielhof, M. (1995). *De Hollandse graanhandel, 1470-1570 [The Dutch Grain Trade, 1470-1570]*; Koren op de Amsterdamse molen. De Bataafsche Leeuw, The Hague.

Van Tielhof, M. (2002). 'Een open economie, in voor- en tegenspoed' [An open economy through thick and thin]; De economische ontwikkeling van Holland. In: De Nijs, T. and Beukers, E. (Eds) *Geschiedenis van Holland [History of Holland]. Deel 1: tot 1572*. Verloren, Hilversum, 135–180.

Wagenaar, M. and Van Engelsdorp-Gastelaars, R. (1986). 'Het ontstaan van de Randstad, 1815–1930' [The origin of the Randstad, 1815–1930], *KNAG Geografisch Tijdschrift*, 20(1), 14–29.

Zweerink, K. (2011). 'De ruimtelijke volwassenwording van de Hollandse stad (1200–1450) [The coming of age of the Dutch town]. Een vergelijkende analyse van het ontstaan van de contouren van de Randstad aan de hand van stadsplattegronden', *OverHolland*, 10/11: 152–172.

3 Urban configurations in a dynamic delta landscape

Han Meyer

Introduction

The development of the collection of Dutch cities, known as the Randstad, is linked strongly to the position of the territory in the delta of the two rivers Rhine and Meuse. Taking this position into account is perhaps enough to understand an important condition for economic and urban development in this region, namely as a strategic interface between overseas shipping routes and the European hinterland. The dynamics of the delta landscape and the specific way that people tried to intervene in this landscape and manipulate it created the conditions for a specific spatial structure. The dynamics of the delta landscape itself are defined by natural processes which are interacting with each other, like climate change (which is as old as earth itself), sea level rise, river discharges, tidal currents, sediment transport by river and sea currents, wind, vegetation and soil composition. These processes result in specific patterns of land formation, which are dynamic because the natural conditions are changing continuously. The interventions and manipulations by people in this dynamic landscape are attempts to control these processes in order to profit from the favourable qualities of the landscape (for agriculture, fishing, trade, etc.), and to provide safe living conditions, especially against flooding. Often, these interventions have led to unexpected side effects, like serious subsidence because of the drainage of peat and clay soils or salt intrusion because of the dredging of river mouths, which in turn lead to new interventions to tackle the side effects. The specific ways of intervening and manipulating in the delta are dependent on economic and technical conditions and contexts, which also have changed through history. Finally, the answer to the questions of why, how and where interventions and manipulations are developed and applied depends strongly on the organisation of society, particularly the organisation of governmental and legal structures and cultural positions, all of which are also changing through history.

This chapter seeks to show how the development of the spatial structure of the Randstad can be regarded as the outcome of three processes: (1) the dynamics of the landscape; (2) the changing economic and technical conditions; and (3) changing societal conditions. The combination of these three processes has resulted in different development-stages of the Randstad region, each time with a specific spatial structure as an outcome. The change from one stage to another can be regarded as a critical transition (Scheffer, 2009), which is the crucial process of finding a new balance among the three processes, which results in a new urban spatial pattern. The following sections will describe five successive stages concentrating on the transition from one stage to another. Each section contains a map, which shows the main spatial characteristics of the stage. This series of sections will finish with the current situation, which also can be considered as a situation of transition. The concept of the 'Randstad' is a result of the previous stage, while the conditions in all three processes (nature, economy and technology, and societal organisation) are changing fundamentally and force again the search for a new balance – possibly resulting in a completely new spatial structure.

The 'big exploitation' with the Rhine as main corridor

The formation of the territory of the present Randstad area is the result of a long process starting with the last ice-age 10,000 years ago. While the North Sea basin was filled with water as a result of melting ice caps, a series of barrier islands was formed by the combination of strong sea currents and sediment transport. Through the centuries, these barrier islands were linked to each other and formed a closed sandy coastline with beaches and dunes, interrupted by the outlets of the rivers Rhine, Meuse and Scheldt. Behind this coastline, a large lagoon with marshlands created the condition for sediment-deposits of the rivers and for vegetation, resulting in the formation of alluvial soils of clay and peat (Van de Ven, 2004; Saeijs, 2006; Wong *et al.*, 2007). This was the landscape which the Romans found when they conquered this part of Europe around the start of our calendar. The Romans considered especially the embankments of the river Rhine and Meuse as interesting possibilities for fortified settlements. The whole stretch of the Rhine located in what now is known as the Netherlands functioned as the borderline of the Roman Empire (the *limes ripa*), while in the Dutch context, the embankments of Rhine and Meuse, relatively high elevations in the middle of muddy marshlands, were the most attractive places to settle. In this period, a number of present Dutch cities found their origin. For our story especially, the foundation of a series of fortified settlements at the embankments of the Rhine is important: Utrecht, Woerden, Alphen, Leiden and Katwijk (Colenbrander and MUST, 2005). This branch of the Rhine, now known as the *Oude Rijn* (Old Rhine), was the main outlet of the Rhine and of great importance from a military as well as economic point of view: the Rhine functioned as a defendable borderline and as an economic transport axis.

When the Romans were gone and a new wave of settlers showed interest in this territory eight centuries later, this branch of the Rhine still functioned as a main corridor in the region. The governmental situation was changed in a way that the most western part was defined as the county of Holland, while the region around the city of Utrecht had the status of a diocese. The territo-rial conflicts between the Count of Holland and the Bishop of Utrecht were numerous during the ninth and tenth centuries (Blockmans, 2010). In this period both authorities started an active policy to develop the uninhabited marshlands of Holland and Utrecht into productive farmland. This project of the 'big exploitation' (cf. Van Tielhof and Van Dam, 2006) was only possible with the layout of an extensive drainage system, which was developed by the farmers themselves. The new settlers came from all over north-west Europe, attracted by the condition that they would get a status of *free* farmers and would become private owners of their land. They could buy concessions to exploit parcels of marshland, under the condition that they would contribute to the layout of the necessary drainage system. In this way most of the terri-tory of Holland and Utrecht was transformed from swampy marshlands into rationally parcelled farmland from the ninth to the thirteenth century. The farmers were obliged to form communities (*ambachten* or shires in English) which took care of the coordination of layout and maintenance of drainage systems at the local scale. Water boards were responsible for water manage-ment at the scale of a coherent water system. There were thousands of boards; in fact until the 1950s, more than 2,500 water boards were active in the Neth-erlands (Van de Ven, 2004; Van Tielhof and Van Dam, 2006). Since then, a process of mergers has taken place, resulting in 21 water boards by 2019.

The river Rhine (the present Oude Rijn) again played a main role. First, the river was the central axis of the complex of drainage systems in the whole region. All the superfluous water from central Holland and Utrecht was transported to and drained into this river by the newly dug drainage systems. Second, because of the growing population and increasing economic activity in the region, the cities along the river gained in importance as regional and trade centres. With hindsight it now seems self-evident that the stretch of cities along the Rhine branch, from Utrecht to Katwijk, would become the urban corridor of Holland and Utrecht par excellence (see Figure 3.1).

The delta landscape turning inside-out

From the eleventh century some important changes took place which forced a reorganisation of the whole spatial system of central Holland and Utrecht. The first change was formed by the process of silting up of the Rhine and the shift of the main discharge of the river southbound via the branch *Lek,* finally merging together with the mouth of the river Meuse. There were several rea-sons for this process. Some extreme storm events in the eleventh century led to an input of large amounts of sediments in the Rhine mouth. Because these sediments blocked the discharge of river water, the water level in the Rhine raised, resulting in several floods. In order to tackle this problem, a dam was built in the Rhine near the town Wijk bij Duurstede, forcing the river water to flow through the Lek branch (Van Tielhof and van Dam, 2006). The dis-charge of the Rhine southbound was stimulated by the coming into existence

Figure 3.1 The Netherlands ca. 1000, for explanation see text.
Source: Teake Bouma, TU Delft.

of the south-west delta. This area of the outlets of the rivers Meuse and Scheldt was transformed into a system of estuaries and islands, as a result of the combination of several storms and the increased vulnerability of the land because of human occupation and exploitation. The drainage systems had led to subsidence of the land. Moreover, people dug large parts of the land for the purpose of salt extraction. The subsiding and partly excavated land was not protected very well against the furious storms in the period 1100–1500. Large amounts of land were washed away, which contributed to the creation of this system of estuaries, which we now call the 'South-west Delta' (Van de Ven, 2004; Saeijs, 2006). Finally, the moving of tectonic plates tends to result in a 'tilting' of the Dutch territory, which creates steady elevation of the north-east part of the Dutch territory and a lowering of the south-west part. Also, this process contributed to a southbound moving of the Rhine mouth (Wong *et al.*, 2007).

The second important change was the creation of a large lagoon north of Utrecht, the *Zuiderzee*. Until the tenth century, there was an inner-lake called Almere north of Utrecht. Again, as a consequence of periods of heavy storms which washed away large amounts of land, this lake came in open connection with the sea and got the name Zuiderzee ('Southern Sea'). This sea came also into connection with the former Lake IJ, which was extended by several storms and reached to the northern edge of the central Holland area as shown in Figure 3.2. These changes created problems but also new opportunities. The first problem was a further decay of the Rhine (Oude Rijn) as a main transport corridor for navigation and trade. Until the sixteenth century, several attempts were made to reopen the river mouth near Katwijk, however, without success (Bisschops, 2006). The second, related problem was the decreased possibility to use the Oude Rijn as the main discharge axis of the drainage system of the whole region. With the silting up of the river mouth, it became even more of a problem to keep the Rhine water out of the land. The third problem was the immediate threat of flooding by the sea inlets of the Zuiderzee and the Southwest Delta. Instead of a relatively safe land behind the dunes, central Holland had become a vulnerable territory, threatened by flooding in the north by the Zuiderzee and IJ and in the south by the branches of the Southwest Delta. Moreover, this vulnerability for flooding was increased because of the serious land subsidence, caused by the large-scale drainage systems. The continuous drainage of peat-land resulted in the oxidation of the dry peat, which leads to shrinkage of the volume of peat and consequently to land subsidence, with large parts of land falling below sea level (Van de Ven, 2004).

The new sea inlets of the Zuiderzee and the Southwest Delta however offered also new opportunities, for trading routes as well as for discharge of the drainage systems. In order to profit from these opportunities, a complete reorientation of the drainage system as well as of the spatial structure of the urban system was needed. At the same time, it would be necessary to create a defence against flooding from the IJ and from the Meuse mouth. This is exactly what happened from the thirteenth century onwards, coordinated and stimulated by the Count of Holland and the water boards. The drainage systems were indeed reorganised and linked to the IJ and the Meuse, which got a new role as main discharge channels of central Holland. This project was only possible with a new role of the water boards. Until then, their role was to create and to control rules for drainage systems. With the big new project, which aimed to turn the whole existing drainage system inside out, water boards started to work together in order to be able to turn around the drainage systems of several contiguous water districts. These collaborations resulted in the founding of new, regional, authorities: the *heemraadschappen*, which started to play a role as planning institutions and executive boards at a regional scale (Van Tielhof and Van Dam, 2006). Around the same time, the Count of Holland initiated dike construction along the IJ and the Meuse-mouth. Two long stretches of dikes were built to protect the central Holland area from flooding (Van de Ven, 2004).

Finally, small local communities along the IJ and the Meuse started to take profit from the favourable position at the sea inlets. The resulting cities played a crucial role in the new water management system. Most of them were located at strategic sites where small peat-rivers flow into larger rivers or sea-arms: Amsterdam and Haarlem at the edges of the IJ, Rotterdam, Schiedam, Vlaardingen at the edge of the Meuse-mouth (Borger *et al.*, 2011). The peat-rivers, like Amstel, Rotte, Schie and Spaarne, played a role as main-elements of the drainage systems but also as navigation routes for trade and transport. The constructing of dams in the mouths of these peat rivers had three functions: (1) they were part of the flood defence system along the larger water; (2) the drainage could be controlled with the dams; and (3) trade traffic could be controlled. These dams were the origin of a series of new urban settlements, as the names show: Amsterdam, Rotterdam, Schiedam, Gouda (originally Goudam), etc. When the territory of central Holland became one large drainage-machine, the cities became the switches to steer and control this machine. The dams and linking water-systems were the main-elements in the spatial structures of these cities (Hooimeijer *et al.*, 2005; Hooimeijer, 2011, 2014). Right up to the present day, the Dam Square of Amsterdam can be regarded as one of the most important urban public spaces of the Netherlands. So next to the water boards, the cities started to play an important role in the lay-out and control of the drainage system. This double-responsibility led to many frictions and conflicts between water boards and city authorities however (Van de Ven, 2004; Bos *et al.*, 2008). The Count of Holland decided to choose a relatively high and dry location in the dunes as comfortable location for his residence: The Hague. So also, this city originates from the thirteenth century.

This radical turning inside out of the region of central Holland resulted in the disappearance of the Oude Rijn as a central corridor and a new emphasis on the meaning of the edges of the region, as shown in Figure 3.2. Thus, the main spatial frame for the present Randstad was founded. During the seventeenth century, Amsterdam and Rotterdam in particular were able to take profit from their new favourable positions, with good accessibility via the Zuiderzee and the mouth of the Meuse, and at the same time, being well connected to the other cities in the central Holland area by a network of ca-nals. The result of the concentration on 'the edges' made the most urbanised region of the world with the 'first modern economy' (De Vries and Van der Woude, 1997). In the framework of the Dutch Republic, composed by seven provinces, Holland was by far the richest and most powerful. The cities in the central part of the province, headed by Amsterdam, reached enormous power and wealth (Brand, 2012; see also Chapter 2 in this volume). However, the mighty cities of Holland still had to fear some competition from cities in the province of Zeeland (Middelburg and Vlissingen) as well as in the northern part of Holland (Hoorn and Enkhuizen). These cities collaborated also with the cities of central Holland in the first large shareholder company, the VOC: *Verenigde Oost-Indische Compagnie* (United East-Indian Company).

The manipulation of the water levels and drainage systems reached an ex-tremely high level of sophistication from the sixteenth century. This was stimulated by the almost continuous state of war when the Dutch Republic fought for its independence from the Habsburg Empire, and also became in-volved in many conflicts with other European powers during the seventeenth

Figure 3.2 The Netherlands ca. 1600, for explanation see text.
Source: Teake Bouma, TU Delft.

and eighteenth centuries (Israel, 1995). The techniques of land-inundation became a notorious but highly effective instrument to stop invaders and were used to develop a complete system comprising a water defence line at the east-side of central Holland and Utrecht (Steenbergen *et al.*, 2009a).

Exhausting the centre of the Randstad

The growth of urban development, especially along the edges of the IJ and Meuse, produced a new problem: the need for energy for the new urban industries, for heating the houses and for cooking. The energy source was found in the territory itself. Peat, when dug and dried, appeared to be an excellent fuel. A large industry of peat-exploitation was developed between the fifteenth and eighteenth centuries, digging the peat in large parts in the countryside between the cities until there was almost nothing left but water (Borger, 1992; Van de Ven, 2004; Van Tielhof and Van Dam, 2006). Thus, large parts in the central area of Holland were ruined completely and transformed into extensive water bodies. A positive effect was that these new lakes could be added to the networks of waterways which already connected the

Dutch cities with each other. A negative effect was that the new lakes resulted in substantially more land loss as the peat edges of the lakes crumbled away during storms. This process threatened many villages and small towns, but finally also the larger cities like Amsterdam and Leiden. In particular, the Haarlemmermeer and the Leidsche Meer, both results of peat digging, became larger in size after every storm and became linked to each other in a gigantic so-called 'water wolf', seriously threatening the cities Amsterdam and Leiden (Rooijendijk, 2009). Attempts and proposals to reclaim these waters were frustrated for two reasons: first, by the resistance of tradesmen and shipowners, who considered the lakes as essential parts of their transport infrastructure (and cheap, without any maintenance costs); and second, by the lack of sufficient technological means. It is true that reclaiming lakes by using windmills had already begun in the seventeenth century creating famous polder areas as the Beemster, the Schermer and the Purmer in the northern part of Holland (Steenbergen *et al.*, 2009b). However, windmill technology was not able to deal with the size of a lake like the Haarlemmermeer. The necessary power to reclaim larger lakes only came into reach with the introduction of steam energy in hydrological technology of the nineteenth century. With the building of the largest steam-powered pumping engines in the world, engineer Beijerinck was finally able to reclaim the Haarlemmermeer in 1850 (Rooijendijk, 2009).

Before the mid-nineteenth century, the centre of Holland, which today is known as the Green Heart, was mainly blue, as shown in Figure 3.3. This process of exhausting the central territory demonstrates the absence of any interest to urbanise this central part of the region; its most important function was to use the peat to enable the ongoing urbanisation at the edges.

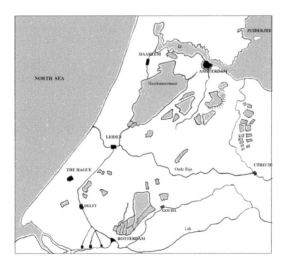

Figure 3.3 Central Holland ca. 1800, with the lakes as a result of peat digging.
Source: Author.

A national policy: the reconnection with the world

The exhaustion of the centre of Holland was one matter of increasing concern for the cities of Holland from the eighteenth century onwards. Another matter of increasing concern was the decreasing navigability of the Meuse mouth and of the Zuiderzee because of ongoing silting up processes. When steam-technology enabled the building of larger ships which needed deeper water channels, the accessibility of the two largest ports of the Netherlands, Amsterdam and Rotterdam, became a problem. Sea vessels heading to Rotterdam had to make long detours through the estuaries of the Southwest Delta (Balk, 1985). Also, the route to Amsterdam through the Zuiderzee became a problem. The island Pampus in the IJ, with a number of sandbanks blocked the entrance of the Amsterdam harbour during low tide, and became proverbial in 'lying for Pampus', a Dutch expression of lethargy. The solution of these problems needed a new authority and a new technology. Digging new entrances from the sea to the ports was too complex and too expensive for the local authorities of the cities, and also for the regional authorities of the provinces and water boards.

There was another problem which also needed to be solved. The silting up process of the Southwest Delta resulted frequently in serious flooding in upstream areas. Also, the provinces Utrecht and Holland were threatened by flooding of the rivers: now the water would come from the east. So, instead of flood danger from the West (sea), the North (IJ) and the South (Southwest Delta), the main danger of flooding for central Holland in the eighteenth and nineteenth centuries came from the interior (the peat lakes, especially the Haarlemmermeer) and the east (the upstream river area).

When the Dutch Republic came under French command during the Napoleonic period, the process of national unification accelerated. An important measure was the foundation of a national Water Management Agency in 1798, later named *Rijkswaterstaat* (Bosch and Van der Ham, 1998). After 1814, when the Netherlands became a Kingdom, this process of national unification was continued. Confronted with the problems of Holland and especially with the decay of the accessibility of the seaports, the prime-minister Thorbecke (three times prime-minister in the period 1849–1872) tried to develop a strategy comparable with the big 'turning inside out' project of the thirteenth century. He proposed to remove the seaport activities from Rotterdam and Amsterdam to the cities of Vlissingen in the southwest and Harlingen in the north of the country (Van der Woud, 2006). Vlissingen was especially regarded as a potential mainport situated next to a deep channel which guaranteed permanent accessibility. During the 1860s, a special railroad was constructed to link Vlissingen with the German hinterland, and a series of new harbours were planned around the city.

However, this second turning inside-out was not realised. The established powers of port and trade companies of Amsterdam and Rotterdam did not agree with a total removal to the periphery of the country. Moreover, this proposed repositioning of the ports would not solve the increasing flooding problems of the upstream river areas. It was the engineer Caland who showed that digging a new waterway from the sea to Rotterdam could solve two problems: it would create a new access to the Rotterdam port and it would function as a new discharge channel, which would relieve the upstream areas from the surplus river-water. By studying historic maps, Caland discovered the tendency of the Rhine to move its mouth southbound. First the Old Rhine silted up, now the same happened with the mouth of the Meuse. By digging the New Waterway (*Nieuwe Waterweg*), he tried to fix the outlet of the Rhine (Ten Horn van Nispen *et al.*, 1994; Van de Ven, 2008). In 1872 the Nieuwe Waterweg was opened. In order to avoid a negative effect on Amsterdam, this city was also provided with a new entrance from the sea by digging the North Sea Canal (*Noordzeekanaal*), which was opened in 1876 (Van der Geest *et al.*, 2008).

The Nieuwe Waterweg and North Sea Canal were part of a large series of canal and canalisation projects in the river area, providing better navigability as well as improved discharge of the rivers (Ten Horn-van Nispen *et al.*, 1994). However, it is important to keep in mind an important difference between *Nieuwe Waterweg* and North Sea Canal. The New Waterway is essentially a new, artificial, mouth of the rivers Rhine and Meuse. It means that the water levels in the Nieuwe Waterweg, Nieuwe Maas and the more upstream river stretches, are influenced by the sea as well as by the discharge of the rivers. Because of the construction of the Nieuwe Waterweg, the tidal range in the Nieuwe Maas increased from 1.1 to 1.8 metre. During storm surges, the water levels in the Nieuwe Maas can go up to more than 3 metres above mean sea level.

The North Sea Canal is quite another story. The canal is not an outlet of a river system, but a connection between the North Sea and the IJ. The dunes were cut through, and the existing IJ was reclaimed, leaving a stretch which connects the new canal with the port of Amsterdam. As well at the west as at the east, the canal was provided with lock systems. So, the water level in the canal is a controlled water level, independent from and not influenced by water levels of the sea or any river.

Together with the previously mentioned reclamation of the Haarlemmermeer and other dug peat lakes, the new canal projects resulted in a huge transformation of the area of central Holland. The port activities of Amsterdam and especially of Rotterdam exploded; while the other Dutch ports north and south of central Holland declined. After the reclamation of peat lakes in the interior of the region, agriculture increased again. And perhaps more importantly, the reclaimed Haarlemmermeer offered vacant lots to start the first Dutch airport Schiphol, southwest of Amsterdam (Bosma and Makhloufi, 2012).

Figure 3.4 shows central Holland as more than ever the central economic region of the Netherlands, while adjacent regions became more than ever peripheral areas and fell into poverty (Brusse and Van den Broeke, 2006).

Figure 3.4 The Netherlands ca. 1900, new sea canals improve the position of
Amsterdam and Rotterdam.
Source: Teake Bouma, TU Delft.

National unification, against the rise of a metropolis

The attempt of Thorbecke to remove the centre of economic activities to the
outward periphery is illustrative for the concern in Dutch government in that period about the increasing contrast between the urbanised and rich centre of Holland and the rest of the Dutch territory, which was still an 'empty land' and very
poor (Van der Woud, 1987). However, the new hydraulic projects of the 1870s
enforced this contrast by stimulating economic and urban growth in the area of
central Holland. The concern with this contrast was continued and increased in
the twentieth century. At the same time, the need for a radical modernisation of
the flood defence infrastructures was formulated. While the number of people
and the invested capital in the western part of the Netherlands had increased
substantially, the flood defence structures around central Holland still dated from
the fifteenth and sixteenth centuries. The flood defences around the Zuiderzee
and in the Southwest Delta were especially considered as insufficient. From 1879,
a special organisation headed by engineer Lely pleaded for the construction of
a closing dam in the Zuiderzee (Van de Ven, 2004; Van der Geest *et al.*, 2008).

The vulnerability of both aspects (the concentration of population in Holland, and the weak flood defences) was demonstrated during the First World War. The Netherlands took a neutral position during this war, but was deprived of the import of food from other parts of Europe. The cities in Holland in particular were starving seriously during the last years of the war. Moreover, the Zuiderzee area was confronted with two heavy storms in 1916 and 1917, which inundated large parts of the northern part of Holland, including some parts of Amsterdam, and led to 50 deaths, many drowned cattle and ruined agricultural land.

Both events, the famine and the floods, were reasons to accept finally the proposals of Lely and his associates to close the Zuiderzee with a dam and to reclaim large parts of this inner sea for agricultural purposes (Van der Geest et al., 2008). The construction of the *Afsluitdijk* (literally: closing dike) resulted in a shortening of the coastline and a transformation of Zuiderzee into a fresh water lake. An important reason for the giant project of damming and reclaiming the Zuiderzee was the extension of the agricultural area. By closing the Zuiderzee and reclaiming a large part of this sea during the twentieth century, the agricultural land of the Netherlands would be extended by 1,650 km^2 (4 % of the land surface of the country). The Zuiderzee was renamed in *IJsselmeer* (Lake IJssel). The new Ijsselmeer polders became the prestigious and exemplary model of modern agriculture, showing a new type of efficiently parcelled agricultural land. It also provided an opportunity for an experiment with comprehensive spatial planning. A system of new towns and villages was carefully planned and designed. The ambition to define a harmonious spatial relationship between townscape and (polder) landscape played an important role in these plans (Van der Wal, 1998).

Combined with a policy regarding the selection of the farmers, the new polders became a model of spatial planning as the central discipline which integrates agricultural and economic policy, town planning and urban design, hydraulic engineering, and demographic and social strategies (Bosma, 1993; Andela, 2000). During the Second World War, the German occupiers showed special interest in the Ijsselmeer polders project. They considered it an interesting model, which could be applied in their strategy to colonise large parts of Eastern Europe (Bosma, 1993). For the Dutch, the polders became a testing ground for a comprehensive spatial planning approach which would be applied for the nation as a whole some years later.

In 1924, Amsterdam hosted a conference of the International Garden Cities and Town Planning Association where the need for not only regional plan-making but also a National Spatial Plan was formulated (Bosma, 1993; Faludi and Van der Valk, 1994). The purpose was to reach a more equal distribution of economic activity and welfare on the national territory. During the following years, this idea was elaborated in several studies, for instance by De Casseres (1926) and Kloos (1939). The possibility to prepare a National Plan arose during the Second World War, when the *Rijksdienst voor het Nationale Plan* (Bureau for the National Plan) was founded. After the war, plans were prepared to repeat the concept of the Zuiderzee to the Southwest Delta: closing the estuaries with dams. Engineer Van Veen, who was in charge of this giant project, emphasised that the meaning of such a work would be far more than just delivering safety for the urbanised centre of Holland. In 1950, he published his book 'Drain, Dredge, Reclaim: the Art of a Nation' (Van Veen, 1950), which emphasised the meaning of a large-scale flood defence structure around the Dutch territory as an expression of national unification and national identity. Van Veen had to wait until the flood disaster of 1953, causing 2,000 deaths in the Netherlands as well as casualties in Belgium, before the national government was fully convinced of the necessity of what became known as the Delta Works.

During the 1950s, plans for closing the estuaries of the Southwest Delta were prepared in combination with plans to extend the urbanisation of the Randstad with a series of new towns and industrial areas in the Southwest Delta and the IJsselmeer reclamations. Government institutions warned that an ongoing urbanisation of the cities of the Randstad would lead to a drawing together of the Randstad cities and finally to one giant and uncontrollable metropolis, with all the problems of congestion, social disparities, poverty, diseases, and criminality. The first two national reports on spatial planning (1960 and 1966) were dominated by the search for a way to prevent the development of such a metropolis. (Van der Cammen and De Klerk, 2012). As was said in several documents, the new *IJsselmeer* project and Delta Works delivered an excellent condition for a new spatial policy, using the reclaimed and protected land for new urban and economic development (Provincie Zuid-Holland, 1957; Constandse, 1976).

So after the proposal of Thorbecke for a reorganisation of the main ports in the nineteenth century, a second attempt took place to dismantle the concentration of urbanisation and economy in the Randstad. This time, it was more embedded in a more institutionalised and legal structure of plan-making and implementation, while the projects of IJsselmeer polders and Delta works delivered the physical conditions for this policy (Figure 3.5). The result was rather successful, with a series of new towns in the IJsselmeerpolders and elsewhere. Almere became the largest one and still plays an important role in relieving the pressure on the Amsterdam housing market (Berg *et al.*, 2007).

Also, for the Southwest Delta a new 'Delta-City' south of Rotterdam was planned, together with an enormous extension of the Rotterdam port and industrial areas (Provincie Zuid-Holland, 1957). However, this city was never realised. Labour productivity in the post-war port and industrial areas was much higher than originally calculated, while demographic growth was much less than expected. Nevertheless, the Southwest Delta was transformed from a poor and peripheral series of isolated islands to an industrialised, wealthy, and integrated part of the nation. The New Waterway increased in importance; instead of an entrance it became the central axis of a 100 km^2 industrial port area, with (at the time of writing) the largest port of Europe and the second largest petrochemical refinery centre of the world. Also, in other parts of the

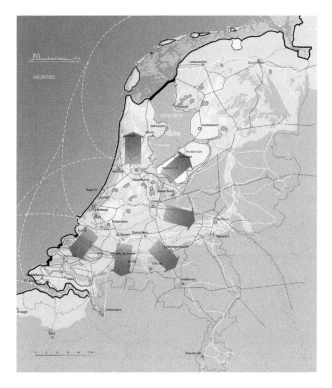

Figure 3.5 The Netherlands ca. 1980, a drastically shortened coastline makes an outward growth of the Randstad possible.
Source: Teake Bouma, TU Delft.

Southwest Delta several new industrial areas were developed, while agriculture took profit from the new fresh water basins in the area resulting from
the damming of the estuaries. Furthermore, the Southwest Delta became an
important destination for tourism and recreation. The basic condition for these
developments was the combined construction of the new system of dams with
a new road network, which made the islands accessible for car traffic.

For The Hague, an outward extension into the sea was proposed. During
the 1980s the engineer and politician Ronald Waterman proposed extensive
reclamation along the coastline of The Hague, offering the possibility for
new urban development at the seaside (Hooimeijer *et al.*, 2005). The proposal
never materialised.

The Randstad and the new Delta programme in the twenty-first century

Until the 1960s national politics put a strong emphasis on national economic
independence. This policy was based upon a rationalised and holistic programme in which agriculture and industrial policy, efficient road systems,

modern town-planning, and hydraulic engineering were interwoven. From the 1970s, all these elements became subject of doubt, resistance, and reconsidering. The last three decades of the twentieth century show a transition to another reality, a farewell to industrial and agricultural independence, rationalised town planning and national hydraulic engineering, and a reform of the welfare state.

Several new trends undermined the existing consensus and paradigms of urban planning and hydraulic engineering as a nucleus of societal and spatial coherence. These trends are based upon: (1) economic motives; (2) ecological and cultural motives; (3) political and financial motives; and (4) spatial development motives. Last but not least, climate change has become a fifth motive since the late 1990s, forcing drastic changes in the policies concerning spatial planning and hydraulic engineering (see Meyer, 2009 and the chapter by Hooimeijer in this volume). Here, it is important to focus on the changes in the Dutch culture of spatial planning and urban design as well as in hydraulic engineering and water management.

Regarding spatial planning, the policy of the Dutch government has changed substantially over the turn of the century. First, the main forces in politics tend to a radical reform of the welfare state as in many other western countries. The embracing of neo-liberal concepts resulted into the decline of the central position of national government in spatial policy. Prepared during the nineties and formalised since then with two successive spatial planning reports, national government has moved many responsibilities to the municipal and provincial authorities and stimulates the role of the market in spatial development (see the Chapter by Zonneveld in this volume).

Second, an essential exponent of the disappearance of a consensus regarding spatial planning is the erosion of the Randstad concept. Since the 1990s, the individual cities are more involved in competition with each other (in which Amsterdam is more and more the winner) than tending to become a coherent region (Ritsema van Eck *et al.*, 2006). The Randstad area tends to be divided into a Metropolitan Region Amsterdam in the north and the Metropolitan Region Rotterdam-The Hague in the south (see the chapter by Spaans *et al.* in this volume). Especially remarkable is the change of meaning and appraisal of the word 'metropolitan'. While it was an indication of what the Randstad should *not* become during the post-war decades, it is used now as an advertisement and indication of what the cities *do* want to be.

Regarding the ambition of the big cities to play a central role in the development of regional entities, large-scale water-systems and water-landscapes are proposed as important potential carriers of regional spatial structures. Already from the 1980s, an impressive transformation of former docklands has taken place in Amsterdam and Rotterdam. 'Eastern Harbours' and the construction of a large-scale new reclamation for the new urban district *IJburg* in Amsterdam and the *Kop van Zuid* ('Head of the South') project in Rotterdam show a new focus on water-related areas for urban development, with the new Erasmus Bridge in Rotterdam becoming a symbol of the rediscovery of the river as the heart of the city. The Hague realised a new boulevard in Scheveningen, emphasising that it wants to be a 'World-City at the Sea' (Gemeente Den Haag, 2005). Also, for the future these cities are developing strategies based upon the spatial development of regional water-structures: in Amsterdam along the IJ and Lake IJ, in Rotterdam along the river Nieuwe Maas and The Hague, as said, at the seafront (Meyer, 1999, 2007).

These ambitions and policies have not been without results. Together with a recovering economy after 2015, economic and urban development in the cities of the Randstad has been exploding. Amsterdam is confronted with a population growth of more than 10,000 people per year from 2015–2019. Also, the other cities of the Randstad are growing again and are looking for new possibilities for urban expansion and densification. The Netherlands Environmental Assessment Agency calculated in 2016 that the Randstad area needs an additional 1 million new houses by 2030 to be able to deal with the increasing need for housing (PBL, 2016). The question is where space can be found for these new urban developments.

Parallel to this process of urban and metropolitan development, the ideas and conceptions of flood-defence and water management have changed substantially. The central role of the state as organiser of the welfare state is weakening, decreasing, and changing. Large flood defence works will not have the same meaning anymore as elements of 'nation-building' as they had in the 1950s and 1960s.

This process started in the early 1970s, when environmental action groups protested against the completion of the Delta Works and IJsselmeer polders. As a result, the two last masterpieces of these projects, the East Scheldt Dam and the Markerwaard in the IJsselmeer, were cancelled. The protection of the areas at the East Scheldt was solved with an alternative solution, a storm surge barrier, which maintained the tidal currents in this basin, saving the existing ecosystems with the mussel-, oyster-, and lobster-cultures (De Schipper, 2008). The fourth *IJsselmeer* reclamation, *Markerwaard,* was not implemented, partly also because of the disappearance of the immediate necessity of new agricultural land (Van der Wal, 1998). Only the surrounding dam '*Houtribdijk*' was realised, cutting the IJsselmeer into two separated water bodies. Since then, the Markermeer in particular is suffering serious ecological problems because of the absence of currents and the shallowness of the lake. According to the European Union Water Framework Directive action is mandatory (Lammens *et al.*, 2008).

The attention to nature-based values and ecological qualities has become an important issue in water management policies. In 1986 a design-competition concerning a new lay-out for the river area near the city of Arnhem resulted in the first prize winning design '*Plan Ooievaar*' ('Plan Stork'), which aimed to repair retention areas and wetlands, resulting in a rejuvenation of the ecological balance of the river area before canalisation (De Bruin *et al.*, 1987; Buijse *et al.*, 2002). It was the start of a series of 'de-polder'-projects in the river and delta areas proposed over coming decades, which aim to create new wetlands, provide more room for river water, and the improvement of environmental qualities.

In this changing context, some extreme high-water situations in the Dutch rivers in 1993 and 1995, as well as the disaster with hurricane Katrina in New Orleans in 2005, were stimulating policies for updating the quality of the flood defence structures in the Netherlands. Two ambitious programmes were started by the government: *Ruimte voor de Rivier* (Room for the River) in 2005 (and completed in 2015) and the Delta Programme in 2009. For both programmes, it was and is the question of how to integrate the new environmental issues in an overall flood defence programme. The Delta Programme will have particular consequences for the spatial structure of the Randstad, while Room for the River can be considered as a preliminary laboratory to test new concepts (see Figure 3.6).

The programme Room for the River focused on the river landscapes in the centre and the east of the Netherlands, where a series of medium-sized towns are regarded as bottlenecks in periods of extreme river-discharges. The policy itself and the projects along the rivers are dominated by the ambition to combine new flood defence measures with an improvement of the conditions for environmental and spatial quality (Klijn *et al.*, 2013). In several cases, the programme forced city authorities to reconsider waterfront-plans fundamentally, in order to create more space for the flow and temporary storage of river water (Harsema, 2017; Klijn *et al.*, 2018). This holds well also with regard to the starting report of the 'Second Delta Programme', which is subtitled 'working together with water' (Delta Committee, 2008). At first, the aim of the Delta programme was to prepare the Netherlands for a future (2100) when extreme river discharges through the Rhine might be increased

Figure 3.6 The 'Room for the River' programme, sites for widening river beds.
Source: Directorate General for Public Works and Water Management.

from 12,000 m^3/sec to 18,000 m^3/sec, and when sea level might have risen 130 cm above the current mean. However, these assumptions already had to be adjusted in 2018, when the Dutch water research agency Deltares calculated that more extreme water levels need to be taken into account: a 3 metre sea level rise might be possible in 2100; 5–8 metre might be possible in 2200 (Haasnoot, 2018). What was considered a 'worst case scenario' in 2008 (130 cm sea level rise by the year 2100) has changed into a minimum assumption ten years later.

New measures will be necessary to be able to deal with these changing conditions concerning the river area, the coastline, the Southwest Delta, the Green Heart and the IJsselmeer area. Important questions are: (a) will the coastline be able to withstand heavy storm surges in the future (when the sea level is expected to be much higher); (b) will the river area and the Southwest Delta be able to endure unprecedented discharge volumes; (c) will it be possible to stop the ongoing subsidence of the central part of Holland; and (d) will it be possible to provide enough fresh water, also in periods of long-lasting drought? In 2018, Europe experienced an extremely long period of drought and heat when the urgency of a fourth issue became clear. An important sub-question in all these issues is: can we develop sustainable strategies with the new paradigm of 'working with water' and 'building with nature', or is it necessary to return to the proven methods of 'hard core' civil engineering? We will address these four questions one by one.

a   *The future of the coastline*
     The erosion of the Dutch coastline is a process which was already underway in the twelfth century. From that time, the sea level has become so high that currents are not able to transport sand from the seabed and deposit it at the coastline. Instead, waves and currents start to remove more sand from the coast than to add. Since then, different attempts have been developed to stop the erosion. It has the effect at most in a delay of the process of erosion, not in stopping this process completely. In 1990, the Dutch government defined a 'basic coastline' (*Basis Kustlijn*), which should be maintained by artificially supplementing sand repeatedly (Ministerie V&W, 1990). Since then, dredging ships take 7 million m^3 sand from the sea bed every year, and dump it on the beaches and on the foreshores, just in front of the beaches. It means that a small ecological disaster takes place each year: the flora and fauna of the tidal areas of the coastline are ruined completely by the addition of the enormous amounts of sand and can barely recover before new additions in the following year.

     In 2011, Rijkswaterstaat started a new experiment with a 'sand motor'. Dredging ships created a new, artificial island, composed of 21.5 million m^3 sand, dredged from the sea bed. The new island is situated in front of one of the weakest parts of the coast, just south of The Hague. Currents and wind are supposed to transport the sand to the coast gradually, in a time-span of 10–20 years. The findings of the monitoring processes are reasons for optimism: the beaches and dunes north of the sand motor are not eroding anymore but growing, and the ecosystem of the coast is not disappearing anymore but revitalizing (Taal *et al.*, 2016). However, the new projections concerning increasing sea level rise (Haasnoot, 2018) mean that many sand motors will be necessary in the near future, and that the coastal zone should be reserved for the dynamic processes of dune growth and beach enlargements. The current question is whether this policy should be applied along the whole coastline. The follow-up question is whether urban expansion in this coastal zone (including beach resorts) should be reduced to a minimum? Or is it possible and even desirable to develop a more differentiated coastal zone, which creates possibilities for new urban development at strategic sites? In 2012–2014 the *Atelier Kustkwaliteit* (Studio Coastal Quality, a collaboration of National Delta Programme, TU Delft, provinces, municipalities and dredging companies) explored this question and suggested a new type of coastline, composed of a variety of bays and capes (Brand *et al.*, 2014; see Figure 3.7). The feasibility of this concept is the subject of current research (Wijnberg *et al.*, 2017).

b   *The future of river discharges and temporary storage of river water*
One of the fundamental questions for the Dutch delta is if the delta will be able to deal with the worst-case scenario of a coincidence of an extreme storm surge and an extreme river discharge. In this case, especially the Southwest Delta (including the Rotterdam-region) should be able

Figure 3.7 Sketch of design exploration for an 'undulating coastline'.
Source: Studio Coastal Quality, 2013.

to provide extra storage capacity for river water, which only can be discharged into the sea when the storm surge is over. Specifically, the future of the mouth of the Rhine has returned to the agenda. This can be regarded as the most fundamental subject of the Delta Programme, because it touches upon the whole Dutch river system as well as the economic and urban system of the Randstad area, especially the southern part.

As we have seen before, the river mouth tends to move southward. In the nineteenth century, Caland fixed the location of the river mouth by digging the New Waterway. This intervention has brought a lot of economic activity and prosperity to the Rotterdam region. But it created also an increased vulnerability for flooding in the area as well as an increase of salt sea water intrusion. The vulnerability for flooding has become a problem especially since large areas of former docklands, unprotected by dikes, have been urbanised from the 1970s. In 2019, approximately 60,000 people are living in these unprotected areas in the Rotterdam region. It is true that the New Waterway has been provided with the *Maeslant* storm surge barrier in the 1990s, which can be closed during heavy storm surges, preventing flooding of the outer-dike areas. However, because of sea level rise this barrier will have to close more frequently in the future, which will be conflicting with the goal to maintain the accessibility of the port in all circumstances. Reducing the frequency of closures of the barrier will mean that the outer-dike housing areas should be provided with adaptive measures. The alternative is to build a lock-system in the New Waterway, forcing the port to concentrate all port terminals at the west-side of the locks. A variation on this alternative is to allow the natural process of silting up of the New Waterway and Nieuwe Maas, by a radical reduction of the dredging activities. Both variations (lock-system or allowing silting up processes) will mean that the southern estuaries of the Southwest Delta, especially the Haringvliet, will take over the role of main discharge outlet of the rivers. These southern estuaries should also play a main role in the temporary storage of river water in times of extreme discharge and storm surge. A research group led by TU Delft has shown that this can be combined with the goal of repairing the estuarine eco-systems in these estuaries by using the zones between old dikes and the recent main dikes as 'adaptive' zones, which can create space for agriculture, recreation, nature, and temporary water storage (Meyer *et al.,* 2015; see Figure 3.8).

c   *The future of ground levels of central Holland*
Land subsidence in the Netherlands is a result of continuous drainage processes, intending to make the land useful for agricultural, urban, or industrial purposes, and leading to oxidation and shrinking of the peat-soils. It is not a unique phenomenon, but can be found in many urbanised deltaic regions in the world, resulting in 'relative sea level rise', which is the combination of sea-level rise and land subsidence (Syvitski and Higgins, 2012;

Figure 3.8 Proposal for a redesign of the Southwest Delta, south of Rotterdam.
Source: Meyer *et al.*, 2015.

Tessler *et al.*, 2015). Where 'peat-pillows' raised 4 to 8 metres above mean sea level a 1,000 years ago (Van de Ven, 2004), the land has dropped to 6 metres below mean sea level in some parts of Holland currently. This leads to increasing vulnerability for flooding (De Moel *et al.*, 2011), but also to a substantial amount of CO^2 emissions (Langeveld *et al.*, 1997) and sagging problems in urban areas. The structural solution to this problem is the substantial reduction of drainage and the elevation of groundwater levels – in rural as well as in urban areas (Wardekker *et al.*, 2010). This means a structural change of the type of agricultural business in the rural areas (Verhoeven and Setter, 2010) and new spatial concepts for rural and urban areas, with a substantial role for surface-water as a main-ingredient of public space (see the chapter by Hooimeijer in this volume]). Since the early twenty-first century, urban and regional authorities are concentrating on the realisation of 'green-blue networks', which should play a main role in elevating groundwater levels and in the temporary catchment of storm water. An example is the plan of the Province of South-Holland for a 'metropolitan landscape park' in the Rotterdam-The Hague region (see Figure 3.9).

Figure 3.9 The 'metropolitan landscape park' proposed by the Province of South-
Holland, 2017.
Source: Marco Broekman – urbanism research architecture and NOHNIK Architecture &
Landscapes.

d   *The future of the IJsselmeer as national fresh water storage basin*
Alongside safety for flooding and land subsidence, the availability of
fresh water is a main issue in any deltaic region – and also for the Netherlands at large and the Randstad in particular. The damming of the former Zuiderzee created the large fresh water basin IJsselmeer. Extending
the storage capacity of the IJsselmeer is under consideration for several
reasons. First, together with the storage capacity of the Southwest Delta
(see above), the IJsselmeer is an important buffer to store river water in
times of a coincidence of peak discharges of the river and a storm surge,
resulting in an extremely high sea level. This problem will increase in the
future, when sea level rise will increase and the period in which it is not
possible to discharge to the sea. Second, the IJsselmeer plays an important
role as supplier of fresh water in periods of draught. The surrounding
provinces are using the fresh water of the IJsselmeer for agriculture (wa-
tering crops, maintaining the groundwater levels, and avoiding increasing salt intrusion) and drinking water supply. This need for fresh water
will become more urgent in the future when periods of draught and
extremely low supply of river water will increase (Spinoni *et al.*, 2018).
This urgency became clear during the Summer of 2018, when the long-
est rainless period since 1976 took place and the fresh water supply in the
Netherlands approached a critical limit (Government Commissioner for
the Delta programme, 2018).
     At first, the report of the Delta Committee (2008) recommended ex-
tending the storage capacity of the IJsselmeer by raising the dikes by 1
to 1.5 metres. During the following years, the focus changed towards a

policy to reconnect the IJsselmeer and Markermeer. The Markermeer was until recently a heritage of the cancellation of the Markerwaard, the last part of the reclamations of the IJsselmeer works as we have seen. It was an 'orphaned' lake, waiting for a final destination and, in the meantime, a victim of pollution because of a wild growth of nutrients in the shallow and stagnant waters. Reconsidering the relation between IJsselmeer and Markermeer became also a central issue in the debate on the role of these lakes in relation to the urban growth of the Amsterdam region. A study by urban designer Frits Palmboom plays an important role in this debate. He pleas for considering the IJsselmeer area (including the Markermeer) as a 'metropolitan breathing space', which should be maintained and strengthened to compensate the crowded and busy world of the metropolis itself (Palmboom, 2018; see Figure 3.10).

How to deal with the demand for more space?

All these developments together mean that the main consequence of the new 'building-with-nature' approach is that it needs more space: more space for a dynamic management of the coast; more space for rivers and for temporary storage of extreme discharges; more space for groundwater elevation in the Green Heart; more space for fresh water storage in the Ijsselmeer; and also more space in the cities for temporary storm water storage. The need for more space for sustainable flood defence systems and water management is at odds with the increasing demographic and economic growth in the Randstad area, which also needs more space.

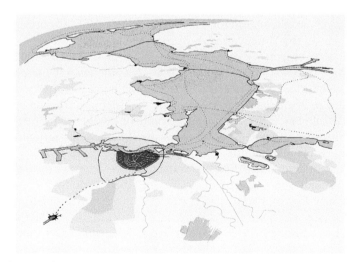

Figure 3.10 The IJsselmeer area as a 'metropolitan breath of fresh air'.
Source: Frits Palmboom and Daan Zandbelt, TU Delft.

This need for more space for water management and flood defence is an important different condition in comparison with the greatest part of the twentieth century when a civil engineering approach dominated. This approach aimed to create as much as possible land for urban, industrial, and agricultural purposes. The current approach of 'building-with-nature' is no longer subservient to urban development, but often competing with urban development. The apparent contradiction of the need of more space for water management and the need for more space for urban and economic expansion can only be solved by looking for new concepts of double land use and flexible land use.

Double land use has been developed in many experiments such as the combination of storm water storage and housing in cities by building housing complexes with 'green roofs' able to store large quantities of water temporarily; building a parking garage in a new dune-landscape, as has been realised in the coastal town Katwijk; or a combination of a new shopping centre and a new flood defence structure in Rotterdam (Van Veelen *et al.*, 2015; Voorendt *et al.*, 2017). Also experiments with floating houses or buildings on piles in riverbeds of flood-prone areas are examples of double land use (Nillesen and Singelenberg, 2010). Experiments with new types of agriculture (flood tolerant or salt water tolerant crops; see Verhoeven and Setter, 2010) are under development and create new perspectives for a combination of agriculture with elevated groundwater levels in the Green Heart and with the repair of estuarine ecosystems in the Southwest Delta.

Flexibility in land use is also an increasingly important issue in design and planning and is already applied and tested in many Room for the River projects: grasslands in the river zone can be used for agricultural or recreational purposes in normal conditions, but should be available for the temporary storage of river water once in 5 or 10 years (Klijn *et al.*, 2013, 2018; Harsema, 2017). In the urban context, 'water squares' have been built, functioning as public spaces and playgrounds in normal conditions, but prepared to store large amounts of water in periods of heavy rain storms (Molenaar and Gebraad, 2014).

This new emphasis on the need of double land use and flexibility means a new attention to spatial quality, combined with new governance arrangements. Water storage areas or flood defences cannot be assessed anymore on the basis of functional and technical criteria only, but should also be appreciated as valuable additions to the public realm of cities and landscapes. This needs new instruments and methods of design and design-assessment (Klijn *et al.*, 2013, 2018; Nillesen, 2019). New governance arrangements are needed resulting in clear agreements between stakeholders on the division of tasks and their role in the management of land and water (Meyer *et al.*, 2015).

Altogether this means that a transition is necessary from a culture of mono-functional solutions and monodisciplinary approaches towards more multi-functional solutions and multidisciplinary and interdisciplinary approaches of professionals and institutions. Civil engineers, urban designers, urban planners as well as landscape architects are no longer able to do 'their own thing', but to look beyond the limits of their own discipline, to work together and search for integrated solutions. This is to be enhanced in practice as well as in education and research in higher education (Nillesen *et al.*, 2016).

Conclusions and discussion

Overlooking a 1,000-year history of urbanisation of a delta-area, we can see the influential and decisive role of changes in the nature of rivers and sea, and the importance of the way that mankind has tried to deal with these changes. There have been several episodes of 'critical transition', with crucial tipping points. The way of intervention by mankind was decisive for the final outcome of the transition and smoothed the way for new urban patterns and economic activities. However, these interventions were never self-evident, neither can the series of interventions over a thousand years be regarded as a logical or linear story. Every intervention was a choice; the sequence of these choices shows a rather fickle development of spatial configurations.

Originally, the corridor of former Roman settlements along the river Oude Rijn seemed to be predestined to become the central axis of urbanisation in the region. But the silting up of the Oude Rijn and the development of new sea-inlets in the southwest and the north changed the conditions for urbanisation and economic development completely. The way that people answered these changes, by turning around the whole drainage system of central Holland, and by constructing dikes along the IJ and the Meuse-mouth, created the condition for a new urban system, which eventually became the foundation of the Randstad pattern. Not only in spatial terms, but also in governance terms the rise of cities and the power they acquired to manipulate the hydraulic systems in this period was important. The Randstad area was and is still more a collection of cities then a coherent metropolitan region.

It is true that the Randstad pattern was not planned, but it is important to see that the conditions for this pattern were created by new hydrological interventions. The digging of the peat lakes in-between the cities emphasised the relative importance of the middle area for urbanisation and created the condition for the later 'Green Heart' of the Randstad.

The silting up of the Meuse mouth and the Zuiderzee in the eighteenth and nineteenth centuries posed again the question of how to react. A second relocation of urban and economic centres of gravity was not unthinkable and was a concrete proposal. However, the pressure of established powers, the rise of the nation-state, and the new hydrological technology created the possibility for digging new canals to the existing centres Amsterdam and Rotterdam.

The decisions and choices in the twelfth and thirteenth centuries and later in the nineteenth century were by no means unavoidable. Other decisions were also possible and were proposed. If these other decisions concerning hydrological infrastructures would have been taken, the Randstad region would have developed a quite different spatial structure. Consider if it would have been possible to dig a New Waterway near Katwijk in the twelfth century.

It could have maintained the mouth of Old Rhine and created a long linear urban corridor along the river. Or suppose that Caland was not able to get support for digging the New Waterway in the nineteenth century? The rise of Vlissingen and Harlingen as new main ports would have been more likely.

Also, the damming of the Zuiderzee and the construction of the Delta Works were not self-evident as they were the result of long periods of public and political debates which could have taken a different path. Finally, they contributed to an important transition of the Randstad. Instead of only a densification of the Randstad area itself, also an outward extension became possible. Moreover, the large infrastructure projects contributed to a further rise of the nation state and to a new balance between central state power and local communities.

However, in the context of a 1,000-year development, the period of national spatial planning in the twentieth century seems to have been an intermezzo. The idea to stop the concentration of urban development in the Randstad area, and to realise a more equal distribution of urban development across the national territory, was embraced and implemented by national politics during not more than 40 years (1960–2000) and was abandoned subsequently. Currently metropolitan development is no longer a spectator but has become a highly desirable perspective.

In the beginning of the twenty-first century, the Dutch delta finds itself in a transition stage again. Also, now the choices are not self-evident. A renewal of the water management and flood defence system can function as the engine of a reconfiguration of urban structures, this time by strengthening the metropolitan regions of Amsterdam and Rotterdam-The Hague. This might also contribute to and fit a new balance between central state responsibilities and local or regional responsibilities – both concerning spatial planning as well as hydraulic engineering. However, this requires that politicians, planners, hydraulic engineers and urban designers are able to see these possibilities at the regional scale, to create strong collaborations and to discuss the different possible perspectives with the public at large, as we have underlined above.

This is increasingly relevant in current times, when, next to the issues of water management and flood defence, several other issues have arrived on the agenda of national politics: the increasing economic, demographic, and urban pressure on the Randstad area; the energy transition; the 'next economy'; and need to restructure the intensive agricultural system which is typical for the Netherlands. A new, comprehensive national Environment and Planning Act on the environment will come into effect in 2020 (or 2021) as a substitute for the many laws on aspects of the environment. This act requires the making of a 'National Vision on the Environment' (NOVI: *Nationale Omgevingsvisie*) of which a draft was published in 2018 (the final version was published Autumn 2020). A new national strategy on water management and flood defence could function as a new guiding framework for this vision.

Two questions remain unanswered in this overview. First: what will be the new, comprehensive strategy on water and flood defence, and how will it lead towards a new spatial configuration of the Randstad? Second: how will it be possible to maintain the Randstad metropolis in this increasingly vulnerable delta landscape in the future, when the conditions will become more extreme: with rising sea levels, increasing river discharges, intensification of rainstorms, and increasing periods of draught? Or should the Dutch be prepared to move their homes, after 1,000 years of living in the lowest part of the delta, to the higher and dryer land in the East? According to Johan van Veen, the 'godfather' of the Delta Works, the question is not if the Dutch should move their habitat to the east, but the question is when this moment will arrive.

References

Andela, G. (2000). *Kneedbaar landschap, kneedbaar volk [Malleable landscape, malleable people]; De heroïsche jaren van de ruilverkavelingen in Nederland*. THOTH, Bussum.

Balk, J. Th. (1985). *Onze Havens [Our ports]*. Publiboek/Baart, Soest/Deurne

Berg, J., Franke, S. and Reijndorp, A. (Eds) (2007). *Adolescent Almere; Hoe een stad wordt gemaakt*. NAi Uitgevers, Rotterdam.

Bisschops, T. (2006). 'Een Zeehaven voor Leiden? [A seaport for Leiden?]; De vroegste doorgravingen bij Katwijk herbekeken (1404–1572)', *Tijdschrift voor Zeegeschiedenis*, 25(1), 33–47.

Blockmans, W. (2010). *Metropolen aan de Noordzee [Metropoles at the North Sea]; De geschiedenis van Nederland 1100–1560*. Bert Bakker, Amsterdam.

Borger, G.J. (1992). 'Draining, digging, dredging. The creation of a new landscape in the peat areas of the low countries'. In: Verhoeven, J.T.A. (Ed.) *Fens and bogs in the Netherlands; Vegetation, history, nutrient dynamics and conservation*. Kluwer, Dordrecht/Boston/London, 131–171.

Borger, G., Horsten, F., Engel, H., Rutte, R., Diesfieldt, O., Pané, I. and De Waaijer, A. (2011). 'Twelve centuries of spatial transformation in the western Netherlands, in six maps: Landscape, habitation and infrastructure in 800, 1200, 1500, 1700, 1900 and 2000', *OverHolland*, 10/11, 5–127.

Bos, D., Ebben, M. and Te Velde, H. (2008). *Harmonie in Holland [Harmony in Holland]; Het polder model van 1500 tot nu*. Bert Bakker, Amsterdam.

Bosch, A. and Van der Ham, W. (1998). *Twee eeuwen Rijkswaterstaat 1798 – 1998 [Two centuries Directorate General for public works and water management 1798–1998]*. Europese Bibliotheek, Zaltbommel.

Bosma, K. (1993). *Ruimte voor de nieuwe tijd [Room for a new era]; Vormgeving van de Nederlandse regio 1900–1945*. NAi Uitgevers, Rotterdam.

Bosma, K. and Makhloufi, A.E. (2012). 'De ruimtelijke metamorfose van Schiphol: Van polderdorp naar nevelstad' [The spatial metamorphosis of Schiphol. From polder village to diffuse city]. In: Taverne, E., De Klerk, L., Ramakers, B. and Dembski, S. (Eds) *Nederland Stedenland [The Netherlands, land of cities]; Continuïteit en vernieuwing*. NAi Uitgevers, Rotterdam, 124–138.

Brand, N. (2012). *De wortels van de Randstad [The roots of the Randstad]; Overheidsinvloed en stedelijke hiërarchie in het westen van Nederland tussen de 13de en de 20ste eeuw*, PhD thesis TU Delft, A+BE 2012 #02. Faculty of Architecture and the Built Environment, Delft.

Brand, N., Kersten, I., Pot, R. and Warmerdam, M. (2014). 'Research by design on the Dutch Coastline: bridging flood control and spatial quality', *Built Environment*, 40(2), 265–280.

Brusse, P. and Van den Broeke, W. (2006). *Provincie in de periferie [Province in the periphery]; De economische geschiedenis van Zeeland 1800–2000*. Matrijs, Utrecht.

Buijse, A.D., Staras, M., Jans, L.H., Van Geest, G.J., Grift, R.E., Ibelings, B.W., Oosterberg, W. and Roozen, F.C.J.M. (2002). 'Restoration strategies for river floodplains along large lowland rivers in Europe', *Journal of Fresh Water Biology*, 47(4), 889–907.

Colenbrander, B. and MUST (2005). *Limes Atlas* [In Dutch]. Uitgeverij 010, Rotterdam.

Constandse, A.K. (1976). *Planning en vormgeving – Ervaringen in de IJsselmeerpolders [Planning and design – Experiences in the IJsselmeer polders]*. Rijksdienst voor de IJsselmeerpolders, Lelystad.

De Bruin, D., Hamhuis, D., Van Nieuwenhuijze, L., Overmars, W., Sijmons, D. and Vera, F. (1987). *Ooievaar. De toekomst van het rivierengebied [Stork. The future of the river area]*. Stichting Gelderse Milieufederatie, Arnhem.

De Casseres, J.M. (1926). *Stedebouw [Urbanism]*. S.L. van Looi, Amsterdam.

De Moel, H., Aerts, J.C.J.H. and Koomen, E. (2011). 'Development of flood exposure in the Netherlands during the 20th and 21st century', *Global Environmental Change*, 21(2), 620–627.

De Schipper, P. (2008). *De slag om de Oosterschelde [The battle of the East Scheldt]; Een reconstructie van de strijd om de open Oosterschelde*. Atlas, Amsterdam/Antwerpen.

De Vries, J. and Van der Woude, A. (1997). *The first modern economy; Success, failure and perseverance of the Dutch Economy, 1500 – 1815*. Cambridge University Press, Cambridge.

Delta Committee (2008). *Working together with water; A living land builds for its future, Findings of the Deltacommissie 2008*. Delta Committee, The Hague.

Faludi, A. and Van der Valk, A. (1994). *Rule and order: Dutch planning Doctrine in the Twentieth Century*. Kluwer Academic Publishers, Dordrecht/Boston/London.

Gemeente Den Haag (2005). *Wèreldstad aan Zee [World city at the sea]; Structuurvisie Den Haag 2020*. Gemeente Den Haag, Den Haag.

Government Commissioner for the Delta Programme (2018). *Delta plan on freshwater supply*. Ministry of Infrastructure and Water Management, The Hague.

Haasnoot, M. (2018). *Mogelijke gevolgen van versnelde zeespiegelstijging voor het Delta-programma [Possible consequences of accelerated sea level rise for the Delta-programme]*. Deltares, Delft.

Harsema, H. (Ed.) (2017). *Room for the river; Beautiful and safe landscape*. Blauwdruk, Wageningen.

Hooimeijer, F. (2011). *The tradition of making polder cities*, PhD Thesis TU Delft. Repository TU Delft, Delft.

Hooimeijer, F. (2014). *The making of polder cities; A fine Dutch tradition*. Jap Sam Books, Heijningen.

Hooimeijer, F., Meyer, H. and Nienhuis, A. (2005). *Atlas of Dutch Water Cities*. SUN, Amsterdam.

Israel, J., (1995). *The Dutch Republic; Its rise, greatness, and fall 1477–1806*. Oxford University Press, Oxford.

Klijn, F., De Bruin, D., De Hoog, M.C., Jansen, S. and Sijmons, D. (2013). 'Design quality of room-for-the-river measures in the Netherlands: role and assessment of the quality team (Q-team)', *International Journal of River Basin Management*, 11(3), 287–299.

Klijn, F., Asselman, N. and Wagenaar, D. (2018). 'Room for rivers: risk reduction by enhancing the flood conveyance capacity of The Netherlands' Large Rivers', *Geosciences*, 8(224), 1–20.

Kloos, W.B. (1939). *Het Nationaal Plan [The National Plan]; Proces eener beschrijving der planologische ontwikkelingsmogelijkheden van Nederland.* Samsom, Alphen aan den Rijn.

Lammens, E., Van Luijn, F., Wessels, Y., Bouwhuis, H., Noordhuis, R. and Portielje, R. (2008). 'Towards ecological goals for the heavily modified lakes in the IJsselmeer area, The Netherlands', *Hydrobiologia*, 599, 239–247.

Langeveld, C.A., Segers, R., Dirks, B.O.M., Van den Pol-van Dasselaar, A., Velthof, G.L., and Hensen, A. (1997). 'Emissions of CO2, CH4 and N2O from pasture on drained peat soils in the Netherlands', *European Journal of Agronomy*, 7(1–3), 35–42.

Meyer, H. (1999). *City and Port; Transformation of Port Cities London, Barcelona, New York, Rotterdam.* International Books, Utrecht.

Meyer, H. (2007) 'The search for new structure and the regional context of Dutch cities'. In: La Greca, P., Albrechts, L. and Van den Broeck, J. (Eds) *ISOCARP review nr.03 – urban trialogues; Co-productive ways to relate visioning and strategic urban projects.* ISOCARP, s.l., 78–93.

Meyer, H. (2009). 'Reinventing the Dutch Delta: complexity and conflicts', *Built Environment*, 35(4), 432–451.

Meyer, H., Bregt, A., Dammers, E. and Edelenbos, J. (Eds) (2015). *New perspectives on urbanizing deltas: A complex adaptive systems approach to planning and design.* Must Publishers, Amsterdam.

Ministerie V&W (Verkeer en Waterstaat) (1990). *Eerste Kustnota [First memorandum on the coast].* Ministerie V&W, The Hague.

Molenaar, A. and Gebraad, C. (2014). 'Rotterdam Resilient Delta City; Connecting water and adaptation with opportunities', *Water Governance*, 2014(1), 43–47.

Nillesen, A.L. (2019). *Spatial quality as a decisive criterion in flood risk strategies;* An integrated approach for flood risk management strategy development, with spatial quality as an ex-ante criterion, PhD thesis TU Delft, A+BE 2019 #01. Faculty of Architecture and the Built Environment, Delft.

Nillesen, A.L., Kothuis, B., Meyer, H. and Palmboom, F. (2016). *Delta interventions; Design and engineering in urban water landscapes.* Delft University Publishers, Delft.

Nillesen, A.L. and Singelenberg, J. (2010) *Amphibious housing in the Netherlands; Architecture and urbanism on the water.* NAi Publishers, Rotterdam.

Palmboom, F. (2018). *IJsselmeer; A spatial perspective.* VanTilt, Nijmegen.

PBL, Planbureau voor de Leefomgeving (2016). *Transformatiepotentie: woningbouwmogelijkheden in de bestaande stad [Transformation potential: the possibilities for home building in existing urban areas].* PBL, Den Haag.

Provincie Zuid-Holland (1957) *Randstad en Delta [Randstad and Delta]; Een studie over de ontwikkeling van het Zuid-Hollandse Zeehavengebied.* Provincie Zuid-Holland, Den Haag.

Ritsema van Eck, J., Van Oort, F., Raspe, O., Daalhuizen, F. and Van Brussel, J. (2006). *Vele steden maken nog geen Randstad [Many cities do not make a single Randstad].* Ruimtelijk Planbureau/ NAi Uitgevers, Den Haag/Rotterdam.

Rooijendijk, C. (2009). *Waterwolven. Een geschiedenis van stormvloeden, dijkenbouwers en droogmakers [Water wolves. A history of storm surges, dike builders and reclaimers].* Amsterdam Atlas, Amsterdam.

Saeijs, H.L.F. (2006). *Turning the tide; Essays on Dutch ways with water.* VSSD, Delft.

Scheffer, M. (2009). *Critical transitions in nature and society.* Princeton University Press, New Jersey.

Spinoni, J., Vogt, J.V., Naumann, G., Barbosa, P. and Dosio, A. (2018). 'Will drought events become more frequent and severe in Europe?' *International Journal of Climatology*, 38(4), 1718–1736.

Syvitski, J. and Higgins, S. (2012). 'Going under: The world's sinking cities', *New Scientist*, 216(2893), 40–43.

Steenbergen, C., Gessel, M., Van der Zwart, J. and Grootens, J. (2009a). *Atlas Nieuwe Hollandse Waterlinie [Atlas of the New Dutch water defence line].* Uitgeverij 010, Rotterdam.

Steenbergen, C., Reh, W., Nijhuis, S. and Pouderoijen, M. (2009b). *Polderatlas van Nederland [Polder atlas of the Netherlands]*; Pantheon der Lage Landen. THOTH, Bussum.

Taal, M.D, Löffler, M.A.M., Vertegaal, C.T.M., Wijsman, J.W.M., Van der Valk, L. and Tonnon, P.K. (2016). *Ontwikkeling van de Zandmotor [Development of the Sand Motor]; Samenvattende rapportage over de eerste vier jaar van het Monitoring- en Evaluatie Programma (MEP).* Deltares, Delft.

Ten Horn-van Nispen, M L., Lintsen, H.W. and Veenendaal A.J. (Eds) (1994). *Wonderen der Techniek [Miracles of Technology]; Nederlandse ingenieurs en hun kunstwerken, 200 jaar civiele techniek.* Walburg Pers, Zutphen.

Tessler, Z.D., Vörösmarty, C.J., Grossberg, M., Gladkova, I., Aizenman, H., Syvitski, J. and Foufoula-Georgiou, E. (2015). 'Profiling risk and sustainability in coastal deltas of the world', *Science*, 349(638), 638–643.

Van de Ven, G.P. (Ed.) (2004). *Man-made lowlands; History of water management and land reclamation in the Netherlands.* Matrijs, Utrecht.

Van der Cammen, H. and De Klerk, L. (2012). *The selfmade land; Culture and evolution of urban and regional planning in the Netherlands (with Dekker, G. and Witsen, P.P.).* Unieboek/Het Spectrum, Houten/Antwerpen.

Van der Geest, L., Berkhof, M. and Meijer, M. (2008). *Het hoofd boven water [The head above the water]; Tweehonderd jaar investeren in waterwerken.* Nyfer, Utrecht.

Van der Wal, C. (1998). *In praise of common sense; Planning the ordinary. A physical planning history of the new towns in the IJsselmeerpolders.* 010 Publishers, Rotterdam.

Van der Woud, A. (1987). *Het Lege Land [The empty land]; De Ruimtelijke Orde van Nederland 1798–1848.* Meulenhoff, Amsterdam.

Van der Woud, A. (2006). *Een Nieuwe Wereld [A new world]; Het ontstaan van het moderne Nederland.* Bert Bakker, Amsterdam.

Van Tielhof, M. and Van Dam, P. (2006). *Waterstaat in Nederland [Water governance in the Netherlands]; Het Hoogheemraadschap van Rijnland voor 1857.* Matrijs, Utrecht.

Van Veelen, P., Voorendt, M. and Van der Zwet, C. (2015). 'Design challenges of multifunctional flood defences. A comparative approach to assess spatial and structural integration', *Research in Urbanism Series*, 3(1), 275–292.

Van Veen, J. (1950). *Dredge, drain, reclaim; The art of a nation.* Martinus Nijhoff, The Hague.

Van de Ven, G.P. (2008). *De Nieuwe Waterweg en het Noordzeekanaal [The New Waterway and the North Sea Canal]; Een waagstuk, Onderzoek in opdracht van de Deltacommissie.* Deltacommissie, Den Haag.

Verhoeven, J.T.A. and Setter, T.L. (2010). 'Agricultural use of wetlands: opportunities and limitations', *Annals of Botany*, 105(1), 155–163.

Voorendt, M., Vrijling, H. and Voortman, H.G. (2017). 'Structural evaluation of multifunctional flood defences using generic element types'. In: Wallendorf, L. and Cox, D. (Eds) *Coastal Structures and Solutions to Coastal Disasters*; Papers from the Coastal Structures and Solutions to Coastal Disasters Joint Conference 2015, Boston, Massachusetts, September 9–11, 2015, 365–374.

Wardekker, J.A., De Jong, A., Knoop, J.M. and Van der Sluijs, J. (2010). 'Operationalising a resilience approach to adapting an urban delta to uncertain climate changes', *Technological Forecasting and Social Change*, 77(6), 987–998.

Wijnberg, K.M., Nijhuis, S., Hulscher, S.J.M.H., Mulder, J.P.M., Van Bergen, J., Meyer, H., Hoonhout, B., Janssen, M., Hoekstra, J.D., De Groot, A.V., Goessen, P. and Van Gelder-Maas, C. (2017). 'ShoreScape: sustainable co-evolution of the natural and built environment along sandy shores'. In: NCK, Netherlands Centre for Coastal Research, *Book of Abstracts NCK Days 2017*, Repository Wageningen University & Research, 102.

Wong, T.E., Batjes, D.A.J. and De Jager, J. (Eds) (2007). *Geology of the Netherlands*. Royal Netherlands Academy of Arts and Sciences, Amsterdam.

4 Rotterdam

A dynamic polder city in the Randstad

Fransje Hooimeijer

Introduction

The famous saying 'God created the world, but the Dutch created Holland' is about the two provinces called North and South Holland that make up the Randstad. The Dutch have a rich and internationally renowned 'fine tradition' in dealing with the characteristics of their territory when it comes to the intense relationship between urban (landscape) development and civil engineering. Their expertise and knowledge of hydrological principles have helped them successfully to make land out of water through the ingenuous technology of polders. The dynamics of the regional water system, which include groundwater and rainwater in combination with surface water in a lowland delta facing the North Sea, is crucial for the process of development and urbanisation of the Dutch polders. Dutch cities, especially in the Randstad, are hydrological constructions with a spatial layout that is strongly connected to the division of land and water on regional and local scales through civil construction and building site preparation (Hooimeijer *et al.*, 2005). In the lower parts of the Netherlands, the relation between technical efficiency and the specific characteristics of the territory as well as the way cities and landscapes are designed and have evolved over time.

In the post-war era, the characteristics of the low-lying Dutch territory were altered with the use of far-stretched technology, and the landscape and cities designed with a high degree of rationality. The natural conditions of the territory were made subordinate to the thriving principle of a societal culture, in Dutch, the *maakbaarheids* principle ('makeability'). Technology seems to make everything possible, but is very inflexible to change. Climate change is currently putting pressure on the hydrological system. More severe and frequent rainstorms, a higher sea level, more water running down the rivers, high temperatures, and drought are very influential on the hydrological system, but technical parts of that system cannot adapt.

This chapter will examine the case of Rotterdam as one of the most representative cities in the Randstad in dealing with water and adapting to the current challenges. The city pays a lot of attention to water and to climate change. In 2009, it was the very first Dutch municipality to install a climate

director as all pressures to the hydrological system mentioned above are present in the city. However, to be better equipped to handle the hydrological
changes, a clear view is needed on the relation between the civil engineering
and urban design and planning professions that are responsible for managing
building on wet and soft soil and balancing the conditions of land and water.
This investigation of the historical relation between urban design culture and
the wet circumstances of the territory shows historical principles on which it
is possible to draw a line into the future.

To structure the investigation, time is defined in separate phases (based on
Van der Ham, 2002: 31 but altered for this perspective) characterised by the
availability of technology, the attitude towards the natural system, and consequently, the urban design. The phases are natural water management (until
1000), defensive water management (1000–1500), anticipative water management (1500–1800), offensive water management (1800–1890), manipulative
water management (1890–1990), and adaptive manipulative water management (1990 until today). For each phase a representative case in Rotterdam is
chosen to show the relation between land and water and how this influenced
urban development. The first three phases are discussed in the next section.
The other phases are discussed in separate sections. The chapter rounds off
with a brief conclusion.

Natural, defensive, and anticipative water management (until 1800)

Until the eighth century, the Dutch lowlands were uninhabitable marshlands
where the forces of water and wind had free rein. People learned to adapt
ways of living to the wet surroundings. Van der Ham described this period
of time until the year 1000 as distinguished by 'natural water management',
as nature ruled over culture (Van der Ham, 2002). There were initiatives to
control the natural landscape by digging drainage ditches to grow crops in
the fields, but for the people living in the lower Delta, there were no means
of protection from the water. This was mainly due to the lack of a community, as people were living in small groups with little power to change natural
conditions.

The Frisians were an exception. They were more organised in, for example, fighting Viking attacks, and altering nature for their benefit by creating
mounds. The first form of building site preparation began in Friesland from
900 AD. Mounds were created that functioned as refuges in times of high
tides, and the first buildings on them were churches, symbols of community
where the whole village could find shelter in times of flooding. Later mounds
became larger and settlements arose.

All settlements in the Netherlands started on higher ground, along rivers,
the sandy ridges at the coast, and on sandy soil between dunes and later the
hinterland (the so-called *geestgrond*). Settlements expanded in the eighth and

ninth centuries for military and, later, economic reasons. Villages were created on economic routes and military boundary lines.

The physical characteristics of settlements during the time of natural water management have two important spatial characteristics. First, the settlement is positioned within the most geographically convenient physical circumstances in the region. Second, this location must be close to water, but water must not be part of the layout of the settlement, since that would make the settlement more vulnerable.

The change in attitude towards the natural system from natural water management to defensive water management occurred around the year 1000, when dikes were introduced as a means of protection (Van der Ham, 2002). This new technology directly affected the location and establishment of settlements. The dike on the one hand protected larger areas to live in and on the other, enabled water in the form of a harbour to be introduced into the settlement. Many dike and dam cities were created in the thirteenth and fourteenth centuries, and the sites along the dikes were prepared for building by raising them with debris.

The dam town

The conceptually most interesting type of water city of the defensive phase is the dam town, like Rotterdam because of its connection to the larger water management scale and the integration of technological intervention with economic and social structures. Figure 4.1 shows the development of Rotterdam, which started as a fishing settlement. The first map depicts the situation around the year 1000; the peat area along the Maas and the Rotte is still under free rein of the water. The first mentioning of the settlement 'Rotta' is in 1028, but centuries before that, there were people living on the banks of the peat river Rotte, where it flows into the river Maas. In the second half of the eleventh century, the first dike ring was built. However, it did not offer enough protection, and the settlement Rotta was lost. Studies of the Rotte and its first settlement proved that in the first half of the twelfth century, people had already started to use piles and mats of woven ash wood to prepare sites for building (Guiran, 2004).

By about 1270, the third dike ring – the *Schielands Hoge Zeedijk* ('High Sea Dike') – was built, and a dam was constructed where the dike crossed the Rotte (Van der Schoor, 1999: 21). Dam cities were established in the most rewarding places where smaller rivers flowed into a larger river. A dike at these points was the most important requirement for the creation of towns in the polders because soil compaction and subsidence resulting from the drainage of peat for agriculture made these areas vulnerable to flooding. The dam had a water-defence function, but with a drainage sluice, it also took care of discharging water from the smaller river originating in the peat area onto open water. A combination of the scouring effect of the sluice water and the tidal

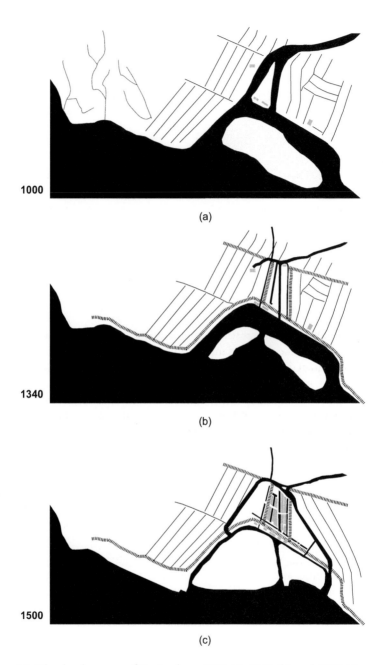

Figure 4.1 The development of Rotterdam: 1000 (a), 1340 (b), and 1500 (c).
Source: Hooimeijer *et al.*, 2005.

movement was cleverly used to maintain the harbour at the correct depth and to make the town accessible to seagoing ships.

The economic importance of regional water transport between the sea and the hinterland was embodied in the dam with its drainage sluice. The dam and the sluice became the heart of the town. The drainage sluice was only able to accommodate relatively small ships, and the cargo from larger ships had to be transferred or traded on the dam. The dam became a market, and the peat river estuary outside the dike became a sheltered harbour. The dam town and the polder were therefore bound closely together, not only in hydrological terms but also in economic and social terms, and in connecting the regional and the urban scale (Van der Schoor, 1999: 21). For the cities in the Randstad this was obviously a very prosperous situation as the wider region came together in these places. The larger scale that these dikes introduced in organising the landscape also had a great effect on the northern provinces like Friesland: the mounds came out of use and were no longer the key to strategic settlements.

Polder city and 'Waterstad'

Windmills came into use on a larger scale around 1500, marking the technological transformation to the next phase, anticipating water management. This phase is characterised by a better understanding of the nature of water systems and by people working with this knowledge. With windmills, larger volumes of water could be moved, so a more effective method was offered to keep large-scale areas and towns dry. The power created by uniting the mills with new hydrological instruments, such as sluices and dams, changed the approach towards the water from defensive to anticipative. The establishment of the Republic of Seven United Provinces accelerated knowledge development by establishing the army: the institution where knowledge about wet and soft soils was developed. The power of political unity represents an enlargement of society, a new relation between regions and cities as water systems were organised on a larger scale than before. The protection of a single plot grew into the protection of a polder, and the protection of a polder grew into the control of whole rivers. The phase of anticipating water management is the phase of the *polder city*, where the polder is not only a physical phenomenon but also the literal representation of the social phenomenon: the power of political unity.

The settlements of the two first phases, mound, river, coast, military stronghold (*burcht*), *geestgrond*, dike, and dam towns, form the first important characteristic of the polder city: the higher-level 'dry core' on which the settlement started. Prosperity and growth led to expansion of built-up areas on the surrounding wet soil, derived from peat or already prepared for cultivation, but not yet prepared to be built upon (Burke, 1956).

Of the various dry cores on which the peat polder cities were developed, the dam town is the most meaningful. One could say that dike residents, who lived alongside a peat bog and controlled the water by building a dam together, were conceptually ahead of the peat polder city dwellers. This is where a second important characteristic can be seen: the need for 'strict control', as the expansion of the polder city needed to be realised cautiously. First, the size of the expansion needed to be determined; this needed to comply not only with the requirements of that time but also with those for the time to come as the necessary works were vast and costly. Second, a technical plan was needed to ensure that water could be discharged and controlled and that city canals could maintain a constant water level. In most cases, expansion was initiated by building an encircling outer canal which was connected through the outer area by means of a sequence of parallel canals. The outer canal was primarily built for drainage but also had a military or defensive function as well as a transport function with access to warehouses (Burke, 1956). The water level of the canal system was regulated, and excess water was discharged by means of sluices and windmills which were often located on top of city walls, as in Amsterdam and Delft. Then, the reclaimed land needed to be raised to the required protection level, and was consolidated, and prepared for building. Mud excavated from the canals was used for raising the land level and was supplemented by fill, which often needed to be transported from far away. In the ground, long wooden foundation piles were driven in order to stabilise buildings in the deep-set stratum of sand.

Since the mid-thirteenth century, a dike had stretched out along the Hoogstraat ('High Street') in Rotterdam, with a dam in the Rotte providing the settlement with its name. Before the invention of the windmill, only direct discharge into the river could keep the water in the polders at the most convenient level for growing crops. The discharge rivers all flow through the settlement in the same north–south direction, steering the way the city developed. Also, roads were laid out at right angles to the river (Van Ravesteyn, 1928: 114).

When the settlement was granted town privileges in 1340, its burghers needed a ring of protecting water. Two moats, Coolvest to the west and Goudsevest to the east, gave the settlement its characteristic triangular shape; see Figure 4.1a (Van Ravesteyn, 1928: 134). However, polder expansion turned out to be less attractive than the waterside, where business was centred along the Maas. So, instead of building into subsiding polders like Amsterdam did, the people of Rotterdam decided to expand the city into the river Maas. Already, in the thirteenth century, people had started to use the salting outside the dike for harbour activities (Van Ravesteyn, 1928: 105). The new quarter was appropriately named *Waterstad* ('Water City'). It was a bustling centre of shipyards, warehouses, sail-making, and rope-making and later grand merchants' houses.

The layout of the new part of the city was very simple, and before the sixteenth and seventeenth centuries, there was actually no plan. The houses grew together following the shape of the river and the harbours. Parts were inside the dike and parts outside, making dikes important urban elements of the layout (Van Ravesteyn, 1929: 22).

The simple layout is directly related to the costs for building site preparation: the wider the house, the more expensive the foundation. The importance of the harbour is represented by its size. It was made very spacious, which was useful when the ships grew larger into the nineteenth century. The result was a spacious Waterstad that had a high quality of special environment and moreover clean water in the canals, especially compared to the dense inner city north of the Hoogstraat. It was taken for granted that the Waterstad, located outside the dike, was vulnerable to flooding from the Maas. Meanwhile, space and clean water became more progressively more problematic in the inner city and especially when industrialisation took force (Van Ravesteyn, 1929; Van der Schoor, 1999; Schadee, 2000).

By creating the Waterstad area, Rotterdam took profit from its strategic position in the Randstad Delta. It introduced the possibility for Rotterdam to develop a flourishing port economy and trade economy, competing with established port cities like Antwerp and Amsterdam.

Offensive water management (1800–1890)

The contour and layout of all the principal water city types that were prior expansions of the polder city were preserved far into the nineteenth century. After the Golden Century of the seventeenth century, when most of these expansions were built, the Republic suffered from political decay and economic stagnation and later the French invasion. The deterioration of conditions ended in 1814 when the monarchy was instated, but only after 1850 did city development restart. A new phase of offensive water management began, made possible by the power of the steam engine. Industrialisation turned Dutch cities into places where people were concentrated around jobs in the factories and the ever-growing harbours. The social and functional change of cities in this era, where people from the countryside were suddenly packed together in dense neighbourhoods, cannot be underestimated. The new steam power started a scale enlargement and acceleration of the growth of cities as well as massive interventions in the water system. Water could be moved in a controlled way with much greater power. Almost everything became possible, from the building of water channels, the closing of sea arms, and the artificial lowering or raising of groundwater levels.

The Waterproject

The first large-scale city development in the Netherlands was the expansion of Rotterdam with the plan called *Waterproject*, designed by military engineer and city architect W.N. Rose (1801–1877) (see Figure 4.2). The urban expansion was interwoven with the aim for better water management in the city. Many people had died from cholera because the water in the inner city was contaminated. In the dense city, the river, the canals and the groundwater

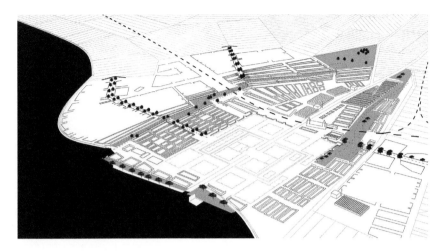

Figure 4.2 Principle drawing of the Waterproject.
Source: Hooimeijer *et al.*, 2005.

were used for everything, producing highly unpleasant smells and an unhealthy living environment.

Rose's answer to this problem was the design of a city water system entirely independent from the regional water system, where water management served the interests of agriculture. Rose, together with landscape architects J.D. and L.P. Zocher, designed the *Waterproject* as an ingenious plan, combining the preparation of the surrounding wet and soft polders together with a new water management system into an integrated urban design.

The first aim was to flush water through the entire inner city to improve water quality. The second aim was the desperately needed expansion. Rotterdam was digging harbour after harbour, and many people were attracted to the jobs this brought. Only the lowering of the groundwater level in the polders made it possible to build new houses there.

Rose asked the Zochers to draw the plan with a park for walking for the poor and living quarters for the rich, which also made the project profitable in improving urban quality. The plan combined the most important urban tasks of that time, while integrating the characteristics of the territory with the technology available within an urban design. The location of the dike that was necessary to build an independent water system and the new polder areas, was carefully situated from one existing dike to another. Along the dike, a waterway was dug that collected all the water from the new expansion that flowed from the higher inner dam city through ditches and culverts. There was an intensive investigation done into the surface levels to accommodate the water flow (see Figure 4.3). Where the waterways reached the Maas, the new power of two steam engines pumped water that was let into the inner city into the river (see Berens, 2001; Hooimeijer and Kamphuis, 2001).

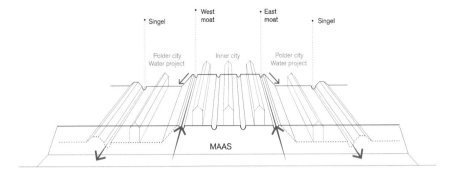

Figure 4.3 The various heights in the Waterproject.
Source: Own illustration based on Van den Noort, 1990.

The Waterproject represents the available technology and the grand issues of urban planning during the era of offensive water management. It
also shows how cities were developed during this period. Main infrastructures were built by the municipality while the areas in between were filled
in by private developers. Here, the building blocks were situated in line
with the original polder pattern. This century-old structure represents the
integrated culture of the water system, the division of land and water, and
the pattern of ownership. In these areas, the municipality built sand strips
under the planned roads, and developers the roads, and afterwards, the
municipality took over the maintenance. Houses were built on piles above
the ground floor, and because the backyards were not raised, the space in
the basement could be used for living, usually as a bedroom. This way of
preparing an area for building influenced the design and use of the city on
all scales.

Manipulative water management (1890–1990)

At the end of the nineteenth century, explosive urbanisation and technological prosperity put pressure on the polder cities. The manipulative era
(1890–1990) is marked by the introduction of the engine and electricity,
which had an immense influence on the city and the water system. The
car, industry, and industrialised building processes and technology created a
new spatial order. This resulted in a situation when technically everything
was possible and there was no connection to the 'natural' laws of the water system. The building of sanitation and drinking water infrastructures
brought segregation between the systems for groundwater-level control, the
discharge of waste water, and the supply of drinking water. The larger part
of the urban water system disappeared underground. At the same time, industrialisation brought the car, claiming more and more space. Many open
waters, bad smelling or dangerous due to bad street-lighting, were filled in,

leading to a reduction of the ratio of open water in the city (De Vries, 1996). Even though the water structure of the polder city remained important for drainage, discharge, and storage, it was no longer used as an element in the urban design of the city.

Blijdorp

At the beginning of the twentieth century, two main forces changed urban development practice in the Randstad and Rotterdam immensely. First was the adaptation to regional infrastructure in dealing with train tracks and later provincial car infrastructure. Second was the 1901 Housing Act that made it mandatory for a municipality larger than 20,000 inhabitants to make expansion plans. This law gave a boost to the new profession of urban design while previously engineers and architects had built cities. Considering the new way neighbourhoods were built, by private entrepreneurs, it was very hard for the municipality to create a plan and make all the developers abide by it. The first expansion plan for Rotterdam (1906), Blijdorp, was more a combination of plans of private developers than an independent urban design. Eleven years after this and many more plans (and a lot of misery trying to get landowners and property developers on the same page), the municipality decided to buy all the land and develop the area themselves. The possibility to prepare the whole site at once with the new technology of hydraulically filling the land with sand from the harbours was an added advantage of this decision. The largest advantage of this technology was by the fact that there was no need to agree on an urban plan *before* applying the layer of sand because any plan could be realised on it. Here the urban design and realisation was disconnected from the polder pattern, the historical pattern of land and water and land ownership. Building site preparation and the technology of balancing out land and water became disconnected from urban design (Gemeentewerken Rotterdam, 1984: 14).

Blijdorp was the first large-scale hydraulic filling project in Rotterdam. The south side of the Schie was done in 1924. During the filling of the north side, water was used to keep the sand in place. The disconnection of building site preparation from the urban design meant that the characteristics of the territory played no role in the design. This is clearly the case for Blijdorp and also for the famous Plan South for Amsterdam by H.P. Berlage that looks just the same (Heeling *et al.*, 2002). Car infrastructure is the backbone in both plans, and the water and green structure is like a 'shadow'. Technology at this time was not perfected yet and the water system was still a part of the urban plan. Industrialisation brought the larger scale into urban development and a new organisation of city development in which the issue of how to deal with water management faded into the background, and issues related to car traffic, road, and rail infrastructure related to the wider Randstad development moved to the foreground.

Lage Land and Ommoord

The enlargement of urban scale and the disconnection of urban design from the characteristics of the land dominated in the post-war era. Water as an urban element is almost completely insignificant when situated on the top of the layer of sand. Indeed, the water system becomes completely artificial. This fulfilled the *makeability* principle, a paradigm of belief in a manmade culture that relies on technology and systematic approaches. This was applied to all aspects of society: social cohesion, social facilities, and control of the city as well as the water system (Cornelis, 2000). During this phase, the spatial order of the Netherlands was fundamentally changed. The large projects of urban expansions, recreation, infrastructure, and land consolidation in agricultural areas led to a completely different landscape.

In his inaugural speech on 12 November 1975, titled *Spel met water, grond en land* ('Game with water, soil, and land'), W.A. Segeren, Extraordinary Professor in Water Construction and Polders in Delft, recognised a direct relation between the location of the settlement, the way of life, and the surroundings. After the Second World War, the process of city expansions was to decide on location, the soil and the water system were investigated, and then the civil and technical interventions were determined to improve the soil conditions. Weak soils were strengthened with sand, calculations for foundation piles were made, and measures were taken for the discharge and drainage of the built area (Segeren, 1975). The hydraulic filling with sand meant that urban designs could be uniform on any soil condition. There was no incentive to react to specific conditions with the urban design because all conditions became the same. Industrial building influenced the standardisation of urban design and planning through the uniform production of apartment buildings and houses, denying any local characteristics to the urban expansions (Segeren, 1975).

In Rotterdam, expansions were made on the south bank and east of the city in the drained lake Alexanderpolder. Lotte Stam-Beese, senior architect and urbanist at the Rotterdam municipality, and Jaap Bakema, independent architect and urban designer, made visionary plans for Alexanderpolder, called the *Lage Land* (the 'Low Land'), and presented these at the *Congrès Internationaux d'Architecture Moderne – CIAM* (International Congresses of Modern Architecture) in Aix-en-Provence in 1953. They chose this site in collaboration with the director of the city development office, Cornelis van Traa, because a great task was set to design a sub-city in these low-lying polders for the ever-growing number of residents of Rotterdam. The city could not expand north while the city centre was moving to the west, so city planners considered an eastern expansion, even in deep, wet polders, as the best counterbalance. The plans were extraordinary because they combine a radical way of building preparation, building on piles, and lowering of the water table, with an internationally inspired vision on urban development.

Bakema's concept of the 'visual unit', a vertical city built-up of high-rise towers, was connected to the 'district idea', where residential neighbourhoods merge harmoniously into a concentric and hierarchical whole. It was a construction on the flat surface of the city map. The 'visual units' made this a three-dimensional composition by introducing a sort of vast elementary sculpture in which architecture and urban design converged. In the plan for Alexanderpolder, these visual units were directly linked to the larger scale of the highway and functioned as autonomous urban units. The geographical circumstances of the deep-lying polder and the poor soil condition were the reason that Stam-Beese and Bakema introduced the idea of vertical neighbourhoods (Schilt, 1982). By founding the highway and these 'Mammoths', as Bakema called them, on piles, the city was disconnected technically from its landscape, which could be used for agriculture and recreation. These mammoths of vertical neighbourhoods were, according to Bakema, the best solution in dealing with the bad soil conditions in the Lage Land. People with an open state of mind and life-style could live in this city on piles with a view of the open agricultural landscape (Palmboom, 1993). Eventually, when Stam-Beese designed the executed plan for *Lage Land*, only a very small part of the Mammoth concept remained in the shape of four large flats that are positioned in the form of a mill wing.

The executed design of *Lage Land* is interesting in two ways. For building site preparation, the choice was made to lower the water table, at a time when the usual practice was the raising of land with sand, and the dimensions of the urban design were very much related to the dimensions of the original polder pattern. Stam-Beese was assigned to design a city that was endless; the polders in the Netherlands, due to the orthogonal structure and quantity, have that characteristic.

After working on the Lage Land, urban designer Stam-Beese also made the design for Ommoord positioned in the same drained lake. She recognised the fact that the technical approach towards the poor soil conditions with layers of sand led to urban designs that do not connect to the *genius loci* (Stam-Beese, n.d.). Stam-Beese tried to establish in Ommoord an urban identity that connects people by the use of a green heart with facilities surrounded by flats that had a view to the surrounding landscape. These parks were made with an irregular surface to make them appear more natural. This and the view were intended to compensate for the lack of private outdoor space (Damen and Devolder, 1993).

This manipulative era urban type, as lucidly described by Stam-Beese, thrives on the perfection of technology and disconnecting settlements from the identity of the landscape. The water problem can be addressed technically and was completely disconnected from the urban plan. This did not add up to the desired urban quality, and this era can be used to make a critical stand against using technology to alter the physical geography of a site.

Zevenkamp

By the 1970s the post-war era was criticised as a time of technocracy and narrow-minded views on social structures. There was a strong urge to free society from these conventions and to search for the 'real identity' of the city. A respect for nature became a theme in reaction to technocracy and manmade culture. The publication by Rachel Carson, 'Silent Spring' (1962), revealed mankind's bad influence on nature. Also, the 1972 report by the Club of Rome, 'Limits to Growth' (Meadows *et al.*, 1972) and the oil crisis in 1973 put the causal relation between economic growth and the effects on the environment in a clear perspective (Meadows *et al.*, 1972). Therefore, in the 1970s nature and ecology became more important in spatial planning, and the landscape architect arrived as a new player. The landscape architect reintroduces water as a spatial element in the city. At the same time, the search for urban identity rediscovered the old water towns which inspired all sorts of plans to bring back the hidden water landscapes.

Zevenkamp is an example development that although it was developed through hydraulic filling of sand, the urban design took an original landscape element, a ditch called the *Ommoordse Tocht*, as the backbone of the plan. The ditch was excavated out of the layer of sand as the central axes of the plan where the most important public space was situated. The new waterway was designed to give identity to the function of the surroundings it flows through. In the centre, it is a canal with brick quays giving the area the identity of a dam city representing the social and economic heart of the expansion. This way, even though the original hydrological system is hidden under a layer of sand, the urban design made a connection to the original landscape and made use of the century-old identity of Dutch towns. It was the first step towards adaptive manipulative water management and new urban types.

Adaptive manipulative water management (1990 to the present)

While adaptive and manipulative may seem contradicting terms, they name the last phase distinguished in this chapter. It indicates that there is no consensus about how to spatially make the right adjustments in order to adapt to climate change. After 1973, the prelude towards the adaptive manipulative phase of water management was initiated, but it took over 20 years for mainstream society to adopt a new spatial attitude towards natural systems as part of policy and practice. The Fourth Assessment Report of the Intergovernmental Panel on Climate Change (IPCC, 2001), in particular, changed the view on the responsibility of people towards nature. The conclusions are quite clear about the impacts of climate change, the vulnerability of natural and human environments, and the potential for response through adaptation.

The first national planning report which supported the rediscovery of water as an element of urban development is the *Fourth Report Extra* or *Vinex* (Ministerie van VROM, 1990), which addresses the expansion of towns concerning living, working and recreation. One million houses were planned for the period up to 2015; a number that was later readjusted to 600,000. The report led to a whole new urban typology, characterised by diversity, called Vinex areas, large-scale developments mainly on the outskirts of larger Dutch cities that were solely allocated to housing. Water is also integrated in other national planning reports like the 1999 so-called *Belvedere Memorandum* (Ministerie van OCW *et al.*, 1999) and new national strategy called (in translation) *Another Way with Water: Water Policy of the Twenty-first Century* (Ministerie van V&W, 2000). The first increases attention towards history and landscape, and the second proclaimed a change in the attitude towards water in response to the near flood disasters in the 1990s. Nature and culture make a strong comeback in the national agenda based on both reports.

Nesselande

In Nesselande, one of the four Vinex areas in Rotterdam, water is introduced as the carrying structure of the plan. Alongside that, the use of ecological sensitive material, a district heating system, and subsidies for the use of solar energy are the starting points to ensure sustainability. A naturally cleaning, independent, open water system for drainage and storage guarantees water quality. The inhabitants have to live by several rules to maintain water quality, such as restrictions on washing cars and materials used in the gardens. Besides the overall importance of water to structure the area, this attempt to make the residents aware of the 'wet' situation of their neighbourhood, located nearly 5 metres below sea level, is expected to change the attitude towards water into a more adaptive approach.

One of the districts in Nesselande is called Water City (*Waterstad*) and is designed by Frits Palmboom and his office, Palmbout Urban Landscapes, together with H + N + S Landscape Architects. Both offices are widely known for their ecology-based design approach. Of interest is that the urban designers reintroduce the mound, or in Dutch *terp*, as a strategy to give open direction to the plan. The surface of the building lots is very low – as said nearly 5 metres below sea level – and is deliberately not raised to remain on the same level as the water to preserve a close relationship between water and garden. The roads are situated on dikes which are 80 cm higher than the lots. The lots are given mounds on the same level as the roads and connected to them to make road, water, and electrical infrastructure possible. Each house needs to be situated somewhere on the mound, but architects can make use of the height difference to create a spatially varied house. In this way, no restrictive rules are needed, and the building site preparation has become an integrated part of the urban design (see Figure 4.4).

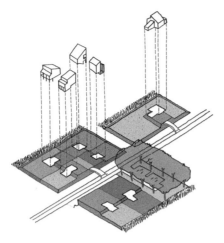

Figure 4.4 Mounds in Nesselande, 1999.
Source: Palmbout Urban Landscapes.

Zestienhoven

The most recent expansion plan of Rotterdam is Zestienhoven, close to Rotterdam The Hague Airport. Here, a park, sports facilities, and allotment gardens are situated next to the airport, and these are expected to roughly stay as they are. The urban design is therefore more a *re*design to make the area available for housing instead of completely new plan for an empty area. This is part of the new strategy of Rotterdam to intensify instead of expanding the existing territory (Gemeente Rotterdam, 2007).

With the development of *Zestienhoven*, water management was also given a leading role due to the fact that the area is very low (about 6 metres below sea level), with a high degree of seepage. From the water management point of view, scenarios were developed, and the optimum one (in relation to the costs and profits as well as functional and ecological aspects) was chosen and worked out in a master plan. This plan brings back the original polder pattern through an open water system forming a grid. Waterways are dug out of the layer of sand put here in earlier years. Building sites are raised with sand to prevent seepage and also to cover soil pollution. Around these sites, the green structure is kept intact. Ten per cent of surface water as demanded by the water board is projected to secure a flexible water structure, meaning that when there is heavy precipitation water can be stored. Figure 4.5 shows the preliminary plan with the building plots and the water grid. Many houses are situated along the water. The park on the west side and the allotment gardens on the south side are kept in their original state. The diagonal is the high-speed train line.

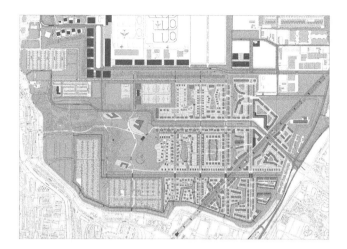

Figure 4.5 Preliminary 2009 plan 'Zestienhoven'.
Source: dS+V, Rotterdam Municipality.

While the master plan is based on the water system and soil conditions, many problems were encountered in the realisation phase, problems that could have been prevented if more detailed data of the water system was taken into the initial planning phase. The 10% surface water that was demanded by the water board is situated at the south side to accentuate a natural height difference. This made a close relation to the existing landscape and created the main ecological and recreational structure. However, the waterway had to be heavily sealed, due to severe seepage. As problems like this manifested themselves in the implementation phase, the realisation grew that it is important not to have a highly detailed master plan in such a complex situation. Instead, it is better to make a much more general and strategic plan with some key guidelines from relevant domains – urban design, engineering, finance – leaving ample room for more specific demands in the implementation phase.

Conclusion

> Without a long start in history, we shall not have momentum needed, in our own consciousness, to take a sufficiently bold leap into the future.
> (Mumford, 1961: 3)

The tight historical relationship between the natural system and the design of polder cities is exemplary for the future. The Netherlands is a water machine of which all cogs are connected to each other. Dutch cities are hydrological constructions, with a spatial layout that is strongly connected to the rules of water. It could be argued that the practice of Dutch urban design as it is today is based on the way the Dutch dealt with the water. This overview in six phases offers insight into a 'fine tradition' and how the self-evident relation between water management and urban design is shaped through time. The main conclusion is that the hydrological system is timeless, forms conditions for human social infrastructure, shapes the dynamics of the city, and sets out clear lines for the future. The landscape as a carrier of the hydrological system, including the original balance between land and water, should be taken on board when designing and redesigning water cities. Various levels of scale are connected to each other, like communicating vessels. The local scale of a new urban extension is connected to the regional scale by the polder system. Together the polders discharge to the channels and rivers as part of the delta in which the Randstad is situated. At this scale the main defence from the sea is crucial, especially when decisions are taken on large new developments while there are predictions of (serious) sea-level rise on the long term.

This chapter shows that each phase puts forth strategies for the future. The eras of natural and defensive water management are examples of how a flexible mental and physical attitude can incorporate uncertainties over time, which in this time frame is rather useful. The anticipative water management phase is an example of how cooperation and boldness lead to making the most of the potential of the territory. It also shows how taking the original waterscape into account can create spatial diversity by the use of technology and landscape while delivering hydrological cities, knowledge development, and prosperity. The offensive phase of water management shows that when the disciplines of engineering and urban design work together, a sound integration of spatial and technical challenges and solutions can be realised. It is clear that the knowledge and impact of water levels should be added to the toolbox of urban planning and design. Engineers should add the spatial consequences of the hydrological system for urban development. Both can, from different angles and closely working together, contribute to new developments as truly urban engineers.

Finally, the last two phases together make for a strategy that first of all must be aimed at developing sound consciousness: consciousness about the impact of technical systems and the vulnerability of the natural system is crucial for new developments. With a critical eye on constructions and with sight not only on the vulnerability of natural system but also moreover on the quality that the natural system can offer urbanity, a new balance can be found.

References

Berens, H. (2001). *W.N. Rose 1801–1877: Stedenbouw, civiele techniek en architectuur [W.N. Rose 1801–1877; Urban design, civil engineering and architecture]*. NAi Uitgevers, Rotterdam.

Burke, G.L. (1956). *The making of Dutch Towns: A study in urban development from the tenth to the seventeenth centuries*. Cleaver-Hume Press, London.

Cornelis, A. (2000). *De logica van het gevoel [The logic of feeling]*; Filosofie van de stabiliteitslagen in de cultuur als nesteling der emoties. Boom Uitgevers, Amsterdam.

Damen, H. and Devolder, A.-M.(Eds) (1993). *Lotte Stam-Beese 1903–1988; Dessau, Brno, Charkow, Moskou, Amsterdam* [In Dutch]. Rotterdamse Kunststichting/Uitgeverij De Hef, Rotterdam.

De Vries, M.L. (1996). *Nederland waterland [The Netherlands: A Waterland]; een nieuw leven voor gedempte grachten, vaarten, havens en beken.* Sdu Uitgevers, The Hague.

Gemeente Rotterdam (2007). *Stadvisie Rotterdam [Municipal vision on Rotterdam].* Gemeente Rotterdam, Rotterdam.

Gemeentewerken Rotterdam (1984). *Methoden van bouw- en woonrijp maken in de gemeente Rotterdam [Methods to prepare land for building in Rotterdam].* Gemeentewerken Rotterdam, Rotterdam.

Guiran, A.J. (2004). 'Op zoek naar Rotte [Searching for the Rotte]; Een huiserf uit de elfde eeuw langs de Binnenrotte', *Rotterdams Jaarboekje*, 11th Series, 2nd Volume, 87–108.

Heeling, J., Meyer, H. and Westrik J. (2002). *Het ontwerp van de stadsplattegrond [The design of the town plan].* SUN, Amsterdam.

Hooimeijer, F. and Kamphuis, M. (2001). *The water project; A nineteenth century walk through Rotterdam.* 010 Publishers, Rotterdam.

Hooimeijer, F., Meyer, H. and Nienhuis, A. (2005). *Atlas of Dutch water cities.* SUN, Amsterdam.

IPCC, Intergovernmental Panel on Climate Change (2001). *Climate change 2001 – impacts, adaptation and vulnerability.* Cambridge University Press, Cambridge.

Meadows, D.H, Meadows, D.L., Randers, J. and Behrens III, W.W. (1972). *The limits to growth; A report for the club of Rome's project on the predicament of mankind.* Universe Books, New York.

Ministerie van OCW (Onderwijs, Cultuur en Wetenschappen), Ministerie van Landbouw, Natuurbeheer en Visserij (LNV), Ministerie van Volkshuisvesting, Ruimtelijke Ordening en Milieubeheer VROM) and Ministerie van Verkeer en Waterstaat (V&W) (1999). *Nota Belvedere: Beleidsnota over de relatie cultuurhistorie en ruimtelijke inrichting [The Belvedere Memorandum: A policy document examining the relationship between cultural history and spatial planning].* Ministeries van OCW, LNV, VROM and V&W, The Hague.

Ministerie van VROM (Volkshuisvesting, Ruimtelijke Ordening en Milieubeheer) (1990). *Vierde nota over de Ruimtelijke Ordening Extra, Deel 1: ontwerp-planologische kernbeslissing [Fourth report on spatial planning extra: Green Paper].* Ministerie van VROM, The Hague.

Ministerie van V&W (Verkeer en Waterstaat) (2000). *Anders omgaan met water: waterbeleid in de 21e eeuw, Beleidsvoornemen [Another way with water: Water policy of the twenty-first century; Green Paper].* Ministerie van V&W, The Hague.

Mumford, L. (1961). *The City in History.* Harcourt, New York.

Palmboom, F. (1993). 'De planningsgeschiedenis van de Alexanderpolder' [The history of planning the Alexanderpolder]. In: Devolder, A.-M. (Ed.) *De Alexanderpolder, waar de stad verder gaat/Alexanderpolder: New urban frontiers.* THOTH, Bussum, 41–49.

Schadee N. (2000). 'Venster op de Rivier; De macht van een metafoor' [Window on the river; The power of a metaphor], *Rotterdams Jaarboekje*, 10th Series, 10th Volume, 441–461.

Schilt, J. (1982). '1947–1957: Ten Years of Opbouw'. In: Beeren, W., Donker Duyvis, P., Schoon, T. and Wiethoff, C (Eds) *Het Nieuwe Bouwen in Rotterdam 1920–1960.* Delft University Press, Delft, 139–157.

Segeren, W.A. (1975). *Spel met water, grond en land [Game with water, soil and land]*; Inaugural speech of extraordinary professor in water construction (polders), November 12, 1975, TU Delft, Delft.

Stam-Beese, L. (n.d.). 'Gedachten rondom de nieuwe wijk Ommoord', [Thoughts about the new district Ommoord], NAi archive Lotte Stam-Beese, no. 120, NAi, Rotterdam.

Van der Ham, W. (2002). 'Een wijd perspectief' [A broad perspective]. In: Van Buuren, M., Van Drimmelen, C. and Iedema, W. (Eds) *Waterlandschappen: De cultuurhistorie van de toekomst als opgave voor het waterbeheer [Water landscapes: The cultural history of the future as an assignment for water management]*, RIZA Werkdocument 2002. RIZA, Lelystad, 107–117.

Van der Schoor, A. (1999). *Stad in aanwas: Geschiedenis van Rotterdam tot 1813 [A growing city: History of Rotterdam until 1813]*. Waanders, Zwolle.

Van den Noort, J. (1990). *Pion of Pionier: Rotterdam – Gemeentelijke bedrijvigheid in de negentiende eeuw [Pawn or pioneer: Rotterdam – Municipal industriousness in the nineteenth century]*, PhD thesis Leiden University, Historische Publicaties Roterodamum, Grote reeks 41. Historisch Genootschap Roterodamum, Rotterdam.

Van Ravesteyn, L.J.C.J. (1928). 'Rotterdam vóór de 19e eeuw; De ontwikkeling der stad' [Rotterdam before the 19th century; The development of the city], *Rotterdamsch Jaarboekje [Rotterdam Yearbook]*, 3rd Series, 6th Volume, 95–144.

Van Ravesteyn, L.J.C.J. (1929). 'Rotterdam voor de 19e eeuw; De ontwikkeling der stad, VII: De oude waterstad'[Rotterdam before the 19th century; The development of the city, VII: The old water city], *Rotterdamsch Jaarboekje [Rotterdam yearbook]*, 3rd Series, 7th Volume, 9–37. Vries, M. L. de (1996). SDU, Nederland Waterland, The Hague.

5 The global petroleumscape in the Dutch Randstad

Oil spaces and mindsets

Carola Hein

Introduction

As a polycentric conurbation in the north-west of the Netherlands, the Randstad is a complex structure that has evolved over centuries under the influence of diverse and shifting actors. It overlaps with numerous economic spaces, including ones for oil. It is home to the Amsterdam Rotterdam Antwerp oil spot market (ARA) that includes Amsterdam, home for refined petroleum products; Rotterdam, the centre for crude; and, crossing the Belgian border to the south, Antwerp, one of the largest petrochemical industrial complexes in the world. This chapter explores how oil companies with the support of public planning and private corporations have co-shaped the landscapes and mindscapes of the Randstad through transformation, transport, consumption, administration, and promotion of petroleum in parallel with other actors. They created what I call a *petroleumscape* that consists of diverse evolving spatial patterns and built forms as well as mindsets.[1] These oil spaces are only partly incorporated into the imaginary of the Randstad. When citizens and tourists think of cities in the Netherlands, few might think of petroleum. Instead, they will probably visualize historic medieval centres with canals and windmills.

Through a close investigation of the multiple dimensions of oil in the Randstad, the chapter highlights the ways in which oil interests have intersected with private and public planning and design paradigms over the last 150 years, establishing patterns that influence spatial practice, including heritage decisions and urban transformation in the future. The chapter further argues that in parallel with the physical construction of oil landscapes the oil companies (with the help of car manufacturers and other enterprises including design) promoted the emergence of a very different mindscape. Distributing free road maps and brochures, for example, that advertise the use of cars to discover the natural landscapes and historical cities in faraway locations, they pursued a major advertisement campaign aimed to change people's behaviours and lifestyles. Highlighting the impact of oil on different parts of the built environment, this chapter raises new questions about spatial formation in the Randstad. The chapter does not claim to provide a complete history: it focuses on Rotterdam and the South Western corner of the Randstad and serves as a call for an integrated study of oil networks and their expression in landscapes and mindscapes on a larger scale.

A comprehensive investigation of the interconnected physical reality of oil and its appearance is ongoing, and the importance of space is receiving more and more attention (Hein, 2010; Hein, 2013; Hein, 2016; Hein, 2017; Hein, 2018a). Diverse groups of scholars concern themselves with select aspects of oil spaces—economic geographers may study oil flows, planning historians investigate urban structures, and cultural historians may consider the lived reality of oil. Historians of the built environment have recognized the impact of oil on a region in specific historic investigations of industrial structures, headquarter buildings, or gas stations, but have yet to explore these impacts in context (Hubbard, 1967; Walker, 1984; Yergin, 1991; Black, 2012). Understanding the changing fabric of the Randstad in light of oil-related structures provides insights on factors external to recognized spatial planning and instead relate to economic policies that drive spatial development. In most instances, oil companies and stakeholders are not planning agents per se, but the flows and the interests related to petroleum have influenced planning practice, directly and indirectly in response to the changing urban environment.

Through four sections—industrial, retail, ancillary, and imaginary—the chapter examines how oil companies and the public sector established the foundations for the Randstad oil cluster in the early years of the industry (from 1862 to the Second World War) and established a petroleumscape that shapes spatial practices and mindsets until today. To highlight how different layers of the petroleumscape have influenced each other, a series of analytical maps shows the various phases in which the industrial, infrastructural, administrative, retail, and ancillary spaces (spatial layers of the petroleumscape) have grown in the era of the car, specifically comparing 1910, 1940, 1970, and 2000 (see Figure 5.1a–d). These maps are based on rich source material, ranging from secondary sources to archival material and telephone book listings of gas/petrol stations. In making the maps we focused on the big picture and broad trends rather than on each location and its historical development. The maps are meant to provoke in-depth follow-up studies. The maps show that installations of oil storage, refining and transport have 'standing power' once established. As the international professional services company Ernst and Young put it: 'Old refineries rarely die' (Ernst & Young, 2012; Hein, 2018b). The fourth section explores the ways in which oil companies have used the landscape in their advertising, focusing on the benefits of oil use rather than the landscape of production. A better understanding of how oil has shaped the spaces and imaginaries of the Randstad helps understand the challenges and opportunities of the ongoing, much-needed energy transition—its spatial, social, and cultural elements.

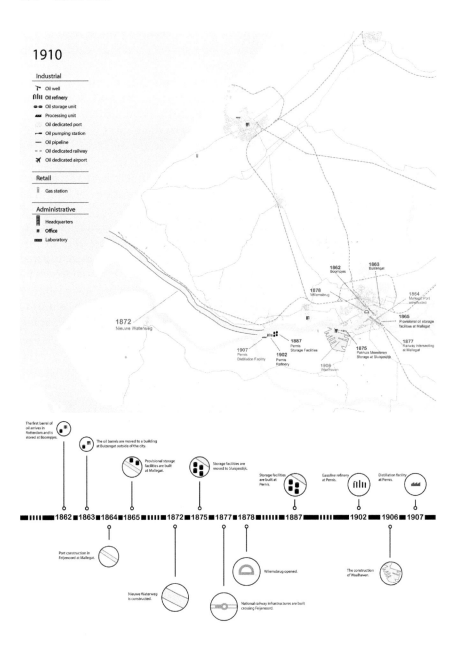

Figure 5.1(a/d) Maps of the petroleumscape of the Rotterdam The Hague area in 1910, 1920, 1940 and 2000.

Source: Carola Hein, Arnaud de Waijer.

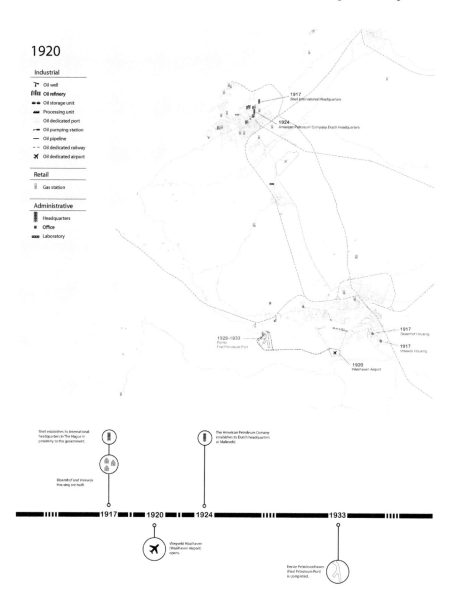

Figure 5.1(a/d) (Continued)

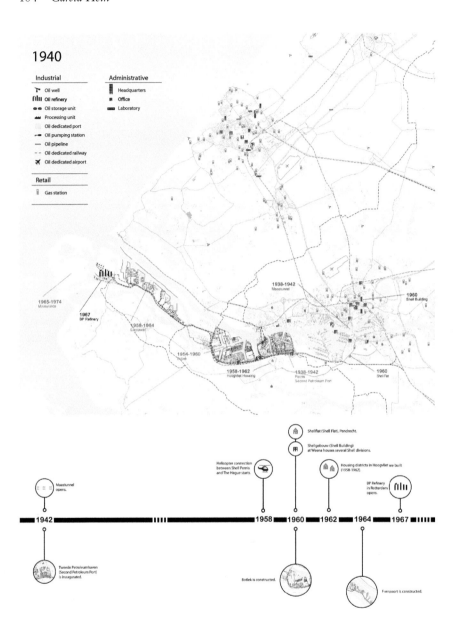

Figure 5.1(a/d) (Continued)

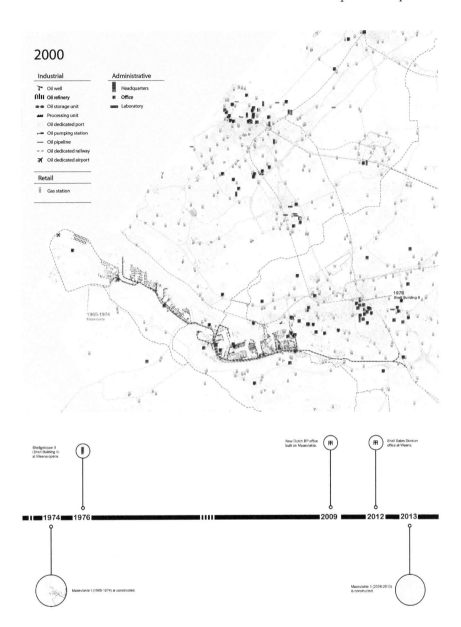

Figure 5.1(a/d) (Continued)

The industrial petroleumscape in the Randstad: building the largest oil port of Western Europe

The first landscape of oil is the industrial footprint of oil, its storage, transformation, and transport. These installations are identical around the globe but largely invisible and inaccessible to the population. They are expansive in the Rotterdam port and clearly visible from the air: port facilities, storage tanks, refineries, pipelines, and other infrastructure spanning from the inner city to the tip of the port, the Maasvlakte II. The production sector is huge in scale with some 5,300 ha for industrial sites and 1,500 kilometres of pipelines within the port, and very costly. Its impact on planning decisions is high, but its visibility for the general public is low and mostly hidden from everyday experience. Most citizens only experience the industrial petroleumscape on the edge of their everyday experience. They might glimpse a refinery or storage tanks at the side of a highway, and they might see a passing train or ship or view the harbour from the air or see the distant light emissions during the night. But little of the larger industrial structure is visible in the everyday environment or part of everyday life (Sijmons *et al.*, 2014). As a result, the huge industrial landscape has little impact on the citizen's mindscape. Some of its infrastructure, notably pipelines (including NATO pipelines) is underground and not visible to the eye—unless a careful observer traces pipeline markers, follows patterns of melted snow across agricultural areas, or accesses relevant data sets. Other parts of the infrastructure, such as important rail and highway networks, are shared with general users and not easily identifiable as part of oil networks either. Other oil-related elements, such as intensive farming in greenhouses that is widely spread in the Netherlands, is also largely dependent on oil (and gas), but rarely associated with the oil industry.

As the map of 1910 shows, it is in the port that oil first arrived in the Netherlands. Small businesses in Rotterdam, Amsterdam, and Antwerp were prominent from the 1860s to the 1880s when American oil entered the European market and as Rotterdam's port evolved into a turntable and transit point for oil heading to the rapidly industrializing areas in western Germany. The use of kerosene to light lamps was growing, creating a market for newly available petroleum. As early as 1862, several hundred barrels and crates of petroleum from America arrived in the Rotterdam port (Loohuis, 1952; Janssen, 1999). Traders in Rotterdam and Antwerp as well as in Hamburg, Bremen, Liverpool, Cork and Marseille had been among the first to import petroleum to Europe, laying the bases for the development of these cities as oil markets. Oil firms were small at the time and focused on transport, storage, and resale as they searched for the fastest and safest transport chains and refining processes. The first shipment of oil was stored by the company *Pakhuismeesteren* in the heart of Rotterdam, paying little attention to its explosive qualities.[2] Only a year later, in 1863, petroleum imports had reached 17,500 barrels of direct and 7,200 of indirect import (Loohuis, 1952). The dangers of the new product—notably flammability and water pollution—became better known which led to its storage outside the city (and similar decisions were made in other cities around the world).

Competition among the port cities in the Randstad and Belgium was fierce in this early period. In 1864 the New York Herald reported growing sales in Rotterdam and moderate activity in Amsterdam.[3] In 1865 Rotterdam received 533,000 gallons, but this was less than half the amount shipped to Bremen or Hamburg, and much less than the over 4m shipped to Antwerp.[4] Indeed, in these early years, Antwerp held the dominant position. But demand in the German and Swiss hinterland spurred the import of oil through Rotterdam in competition with these other ports, alternatively transported via rail and ship. The amount shipped to Rotterdam increased rapidly. Storage facilities had to be expanded and improved. By 1867, imports (107,000 barrels) were double that of 1866 (Loohuis, 1952). In 1870, the Provincial Executive agreed upon the extension of the Rotterdam municipality because of interest in maintaining the port area within the city limits, against the opposition of the municipalities of Charlois and Katendrecht (Schoor, 2013). The opening of the shipping canal, the Nieuwe Waterweg, connecting Rotterdam directly to the North Sea in 1872 facilitated access for the growing number of steamships that transported petroleum and brought about the request for a petroleum port with sound rail and road connections to the German hinterland.

The quick growth of the petroleum trade, and the need for dedicated facilities, necessitated a close collaboration between elite merchants and the municipality. Their work together helped Rotterdam develop into one of the key European oil ports within about a decade of the first oil drilling in Titusville, Pennsylvania in 1859. In Rotterdam, the De Monchy family of merchants owned the firm *Pakhuismeesteren* and emerged as one of the drivers of the Rotterdam port development (Schijf, 2011). They had important political connections, including positions on the Town Council and the Chamber of Commerce. The economic elite was closely associated with the main political forces, including ones driving Rotterdam's annexation of Charlois.[5] The storage of oil was transferred to a new location in the newly built Charlois area by 1876 (near Sluisjesdijk) a location fully in control of *Pakhuismeesteren* (Loohuis, 1952; Van de Laar, 2000; De Klerk *et al.*, 2008). After several years of negotiations in February 1895, Charlois became officially part of Rotterdam and the core of the oil storing and trading (Schoor, 2013). By that time, the Randstad, where railways had first connected the main cities on the Western shore, saw the construction of railway lines towards the border, lines that would also come to serve the oil industry. These choices created the foundation for the long-term development of Rotterdam as oil port just at a time when new global players in oil emerged.

Advances in shipping, transporting and refining, and the advent of major companies who gained control of the entire production and distribution chain extensively reshaped the port and the oil business. Their interests connected various parts of the world through their commodity flows, putting their imprint also on the Randstad. These companies, led by the American Standard Oil Company that monopolized oil interests at the time, intervened also in Europe. In 1885, foreign companies challenged the 23-year monopoly of *Pakhuismeesteren* and started to compete for land allocation in the Rotterdam petroleum port. By 1890, Standard Oil had secured large firms in Bremen and Hamburg and organized them into a stock company, the German American Petroleum Company (DAPG: *Deutsch-Amerikanische Petroleum Gesellschaft*). One year later, Standard Oil, together with four companies from Antwerp and Rotterdam, set up the American Petroleum Company (APC), with headquarters in both cities.[6] Around the same time, several other oil companies settled in the port, including in 1901, the Koninklijke Olie—one of the predecessors of the Royal Dutch Shell (created in 1890 and consolidated in 1907) (Gabriels, 1990). The city on the Maas had emerged as the main Dutch petroleum centre, outpacing Amsterdam, where the local petroleum harbour company had unsuccessfully tried to keep the business to themselves.[7] The presence of oil expanded in the port throughout the nineteenth century, promoting also the construction of select rail and water infrastructures; its impact on built form in the cities remained low though as lighting oil replaced other forms of light.

If demand for lighting oil established Rotterdam as a major oil port, the rapidly growing new demand for benzine as a car fuel triggered its explosive growth. Royal Dutch quickly picked up on the new oil age geared towards cars and built a gasoline refinery in Pernis in 1902. First plans for a large oil port in newly to be annexed Pernis emerged in 1913, but it took more than a decade and pressure from the Royal Dutch to finish what would be called the first petroleum harbour (Van de Laar, 2000). Created in 1907 the *Bataafse Petroleum Maatschappij*, a subsidiary of Royal Dutch Shell, also explored for oil fields in the Netherlands and started drilling—an activity that continues until today.[8] The company, predecessor to the *Nederlandse Aardolie Maatschappij* (NAM), established by Shell and Esso built residences in Hoogvliet near the Rotterdam oil port area for their employees (Van der Schoor, 2013).[9] By 1940, another date captured in the maps, Rotterdam was the third largest port of the world after New York and London (Borghuis, 1987; De Goey, 1990). Oil storage was a major price in the Second World War. The war faring parties tried to keep the German enemy from getting their hands on oil, destroying storage tanks, that had not been bombed (Gabriels, 1990).

In the post-war period, the oil industry brought new demands and opportunities to Rotterdam. The Rotterdam port grew in size, and Pernis, Botlek, and Europoort stand out as the main areas under control by six multinational oil companies. America lost its status as primary oil supplier. With de-colonization in Asia and Africa, oil companies (and their home countries) no longer had access or control over oil resources and had to rearrange their business. Most of the oil started coming from the Middle East; with nationalization of oil there and the creation of OPEC in 1960, demand increased, supply was reduced, and prices rose (Bauer and De Boer, 1981). Post-war development took the expansion of oil to a new scale. Cargo ships grew in size, and some ports, such as Antwerp, accessible only through an estuary (or Amsterdam, a closed port only accessible through a coastal lock complex), could no longer accommodate them, much unlike Rotterdam with its direct access to the sea.

The Rotterdam port grew rapidly in the post-war period as shown in the map of 1970, thanks to its geographical advantage, seaport infrastructure, collaboration among its corporations, subventions promoting investment, a sufficient labour market, and growing demand. The port grew so quickly that the province could not keep up with its growth in regional spatial plans. Meanwhile, new types of refining processes created diverse novel products and further demand for them, notably in the field of plastics. Since the 1960s, the chemical industry has blossomed, indicating another major change in the petroleum industry. According to Dutch historian De Goey, the construction of refining compounds (petrochemical complexes) was the major difference between the pre- and post-war (De Goey, 1990; De Goey, 2004; Van de Laar and Loyen, 2004). The oil crisis of the 1970s seems to have had only a fleeting impact on Rotterdam.

The demands of the oil industry and the needs of shipping companies that require deep access continued to be key to planning and land allocation in the Rotterdam area. A regional plan for West Brabant published around 1969 allowed for a new Shell refinery in Moerdijk and provided space for future expansion (Van der Cammen and De Klerk, 2012). Opening this land for the oil company ultimately led to the creation of a new binding national spatial planning procedure: the 'national planning key decision' (*planologische kern-beslissing*) as the site, located in a designated green belt, was in clear conflict with national spatial planning policy, and the parliament decided that such 'flexibility' should be curtailed by statutory planning decisions in which the parliament has a final say. The port continued to grow, separating it from the city. Several studies document the overlapping interests of Shell and the Rotterdam Port Authority (Chapman, 1976; Meyer, 1999; Merk and Notteboom, 2013). From the 1970s, pipelines became the main carrier for oil, notably crossing borders towards Antwerp in Belgium and the German Ruhr area (cheaper than train or ship) long before the Schengen agreement provided for the free circulation of people (Boon, 2014). The construction of the pipeline from Rotterdam to the Rhine, instead of from Wilhelmshaven in the north of Germany, was influenced by Shell Netherlands' intervention (Boon, 2014).

The map from 2000 shows the rapid growth of industrial oil infrastructures. Today, the refineries in Rotterdam have a combined distillation capacity of 58 million tonnes.[10] In the Netherlands, Belgium and Germany another five refineries are supplied with crude oil via pipelines from the port of Rotterdam. Oil production in the Netherlands itself is limited, but ongoing. The enormous impact of the port and its petroleum installations on the spatial development and the environment of the Netherlands and the extent of the port, are rarely visible to citizens. Most recently, the impact of the port in terms of CO_2 output—about 18% of Dutch emissions are produced by the port of Rotterdam—and its slow reduction have captured the attention of the public.[11] Nonetheless, an end of the oil era does not seem in immediate sight—fracking has increased production in the United States—but the fact that the Rotterdam Q8 refinery has been for sale since 2014 indicates changes in the industry.[12] Aging European refineries suffer competition from modern facilities in other parts of the world. For example, the activity of the Kuwait-owned Q8 refinery has relocated to the Middle East raising the question of whether other companies interested in refining will purchase the refinery, or what activities will follow in its footsteps. The ongoing efforts for an energy transition in both the port and city of Rotterdam require awareness of the scale and impact of these installations.

The retail petroleumscape: gas stations

Parallel to the industrial petroleumscape, with its spaces of production and transport that includes elements such as refineries with a long span of life, another petroleumscape emerged that was more short-lived and much closer to the consumer: gas or petrol stations (known in the Netherlands as *benzine stations*). The retail network of oil is so mundane as to generally escape comment. Since the beginning of the twentieth century, retail networks of gas stations have spread throughout cities and rural areas. These structures have evolved over time with the transformation of cars, road infrastructures and user needs. Today, the norm for the Randstad is one petrol station about every 20 kilometres of road.[13] They can take on a regional flavour, adapt to local urban forms or changing consumer preferences, while boasting the names and colours of oil companies. Their forms are not identical, but they are easily identifiable through their colour and general basic typology (a canopy on stilts), which inscribe the oil companies' names into everyone's mindscape. Unlike other countries, the Netherlands adopted specific aesthetic guidelines regarding the design of gas stations and thus the public face of oil. As places of contact with the consumer, gas stations are ideally suited for brand marketing to adults and children through free toys and other items.

The invention of the light bulb in 1879 and the spread of electric lighting had started to challenge the oil industry, but oil's days were far from over as benzine emerged as the fuel for cars. The first cars entered the Netherlands in 1895, and their owners purchased fuel in pharmacies or in containers from street cars (Aertnijs, 1948). Users carried it in open buckets; later, companies built gas pumps to fill cars and then specialized gas stations (Vieyra, 1979; Boy and De Voogd, 2015). As the use of the car spread in the beginning of the twentieth century, gasoline, formerly a by-product of the kerosene production, saw a major expansion. The next challenge was to dispense the gasoline directly from storage to the car. The Continental Petroleum Company (CPC), part of the Texas (fuel) Company, opted to import pumps from the United States and to have them installed by local entrepreneurs (Van Santen,

2013). In 1907, the first gas station opened in St Louis, and mass fabrication of Ford cars starting in 1913 led to a rapidly growing number of users. The First World War slowed down petroleum activities in the Netherlands, but the rise of the car as a widespread means of transport took the petroleum industry to a new level. Maps of oil-related buildings in the area of Rotterdam and The Hague suggest that no gas stations existed in 1910. The only icon on the map is derived from a postcard that shows the label *De Benzine Automaat* (The Benzine Slot Machine) possibly a predecessor of Standard Oil. There may have been free-standing pumps and depots that the research underlying this chapter has not detected.

Gas pumps with underground storage tanks emerged mostly in places where people could afford to buy or use cars (and they came to serve as an indicator of the presence of such wealth). Shelterless, they often stood alongside the street, sometimes in a line-up of different brands. Before 1940, pumps were often an additional service rather than the core purpose of a business. Hotels, garages, or bike shops would set up gas stations. A well-known picture shows a pump attached to the garage of Willem van Setten near the hotel and restaurant Pabst in Zeist.[14] The map of the Randstad from 1940 suggests that gas pumps and stations appeared first in or near cities. They also indicate that some cities had higher densities of gas dispensers than others. Vehicles did not travel far on a few litres of gasoline until they needed to be refilled, so people must have been going from city to city where pumps were located (or they used rural petroleum depots that the research has not detected). The map of 1940 shows more than ten gas pumps in the capital city of The Hague, where decision-makers of the corporate and public sector congregated and where wealthy people traditionally lived. Photographs of gas pumps in The Hague survive because they were taken as part of applications for permission to install advertisement panels. The mapped locations in The Hague include places where businesses provided gas pumps as a convenience for a rich clientele. Hotel Zeerust on Keizerstraat, near the beach, for example, had its own Shell pump. Garages in the 1920s and 1930s hosted gas pumps and provided rental vehicles. A Shell pump stood near the Thiessens garage on Stephensonstraat 92–98 in the centre of The Hague. The building featured multiple garage doors, suggesting that the establishment also provided storage and repair. The map of 1940 suggests that Rotterdam at that time had fewer gas pumps. Although petroleum entered the region through Rotterdam's port, the city was predominantly working class, and therefore there were probably fewer cars.

The European development of the automobile was slower than in the United States, but what started as an elite pastime rapidly spread to a larger population group. Rapidly growing numbers of people clamoured for the construction of car-usable surroundings supporting the interests of the oil companies. Oil companies started to develop an integrated distribution system for the new fuel, building over time a dense network of gas stations in and around the Randstad. Meanwhile, the *Nederlandsche Automobiel Club* (later

(*Royal: Koninklijke*) KNAC) and the Royal Dutch Touring Club ANWB (*Algemene Nederlandsche Wielrijdersbond*, an association founded in July 1883 for bikes), became key players in developing landscapes for driving, even controlling the quality of benzine, developing depots, and organizing benzine resale. [15] By the 1920s, streets were improving and gas stations were popping up as prefabricated objects. Designers rapidly developed gas stations as a new typology, a place where the attendant could find shelter, where people could restart their cars under cover and expect services (hence the name service station) such as cleaning windows and small repairs. Painted in the colours of their company and a promotional tool, these stations were eye-catching and a photographic subject.

Street-side pumps started to occupy public space but they could not satisfy the growing customer base. Safety concerns also arose and led to the construction of pumps on small islands next to the streets. Gas stations that resembled the structures we know now emerged in the United States around 1910. Instead of a shelterless roadside pump, companies built access from the road to a dedicated lot with distinctive new features. It included pumps on an island, a canopy sheltering the employee and customers while the car was being served, and a small building for the employees. Many gas stations in the United States were commercially built structures, but architects also seized the opportunity to design buildings with a new function—creating iconic buildings or fitting them with the architecture of the surroundings. At the time, US gas stations, including ones built by Shell, aimed to attract customers through architectural surprise: they appeared along the road in a range of shapes from a teapot to a sphinx, including a shell-shaped one in North Carolina (Jonker and Luiten van Zanden, 2007). The company had used the Shell name in California since 1912, but it took until 1925 to establish the name and the logo in the Netherlands where gasoline sold under different names, such as Aceylena, Autoline, or Sumatrinegasoline rather than the Royal Dutch name. The rapid propagation of these structures, sited every 10–20 kilometres, brought opposition from Bond Heemschut, an organization established by citizens in 1911 to protect the appearance of the Dutch landscape. Its commission on *De Weg in het Landschap* (The Road in the Landscape) specifically asked provincial administrations to intervene with the oil companies to improve the aesthetics of gas stations (Van Lanschot and Cleyndert, 1939; Segers, 1984). They ultimately succeeded in changing the appearance of the new building type and establishing an 'aesthetical petroleumscape' in the Randstad.

In the Netherlands, as car traffic became denser in the 1920s, dedicated gas stations began appearing in urban spaces. The new typology colonized traditional streets and town squares and facilitated new lifestyles. The new architecture allowed the customer—or chauffeur—to drive under a roof and be served—in some places day and night, such as at the Shell Station Rijswijkseweg, which opened in 1928. These new forms for dispensing petroleum needed more space, and at times, construction coincided with street widening or building. The oil companies in the Netherlands decided to invite local architects to design them. As a result of particular Dutch aesthetic guidelines uniquely designed gas stations heralded the main company's names throughout the Randstad and beyond (many at its outskirts). Starting in the 1920s, petroleum stations became the signboard of the enterprise. The Dutch opted for a functionalist approach and the architect Sybold van Ravesteyn, architect of numerous buildings of the Dutch railway, was among the first architects to design for this new typology in 1935 when he created a (non-permanent) pump island with a roof (Verweij, 1997; Scharlemann and Koudijs, 2005; Rouw, 2014). The aesthetic control exercised in the Netherlands prompted Esso to hire the modernist Dutch architect W.M. Dudok to produce a gas station prototype. He designed a V-shaped construction that sheltered the pump island and allowed for a translucent façade underneath. Over 100 such structures were built from the 1950s to the 1970s. This and other buildings celebrated the advent of oil in spectacular architectural ways and wrote oil into the mindscapes of the general public.

After the Second World War, cars became an everyday mode of travel for a large part of the general population in many industrialized countries, including the Netherlands. Gas stations became even more intimately tied to the freedom of driving and the joy of leisure. Cars, roads and gas stations allowed people to explore and occupy rural areas. They facilitated the expansion of suburban landscapes and new cultural practices. In the Netherlands, new car owners practised so-called 'berm tourism', that is, they held picnics on the side of roads to watch other cars drive by. As people travelled farther and more often, they also celebrated their experiences. Photographs (as well as postcards) of leisure spots and iconic buildings—including the Scheveningen beach with the Kurhaus near The Hague—at times feature gas stations. Characteristic of the 1950s and 1960s is the way in which the sand of the beach sided the asphalt band of the street, and the pedestrian promenade was hemmed in between flowing traffic and parking spaces.

Since these early years, gas stations in the Randstad and the Netherlands in general have seen multiple changes. As cheaper self-service gas stations became dominant, the architecture changed. Marketing wars led to greater attention to logo and colours, and Shell globally adopted a standard banner to surround its buildings. The First National Highway Plan (1927) implemented in the 1960s provided room for more traffic and did so largely outside the spatial planning system (Hoogenberk, 1980; Van der Cammen and De Klerk, 2012). The map of 1970 shows that new gas stations were built together with the streets, occupying rural areas. Changes in car construction allowed cars to cover greater distances; consumers' expectations of what products can be bought in a shop at the gas station, shaped by competition and advertisement, influenced changes in gas station location, form and function that merit further study and evaluation. Small street-side stations vanished as larger gas stations were erected near new highways. Today, the Randstad continues to feature a higher density of gas stations than the rest of the Netherlands.

Despite the availability of public transport in dense cities and in the Randstad in particular, the places where people live and work are those where they also park and refuel their cars. The major cities of the Randstad have a high level of mobility as well as of access to gas stations. A detailed analysis of historical changes of gas stations within cities, their (re-)location over time, and in relation to each other as well as their accessibility, still has to be done. While gas stations are available throughout the country alongside major roads and highways, inner-city gas stations impact urban development and urban form through their traffic, environmental and security impact in ways that still have to be researched.

Compared to the stable and fixed industrial oil landscape, the gas stations form a more flexible and fleeting landscape, albeit one with a strong impact on the mental mindscape of the citizens of the Randstad. Gas stations are designed to be steps along a way, a secure companion on long trips as well as in the neighbourhood. Policy changes in the Netherlands now promote a change from gas-fuelled to electric cars.[16] Recent years have seen changes in oil company strategies. Exxon/Mobil has decided to shut down its Dutch gas stations (while maintaining the logo for some time to come), signalling a change in organization that traditionally aimed to be present throughout the commodity chain. [17] Shutting down gas stations that no longer fit a company's economic model requires interventions from specialists in soil clean-up to allow for new uses as well as from heritage specialists (Van den Anker, 1988). A system of electric cars will not need the gas stations that have become the signboard for oil. And plans will have to be made to adapt streetscapes, building quick electric loading stations while also providing street space for loading. An explosive growth of electric cars may put an end to the free parking spaces that are available for them today in the Randstad. The term *laadpaalklever* meaning someone occupying an electric charging space longer than necessary became the word of the year in 2018.[18] Clearly, a new mindscape is emerging around the spaces of green energy.

The administrative petroleumscape: headquarters

The Randstad is home to major oil-companies headquarters and research centres, establishing yet another face for the oil industry. Separated from the physical streams of oil, companies translate the physical presence of oil administration into more distinctive urban and architectural spaces, creating additional layers of the petroleumscape. In contrast to the gas stations that are present throughout the country but have a largely utilitarian character, oil companies' large administrative and research facilities, notably those of Royal Dutch Shell, are in prestigious locations in The Hague, Amsterdam and Rotterdam. While the presence of the port and transport infrastructure was key to the physical networks of oil, proximity to the national government and its relevant ministries drove the settlement patterns of the oil company headquarters. In contrast to the hidden sites of the oil industry, several of the administrative and research buildings are urban icons and well-known to locals. Less visible are the additional demands for employee housing, education, or leisure facilities that these activities generate and that often also accommodate other people. They only occupy a small portion of their host cities, but can drive up prices in the housing sector—an effect that merits further study and that is largely excluded in this piece.

The landscapes of production and retail are complemented with administrative and research facilities. Oil companies not only developed the port (and its key infrastructure) and set up a retail system, they also inscribed their interests into a corporate landscape of headquarters. The economic fates of the two systems are closely intertwined, while their spatial location and their visibility are different, industrial buildings on the one hand, monumental ones on the other. In response to the fusion of Royal Dutch with the British Shell Transport Company in 1907, the new company constructed headquarters for the *Bataafsche Petroleum Maatschappij* in The Hague (and in London) as seen in the map of 1910. Over the following decades, the Shell Company expanded its headquarters building (1928–1930) and bought and built several others around it creating an administrative core that is still the company's central location. The company promoted pectons, the symbol of Shell, as part of the ornamental imagery, as seen in several of the buildings in The Hague. Other buildings belonging to the Shell group include Wassenaarseweg 80 erected in 1938–1946 by the leading Dutch architect J.J.P. Oud (Taverne and Broekhuizen, 1995). Today it is a classified monument.

Though Shell sold several of its inner-city locations in The Hague, it held on to its headquarters and recently restored and upgraded them. Meanwhile, Esso sold its former headquarters in The Hague known as the Red Elephant, and the company Spaces uses the building today to rent out flexible office and meeting spaces. The destruction of Rotterdam in the Second World War set the stage for modernist approaches in architecture. The rebuilding around the Hofplein, south of the train station on the way to the redesigned Lijnbaan, provided the space for a 90 metre high-rise featuring the Shell logo on the top and a gas station underneath. The construction of this so-called 'Shell Toren' in 1960 signalled the pressure that a company of this scale can put on the city. As the maps demonstrate, the physical space of the headquarters is minimal, but through their close connection to decision-makers, their impact is huge.

Headquarter location and design remain of iconic importance for the oil companies, but it is ultimately only a small part of their portfolio. The spatial impact of the company is mostly visible in the real estate it owns, but a list of the sites Shell or other companies own does not tell the full story. These institutions, like other global companies, generate a secondary petroleumscape through their demands for housing, schooling, and leisure facilities for their employees. As a global company, Shell employs many expatriates, who expect appropriate educational facilities and other amenities for themselves and their families. Combined with the presence of employees of many other international institutions, their presence also supports the large number of international schools in The Hague, and the high prices for housing, a topic that merits further exploration. Shell sold much of its housing and today expats typically find housing on the private market.

The representational petroleumscape: maps and booklets

Whereas the first three layers of the petroleumscape are about the physical impact of oil companies on the built environment, their meaning for the general public goes beyond the fuel itself. It includes the construction of space and identity as well as culture in and for spaces far beyond the ones that they actually occupy. These depictions and narratives construct a mindscape of oil that is different from the one that they actually build. In this case, the road atlases, booklets and brochures, and more recently, apps produced by the oil companies link the company logo to everyday practices and Dutch traditions, providing driving and gas station maps, tourist guides, and information on history and technology (including that of petroleum). The status of Royal Dutch Shell as a household name and one might say a national icon, similar to KLM, further increases the power of this company to transform landscapes, through interventions at the governmental level in regard to, for example, pipeline construction or through the transformation of mindscapes and citizen attitudes.

Selective representations and connections between company logos and territory can create novel understandings of space. In their marketing, oil companies have used this power to position themselves in a space that is quite different from the one they occupy. Map-makers have a powerful tool to help users understand space but also to create imagined geographies (Wood, 1992). Atlases, maps, brochures, and booklets produced by oil companies rarely depict refineries or headquarters; instead they tie company colours and logos to traditional landscapes, to tourist destinations, to historical, scientific, or cultural explorations.[19] Since the 1930s, oil companies have used maps to fuel the general public's desire to explore the Dutch landscape (for example: Shell started in 1931, Texaco in 1935). They sold or freely distributed road maps that tied the company name to the experience of driving and visiting. Esso's map of 1957 and other examples show oil companies establishing a relationship between modern technology (streets) and traditional Dutch features: a Dutch windmill appears next to an oversized car and tiny highway on the Shell map.[20] Tying the oil companies company to traditional landscapes rather than the industrial ones that petroleum generates, (early) road map covers also promote the car as a means of freedom and discovery. Some maps do show the connection between the physical presence of oil production and maps, notably those made by the City and Port of Rotterdam and by companies who are catering to the refineries, such as engineers, or car rentals. These maps demonstrate the importance of the refineries to the local business community. They depict oil installations, even indicating the refineries by name and proudly displaying imagery of the refineries. The yearbooks produced by Rotterdam Europoort emphasize the importance of the refineries and of the highway infrastructure that serves the port and the city.[21]

Oil companies also carefully established their images with their own employees and regular customers, once again with a focus on Dutch culture, history, and technology and promotion of driving as a new lifestyle. A full examination of the companies' publications remains to be done, but the *Shell Journaal*—a yearly booklet distributed to its regular clients (not at the gas station), published between 1961 and 1993, and still available on second handbook sites—is suggestive. A common message of these booklets is the historical qualities of the Dutch cities and landscapes as tourist attractions. Other publications include engineering topics: bridges, buildings, themes of trade, and change. A 1989 publication, entitled *Snelweg naar Europa* (Highway to Europe) put forward a vision for the Netherlands as a logistics centre and praised the advantages of petroleum (Van Rooijen, 1989). Another late 1980s series, *Shell helpt u op weg* (Shell helps you on the road), was also geared to a general public as the various volumes highlighted all sorts of tourist and leisure attraction across the country. Originally meant as advertisement objects, these publications have become collectibles sold on Ebay.

To increase customer bonding, oil companies have adopted diverse strategies, producing toy gas stations with company logos, developing board games, or games to play during car rides or bonus cards. They have published car humour books and booklets educating children about urban car traffic. They even organized art exhibitions.[22] Overall the publications promoted the idea that companies like Shell were essential to the well-being of the people in the Netherlands. The focus of these publications has changed over time, adjusting to the interests of the general public. They were abundant from the 1960s to the 1990s and have not yet been studied or even acknowledged as an important agent in the construction of modern cities and lifestyles. These publications have since made their way to social media and apps, which are more volatile. Free locator apps direct customers to the company of their choice with information on the services available.[23] Other activities are geared to current issues and questions of sustainability, such as the eco-marathon sponsored by Shell.[24] The expansion of shops for articles of daily consumption, the inclusion of coffee bars or free Wi-Fi are all tools that are not related to its core-business but important in terms of image building, as the recent ads of the Shell company demonstrate.

Conclusion

The built environment is shaped by multiple, sometimes opposing functions. Commodity flows tie production and consumption, administration, research, and culture together under a single commodity such as oil, creating parallel, and occasionally intertwined built forms that are rarely (if ever) explored in conjunction. Some institutions are active in many or all of these domains and transform our built environment on multiple, interconnected scales. Major oil corporations are among these actors. The history of their interventions in urban form documents the revolutionary impact that such institutions can have on the built environment. In several instances, the oil companies generated major changes in the built environment. Examples such as the refinery in Moerdijk and the intervention by the aesthetic commission mentioned above demonstrate that the landscape of oil sometimes sits uneasily with local planning policies and interest, but also that it is powerful enough to generate major changes. Oil companies own huge and expansive structures in the Rotterdam port. These are the core company business, but they are hidden from most viewers. Other built artefacts are closer to the consumer: these include iconic headquarters and functional gas stations. Both structures take up less space and are relatively less costly.

Understanding the changing fabric of the Randstad in light of oil-related structures provides insights on factors external to recognized planning that drive spatial development. Private companies have shaped infrastructure growth, land use, or urban development through their own means without the traditional tools of spatial planning. Through their consumption behaviour, citizens further enhanced or even initiated these changes. Spatial development plans often accommodated these pressures and developments, trying to channel them into comprehensive development for economic growth. The planning of the Randstad was a key theme for national plans and industrialization policies aimed at balancing population growth and notably for the port of Rotterdam. Much of the petroleum development was driven by private actors, but the government accommodated the growth of the petroleumscape through its support of the development of the port. From the 1950s to the 1980s industrialization policies such as the Deltaplan in 1958, the Seaport Report (*Zeehavennota*) of 1966 and its successor, the Second Structural Scheme for Seaports (*Tweede Structuurschema Zeehavens*, 1989), and the national Fourth Planning Report of 1988, aimed to balance the concentration of industrial and economic forces around the growing port and the desire for decentralization in and of the Randstad. The Delta Plan, for example, proposed separation of port and city and the creation of a Delta-city (*Delta-stad*) to counter traffic problems, to avoid the mixing of working and living areas, to address problems of governance, to reduce the distance to agricultural areas, and to address flood risk issues. This proposal was not realized but led to the establishment of growth centres such as Spijkernisse and Hellevoetsluis (Ministerie van Verkeer en Waterstaat, 1958). Dutch planners anticipated the growth of the Rotterdam port in the Zeehavennota of 1966 and proposed to provide additional development opportunities in the Eemshaven area and in Zeeland (Zonneveld, 1991). The concept of the mainport, developed in the 1980s (see Chapter 8) and the recognition of relevant hinterland infrastructures, for example, further strengthened the role of the port as petroleum throughput centre.

The court rulings from 2015 and 2018 requiring the Dutch government to reduce greenhouse gas emissions may indicate a sea change.[25] If and when a major change in use occurs, this industrial petroleum landscape will need to be redesigned and reused. This history of how private and public petroleum actors have helped to build the Randstad also raises questions about the changes on all levels of the built environment that new sustainable energy will bring. As the landscape of energy production and consumption changes, it will be necessary to rethink the workings of the Randstad: to what degree is the oil infrastructure geared to transitioning products or to ones that remain in the area? New energy sources, such as biofuels and biochemicals may bring about less concentrated landscapes. The choice of hydrogen for energy generation, however, could continue the current centralization pattern through a reuse of existing gas networks. To what degree local energy transformation impacts the workings of the oil port remains to be seen. Changing local patterns do not necessarily imply that the end of the oil port is in sight (Noorman and De Roo, 2011). It also raises questions on land ownership of refinery sites, responsibilities for their clean up, and the importance of existing and expensive refining structure for the future development of cities.

Notes

1 The article draws from material published notably in Hein (2018a).
2 125 Jaar Pakhuismeesteren 1818–1943; 1943. Vopak: Our History, https://www. vopak.com/at-a-glance/our-history (accessed 10 October 2019).
3 'Petrolia. Another peep into the hidden land', *New York Herald*, 14 October 1864, p. 10274.
4 [Boston]; Age, published as *The Daily Age* 17 January 1865; Philadelphia, Pennsylvania Press, published as The Press; Date: 06 January 1865; 1; Philadelphia, Pennsylvania.
5 'Familie de Monchy' [Family de Moncy], http://www.top010.nl/html/monchy. htm (accessed 15 July 2015); Succesvolste havenbaronnen [Most successful port barons], http://www.top010.nl/html/succesvolste_havenbaronnen.htm (accessed 15 July 2015).
6 'A gigantic monopoly. The standard oil company has practically secured control of the trade of the world'. *Idaho Statesman, published as Idaho Daily Statesman*, 01 July 1891.
Neptune kind to him; Article Type: News/Opinion Paper: *Dallas Morning News*, 25 August 1902.
7 'Favor a rejection. Authorities denounce the proposal to grant the standard oil company privileges'. *Patriot*, 15 July 1891.
8 For a map of contemporary oil drilling in the Netherlands, see NAM, Locaties Oliewinning: https://www.nam.nl/gas-en-oliewinning/aardolie/locaties-oliewinning.html#iframe=L21hcHMvb2xpZS1rYWFydC8 (accessed 17 February 2020).
9 'Woningen Voor Personeel Van De Bataafsche' [Homes for personnel of the Banier: staatkundig gereformeerd dagblad, 09 September 1935.
10 Port of Rotterdam, Oil refineries, https://www.portofrotterdam.com/en/ doing-business/setting-up/existing-industry/refining-and-chemicals/oil-refineries (accessed 17 February 2020).

11 Port of Rotterdam, All roads lead to a sustainable port by 2050, https://www. portofrotterdam.com/en/news-and-press-releases/all-roads-lead-to-a-sustainable-port-by-2050; Port of Rotterdam, CO2 Footprint Port of Rotterdam Authority (accessed 17 February 2020), https://www.portofrotterdam.com/sites/default/files/downloads/co2_footprint_en_factsheet-2017.pdf (accessed 17 February 2020).

12 Hess wil Rotterdamse raffinaderij Q8 kopen [Hess seeks to buy Rotterdam Q8 refinery], FD 13 April 2015, http://fd.nl/frontpage/economie-politiek/899643/ rotterdamse-raffinaderij-q8-staat-op-de-tocht; http://fd.nl/ondernemen/1100174/ overslagbedrijf-hes-wil-bieden-op-rotterdamse-raffinaderij-q8 (accessed 3 October 2019).

13 Bart van Zoelen, 'Ouder-Amstel wil bouw benzinestation voorkomen om bomen te redden' [Ouder-Amstel seeks to prevent the arrival of a new petrol station to protect trees], https://www.parool.nl/amsterdam/ouder-amstel-wil-bouw-benzinestation-voorkomen-om-bomen-te-redden~bef05f07/ (accessed 17 February 2020).

14 *Volgooien maar!!*; Tanken Vroeger en Nu: Geschiedenis van het tanken [Fill it up!!; Tanking then and now; A history of tanking], http://www.grootveld.net/ tankstat/historie.htm (accessed 17 February 2020).

15 Koninklijke nederlandsche automobiel club (1938) *40 Jaar K.N.A.C. 1898–1938* [40 Years K.N.A.C.], Jubilee issue of *Auto*, 35 (26 June 1938); *KNAC*, CLUB, F. A. K. N. A. *100 Jaar Knac: Clubtocht Door Een Eeuw Heen,* Utrecht, Kosmos-Z&K uitgevers B.V.

16 The Dutch administration is carefully tracing the growth of electric vehicles and charging stations: Rijksdienst voor Ondernemend Nederland Januari 2019 Pagina 1/5 Elektrisch Rijden—Analyse over 2018 Elektrisch Rijden— Personenauto's en laadpunten Analyse over 2018, https://www.rvo.nl/sites/ default/files/2019/01/Elektrisch%20Rijden%20%20Personenautos%20en%20 laadpunten%20%20Analyse%20over%202018.pdf (accessed 17 February 2020).

17 Tankpro, 'Esso Nederland verkoopt ruim honderd stations aan NRG Value' [Esso Netherlands sells 100 petrol stations to NRG Value], http://www.tankpro. nl/specials/2015/02/16/esso-nederland-verkoopt-ruim-honderd-stations-aan-nrg-value/ (accessed 17 February 2020).

18 Laadpaalklever is het woord van 2018 volgens Onze Taal. *Het Parool*, 29 December 2018, https://www.parool.nl/kunst-media/laadpaalklever-is-het-woord-van-2018-volgens-onze-taal~b8bf2306/ (accessed 17 February 2020).

19 For map covers and the exception of the Rotterdam refinery map by BP 1970, see Oil Company Roadmaps from the Netherlands, http://www.petrolmaps. co.uk/country/maps-nl.htm (accessed 15 July 2015).

20 For classic oil company roadmaps from the Netherlands, see http://www. petrolmaps.co.uk/country/maps-nl.htm (accessed 17 February 2020). The 2010 final edition of the Shell road led to newspaper articles: http://www.ad.nl/ad/ nl/5597/Economie/article/detail/2424235/2011/04/16/Shell-Stratenboek-verleden-tijd.dhtml (accessed 17 February 2020).

21 Rotterdam Europoort, Yearbook/Jahrbuch Information 1983.

22 In 1959, Shell Nederland organized: 'Aardolie-tentoonstelling: van put tot pomp' [Oil exhibition: From well to pump].

23 Esso developed: http://www.essofuelfinder.nl/; Shell: https://www.shell.nl/ consumenten/shell-station-locator.html#iframe=Lz9sb2NhbGU9bmxfTkw jL0A1Mi4zMTE4NCw1LjEyNTEyLDh6 (accessed 17 February 2020).

24 Shell, Shell Eco-Marathon https://www.shell.com/make-the-future/shell-ecomarathon.html (accessed 17 February 2020).

25 John Schwartz, 'Ruling says Netherlands must reduce greenhouse gas emissions', *New York Times*, 24 June 2015, http://www.nytimes.com/2015/06/25/science/ruling-says-netherlands-must-reduce-greenhouse-gas-emissions.html?_r=0 (accessed 17 February 2020). See also Climate Liability News, Dutch Court upholds Urgenda; says government must reduce emissions, https://www.climateliabilitynews.org/2018/10/09/urgenda-netherlands-climate-emissions/ (accessed 17 February 2020).

References

Aertnijs, M.W. (1948). *Hoe De Auto in Ons Land Kwam [How the car arrived in our country]*. Hafkamp, Amsterdam.

Bauer, C. and De Boer, M. (1981). *Energie [Energy]*. Shell Nederland, s.l.

Black, B.C. (2012). *Crude reality: Petroleum in world history*. Rowman & Littlefield, Lanham.

Boon, M. (2014). *Oil pipelines, politics and international business: The Rotterdam oil port, royal Dutch shell and the German Hinterland, 1945–1975*, PhD Erasmus School of History, Culture and Communication. Erasmus University, Rotterdam.

Booy, R. and De Voogd, B. (2015). *Van blik naar pomp [From can to pump]*; Hoe benzine en auto elkaar vonden: een fascinerende zoektocht over benzineverkoop van 1885 tot 1940. Ad. Donker, Rotterdam.

Borghuis, G.J. (1987). *Veertig jaar NAM. De geschiedenis van de Nederlandse Aardolie Maatschappij 1947–1987 [Forty years NAM. The history of the Nederlandse Aardolie Maatschappij]*. NAM/Van Gorcum, Assen.

Chapman, K. (1976). *North Sea oil and gas; A geographical perspective*. David & Charles, Newton Abbot.

De Goey, F. (1990). *Ruimte voor Industrie: Rotterdam en de Vestiging van Industrie in de Haven 1945–1975 [Room for industry: Rotterdam and the location of industry in the port 1945–1975]*, PhD Erasmus University Rotterdam. Eburon, Delft.

De Goey, F. (2004). *Comparative Port History of Rotterdam and Antwerp (1880–2000): Competition, cargo and costs*. Amsterdam University Press, Amsterdam.

De Klerk, L., Van de Laar, P. and Moscoviter, H. (2008). *G.J. de Jongh: Havenbouwer en Stadsontwikkelaar in Rotterdam [G.J. de Jongh: Port builder and city developer in Rotterdam]*. Thoth, Bussum.

Ernst & Young (2012). *The oil downstream: Vertically challenged?* Ernst & Young, s.l.

Gabriels, H. (1990). *Koninklijke Olie: de eerste honderd jaar 1890–1990 [Koninklijke Olie: The First hundred years 1890–1990]*. Shell, The Hague.

Hein, C. (2010). 'Global landscapes of oil', *New Geographies*, 2, 33–42.

Hein, C. (2013). 'Between water and oil: The logistical petroleumscape'. In: Bhatia, N. and Casper, M. (Eds) *The petropolis of tomorrow*. Actar/Architecture at Rice, New York, 436–447.

Hein, C. (2016). 'Refineries (oil)'. In: *The Encyclopedia of Greater Philadelphia*, http://philadelphiaencyclopedia.org/archive/refineries-oil/ (accessed 1 July 2020).

Hein, C. (2017). 'Oil in oil (and other art media): Painting the petroleum port', *PORTUS: The online magazine of RETE*, XVII (33), 1–5.

Hein, C. (2018a). 'Oil spaces: The global petroleumscape in the Rotterdam/The Hague area', *Journal of Urban History*, 44(5), 887–929.

Hein, C. (2018b). '"Old Refineries Rarely Die"': Port City refineries as key nodes in the global petroleumscape', *Canadian Journal of History*, 53(3), 450–497.

Hoogenberk, E.J. (1980) *Het Idee van de Hollandse Stad: Stedebouw in Nederland 1900–1930 met de internationale voorgeschiedenis [The notion of the Holland town: Town planning in the Netherlands including the international previous history]*. Delftse Universitaire Pers, Delft.

Hubbard, M. (1967). *The economics of transporting oil to and within Europe*. Maclaren & Sons, London.

Janssen, J.H.M. (1999). 'Het petroleumvertier: Rotterdams ongemakkelijke kennismaking met de aardoliehandel' [Petroleum entertainment: The uncomfortable acquaintance of Rotterdam with the trade in oil], *Rotterdamsch Jaarboekje*, 7, 289–311.

Jonker, J.P.B. and Luiten van Zanden, J. (2007). *Van nieuwkomer tot marktleider, 1890–1939. Geschiedenis van Koninklijke Shell, Deel 1 [From novice to market leader, 1890–1939. History of Royal Shell, Part 1]*. Boom, Amsterdam.

Loohuis, J.G. (1952). *Rotterdam als Petroleumhaven in de Negentiende Eeuw [Rotterdam as oil port in the nineteenth century]*. Ad. Donker, Rotterdam.

Merk, O. and Notteboom, T. (2013). *The competitiveness of global port-cities: The case of Rotterdam, Amsterdam – the Netherlands,* OECD Regional Development Working Papers, 2013/08. OECD, Paris.

Meyer, H. (1999). *City and port; Transformation of port cities London, Barcelona, New York, Rotterdam*. International Books, Utrecht.

Ministerie van Verkeer en Waterstaat (1958). *Het Deltaplan [The delta plan]*. Ministerie van Verkeer en Waterstaat, Deltadienst van de Rijkswaterstaat, The Hague.

Noorman, K.J. and De Roo, G. (Eds) (2011). *Energielandschappen – de 3de Generatie [Energy landscapes – the 3rd generation]; Over regionale kansen op het raakvlak van energie en ruimte*. Provincie Drenthe/Rijksuniversiteit Groningen, Assen/Groningen.

Rouw, K. (2014) *Sybold van Ravesteyn – Architect*. nai010 uitgevers, Rotterdam.

Scharlemann, M. and Koudijs, J.-D. (2005). *S. van Ravesteyn (1889–1983); De meester van de gebogen lijn*. Stichting BONAS, Rotterdam.

Schijf, H. (2011). 'Mercantile elites in the ports of Amsterdam and Rotterdam, 1850–1940'. In: Hein, C. (Ed.) *Port cities: Dynamic landscapes and global networks*. Routledge, London. 104–115.

Segers, J. (1984). 'Benzinestations. Een geschiedenis van de benzinedistributie in Nederland' [Petrol stations. A history of the distribution of petrol in the Netherlands], *Industriële Archeologie*, 4, 164–180.

Sijmons, D., Hugtenburg, J., Feddes, F. and Van Hoorn, A. (Eds) (2014). *Landscape and energy: Designing transition*. NAI Publishers, Rotterdam.

Taverne, E. and Broekhuizen, D. (1995). *Het Shell-Gebouw van J.J.P. Oud. Ontwerp en Receptie/J.J.P. Oud's shell building. Design and reception*. NAI Publishers, Rotterdam.

Van de Laar, P. (2000). *Stad van formaat: Geschiedenis van Rotterdam in de negentiende en twintigste eeuw [A great city: History of Rotterdam in the nineteenth and twentieth century]*. Waanders, Zwolle.

Van de Laar, P. and Loyen, R. (Eds) (2004). *Trade and transhipment in Antwerp and Rotterdam. Port competition and the load factor (1900–1940)*. Aksant/Amsterdam University Press, Amsterdam.

Van den Anker, M. (1988). *Benzeen rondom benzinestations [Benzene around petrol stations]*. Rijksinstituut voor Volksgezondheid en Milieu, Bilthoven.

Van der Cammen, H. and De Klerk, L. (2012) *The Selfmade Lan; Culture of urban and regional planning in the Netherlands (with Dekker, G. and Witsen, P.P.).* Spectrum, Houten/Antwerpen.

Van der Schoor, A. (2013). *De Dorpen van Rotterdam: van Ontstaan tot Annexatie [The villages of Rotterdam: From origin to annexation].* Ad. Donker, Rotterdam.

Van Lanschot, F.J. and Cleyndert, H. (1939) 'Benzinestations' [Petrol stations], *Heemschut, Orgaan van den Bond Heemschut*, 16(1), 30–31.

Van Rooijen, M. (1989). *Snelweg naar Europa; Over Nederland als distributieland [Highway to Europe: About the Netherlands as a distribution country], Shell Journaal* 1989. Shell Nederland, s.l.

Van Santen, B. (2013). *'t Komt in orde. Het ware verhaal achter Villa Jongerius [It's going to be all right: The true story behind Villa Jongerius].* Matrijs, Utrecht.

Verweij, M.S. (1997). 'Sassenheim en Arnhem: twee benzinestations naar ontwerp van ir. S. van Ravesteyn (1889–1983)' [Sassenheim and Arnhem: Two petrol stations designed by S. van Ravesteyn], *Bulletin KNOB*, 96(1), 12–25.

Vieyra, D.I. (1979). *Fill 'er Up: An architectural history of America's gas stations.* Macmillan, London.

Walker, A.R. (1984). 'Oil-dependent economies and port development'. In: Hoyle, B.S. and Hilling, D. (eds) *Seaport systems and spatial change: Technology, industry and development strategies.* John Wiley & Son, Chichester. 179–197.

Wood, D. (1992). *Power of maps.* Guilford Press, New York/London.

Yergin, D. (1991). *The prize: The epic quest for oil, money, and power.* Simon & Schuster, New York.

Zonneveld, W. (1991). *Conceptvorming in de ruimtelijke planning: Encyclopedie van planconcepten [Conceptualisation in spatial planning: Encyclopedia of planning concepts],* Appendix PhD thesis University of Amsterdam. Planologisch Demografisch Instituut, Universiteit van Amsterdam, Amsterdam.

Part III

The dynamics of a complex metropolitan region

6 Randstad Holland between functional entity and political desire

Evert Meijers, Martijn Burger and Frank van Oort

Introduction

The attention given to the Randstad Holland as a key concept in urban and regional development strategies of the Dutch national government has come in waves over decades. The status of the Randstad concept largely depends on the ruling coalition in the Dutch parliament and can be explained by the location of liberal, socialist and confessional voters (Frieling, 2009). Liberal voters are overrepresented in the Randstad in general, with social-democrat voters being strongly present in the Randstad's major cities. Confessional voters are overrepresented in the areas outside of the Randstad and also in its Green Heart. Ideologically, and at risk of an overly simple generalisation, liberals and social-democrats favour an urban culture, in contrast to confessionals who prefer more orderly urban patterns and are more rooted in rural culture. Over the years, the Netherlands has been governed by coalitions involving changing combinations of two of these three parties, sometimes with additional smaller parties. Involvement of the liberals in these coalitions generally led to a fostering of the (economic) position of the Randstad in the Netherlands (national concentration), while involvement of the socialists particularly strengthened the position of cities within regions (regional concentration), and confessionals adhere to policies of dispersal, either at the national scale (when in a coalition with social-democrats) or at a regional scale (when ruling together with liberals). It follows that the Randstad gets most emphasis under liberal–social-democrat rule. It is less on the agenda under confessional–socialist rule, when instead the focus is more on the individual cities. As none of these coalitions tends to be in place for longer than eight years, it follows that attention to the Randstad, and how it is translated into policies, comes in waves.

However, the picture has become more complicated in recent years. The political landscape has become more fragmented and populist parties have risen to prominence, particularly those on the right of the political spectrum. These tend to get relatively many more votes from the southern, formerly catholic part of the country, as well as from particular neighbourhoods, suburbs or post-war satellite towns of the larger cities of the Randstad

(De Voogd, 2016). According to Rodríguez-Pose (2018), populist movements find their roots in places that feel or get told that they do not matter, which subsequently take 'revenge' through the ballot box. Even though
right-wing populist parties address rather urban themes such as immigration
and integration, they do challenge the urban cosmopolitan perspective dominant in larger cities and college towns in the Randstad. Coupled with their
large support base also outside the Randstad, it follows that attention for the
development of the Randstad as a whole will be limited, even though there
will be attention for problematic neighbourhoods in its cities. While these
parties have so far not joined a ruling coalition at the national level, they have
drawn attention away from planning at a pan-Randstad scale.

Academics play a potential counterweight role to the dynamic interplay of
political forces in that they can provide a more consistent rationale as regards
the need and relevance of conceptualising the Randstad as a single entity or
whether a focus on its main cities, or some of its neighbourhoods is more relevant. For sure, the functional rationality of the Randstad concept has been
contested ever since it rose to prominence in public and policy circles in the
1950s (e.g. Werkcommissie Westen des Lands, 1958; Steigenga, 1972; Bours
and Lambooy, 1974; Wagenaar and Van Engelsdorp Gastelaars, 1986; Brand,
2012; Maessen, 2013). Over many years, numerous academic studies have
tried to shed light on these issues, and to some extent, their volume follows
the political discourse as attention to the Randstad comes coupled with more
research funding opportunities as well.

Some of the studies into functional coherence have been very influential to the political discourse. Arguably, the most influential one is a study
by (the predecessor of) the Netherlands Environmental Assessment Agency
(Ritsema Van Eck *et al.*, 2006) that concluded essentially that the Randstad
was not a functional entity (see Chapter 7). It was the prelude to the ending
of the period of renewed interest in the Randstad concept that had started
with the rise of the Delta Metropolis Association at the end of the 1990s
(see Chapter 11) and ended with the never-put-into-practice proposal for a
Randstad Province in 2007 (CVR, 2007). In subsequent years, two new so-
called 'metropolitan areas' were defined centred on Amsterdam (the so-called
North Wing of the Randstad but excluding Utrecht) and Rotterdam/The
Hague (the South Wing of the Randstad; see Chapter 12) partly because research had shown that these scales were more relevant functional entities than
the Randstad as a whole (Van Oort *et al.*, 2013). Van den Berg (1957) and the
1966 Second National Report on Spatial Planning presented the North Wing
and South Wing already as possible development entities; the North Wing
also incorporating the cities of Utrecht, Amersfoort, Hilversum and Alkmaar
and the South Wing also incorporating the cities of Leiden and Dordrecht.

It is interesting to note the difference in perspective for insiders and outsiders. While many public actors and residents in the Randstad identify and associate more with smaller spatial entities within the Randstad, outsiders tend

to see the region more often as a whole. In the rest of the Netherlands, the Randstad toponym sometimes denotes the (too) dominant economic and political power concentrated there. But many studies tend to consider the region as an entity (e.g. Hall, 1966; BBSR, 2011; see also various projects within the ESPON programme), with the associated advantage that this makes the region look more prominent in any competitive ranking of cities or regions.

The relevance of studies into functional coherence goes far beyond catering to political whims. Whether or not the Randstad is a functional entity is believed to be critical to its economic, social and environmental performance (Shachar, 1994; Lambooy, 1998; Meijers, 2007a; OECD, 2007). More generally, it has been suggested that flows, and especially a city's embeddedness in these flows, are critical to understanding its performance (Taylor, 2003; Hall and Pain, 2006; Neal, 2013). As regards this embeddedness, often, an analogy is drawn with firm networks: the potential importance of global economic networks in shaping a firm's competitiveness and performance potential has often been mentioned (e.g. Malecki, 2002; Tracey and Clark, 2003). Parallel to these debates, it could be argued that networks between cities, also on the regional scale as for example in the Randstad, are crucial in enhancing its competitiveness. Obviously, without interactions and flows between the Randstad cities, it is hard to imagine that they would gain 'world city' status (Hall, 1966; Shachar, 1994), or that such a loose collection of medium-sized and small cities would be able to organise the agglomeration benefits of a single, large metropolis (Meijers and Burger, 2010). Indeed, a recent study of 117 polycentric urban regions reveals that they are able to organise more agglomeration benefits when they are more strongly functionally and politically integrated (Meijers *et al.*, 2018).

In this chapter, the central aim is to scrutinise the wide variety of studies that have addressed the question of whether the Randstad is a functional entity or not. At first sight, this may appear to be a fairly simple question. However, in practice, we must address theoretical, conceptual and methodological questions that potentially have a strong influence on the answers. The aim of this chapter is to unravel such theoretical, conceptual and methodological issues by discussing existing studies of functional relationships in the Randstad as well as their findings. This will unveil the relational complexity of the Randstad.

The next section comprises the main part of this chapter and presents a selection of some of the most important studies that have been exploring functional coherence in the Randstad at different points in time, culminating in an overview table in which their main characteristics are summarised. While this section is more of a descriptive nature, the section thereafter critically discusses the studies from a conceptual and methodological perspective. This final section considers general conceptual and methodological requirements that need to be adhered to when studying functional coherence in polycentric metropolitan areas such as the Randstad.

The Randstad: a coherent functional entity?

The rise of the Randstad as a territorial, policy and research concept

The Netherlands became a unified state in 1815, but resembled the former federation of provinces until the start of industrialisation. Over several decades, growth was located disproportionally in the entire Randstad. The Hague developed rapidly with the rise of central government and associated functions, the port of Rotterdam thrived, Amsterdam regained its prominence as a financial and colonial trade centre, while Utrecht's central location led to the establishment of many national services in that city (Atzema *et al.*, 1992). Thus, an economically thriving and politically important region in the West of the Netherlands was born. In a way, the development of such a polycentric system of cities is remarkable; as in the nineteenth century, the general trend in surrounding countries was that a primate city developed as countries became more centrally governed (Wagenaar and Van Engelsdorp Gastelaars, 1986; Brand, 2012).

There was a generally felt need to develop a name for this polycentric urban system. The earliest occurrence of the Randstad toponym in newspapers dates from November 1938 and paradoxically has its roots not in a debate that stresses its unity and coherence, but instead, is rooted in a competition between the main cities regarding the location of a national airport (Borger *et al.*, 2011: 87; Meijers, 2019). The national airline, KLM, was not in favour of Schiphol airport at Amsterdam, at that time a small airstrip, and instead favoured a new national airport to be located in the centre of the ring of cities in the West of the Netherlands, and this ring of cities was referred to as Randstad ('rand' means rim). Lobbying together with the city of The Hague, KLM propagated a location not far from Leiden. In the debate, a variety of other names also circulated like 'Zoomstad' ('Edge City'), but 'Randstad' surfaced as the most appealing toponym and quickly became part of the everyday vocabulary, as evidenced by its increasingly frequent appearance in newspapers (Burger, 2018), inside and particularly also outside the area.

After the Second World War, the territorial concept of the Randstad turned into a policy concept (Werkcommissie Westen des Lands, 1958), as growth management was deemed necessary given substantial population increases in the Randstad due to internal migration from rural areas, fuelled by mechanisation of work in agriculture (Lambregts and Zonneveld, 2004). While policy-makers proposed safeguarding the deconcentrated nature of the Randstad, they also foresaw that the Randstad cities would functionally become related to such an extent that the network of cities would be able to rival large metropolises such as London and Paris (Lambregts and Zonneveld, 2004).

Early observations[1]

The entity of a network of cities in the Randstad was not yet in place in the 1950s. In his analyses of the Randstad cities, the geographer Keuning (1955) concluded that the Randstad did not form an integrated urban system. Amsterdam clearly served a wider territory as a commercial and trade centre, but this area was by no means restricted to the Randstad, as the headquarters in the city directed operations in the whole country and the city formed a shopping centre for all Dutch. Rather, he discerned metropolitan areas centred on Amsterdam, Rotterdam, the Hague and Utrecht, while he also points to the city-regions of Leiden and Haarlem as distinguishable units. The pattern in the South Wing (a term already in use in the 1950s) of the Randstad was rather complicated. In addition to the industrial and transport-oriented cluster of activities extending from Delft up to Gouda and Dordrecht, he pointed to the important residential role of (parts of) The Hague and places adjoining such as Wassenaar and Voorburg for the high-level workers in the industrial and transport cluster around Rotterdam. Similarly, the area for which Rotterdam is the centre for services and amenities is different to the area of the industrial-logistical complex, as for example, Delft is more oriented towards The Hague. Likewise, he found that the labour market for the most highly skilled workers such as those working at the universities in Leiden and Delft easily covers the combined metropolitan areas of Rotterdam, The Hague and Leiden. If the Randstad were to be considered an entity, he posed that it would probably be in the area of international tourism, as the prime tourist attractions were concentrated in the area. The hierarchical orientation of flows is presented in Figure 6.1, which shows the spheres of influence of the major Dutch cities according to Keuning (1955).

Luning Prak (1960) made an early contribution in emphasising the value of the concentration of economic activities and agglomeration economies for welfare, arguing against a deconcentration of activities to more peripheral regions and cities which gained considerable political momentum in the late 1950s. Similarly, in Steigenga (1972: 157), the Randstad is introduced as a 'sympolis'. Building on Vance (1964: 89), a sympolis is suggested to work according to the principles of equality and concert, expressing the idea that 'each city in the urban region stands as a functional equal to all other, and that it is the collective and cooperative labors of the lot that give us our urban economy'. Also, an emphasis on equality and concert 'may overcome the implied dependence of the outer parts of the urban region on the centrally located core, a connotation that cannot be winnowed from the term metropolis'. Lambooy (1974) confirms this development view stressing functional and economic complementarities between urban regions in the Randstad.

Urban networks research programme

It was only at the end of the 1980s and beginning of the 1990s that there was a new upsurge in studies addressing the functional coherence of the Randstad (NEI, 1986; De Smidt, 1987; Stam *et al.*, 1988; Van der Knaap and Louter, 1988; Verroen *et al.*, 1988; Knol and Manshanden, 1990; Dieleman and Musterd, 1992). This rise was not a coincidence, as it came coupled with the publication of a new national spatial strategy called the Fourth Report on Spatial

Figure 6.1 Dutch cities and their sphere of influence in the early 1950s.
Source: Keuning, 1955.

Planning (Ministerie van VROM, 1988) in which the then-prevalent political ambition to spread development further over the country was abandoned.
Instead, the focus turned to strengthening the Randstad area given trends
such as internationalisation. Increased functional integration between the
Randstad cities was considered an essential part of this and would also exploit
the clear complementarities in economic profile of the cities. An interesting
anecdote is that in the first 1988 version of this planning memorandum, the
planners of the National Spatial Planning Agency introduced a new version
of the Randstad which excluded Utrecht. The assumption behind this was
that 'top functions' were concentrated in a much more confined area: the
western part of the Randstad. The demotion of Utrecht met heavy political

opposition in and outside parliament and was dropped in later versions (for a full account of this battle, see Van Duinen, 2004; see also Chapter 11).

A new research programme – the 'Urban Networks Research Program' – was set up involving several Dutch universities (Kruyt *et al.*, 1987) and strongly supported by government funding. The outcomes were published in a special issue of the journal *Tijdschrift voor Economische en Sociale* Geografie (TESG) (Atzema *et al.,* 1992). In particular, the study by Cortie *et al.* (1992) focused on the question of whether the Randstad was a functional entity or not. The availability of flow data was an issue for these researchers, forcing them to limit their analysis to migration patterns and daily traffic flows. Descriptive statistics of flows between areas were presented, but the authors struggled with the question of which criterion to use to determine whether the Randstad was integrated or not. In their study, the level of flows within the Randstad was judged against the level of flows within the four largest city-regions, and whether intra-Randstad flows were stronger than between the Randstad and the rest of the Netherlands. While Cortie *et al.* emphasise the need to not just look at flows in terms of absolute numbers but also to control for the size of origin and the distance between them, they only controlled for the size of origin.

As regards migration patterns, it was concluded that migration between the city-regions of the four main cities was limited, and if there was migration, this was predominantly between suburban rings of different cities. In retrospect, one may wonder whether migration was an aptly chosen indicator. After all, if a change of jobs required a household to move house, this is probably more an expression of fragmentation (travel distances, times and costs being too high when commuting on a daily basis) rather than integration. One could even develop an opposing argumentation as the lack of intra-Randstad migration found by Cortie *et al.* could actually be an expression of integration: it shows that it is possible to cover the entire area without having to migrate.

The other indicator available was 'daily travel patterns' in terms of work-related trips (e.g. commuting and business trips), services-related trips (e.g. shopping) and leisure-trips (sports, culture and social visits, among others). Of these trips, work-related trips were over greater distances than the others. This appears to have changed (see Schwanen *et al.*, 2001). Leisure trips account for the largest share of trips and total distance travelled. As could be expected, an analysis of these trips indicated that functional coherence within one of the four city-regions was much stronger than between them. However, it was also shown that the number of trips between adjacent city-regions was higher, providing some evidence of integration at the scale of the southern and northern wing of the Randstad.

Overall, the conclusion was that 'the Randstad cannot be taken as one fully integrated network of cities. It consists of four separate daily urban systems. At most two wings can be distinguished' (Cortie *et al.*, 1992: 284), and this conclusion was similar to studies in the 1970s and early 1980s (Cortie and Ostendorf, 1986). The authors provide two explanations for the lack of coherence.

First, the internal accessibility of the Randstad would be insufficient to enable frequent pan-Randstad travel. Second, the complementarities of the cities would be too limited, which also makes the need for such pan-Randstad travel limited.

Focus on dynamics through time

In the 1990s, several studies were published that took a different approach by comparing functional patterns at multiple points in time, and in the case of Clark and Kuijpers-Linde (1994) by also comparing the Randstad to Southern California. By comparing 1980 and 1990 data on work trips, these authors counter the arguments for maintaining separate city-regions as done by Cortie *et al.* (1992) by pointing at the rising relative number of flows occurring between the four main Randstad city-regions (as well as the Green Heart). In particular, the number of flows out of The Hague, Rotterdam and Utrecht city-regions was increasing, and these were particularly oriented at the closest neighbouring city within the northern wing and southern wing, respectively. Trips from The Hague to Rotterdam increased 75%, the other way around, they almost doubled. Trips from Utrecht to Amsterdam increased by two-thirds over the 10 years and from Amsterdam to Utrecht by almost 50%. Remarkably, integration between the northern and southern wing decreased somewhat. Moreover, 'the evidence for an interconnected urban structure is as strong as in Southern California' (Clark and Kuijpers-Linde, 1994: 475). They make an interesting remark that 'now the issue is the equilibrium at which flows will stabilise' (Clark and Kuijpers-Linde, 1994: 475), which recognises that functional integration is not likely to increase forever, and which suggests that there may be some optimum level of functional integration.

A later study by Limtanakool *et al.* (2009) examines the 1992–2002 period, focusing on flows of people between daily urban systems (identified on the basis of commuting and migration data in Vliegen, 2005; see also Van der Laan, 1998). In the Randstad, nine daily urban systems were identified, in itself an indication of a lack of functional coherence, although these daily urban systems are located adjacent to each other, hence forming a continuous ring around the Green Heart. The study employs an urban systems approach using strength and symmetry of interaction to define the structure of the Dutch urban system. Spatial interaction is measured by commuting and leisure trips of persons. The authors find that the Netherlands urban system is composed of several smaller urban systems, and the Randstad stands out as an identifiable subsystem, in which stronger interaction occurs than in the other subsystems. This is at least partly due to a methodological choice to measure strength of a link between cities as a proportion of total interactions, meaning that mass of origin and destination (which are larger in the Randstad) are not controlled for.

In the 1990s, both Amsterdam and Utrecht started to attract more commuters from elsewhere, and in particular, the pattern of interaction within the northern wing became more complex (notably in terms of leisure flows). An important conclusion drawn is that in the 1992–2002 period especially, commuting interaction between close-by daily urban systems became stronger, more symmetrical and more evenly distributed. Because of this, there appears to have been a rise of the Randstad north and south wing as relevant functional entities. Results for leisure flows gave little evidence of stronger, pan-Randstad integration.

A recent study by Kasraian *et al.* (2018) explored developments in travel behaviour in the Randstad over time (1980–2010). It found a rise in average daily distance travelled until the mid-1990s, which was however followed by a decrease up to 2010. This may suggest that the functional integration of the Randstad has become less strong in more recent periods.

Interlocking network model

The EU co-funded Interreg IIIb project Polynet of the early 2000s set out to explore functional relationships within eight mega-city regions in North West Europe, including the Randstad. Next to descriptive analyses of commuting flows, showing no integration at the Randstad scale, it also extended the interlocking network model of inter-city relations, originally devised to provide a descriptive analysis of how global and world cities are connected at the regional scale or 'inter-locked' with one another (Taylor, 2001) (see Hall and Pain, 2006; Hoyler *et al.*, 2008). The results are extensively discussed in Burger *et al.* (2014b).

The interlocking network model defines two cities as linked in a network to the extent that they host offices of the same firm, assuming that there is likely to be a flow of knowledge between different locations of the same firm. Applying this method, Lambregts *et al.* (2006) found that the strongest intra-firm linkages in the Randstad are between Amsterdam and Rotterdam, meaning that most firms have a simultaneous presence in both cities. Other dense connections include relationships between the four large anchors of the Randstad: Amsterdam, Rotterdam, The Hague and Utrecht. Smaller centres such as Alkmaar and Amersfoort also appear relatively well connected to the other Randstad cities studied, while the remainder cities are less well connected. Following this logic, it would seem that 'a dense and well-spread network of business services flows exists between the main business service centres of the Randstad' (Lambregts *et al.*, 2006: 142). However, based on a series of interviews with policy-makers, the authors of the Randstad study cast doubt over this initial interpretation: perhaps the findings signal

> the existence of relationships at the pan-Randstad level, but simultaneously point at intra-regional fragmentation and 'disconnectedness'. After all, from the practice among firms to have multiple offices in the Randstad area it may be derived that for many firms it is apparently not feasible

to service the entire area from a single office and hence that for many firms the Randstad falls apart into several, separate business markets.

(Lambregts, 2009: 135)

In other words, the business services market in the Randstad appears geographically fragmented, an interpretation which is contrary to the standard interlocking network model perspective that the Randstad is strongly integrated.

Light-intensity at night

A very different perspective is taken by Florida *et al.* (2012). While their prime objective is to measure economic output by focusing on light intensity, they also identify metropolitan areas as completely contiguously lighted areas as seen from space at night. They do so using light emission data for the year 2000. Although no maps are made available, the population number of 7.62 million they found for the Amsterdam-Rotterdam-The Hague area suggests that this corresponds to a broad definition of the Randstad. Obviously, this method, which in many ways is a crude approximation of a functional area, does not allow identifying functional relationships between places.

Integration, specialisation and complementarity

The study that strongly criticised the rise of interest in governmental co-operation at a pan-Randstad scale in the early 2000s was undertaken by the Netherlands Environmental Assessment Agency (Ritsema Van Eck *et al.*, 2006; see also Chapter 7). The conclusion was that the widespread assumption in policy circles at that time that the Randstad was developing into or had already developed into a coherent functional entity characterised by specialisation, integration and complementarities, could not be empirically supported. These firm conclusions are based on a number of observations relating especially to specialisation and complementarities: the economic specialisation and socio-economic composition of cities are converging (in line with: Kloosterman and Lambregts, 2001; Meijers, 2007b), and complementarities (in the sense that specialisations in one place evoke interactions with places that lack these specialisations) with regard to industry and trade seem non-existent. In terms of trips for shopping Ritsema Van Eck *et al.* (2006) conclude that 90% of shopping trips take place within the own city-region and only 5% of shopping trips in another Randstad city-region, while the average distance for such trips is also hardly increasing. Also, input-output relations between firms in the central cities are substantial in absolute terms, but less than expected given their size. Ritsema Van Eck *et al.* (2006) continue by stating that functional coherence at a pan-Randstad level only holds for a limited number of activities, areas and sectors, and furthermore, in these niches, trends were not indicating a further strengthening of coherence.

These niches include commuting, as long-distance commuting was found to have risen, but still, 75% of workers did so in their own city-region. Yet, it is concluded that the Randstad is a relevant scale for the labour market, albeit not the most important scale. Another niche is 'fun shopping' in the northern wing, where specialisation of cities appears to lead to interaction (compare De Hoog, 2013 and Chapter 10 elsewhere in this volume).

In sum, the evidence for functional coherence found was not sufficient to consider the Randstad a functional entity nor is it one in the making. Rather, the report suggests that Amsterdam was, after more than a century, regaining (or continuing) its status as leading metropolis. The rest is history. Amsterdam withdrew from pan-Randstad co-operation platforms and instead, started its own 'Metropolitan Region Amsterdam' incorporating a large part of the northern wing, but not Utrecht. In response, Rotterdam and The Hague joined forces in the 'Metropolitan Region Rotterdam-The Hague' (see Meijers *et al.*, 2014 and Chapter 12).

In a follow-up to this project, and again using the data on input-output relations between firms operating in the Randstad and gravity models, Van Oort *et al.* (2010) concluded that there is a clear ranking of relations in the Randstad: intra-urban and suburban-core relations are stronger in magnitude than could be explained from the gravity variables mass and distances alone, while all inter-urban and core-suburban relations were clearly less than expected. Re-estimating the model while testing for inter-firm flows between municipalities with complementary sectoral specialisations did not alter the outcomes substantially. This suggests that the main Randstad cities (Amsterdam, Utrecht, Rotterdam and The Hague) still predominantly function as monocentric nodes without much division of flows based on economic complementarities for many inter-firm relationships (recall that half of all relations were with partners outside the Randstad).

Multiplexity and heterogeneity

More recently, researchers addressing functional coherence in the Randstad have drawn attention to the issues of *multiplexity* (Burger *et al.*, 2014a) and individual-level heterogeneity (Burger *et al.,* 2014b). Multiplexity refers to the situation where different types of functional linkages do not display a necessarily identical pattern. This means that a region can appear to be spatially integrated based on the analysis of one type of functional linkage, but loosely inter-connected based on the analysis of another type of functional linkage. In the case of the Randstad, it was found that input-output relationships, intra-firm relationships and business travel occur more on a pan-Randstad level than commuting, and much more than social, leisure or shopping trips which have a narrower spatial scope (Burger *et al.*, 2014a). In a follow-up study, it was also shown that individual-level heterogeneity plays a role. This means that, even though a similar type of flow may be taken into account, there may be a wide variety of spatial interaction patterns that can be attributed to differences among people or firms. Burger *et al.* (2014b) demonstrate this for commuting and inter-firm relationships. Commuting patterns are strongly dependent on individual-level characteristics, such as gender, age, income, hours worked, education, having children or not and the type of household to which one belongs. For instance, young, higher-educated and higher-earning men generally tend to commute much more on a pan-Randstad scale than older, lower-education and lower-earning men. The same holds for women. But for them, having children limits their spatial scope. For firms, the odds of having buyer-supplier relationships at the regional scale of the Randstad were dependent on sector, establishment type, size and age of the firm (Burger *et al.*, 2014b).

The turn to 'big data'

Traditionally, it is rather difficult to obtain fine-grained data relationships between cities, but 'big data' is going to change this. An increasing number of resources is becoming available or can be made relevant to study functional coherence of metropolitan regions using, for example, community detection algorithms. A promising method to determine the relatedness of cities is the so-called 'toponym co-occurrence method'. This approach reconstructs the spatial organisation of a territory on the basis of co-occurrences of place names in a text corpus. Studying the relationships between all Dutch places with over 750 inhabitants (#1639) through counting co-occurrence of their names on all Dutch (.nl) websites, Meijers and Peris (2019) reconstruct the spatial organisation of the Netherlands for the year 2017. The residuals of applying a gravity model to this network of relationships can inform whether cities are more or less related with each other than could be expected given their sizes and the distance between them. Meijers and Peris (2019) establish that the relationships in the Randstad region are actually somewhat less strong than expected. Whereas the relation between Rotterdam and Amsterdam is the strongest in absolute terms, it happens to be somewhat less strong than expected (−2.8% to be precise). Within the Randstad region, The Hague stands out as a city that is more related to the other main Randstad cities (The Hague-Amsterdam: +10%; The Hague-Rotterdam: + 7%; The Hague-Utrecht: + 10%). The relations Amsterdam-Utrecht (−3%) and Utrecht-Rotterdam (−4%) are less strong than expected. Places that were particularly more weakly related to other cities than expected tended to be either relatively new suburban places near the main Randstad cities (Capelle aan den IJssel, Spijkenisse, IJsselstein, Hellevoetsluis, Almere), or older places that have always been in the 'agglomeration shadow' (see Meijers and Burger, 2017) of a larger close-by city (Vlaardingen near Rotterdam, Zwijndrecht next to Dordrecht) (Meijers and Peris, 2019). Table 6.1 summarises the findings of the overview of studies presented in this section. The next section elaborates and discusses these findings.

Table 6.1 Overview of studies into functional coherence Randstad

Period studied	Study	Main approach	Indicators and data	Methodological approach	Findings
1930s–1950s	Keuning (1955)	Define hinterlands of individual cities.	Travel patterns: observations	Mostly tacit knowledge.	Randstad fragmented into several separate urban systems (Amsterdam, Rotterdam, The Hague, Utrecht), although Amsterdam has a function as a national service centre. South wing of the Randstad presents a more complex functional pattern and some signs of integration on the (upper level of the) housing market and for higher education. Draws attention to multiplexity.
1970s–1980s	Cortie *et al.* (1992)	Comparing functional integration at different spatial scales.	Actual flows: migration; commuting & business trips; services trips; leisure trips.	Absolute flows standardised by size and origin.	Randstad is not integrated, but fragmented into four city-regions centred on Amsterdam, Rotterdam, The Hague and Utrecht. Limited evidence of increasing functional integration at the scale of the northern and southern Randstad wings.
1980s	Clark and Kuijpers-Linde (1994)	Dynamics in flows through time and comparison between regions.	Actual flows: work-related trips.	Relative distribution of trips out of city-regions over several destinations.	There is evidence for an interconnected urban structure in which functional relations are increasing, in particular at the scale of the northern and southern Randstad wings. These wings are becoming more separated from each other.

(Continued)

Period studied	Study	Main approach	Indicators and data	Methodological approach	Findings
1990s	Limtanakool et al. (2009)	Describing dynamics in urban systems over time.	Actual flows: commuting, leisure trips.	Changes in relative strength of flows between two places in relation to the total number of flows. Symmetry of flows (multidirectional).	The Randstad is an identifiable subsystem in the Dutch urban system. Commuting interaction between close-by urban systems became stronger, more symmetrical and more evenly distributed. Consequently, the northern and southern Randstad wings are becoming relevant functional entities. Results for leisure flows gave little evidence of stronger, pan-Randstad integration.
Early 2000s	Lambregts et al. (2006)	Identification of city networks derived from assumed knowledge flows between offices of advanced producer services (APS) firms.	Intra-firm networks: spatial distribution of offices of APS firms.	Interlocking network model.	Mixed interpretations of findings possible. Standard interpretation of the method suggests that the Randstad is strongly tied together by intra-firm (knowledge) flows. An alternative interpretation leads to opposing findings: that many APS firms have multiple offices in the Randstad suggests fragmentation rather than integration.
1990s– Early 2000s	Ritsema Van Eck et al. (2006); Van Oort et al. (2010)	Search for complementarities, understood as specialisation coupled with integration (interaction).	Actual flows: commuting, shopping; input–output relationships of firms.	Gravity models	The Randstad is not an integrated functional entity characterised by specialisation, integration and complementarities, and is also not developing in that direction. Randstad is composed of subsystems that are linked, but not integrated. City-regions provide for the most appropriate functional entity.

2000	Florida *et al.* (2012)	Defining metropolitan areas based on light intensity at night.	Light intensity: night-time satellite images.	Light emission thresholds based on American metropolitan areas applied globally.	Few details available. The 'Amsterdam–Rotterdam–The Hague' metropolitan area is identified, and its population number (7.62 million) suggests that this is based on a broad definition of the Randstad.
2000s	Burger *et al.* (2014a); Burger *et al.* (2014b)	Demonstrating multiplexity and individual-level heterogeneity.	Comparing functional patterns for different types of actual flows and per flow for different types of actors.	Gravity models, network density and visualisation. Comparing levels of integration at city-region scale versus Randstad scale.	Functional integration on a pan-Randstad scale is limited. Assessments depend on the lens through which it is assessed. Firm-related interactions occur more on a pan-Randstad scale than person-related interactions, but some trip motives (e.g. business trips and commuting) have a greater spatial scope than leisure or social visit trips. Individual's characteristics play an important role. Younger, higher-educated and higher-earning persons tend to operate on a much larger scale than those who are older, less educated and are earning less.
Late 2010s	Meijers and Peris (2019)	Assumption that probability of co-occurrence of place names in texts is higher when they are more related.	Retrieves co-occurrences of place names from large text corporate (often digital archives) and applies machine learning to classify these relationships.	Natural language processing, machine learning, deviations from gravity model.	Randstad is somewhat less coherent than could be expected given a gravity model for the entire Randstad. Provides detailed information on the embeddedness of individual cities in the Randstad.

Conclusion: relational complexity in the Randstad

The research question in this chapter was simple at first sight: is the Randstad a functional entity? The equally simple answer to this question is no. Studies focusing on different indicators of functional coherence tend to show that pan-Randstad functional integration is rather limited and generally point to the relevance of the city-regions centred on Amsterdam, Rotterdam, The Hague and Utrecht as more dominant functional entities, with some indication of an extension of these city-regions into the north wing and south wing of the Randstad (Keuning, 1955; Cortie *et al.*, 1992; Clark and Kuijpers-Linde, 1994; Ritsema Van Eck *et al*, 2006; Limtanakool *et al.*, 2009; Van Oort *et al.*, 2010; Burger *et al.*, 2014a). It is rather striking that this conclusion was already drawn by Keuning and Van den Berg in the 1950s, Steigenga in the 1970s, Cortie *et al.* in the 1980s and Van Rossem (1994) and De Boer (1996) in the 1990s. The use of sophisticated measurement methods in the later decades has not changed this conclusion much. At the same time, some studies emphasise that the Randstad is an identifiable subsystem within the Netherlands (Limtanakool *et al.*, 2009; Florida *et al.*, 2012).

The more nuanced answer is that there is substantial relational complexity in the Randstad, and the answer to the question of functional coherence is very much dependent on the conceptual and methodological approach adopted by the researcher(s) as well as the data being considered. Conceptual approaches define the question of whether the Randstad, or any region, can be considered a functional entity. The first important question is whether the Randstad should actually function as if it were a daily urban system to consider it a functional entity. The choice to study daily flows such as shopping or commuting is obviously an often-implicit indication that the Randstad should be considered a daily urban system. But the alternative is to consider the Randstad more a 'weekly urban system' or perhaps even a 'monthly urban system'. A focus on non-daily flows, such as leisure flows, is perhaps more indicative. At the other end of the spectrum, a focus on migration is perhaps not good either, since the average frequency of moving house is every 10 years in the Netherlands.

This leads to the second issue, which is that it could be argued that some types of flows do not really indicate integration, but rather the opposite, fragmentation. This holds for migration, which could indicate that a region is not sufficiently linked by infrastructure and transit systems making it rather difficult to access the amenities of a place from the previous home. It also holds for the interlocking network model method, where the simple fact that firms in advanced producer services cannot serve the Randstad from one location, but need to establish several branches is rather an indication of fragmentation than integration through knowledge flows between these offices.

The third issue is that studies show that the Randstad has a kind of imbricated structure: close-by pairs of cities tend to show integration, making them all linked in a chain, but not necessarily individually. It is unclear how this should be addressed conceptually.

The fourth issue is that the question of whether a region is integrated or not is strongly dependent on the type of flow being studied (as a result of multiplexity), which necessitates that any answer should be based on analyses of multiple types of flows.

An issue that combines both conceptual and methodological choices is how the reference against which absolute patterns of flows can be judged is set: when is integration 'strong', 'weak' or 'less than expected'? For example, when 75% of people living in a city-region work in another one, then is this high or not? And what if 90% of these people shop in their own city-region? How do we evaluate this? We have seen studies that try to maximise internal coherence relative to external flows. This allows definition of a subsystem, but not the level of integration within it. A more common approach has been to compare the level of intra-city region flows with pan-Randstad flows. But was it really a surprise that such close-by ties were stronger than more distant ones? And can one really infer the conclusion from this that pan-Randstad integration is limited? A seemingly more objective method is to employ the gravity model, which at least controls for the mass of origin and destination, and the distance between them. But one factor is consistently overlooked, namely what Ullman (1956) many years ago defined as 'intervening oppor-tunities' (after Stouffer, 1940): alternative sources of supply and demand. In a polycentric structure like the Randstad with its many cities, there are also many possible origins and destinations for flows. As in and outcoming flows are distributed over so many individual pairs of relations between cities, they can make these individual interactions appear weak when employing the gravity model, even though the sum of all in and outgoing flows can be sub-stantial. It could well be that ignoring this particular feature of polycentric systems has led to a serious underestimation of flows in the Randstad. Finally, considering the evidence for individual-level heterogeneity, how correct is it to take averages of general flows and not take stock of characteristics of the firm or the person involved in the interaction?

Another methodological issue is whether one should not simply consider frequencies of interaction, but also try to give them a different weight. For instance, input-output relationships between firms could be given a weight based on the importance or value of what is being transferred. And, should we weigh the frequency of personal trips perhaps by the time spent at a lo-cation? Getting fresh bread from the bakery around the corner is perhaps something different than an afternoon of fun shopping in another city. One way to do so that has been used is to link interactions to specialisations and complementarities of cities. But here, the specialisation of a city has been judged relative to the whole set of other places in the Randstad, and not rela-tive to an individual place; however, interaction is measured between places.

To conclude, we are not saying that the Randstad is an integrated func-tional entity. What we show here is that conceptual and methodological choices that have been made in many studies of functional coherence in the Randstad have the tendency to underestimate pan-Randstad coherence.

While there has been a search for truly objective methods to measure functional coherence, with big data and data science approaches sparking new hopes of doing exactly that, it could be argued that any method necessarily always involves some normative conceptual and methodological choices. The point is that these always need to be made explicit. As well as studying the question of whether the Randstad is functionally integrated, more time needs to be devoted also to the question of what is an optimal level of functional integration at a Randstad scale. The implicit idea that more pan-Randstad interaction is always better needs to be abandoned: there is a social, economic and sustainability dimension to such functional interaction that has not received full attention yet.

Note

1 This and some of the following subsections are a much elaborated version of Section 2 in Burger, Meijers and Van Oort (2014).

References

Atzema, O., Kruyt, B. and Van Weesep, J. (1992). 'The Randstad today and tomorrow: Introduction to the special issue', *TESG: Tijdschrift voor Economische en Sociale Geografie*, 83(4), 243–249.

BBSR, Bundesinstitut für Bau-, Stadt- und Raumforschung (2011). *Metropolitan Regions in Europe*, BBSR-Online-Publikation, No. 01/2011. Federal Institute for Research on Building, Urban Affairs and Spatial Development (BBSR) within the Federal Office for Building and Regional Planning (BBR), Bonn.

Borger, G., Horsten, F., Engel, H., Rutte, R., Diesfeldt, O., Pané, I. and De Waaijer, A. (2011). 'Twelve centuries of spatial transformation in the western Netherlands, in six maps: Landscape, habitation and infrastructure in 800, 1200, 1500, 1700, 1900 and 2000', *OverHolland*, 10/11, 8–124.

Bours, A. and Lambooy, J.G. (eds) (1974). *Stad en stadsgewest in de ruimtelijke orde [City and city-region in the spatial order]*. Van Gorcum, Assen.

Brand, A.D. (2012). *De wortels van de Randstad [The roots of the Randstad]*; Overheidsinvloed en stedelijke hiërarchie in het westen van Nederland tussen de 13de en 20ste eeuw, PhD thesis TU Delft, A+BE 2012 #02. Faculty of Architecture and the Built Environment, Delft.

Burger, M.J. (2018). *Randstad of Regio: De ontwikkeling van het Randstad concept tussen 1938 en 1994 [Randstad or region: The development of the Randstad concept between 1938 and 1994]*. Honours Programme Technische Bestuurskunde, TU Delft.

Burger, M.J., Van der Knaap, B. and Wall, R.S. (2014a). 'Polycentricity and the multiplexity of urban networks', *European Planning Studies*, 22(4), 816–840.

Burger, M.J., Meijers, E.J. and Van Oort, F.G. (2014b). 'Multiple perspectives on functional coherence: Heterogeneity and multiplexity in the Randstad', *TESG: Tijdschrift voor Economische en Sociale Geografie*, 105(4), 444–464.

Clark, W.A.V. and Kuijpers-Linde, M. (1994). 'Commuting in restructuring urban regions', *Urban Studies*, 31(3), 465–483.

Cortie, C., Dijst, M. and Ostendorf, W. (1992). 'The Randstad a metropolis?' *TESG: Tijdschrift Voor Economische en Sociale Geografie*, 83(4), 278–288.

Cortie, C., and Ostendorf, W. (1986). 'Suburbanisatie en gentrification: sociaal-ruimtelijke dynamiek in de Randstad na 1970' [Suburbanisation and gentrification: Social-geographical dynamics in the Randstad after 1970], *Geografisch Tijdschrift*, 20, 64–83.

CVR, Commissie Versterking Randstad (2007). *Advies Commissie Versterking Randstad [Advisory report 'Committee strengthening Randstad']*. CVA, s.l.

De Boer, N. (1996). *De Randstad bestaat niet: De onmacht tot grootstedelijk beleid [The Randstad does not exist: The incapacity to bring about a metropolitan policy]*. NAi Uitgevers, Rotterdam.

De Hoog, M. (2013). *The Dutch metropolis*. THOT, Bussum.

De Smidt, M. (1987). 'In pursuit of deconcentration: The evolution of the Dutch urban system from an organizational perspective', *Geografiska Annaler: Series B, Human Geography*, 69(2), 133–143.

De Voogd, J. (2016). 'Van Volendam tot Vinkeveen: de electorale geografie van de PVV' [From Volendam to Vinkeveen: The electoral geography of the PVV], *TVS: Tijdschrift voor Sociale Vraagstukken*, 22, December 2016 [available online].

Dieleman, F. and Musterd, S. (Eds) (1992). *The Randstad: A research and policy laboratory*. Kluwer Academic Publishers, Dordrecht/Boston/London.

Florida, R., Mellander, C. and Gulden, T. (2012). 'Global metropolis: Assessing economic activity in urban centers based on nighttime satellite images', *The Professional Geographer*, 64(2), 178–187.

Frieling, D.H. (2009). 'De politieke dimensie van ruimtelijke ordening' [The political dimension of spatial planning], *Rooilijn*, 42(6), 398–405.

Hall, P. (1966). *The world cities*. Weidenfield and Nicolson, London.

Hall, P. and Pain, K. (2006). *The polycentric metropolis: Learning from mega-city regions in Europe*. Earthscan, London.

Hoyler, M., Kloosterman, R.C. and Sokol, M. (2008). 'Polycentric puzzles – Emerging mega-city regions seen through the lens of advanced producer services', *Regional Studies*, 42(8), 1055–1064.

Kasraian, D., Maat, K. and Van Wee, B. (2018). 'Urban developments and daily travel distances: Fixed, random and hybrid effects using a Dutch pseudo-panel over three decades', *Journal of Transport Geography*, 72, 228–236.

Keuning, H.J. (1955). *Mozaïek der functies. Proeve van een regionale landbeschrijving van Nederland op historisch- en economisch geografische grondslag [A mosaic of functions. A trial to describe Dutch regions based on their historical and economic-geographical foundations]*. Leopolds, The Hague.

Kloosterman, R.C. and Lambregts, B. (2001). 'Clustering of economic activities in polycentric urban regions: The case of the Randstad', *Urban Studies*, 38(4), 717–732.

Knol, H. and Manshanden, W. (1990). *Functionele samenhang in de noordvleugel van de Randstad [Functional integration in the north wing of the Randstad]*, Nederlandse Geografische Studies 109. Royal Dutch Geographical Society, Utrecht.

Kruyt, B., Bovenkerk, F. and Dieleman, F.M. (1987). *Stedelijke netwerken: groei, stagnatie en segmentering in de Randstad [Urban networks: Growth, stagnation and segmentation in the Randstad]*. Ministerie van OCW, The Hague.

Lambooy, J.G. (1974). 'Stad en stadsgewest in het perspectief van hiërarchie en complementariteit' [City and city-region from the perspective of hierarchy and complementarity]. In: Bours, A. and Lambooy, J.G. (Eds) *Stad en stadsgewest in de ruimtelijke orde [City and city-region in the spatial order]*. Van Gorcum, Assen, 270–292.

Lambooy, J.G. (1998). 'Polynucleation and economic development: The Randstad', *European Planning Studies*, 6(4), 457–466.

Lambregts, B. (2009). *The polycentric metropolis unpacked: Concepts, trends and policy in the Randstad Holland,* PhD thesis, University of Amsterdam. Amsterdam Institute for Metropolitan and International Development Studies (AMIDSt), Amsterdam.

Lambregts, B., Kloosterman, R.C., Van der Werff, M., Roling, R. and Kapoen, L. (2006). 'Randstad Holland: Multiple faces of a polycentric role model'. In: Hall, P. and Pain, K. (Eds) *The polycentric metropolis: Learning from mega-city regions in Europe.* Earthscan, London, 137–145.

Lambregts, B. and Zonneveld, W. (2004). 'From Randstad to Deltametropolis: Changing attitudes towards the scattered metropolis', *European Planning Studies*, 12(3), 229–323.

Limtanakool, N., Schwanen, T. and Dijst, M. (2009). 'Developments in the Dutch urban system on the basis of flows', *Regional Studies*, 43(2), 179–196.

Luning Prak, J. (1960). *De Randstad Holland en haar belagers [The Randstad and its enemies].* Heijnis, Zaandijk.

Maessen, P. (2013). *De poldermetropool. Wat iedereen moet weten over de Randstad [The polder metropolis: What everybody should know about the Randstad].* Nai010 Uitgevers, Rotterdam.

Malecki, E.J. (2002). 'Hard and soft networks for urban competitiveness', *Urban Studies*, 39(5–6), 929–945.

Meijers, E.J. (2007a). 'From central place to network model: Theory and evidence of a paradigm change', *TESG: Journal of Economic and Social Geography*, 98(2), 245–259.

Meijers, E.J. (2007b). 'Clones or complements? The division of labour between the main cities of the Randstad, the Flemish Diamond and the RheinRuhr Area', *Regional Studies*, 41(7), 889–900.

Meijers, E.J. (2019). 'Herkomst van het concept Randstad: de strijd om de locatie van de nationale luchthaven' [The origin of the Randstad concept: The battle about the location of the national airport], *Geografie*, 28(1), 32–33.

Meijers E.J. and Burger, M.J. (2010). 'Spatial structure and productivity in U.S. Metropolitan areas', *Environment and Planning A: Economy and Space*, 42(6), 1383–1402.

Meijers, E.J. and Burger, M.J. (2017). 'Stretching the concept of 'borrowed size', *Urban Studies*, 54(1), 269–291.

Meijers, E.J., Hoogerbrugge, M.M. and Hollander, K. (2014). 'Twin cities in the process of metropolisation', *Urban Research & Practice*, 7(1), 35–55.

Meijers, E.J., Hoogerbrugge, M.M. and Cardoso, R. (2018). 'Beyond polycentricity: Does stronger integration between cities in Polycentric Urban Regions improve performance?' *TESG: Tijdschrift voor Economische en Sociale Geografie*, 109(1), 1–21.

Meijers, E.J. and Peris, A.F.T. (2019). 'Using toponym co-occurrences to measure relationships between places: Review, application and evaluation', *International Journal of Urban Sciences*, 23(2), 246–268.

Ministerie van VROM (Volkshuisvesting, Ruimtelijke Ordening en Milieubeheer) (1988). *Vierde nota over de ruimtelijke ordening, Deel a: Beleidsvoornemen [Fourth report on spatial planning: Green paper].* SDU Uitgeverij, The Hague.

Neal, Z. (2013). *The connected city: How networks are shaping the modern metropolis.* Routledge, New York.

NEI, Nederlands Economisch Instituut (1986). *De Randstad in economisch perspectief: economische specialisatie, functionele samenhang en ontwikkelingstendenties [An economic perspective on the Randstad: Economic specialisation, functional integration and development trends]*. NEI, Rotterdam.

OECD, Organisation for Economic Co-operation and Development (2007). *Territorial reviews: Randstad Holland, The Netherlands*. OECD Publishing, Paris.

Ritsema van Eck, J., Van Oort, F., Raspe, O., Daalhuizen, F. and Van Brussel, J. (2006). *Vele steden maken nog geen Randstad [Many cities do not make a single Randstad]*. Ruimtelijk Planbureau/ NAi Uitgevers, The Hague/Rotterdam.

Rodríguez-Pose, A. (2018). 'The revenge of the places that don't matter (and what to do about it)', *Cambridge Journal of Regions, Economy and Society*, 11(1), 189–209.

Schwanen, T., Dieleman F. and Dijst, M. (2001). 'Travel behaviour in Dutch monocentric and policentric urban systems', *Journal of Transport Geography*, 9, 173–186.

Shachar, A. (1994). 'Randstad Holland: A world city?' *Urban Studies*, 31(3), 381–400.

Stam, W.J., Kluyver, D., De Smidt, M., Mes, D.L. and Conijn, M.C. (1988). *Dynamiek van het bedrijfsleven in de Randstad [Dynamics of the business world in the Randstad]*, Stedelijke netwerken 7. Ministerie van Onderwijs en Wetenschappen/ Onderzoeksinstituut voor Technische Bestuurskunde, The Hague/Delft.

Steigenga, W. (1972). 'Randstad Holland. Concept in evolution', *TESG: Tijdschrift voor Economische en Sociale Geografie*, 63(3), 149–161.

Stouffer, S.A. (1940). 'Intervening opportunities: A theory relating mobility to distance', *American Sociological Review*, 5(6), 845–867

Taylor, P.J. (2001). 'Specification of the world city network', *Geographical Analysis*, 33(2), 181–194.

Taylor, P.J. (2003). *World city network; A global urban analysis*. Routledge, London.

Tracey, P. and Clark, G. (2003). 'Alliances, networks and competitive strategy: Rethinking clusters of innovation', *Growth and Change*, 34(1), 1–16.

Ullman, E.L. (1956). 'The role of transportation and the basis for interaction'. In: Thom, W. (Ed.) *Man's role in changing the face of earth*. The University of Chicago Press, Chicago, 862–880.

Vance, J.E. (1964). *Geography and the evolution in the San Francisco Bay Area*. Institute of Governmental Studies, University of California, Berkeley.

Van den Berg, G.J. (1957). 'De grote stad in de toekomst' [The large city in the future]. In: Groenman, S. (Ed.) *Problemen van de grote stad [Problems of the large city]*. Het Spectrum, Utrecht, 66–83.

Van der Knaap, G.A. and Louter, P.J. (1988). 'Technologische ontwikkeling en ruimtelijke specialisatie in de Randstad' [Technological development and geographical specialisation within the Randstad], *Geografisch Tijdschrift*, Nieuwe Reeks XXII, 3–14.

Van der Laan, L. (1998). 'Changing urban systems: An empirical analysis at two spatial levels', *Regional Studies*, 32(3), 235–247.

Van Duinen, L. (2004). *Planning imagery: The emergence and development of new planning concepts in Dutch national spatial policy*, PhD thesis University of Amsterdam. Repository University of Amsterdam, Amsterdam.

Van Oort, F.G., Burger, M.J. and Raspe, O. (2010). 'On the economic foundation of the urban network paradigm. Spatial integration, functional integration and urban complementarities within the Dutch Randstad', *Urban Studies*, 47(4), 725–748.

Van Oort, F.G., De Graaff, T., Koster, H., Olden, H. and Van der Wouden, F. (2013). *Ruimte voor de stad als groeimotor [Room for the city as an engine of growth]; Theoretische verdieping, empirische analyse en duiding van beleidsopties voor woon-werkdynamiek in de Randstad*. Faculteit Geowetenschappen, Universiteit Utrecht, Utrecht.

Van Rossem, V. (1994). *Randstad Holland; Variaties op het thema stad.* NAi-Uitgevers, Rotterdam.

Verroen, E., Van der Vlist, M. and Korver, W. (1988). *Interaktiepatronen in de Randstad [Patterns of interaction in the Randstad]; Een verkennend onderzoek naar funktionele relaties binnen de Randstad op bovenstadsgewestelijk niveau.* TNO-Inro, Delft.

Vliegen, M. (2005). *Grootstedelijke agglomeraties en stadsgewesten afgebakend [The delineation of metropolitan agglomerations and city regions].* Centraal Bureau voor de Statistiek, Heerlen.

Wagenaar, M. and Van Engelsdorp-Gastelaars, R. (1986). 'Het ontstaan van de Randstad, 1815–1930' [The origin of the Randstad, 1815–1930], *Geografisch Tijdschrift,* Nieuwe Reeks XX, 14–29.

Werkcommissie Westen des Lands (1958). *De ontwikkeling van het Westen des lands: Rapport [The development of the west of the country: Advisory report].* Staatsdrukkerij, The Hague.

7   Randstad

Spatial planning, polycentrism and urban networks

Jan Ritsema van Eck and Ries van der Wouden

Introduction

Relations between the Randstad urban area and spatial planning are complex. Spatial planning played a role in shaping the urban form of the Randstad, but in turn, the existence of a polycentric urban structure in the densely populated west of the Netherlands also shaped spatial planning. Modern spatial planning in the Netherlands is unthinkable without the Randstad. The Randstad has been on the agenda of spatial planning since the 1950s and has been mentioned in every national spatial planning document from the first published in 1960. Controlling the process of urbanisation in the west of the Netherlands was the most important goal of spatial planning for a long time, and policy instruments were developed to meet this challenge. In this way, the Randstad influenced the concepts, goals, instruments and institutional structure of spatial planning.

The physical structure of the classic monocentric city can be easily discovered by the human eye, whereas that of the polycentric urban region cannot. To be sure, the polycentric pattern in the Randstad area itself has grown in the course of history (Wagenaar and Van Engelsdorp Gastelaars, 1986; Brand, 2012). But the coherence between different parts of the polycentric urban region is not evident; it has to be discovered and constructed and that is exactly what the concept of 'Randstad' is about. Thus, the Randstad started its life as a visionary and abstract concept before the Second World War (Dieleman and Musterd, 1992: 3). The spatial concept of the Randstad was constructed around the existing polycentric urban pattern: a horseshoe-shaped urban ring consisting of large and medium-sized cities around a green open space, the 'Green Heart'. In the years after the War, the Randstad urban region became an essential concept in spatial planning. It also attracted attention abroad. In his book *The World Cities*, Peter Hall praised the Dutch planning system and the advantages of the Randstad polycentric urban order (Hall, 1966). The Randstad has been a central issue in spatial planning for a long time but the visions about its future have changed. For decades, the idea to preserve the polycentric structure and to control the urbanisation process was dominant. There have been voices arguing for a change to the polycentric Randstad into a more coherent metropole, but for a long time they were a minority. Only during the 1990s, the latter vision gained more ground to be replaced by the decentralisation agenda during the 2000s. Also, the dominant scale has changed from time to time from the Randstad as a whole to daily urban systems, cities, international networks and North and South Wings of the Randstad (Lambregts, 2009: 45–72).

In this chapter we discuss two issues: first, what was the role of spatial planning in shaping the urban structure of the Randstad? This issue will be discussed in the next section. Second, how did the polycentric urban structure of the Randstad evolve, and what can be said about the development of urban networks within this polycentric structure? The section thereafter is devoted to these issues. The final section summarises the conclusions.

The Randstad and spatial planning

The Randstad has been a major issue in national spatial planning since the 1950s (Faludi and Van der Valk, 1994). Economic growth triggered migration from other parts of the country to the west of the Netherlands, and the government feared that the population growth would result in uncontrolled urbanisation of the Randstad area. A committee for the west of the Netherlands was formed to advise the Dutch Government on this issue. The committee published its final report in 1958 (Werkcommissie Westen des Lands, 1958). The report recommends that to prevent uncontrolled urbanisation form the Randstad urban ring into the central open space ('the Green Heart'), the government should allow urban growth beyond the Randstad area. This recommendation became part of the First and Second National Policy Documents on Spatial Planning (1960 and 1966, respectively). The aim was to preserve the polycentric character of the Randstad urban ring and the Green Heart, rather than creating a coherent Randstad urban area. For most policy makers megalopolis was dystopia, not utopia.

Migration into the Randstad was followed by another demographic development. Suburbanisation became a mass phenomenon during the 1960s and 1970s. Families that could afford to, left the large cities and moved into homes that had gardens in suburban municipalities. The size of the population of the large Dutch cities peaked in the early 1960s after which it rapidly declined. Over the course of two decades the largest cities combined lost over half a million inhabitants. This process of population decline lasted until the second half of the 1980s, after which their population started to grow again (see also Figure 7.1 and below). Controlling the process of suburbanisation became a major goal in spatial planning.

National spatial planning followed the advice of the 1958 report (discussed above) to allow urban growth in the outer ring of the Randstad but not in the Green Heart. The resulting strategy was a combination of regulation through zoning (defining the Randstad urban ring, Green Heart and green zones between urban areas) and the development of growth centres to control suburbanisation.

But the implementation of this strategy had to wait until the launch of the concept of 'bundled deconcentration' in the Second National Policy Document on Spatial Planning of 1966 (*Tweede Nota over de Ruimtelijke Ordening*; Ministerie van VRO, 1966). At the same time, the spatial planning system had changed. In 1965, the Spatial Planning Act (WRO) came into force. Within the Ministry of Housing and Spatial Planning, the National Spatial Planning Agency (RPD) was created with the objective to formulate, coordinate, implement and evaluate national spatial policy. More importantly, after two decades of national government-dominated spatial policy, the spatial planning system was decentralised, providing the municipalities with more power and providing citizens with more possibilities to participate in the policy process.

The implementation of urban growth centres peaked during the 1970s. Most of the growth centres were located in and around the Randstad area. The choice of having a number of these urban growth centres at a certain distance from the large cities, and for them to function as cities in and of themselves, meant that Dutch urbanisation policy more closely resembled the English new towns rather than the French villes nouvelles, the latter of which were specifically focused on strengthening Paris (Aldridge, 1979; Tuppen, 1983; Desponds and Auclair, 2017). Many of them were along the outer ring of the Randstad but some were located within or adjacent to the Green Heart (Reijndorp *et al.*, 2012). This is rather remarkable given the objective of keeping the Green Heart of the Randstad as open as possible. For the growth centre of Zoetermeer this can be explained because its prime donor city, The Hague, does not have many possibilities to enlarge due to its location between the coast, built-up areas of adjacent municipalities and the Green Heart. Key to implementation was the close collaboration between spatial planning and the public housing sector, combining spatial development and public investment. The funds coming through public housing were a significant instrument in directing the development of the urban growth centres.

In quantitative terms, growth centre policy was a success. The construction of new housing was accelerated despite the collapse of the housing market for owner-occupiers caused by the economic crisis of 1973. The urban growth centre policy remained firmly based on government-funded public housing, which resulted in continued population growth of the growth centres. Job growth however fell short of expectations. For employment, most of the growth centres remained strongly focused on their respective donor cities, thus leading to an increase in commuting to those cities.

The growth centre policy did not stop suburbanisation from the large cities. On top of this, the economic crisis of the 1970s and 1980s resulted in a severe urban crisis. This caused a major change in the national spatial planning strategy during the 1980s. The tide was turned in the 1983 national policy strategy on urban areas (Ministerie van VROM, 1983). The concept of 'bundled deconcentration' was replaced with the 'compact city' policy, the growth centre policy was gradually phased out, and the former growth centres had to make do without additional subsidies.

It took a new policy document, a few years later, to turn the new 'compact city' concept into policy: the 1988 Fourth Report on Spatial Planning (Ministerie van VROM, 1988). The new spatial planning agenda was more metropolitan than before, its aim was to revitalise the cities rather than creating a coherent Randstad. It involved a reorientation of spatial policy, from public housing to economic development and infrastructure. This was considered an urgent matter because the economic crisis of the 1970s and 1980s caused mass urban unemployment, and the cities needed an economic impulse and better infrastructure to face future globalisation. A few years later new elements were added to spatial policy. In 1990, the 'Vinex' policy document was published (Vinex is the Dutch acronym for Fourth Report on Spatial Planning Extra; Ministerie van VROM, 1990), with a focus on limiting mobility growth to benefit the environment, and the development of new residential areas within or nearby urban areas, known as the Vinex locations.

New and better infrastructure had the highest priority in spatial planning. High-quality infrastructure was meant to connect the economic hotspots: the urban areas and the 'mainports' (Schiphol Airport and Rotterdam Harbour; see Boelens and Jacobs in this volume). New railway lines were planned both for passengers and for freight. In the first place a high-speed railway, connecting Amsterdam, Schiphol Airport and Rotterdam to Brussels and Paris, and second, a freight railway line connecting Rotterdam Harbour to Germany (the 'Betuwe line'). Both projects suffered from the 'large projects disease' (Flyvbjerg *et al.*, 2003), they took much more time than foreseen and the necessary investment exceeded planned budgets by far (Van der Wouden, 2015: 119–124). Together with these investments in railway infrastructure, the main railways stations in the cities were renovated, very often in combination with the development of new real estate: offices, retail and sometimes housing.

Transport infrastructure (railways and roads) is important for the growth of urban networks. The central planning of main infrastructure was helped by a new law, the Infrastructure Planning Act (*Tracéwet*, 1994, adapted in 2000) and by the creation of an Infrastructure Fund (known by its Dutch abbreviation MIT, later MIRT). Infrastructure planning was centralised and became less dependent on the consent of municipal governments (De Gier, 2011; Filarski, 2016, 298–300). While the large railway projects received a lot of public attention, the enlargement of the capacity of motorways also progressed quite smoothly. Although some new motorways were realised at important 'missing links' in the network, the adding of new traffic lanes to existing motorways had been the most effective way to expand traffic capacity (Ploeger, 2014).

Urbanisation policy changed after the publication of the Fourth National Policy Document on Spatial Planning. New urbanisation was to take place, in accordance with the 'compact city' concept, either within or near the large cities. In that way, urbanisation concerned both inner-city projects and new greenfield sites around the city with brownfield and greenfield developments part of a single urbanisation concept. The emphasis on implementation led to national government involvement in so-called 'national key projects', strategic urban redevelopment locations, in collaborations with municipalities and private investors. Well-known key projects are located in the port districts of Amsterdam and Rotterdam, the railway station areas of The Hague and Utrecht and the Maastricht district of Ceramique (BSP/TU Delft, 2009; Spaans *et al.*, 2013). National government no longer limited its involvement to the formulation of visions and provision of subsidies but also entered into concrete agreements with local authorities about the realisation and deadlines of certain targets, who in turn, did the same with market stakeholders.

The inner-city projects certainly have been successful. They added new houses to the urban housing stock enabling further urban population increases. Some of the numbers are quite large (e.g. over 8,000 houses around the eastern part of the Port of Amsterdam), and these homes were mostly for the higher income groups. Their consumption contributed to the growth of the local economy. But the suburban greenfield residential locations close to the cities comprise the lion's share of the new houses that were built. After a slow initial start, in part due to new institutional relationships, most quantitative objectives of the Vinex policy were achieved between 1995 and 2005. In total, over the course of this period, more than 650,000 dwellings were built (Korthals Altes, 2006; RIGO, 2007).

From the point of view of spatial planning, the new Vinex locations were in line with the concept of the compact city. Most locations are found in the immediate vicinity of cities, and very often even part of those cities. But a closer look casts some serious doubts. First, the new residential areas hardly became an organic part of existing cities. Usually, there were substantial barriers separating them from the existing cities, such as canals, motorways and railways. In addition, they attracted a relatively large number of residents who would not only exclusively be focused on the nearest city but also on other urban centres and metropolitan areas. Rather than becoming expansion areas of compact cities, the Vinex locations became 'island nations' within the urban network. Second, spatial policy did not stop urbanisation into the Green Heart because many large new residential areas were built close to or even within this area. Also, some of the former urban growth centres close to the Green Heart were allocated new Vinex locations. From a spatial perspective, the urban growth centre policy was being continued by facilitating further growth. Thus, spatial development during the 1990s and 2000s is characterised by two trends: re-urbanisation of the large cities and continuing urbanisation into the Green Heart.

From the beginning of the new millennium, decentralisation of spatial planning from the national government to the municipalities dominated the agenda (Zonneveld and Evers, 2014). Major spatial planning issues such as the development of residential areas and nature conservation, were left to municipalities and provinces roughly from the mid-2000s onwards. In 2008, the financial and real estate crisis followed. It caused severe problems in spatial planning, especially at the local level. Instead of growth, there were vacancies in offices and retail buildings, house prices and new housing construction stagnated, and uncertainty about development prospects increased. But it did not influence the long-term process of re-urbanisation, as became visible after the crisis. The growth of the population of the large cities continued. House prices in the large cities rose sharply, indicating the enduring popularity of urban living.

Polycentrism and urban networks in the Randstad

Differentiated growth

The combination of the process of suburbanisation and spatial planning changed the distribution of the population within the Randstad area. From the 1960s to 1975, there was an almost classic pattern of urban sprawl. The largest cities (Amsterdam, Rotterdam, The Hague and Utrecht) lost a substantial amount of their population, whereas that of many other municipalities grew. The smaller the municipality, the faster the growth. After 1975, the growth centre policy accelerated the growth of the small cities, with a population between 50,000 and 100,000. During the 1980s the medium-sized cities (100,000–250,000) also followed this pattern. From the 1990s onwards, the re-urbanisation of the largest cities started and continued into the new millennium. Nowadays, the population of the largest cities is close to their peak at the beginning of the 1960s. Although the re-urbanisation of large cities fits into a global pattern, it is quite plausible to assume that the Dutch 'compact cities' policy has supported this process. Figure 7.1 summarises the development of the population of Dutch cities and municipalities in different size categories, from 1960 until 2017.

In 1960, 47% of the Randstad population lived in one of large cities Amsterdam, Rotterdam, The Hague or Utrecht. By 2017, their share had decreased to 30%, whilst the share of the other categories of settlement grew. This decentralisation of the population obviously strengthened the polycentric character of the Randstad area. While the number of large cities was restricted to four during those years (during the 1980s and 1990s even three: Utrecht then had less than 250,000 inhabitants), the number of cities between 100,000 and 250,000 inhabitants grew from 2 in 1960 to 11 in 2017 and between 50,000 and 100,000 from 8 in 1960 to 22 in 2017. This is partly caused by natural growth, but also by the merging of smaller municipalities into larger units through administrative reorganisation. The stimulus of growth centre policy also played a role: 4 of the 11 medium-sized cities are former growth centres as well as 6 of the 22 smaller cities. Although polycentrism is not the same as the growth of urban networks, it seems a sound base. The growth of the number of urban centres enhances the potential for the development of urban networks. However, a polycentric urban region may also be a scattered metropolis and not an urban network. Therefore, the final proof

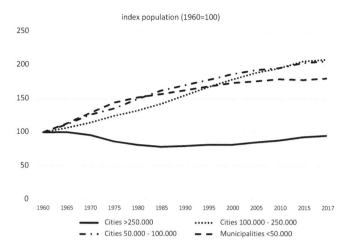

index population (1960=100)

Figure 7.1 Change of the population in the Randstad, according to the size of the city 1960–2017 (municipalities are classified according to their size in 2017).

Source: Authors, based on data from Statistics Netherlands (CBS).

of the growth of urban networks is the connectivity and the intensity of interactions, be it economic or social (Ritsema van Eck *et al.*, 2006, Lambregts, 2009).

The question then becomes one of how to measure the growth of urban networks. Following Castells, the concept of 'networks' connects the 'space of places' with the 'space of flows' (Castells, 1996). Whereas the physical structure of cities and infrastructure belongs to the first category, interactions between companies and people belong to the second. Companies have business relations with companies in other cities, they exchange goods, services or money. People commute from one place to another in order to go to work, to school or university, or to shop for recreation. Those flows of people and the interactions between companies are usually considered the best indicators of the strength and growth of urban networks. These indicators measure the integration of different parts of an urban network. Together with indicators for specialisation, such as the economic specialisation of cities, they measure their complementarity (Ritsema van Eck *et al.*, 2006). However, this also shows a major problem in the measurement of urban networks. For example, the interaction between companies might indicate the existence of an urban network between cities, but the commuting patterns to work or school might not, or the other way around. This is called the *multiplexity* problem. Drawing conclusions on urban networks based on the analysis of one indicator is therefore highly risky. Connected with the multiplexity problem is the (individual) *heterogeneity* (Burger *et al.*, 2014; Meijers *et al.* in this volume). For example, highly educated employees commute over longer distances to their work than members of other groups and therefore form different networks. Both multiplexity and individual heterogeneity have to be taken into account in order to draw valid conclusions on urban networks. In addition, there is also the dimension of time. Do only the daily flows ('daily urban systems') matter or also the weekly or even monthly flows (Tordoir and Regioplan, 2015)? Bearing this in mind, we will first discuss the results of previous research projects on urban networks in the Randstad and/or the Netherlands and second, present findings from analysis of recent data.

Analyses of commuting trends

In 2006, the Netherlands Institute for Spatial Research (RPB) published the results of an analysis of urban networks in the Randstad using indicators on the specialisation of urban regions, the relations between companies, commuting behaviour and shopping behaviour in the period 1992–2002 (Ritsema van Eck *et al.*, 2006). The general conclusion was that there was no tendency towards more specialisation of the urban regions within the Randstad and that there was no significant increase of 'flows' between the urban regions. The only exception was the increase in scale of commuting from home to work: there was a tendency to commute over longer distances. But despite this, the vast majority of commuting behaviour took place within the borders of the urban regions. The urban networks within the individual urban regions remained more important than those on the scale of the Randstad as a whole. But there was another remarkable tendency: the importance of the Amsterdam urban region within the Randstad had increased. The relations from other parts of the Randstad towards Amsterdam were more intense than before, indicating the strong position of Amsterdam in the service and knowledge economy.

Others studied the urban networks within the Netherlands as a whole. In 2015, Tordoir and Regioplan published an analysis of spatial interaction patterns in the Netherlands from 1985 onwards (Tordoir and Regioplan, 2015). They based their research upon data sets of daily mobility of various motives for households moving from one place to another and on changes in working places. They took heterogeneity seriously, distinguishing between levels of education, generations and different types of households. They concluded that there was an increase in the scale of some geographical patterns, especially amongst the young highly educated and the established economic elite. This tendency results in a slow growth of the inter-urban network in the Netherlands, creating a 'new geography'. They also observed the increasing importance of the Amsterdam and Utrecht urban regions (within the Randstad) as well as the Den Bosch region (outside the Randstad).

In the remainder of this section, we analyse some trends in functional relations between urban regions in the Randstad. Figure 7.2 shows the regions of the four large cities, Amsterdam (including Almere), Rotterdam, The Hague ('s-Gravenhage) and Utrecht as well as those of four medium-sized cities Amersfoort, Haarlem, Leiden and Dordrecht, as defined by Statistics Netherlands. Our analysis is based on the mobility surveys OVG (1995–1999) and

OViN (2012–2016), both carried out by Statistics Netherlands (CBS). We combined five years in each period to get a sufficiently large sample; numbers mentioned are thus five-year averages. The mobility surveys contain data on trips for different motives. In this section, we will discuss mainly the commute to work. At the end of the section, we will also briefly show some trends in the commute to higher education, in shopping trips and social visits.

The number of commuters between urban regions has grown from 0.3 million in 1995–1999 to over 0.5 million in 2012–2016 (see Table 7.1). This growth should be seen in the context of the growth of total employment and working population in the Randstad. In the first period the working

Figure 7.2 The eight urban regions of the Randstad.
Source: Authors, based on data from Statistics Netherlands (CBS).

Table 7.1 Commuting to work in the Randstad ×1,000

	1995–1999			*2012–2016*		
	Abs	*% Jobs*	*% Workers*	*Abs*	*% Jobs*	*% Workers*
Within urban regions	1,621	72	78	2,009	66	73
Between urban regions	295	13	14	522	17	19
From elsewhere to urban regions	332	15		519	17	
From urban regions to elsewhere	164		8	233		8
Total jobs in urban regions	2,249	100		3,050	100	
Total workers in urban regions	2,080		100	2,764		100

Source: Authors, based on data from OVG/OVIN Mobility Surveys and LISA employment register.

population in the eight urban regions was 2.1 million and the number of jobs was 2.2 million; in the second period these had increased to 2.8 and 3.1 million, respectively. Within these growing totals, the commuters between the urban regions were the fastest growing group from 14% of the working population living in the Randstad to 19%.

Figure 7.3 shows the spatial pattern of the commute to work between the urban regions. Only flows larger than 2,000 commuters per day are shown. Clearly the network of commuting relations has changed: new flows between urban regions have been added and existing flows have grown. The largest flow, from Haarlem to Amsterdam, has almost doubled from 32,000 to 60,000. Other flows to Amsterdam have also grown considerably, especially those from Utrecht, Leiden and The Hague. These last two blur the traditional distinction between the North and South Wings of the Randstad. Flows between Rotterdam and The Hague (in both directions) also grew. And finally, the map shows a number of new flows from Haarlem, Leiden and Dordrecht to Utrecht as well as from Dordrecht to Amsterdam.

Several factors will be examined to explain these changes. First the change in composition of the working population; second the differences between demographic and economic developments in the urban regions; and last the changing position of the former growth centres.

One often cited cause of this increase in long distance commuting is the growing share of highly educated workers in the Randstad. Since the 1990s, the general educational level of the Dutch workforce has risen considerably. In the Randstad, the share of workers with higher education (university or higher vocational education) has risen from a third to just less than a half. More highly educated people are willing to travel further to their jobs because their travel budget is larger and also because their work is often more specialised. In the Netherlands, the average distance travelled to work is 23.4 kilometres for highly educated workers against 13.9 kilometres for workers with lower education. This

(a)   (b)

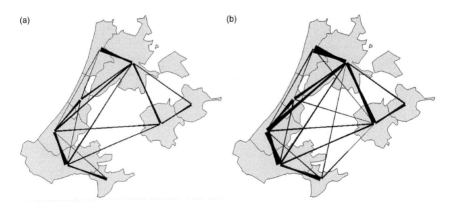

Figure 7.3(a/b) Commuters between the urban regions average 1995–1999 (left) and 2012–2016 (right).

Source: Authors, based on data from OVG/OVIN Mobility Surveys and LISA employment register.

Table 7.2 Educational level of commuters in the Randstad

	1995–1999				2012–2016			
	Lower (%)	Interm. (%)	Higher (%)	Total (%)	Lower (%)	Interm. (%)	Higher (%)	Total (%)
Within urban regions	38	34	29	100	19	38	43	100
Between urban regions	25	30	46	100	11	31	58	100
From elsewhere to urban regions	34	33	33	100	14	36	50	100
From urban regions to elsewhere	35	31	34	100	16	36	48	100
Total jobs in urban regions	35	33	32	100	17	36	47	100
Total workers in urban regions	36	33	32	100	17	36	46	100

Source: Authors, based on data from OVG/OVIN Mobility Surveys.

shows clearly in the composition of commuter flows: people with lower education are overrepresented in the shorter distance trips to work within urban regions, whereas people with higher education are overrepresented in the longer distance trips (see Table 7.2). Therefore, the increase in the share of highly educated workers leads to an increase in the commuter flows between urban regions.

It should be noted that other trends in the composition of the workforce have opposite effects. The shares of women and part-time workers have also increased strongly since 1995–1999. Since these groups generally have (much) shorter travel distances to work than men and full-time workers, this has a dampening effect on the increase of long-distance commuting (Ritsema van Eck and Hilbers, 2018). The changing composition of the workforce by itself is not a sufficient explanation for this increase of commuting between urban regions.

Another cause may be the differential demographic and economic development of the regions in the Randstad. As Figure 7.4 shows, in recent times, economic growth within the Randstad has been strongest in the North Wing of the Randstad, or more specifically in the regions around Amsterdam, Amersfoort and Utrecht. In the urban region of Amsterdam, employment soared from around 700,000 in 1996 to almost 1.1 million in 2016. This growth was strongest in the period from 1996 to 2003 when financial and commercial service industries were booming, but after the Dotcom Bubble had burst, job growth in Amsterdam continued to be strong until the financial crisis of 2008. Population growth was less strong. In the years after 2000, the building of new dwellings fell far short of the increasing demand leading to a strong increase in housing prices (Jókövi et al., 2006). This made commuting to Amsterdam for many people a more attractive (or more attainable) option than moving there. The number of jobs per

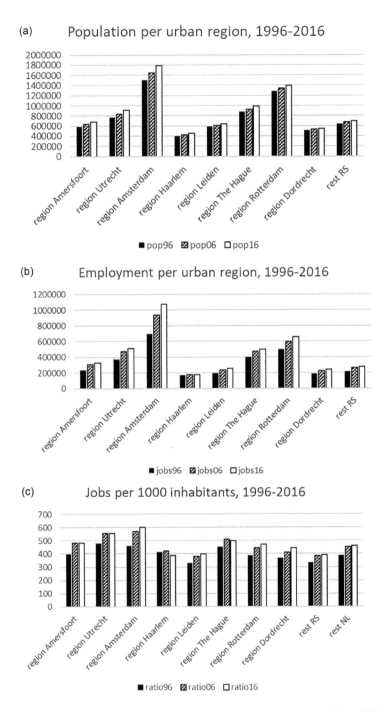

Figure 7.4(a/c) Population and employment in the urban regions: 1996, 2006 and
2016.

Source: Authors, based on data from: CBS Population Statistics and LISA employment register.

1,000 residents rose from 460 to 600. Employment in Utrecht also grew quite strongly, leading via similar mechanisms as in Amsterdam to a ratio of 555 jobs per 1,000 residents. The regions of Amersfoort and The Hague also score above average at around 500. Although labour participation, especially of women, has risen considerably during this period, it is clear that the number of workers living in the regions of Amsterdam and Utrecht has not kept up with the increase in jobs. Net commuting to these regions has increased, contributing to the growth of commuter flows to these regions as shown in Figure 7.4. To facilitate these growing flows, the capacity of transport infrastructure was increased, adding lanes to highways such as the A2 between Utrecht and Amsterdam and the A4 between Leiden and Amsterdam and increasing the frequency as well as the number of seats in intercity trains in the Randstad.

It should be noted that the majority of workers still work and live in the same urban region; indeed the largest group are those who live and work in the same municipality. In 1995–1999, this was 54% of the working force in the Netherlands, but since then this number declined to 46% (Ritsema van Eck and Hilbers, 2018). The second largest group are the people commuting from suburban municipalities to the central city in the same region. The relative size of this group is stable at 23% of the working population in the suburban areas, but there are large differences between locations. An interesting development is that some of the former growth centres have become less exclusively oriented to their original central city. For example, the share of commuters from Almere and Haarlemmermeer to Amsterdam has decreased, likewise the share of commuters from Zoetermeer to The Hague. These former growth centres, which have a relatively central location in the Randstad, have become more diversified in their commuting orientation. For example, commuting from Almere to Utrecht has increased as has commuting from Haarlemmermeer to Haarlem. Almere and Haarlemmermeer also saw a relatively large increase in jobs, leading to an increase in the share of the working population working in the own municipality, against the general trend of increasing commuting. Zoetermeer saw an increase in the share of commuters to Rotterdam, Leiden and Utrecht. In this way, these former growth centres have become new residential nodes in the emerging urban network at the scale of the Randstad.

Analyses of other functional relations outside commuting

In this section we have focused on commuting to work as one of the defining characteristics of the daily urban system. As has been argued, to counter the problem of multiplexity and to get a broader view of the functioning of the Randstad as an urban network, we should also look at other functional relations. We will therefore conclude with a brief look into travel to higher education, shopping trips and social visits.

Higher education (university and higher vocational education) is of course highly concentrated in the urban regions. It has also grown quite strongly since the 1990s from 170,000 students in the Randstad in 1995–1999 to

316,000 in 2012–2016. Here, as in the commute to work, we see an increase in the share of travel between the urban regions, from 15% to 18% of all students studying in the Randstad or from 17% to 21% of those living in the Randstad (Table 7.3). Although we will not speculate here on possible causes of this increase, it is worth mentioning that all students in higher education have a concessionary student travel card, also valid for national rail, as part of student finance arrangements.

Shopping covers a number of rather different activities, varying from the daily visit to the local baker or supermarket through the targeted search for a new car or new furniture to 'funshopping' as part of a day out to another city. The mobility surveys do not allow us to distinguish between these different kinds of shopping. Obviously, the data are dominated by the daily shopping for food. In as far as shopping trips between urban regions do show up, the numbers do not suggest a significant increase in their share (see Table 7.4).

Just as shopping, social visits include a wide range of activities from a quick cup of coffee with the neighbour next door to a multi-day stay with old friends or family in another part of the country. Interestingly, this is the only category where visits from the urban regions to elsewhere are more frequent than the other way around. This probably reflects the effect of people who moved to the Randstad for study or a career move and who still have a social or family network 'back home'. More relevant to the theme of this chapter is the share of social visits between urban regions, which increased slightly from 9% to 10%. This suggests that the Randstad is slowly becoming more

Table 7.3 Travel to higher education in the Randstad (×1,000's of students)

	1995–1999			2012–2016		
	Abs	*% Studying*	*% Living*	*Abs*	*% Studying*	*% Living*
Within urban regions	113	66	78	200	63	73
Between urban regions	25	15	17	58	18	21
From elsewhere to urban regions	33	19		58	18	
From urban regions to elsewhere	8		5	14		5
Total studying in urban regions	170	100		316	100	
Total living in urban regions	145		100	272		100

Source: Authors, based on data from OVG/OVIN mobility surveys and Statistics Netherlands (CBS).

Table 7.4 Shopping trips in the Randstad

	1995–1999		2012–2016	
	% Shopping	% Living	% Shopping	% Living
Within urban regions	94	95	93	94
Between urban regions	3	3	3	3
From elsewhere to urban regions	3		4	
From urban regions to elsewhere		3		3
Total shopping in urban regions	100		100	
Total living in urban regions		100		100

Source: Authors, based on data from OVG/OVIN mobility surveys.

Table 7.5 Social visits in the Randstad

	1995–1999		2012–2016	
	% Visiting	% Living	% Visiting	% Living
Within urban regions	81	79	78	77
Between urban regions	9	9	10	10
From elsewhere to urban regions	10		12	
From urban regions to elsewhere		12		13
Total visiting in urban regions	100		100	
Total living in urban regions		100		100

Source: Authors, based on data from OVG/OVIN mobility surveys.

important as a level of scale for social interaction as well as for more obvious activities such as work or education (see Table 7.5).

Conclusions

The Randstad was introduced as a planning concept in national spatial planning during the 1950s in order to formulate a more coherent policy for the urbanised polycentric western part of the Netherlands. The policy was aimed at controlling the process of urbanisation and preserving the polycentric character of the area, not at creating one large metropolis. In the course of time, the goals and instruments of national spatial planning have changed from controlling suburbanisation by means of growth centres during the 1960s and 1970s to strengthening the urban areas by a 'compact city' policy from the end of the 1980s onwards. In combination with economic and demographic developments, spatial planning tried to influence the urban form of the Randstad area and with that indirectly also the shape of urban networks. The analysis in the previous sections can be summarised in three conclusions.

First, the level of scale of the Randstad. The analyses of urban networks in the previous section indicate a slow growth of the importance of the Randstad as a whole. Commuting relations between urban regions have grown considerably. Over the last three or four decades new commuting flows between urban areas have been added and existing flows have grown. Developments in travel patterns for higher education and for social visits corroborate this pattern. The previous section gives some explanations for this development. It is hard to say in what way spatial planning has influenced this, apart from a possible general effect of the policy to strengthen the urban areas from the end of the 1980s onwards.

Second, there have been changes of position of some of the former growth centres in the urban network. Many of the growth centres started as 'satellite' municipalities in the urban region that is residential areas oriented to the large city. Over the last two decades, the largest former growth centres evolved from satellite cities to 'full-grown' nodes in the urban network having connections with different urban regions. Here, the influence of spatial planning is very plausible because of the decision in the 1960s to control suburbanisation by creating growth centres and then by facilitating their rapid growth. Also, during the 1990s the allocation of Vinex residential areas not only to the large cities but also to some of the former growth centres allowed them to continue their growth and to develop into more mature cities.

Third, the North Wing and especially the Amsterdam urban region within it, has grown in importance. This development was already observed in earlier research projects and corroborated in the analysis of commuting patterns between urban regions. The Amsterdam urban region shows a very strong growth in the number of jobs in combination with a slower pace of growth of the population. This is explained by the booming financial and service industries causing more commuting into the urban region. The spatial planning policy of restructuring inner city areas and allocating Vinex residential areas to the large cities might have facilitated part of the population growth, but clearly not enough to keep pace with job growth.

These conclusions are broadly unchanged since the RPB study (Ritsema van Eck *et al.*, 2006). Commuting flows between the urban regions of the Randstad have continued to grow, especially for the more highly educated part of the workforce. Clearly, an urban network is forming, with Amsterdam as its most important node. Still, 75% of the population in the Randstad lives and works in the same urban region, and for many activities the Randstad is not a relevant level of scale. The name *Randstad* suggests a single city (Dutch *stad*), or at least something that is broadly comparable to a monocentric, continuous urban area. However, the main strength of the urban network in the western part of the Netherlands is the diversity of its small and medium-sized cities, each with its own centre and its own identity, interspersed with natural and agricultural green areas but well connected by infrastructure and close enough to "borrow size" (Meijers and Burger, 2017). This structure of the Randstad area suited the ideas of the majority of spatial planners over the last six decades. For them, a future Dutch megalopolis was a nightmare. Rather than creating a coherent urban area, spatial planning has strengthened the polycentric character of the Randstad.

References

Aldridge, M. (1979). *The British New Towns: A Programme without a Policy*. Routledge and Kegan Paul, London.

Brand, A.D. (2012). *De wortels van de Randstad [The Roots of the Randstad]*; Overheidsinvloed en stedelijke hiërarchie in het westen van Nederland tussen de 13de en 20ste eeuw, PhD thesis TU Delft, A+BE 2012 #02. Faculty of Architecture and the Built Environment, Delft.

BSP and TU Delft (2009). *Evaluatie sleutelprojecten [Evaluation National Key Projects]*. Bureau Stedelijke Planning, Gouda.

Burger, M., Meijers, E. and Van Oort, F. (2014). 'Multiple Perspectives on Functional Coherence: Heterogeneity and Multiplexity in the Randstad', *TESG: Tijdschrift voor Economische en Sociale Geografie*, 105(4), 444–464.

Castells, M. (1996). *The Rise of the Network Society*. Blackwell, Cambridge MA.

De Gier, A.A.J. (2011). 'Kan het tij worden gekeerd?' [Could the Tide be Turned?]. In: *Essaybundel over de decentralisatie ruimtelijk beleid [A Collection of Essays about the Decentralisation of Spatial Planning]*. Raad voor de leefomgeving en infrastructuur, Den Haag, 3–12.

Desponds, D. and Auclair, E. (2017). 'The French New Towns 40 Years Later. New Dynamic Centralities or Suburbs Facing Risk of Marginalization?' *Urban Studies*, 54(4), 862–877.

Dieleman, F. and Musterd, S. (Eds) (1992). *The Randstad: A Research and Policy Laboratory*. Kluwer Academic Publishers, Dordrecht/Boston/London.

Faludi, A. and Van der Valk, A. (1994). *Rule and Order: Dutch Planning Doctrine in the Twentieth Century*. Kluwer Academic Publishers, Dordrecht/Boston/London.

Filarski, R. (2016). 'On the Right Track?' In: Arts, J., Filarski, R., Jeekel, H. and Toussaint, B. (Eds) *Builders and Planners*. Eburon, Utrecht, 279–343.

Flyvbjerg, B., Bruzelius, N. and Rothengatter, W. (2003). *Megaprojects and Risk; An Anatomy of Ambition*. Cambridge University Press, Cambridge.

Hall, P. (1966). *The World Cities*. Weidenfeld and Nicholson, London.

Jókövi, M., Boon, C. and Filius, F. (2006). *Woningproductie ten tijde van Vinex: Een verkenning [The Production of Homes during the Vinex Period: An Exploration]*. Den Haag/Rotterdam: Ruimtelijk Planbureau/NAi.

Korthals Altes, W.K. (2006). 'Stagnation in Housing Production: Another Success in the Dutch "planner's paradise?"' *Environment and Planning B: Urban Analytics and City Science*, 33(1), 97–114.

Lambregts, B. (2009). *The Polycentric Metropolis Unpacked: Concepts, Trends and Policy in the Randstad Holland*, PhD thesis, University of Amsterdam. Amsterdam institute for Metropolitan and International Development Studies (AMIDSt), Amsterdam.

Meijers, E.J. and Burger, M.J. (2017). 'Stretching the concept of 'borrowed size'', *Urban Studies*, 54(1), 269–291.

Ministerie van VRO (Volkshuisvesting en Ruimtelijke Ordening) (1966). *Tweede nota over de ruimtelijke ordening [Second Report on Spatial Planning]*. Staatsuitgeverij, The Hague.

Ministerie van VROM (Volkshuisvesting, Ruimtelijke Ordening en Milieubeheer) (1983). *Structuurschets Stedelijke Gebieden 1983 Deel a: Beleidsvoornemen [National Policy Strategy on Urban Areas 1983: Green Paper]*. Ministerie van VROM, The Hague.

Ministerie van VROM (Volkshuisvesting, Ruimtelijke Ordening en Milieubeheer) (1988). *Vierde nota over de ruimtelijke ordening, Deel a: Beleidsvoornemen [Fourth Report on Spatial Planning: Green Paper]*. SDU Uitgeverij, The Hague.

Ministerie van VROM (Volkshuisvesting, Ruimtelijke Ordening en Milieubeheer) (1990). *Vierde nota over de Ruimtelijke Ordening Extra, Deel 1: ontwerp-planologische kernbeslissing [Fourth Report on Spatial Planning Extra: Green Paper].* Ministerie van VROM, The Hague.

Ploeger, J. (2014). 'Evaluatie 20 jaar Infrastructuurfonds: het geplande wegenbouwprogramma is gerealiseerd' [20 Years Infrastructure Fund Evaluated: The Realisation of the Planned Road Construction Programma], *Tijdschrift Vervoerswetenschappen,* 50(3), 74–87.

Reijndorp, A., Bijlsma, L., Nio, I. and Van der Wouden, R. (2012). *Nieuwe steden in de Randstad [New Towns in the Randstad].* Planbureau voor de Leefomgeving, The Hague.

RIGO (2007). *Evaluatie verstedelijking VINEX 1995 tot 2005. Eindrapport [Evaluation of Urban Development VINEX 1994–2000. Final Report].* Ministerie van VROM (Volkshuisvesting, Ruimtelijke Ordening en Milieubeheer), The Hague.

Ritsema van Eck, J., Van Oort, F., Raspe, O., Daalhuizen, F. and Van Brussel, J. (2006). *Vele steden maken nog geen Randstad [Many Cities Do Not Make a Single Randstad].* Ruimtelijk Planbureau/ NAi Uitgevers, The Hague /Rotterdam.

Ritsema van Eck, J. and Hilbers, H. (2018). *De ene forens is de andere niet: een analyse van twee decennia woonwerkverplaatsingen [Every Commuter Is Different: An Analysis of Two Decades of Commuting],* Paper presented at Colloquium Vervoersplanologisch Speurwerk 2018, Amersfoort.

Spaans, M., Trip, J.J. and Van der Wouden, R. (2013). 'Evaluating the Impact of National Government Involvement in Local Development Projects in the Netherlands', *Cities,* 31, 29–36.

Tordoir, P. and Regioplan (2015). *De veranderende geografie van Nederland; De opgaven op mesoniveau [The Changing Geography of the Netherlands: The Challenges at Meso Level].* Regioplan, Amsterdam.

Tuppen, J.N. (1983). 'The Development of French New Towns: An Assessment of Progress', *Urban Studies,* 20(1), 11–30.

Van der Wouden, R. (Ed.) (2015). *De ruimtelijke metamorfose van Nederland 1988– 2015. Het tijdperk van de Vierde Nota [The Spatial Metamorphosis of the Netherlands 1988–2015. The Fourth Report Era].* Planbureau voor de Leefomgeving/nai010 Uitgevers, The Hague/Rotterdam.

Wagenaar, M. and Van Engelsdorp-Gastelaars, R. (1986). 'Het ontstaan van de Randstad' [The Origin of the Randstad], *KNAG Geografisch Tijdschrift,* 20(1), 14–29.

Werkcommissie Westen des Lands (1958). *De ontwikkeling van het Westen des lands: Rapport [The Development of the West of the Country: Advisory Report].* Staatsdrukkerij, The Hague.

Zonneveld, W. and Evers, D. (2014). 'Dutch National Spatial Planning at the End of an Era'. In: Reimer, M., Getimis, P. and Blotevogel, H. (Eds) *Spatial Planning Systems and Practices in Europe: A Comparative Perspective on Continuity and Change.* Routledge, New York/Oxon, 61–82.

8 The Randstad and its mainports

Towards new heterogeneous discourses in Dutch planning

Luuk Boelens and Wouter Jacobs

Introduction

Arguably one of the most successful planning concepts of the Dutch Randstad is the mainport Policy which began in the 1980s. This policy proposed national advocacy for economic growth through the support for the upgrading of the infrastructure of the port of Rotterdam and Amsterdam Schiphol Airport. This resulted in massive public-private investment strategies and an institutional 'stretching' of governance and regulatory arrangements (Notteboom *et al.*, 2013) through a powerful alliance of public and private actors. The policy can be considered a 'hegemonic discourse' because of its dominance as alternative visions were not supported. A spatial structure formed by a ring of middle-sized cities around a more or less non-urbanised green centre was originally regarded as the major feature of the 'Rim City' or Randstad (in Dutch). Van Lohuizen (1927) was the first to discover this rim-like structure of the Randstad. Sir Peter Hall (1966) included the Dutch Randstad in his seminal piece on *World Cities* (1966). His inclusion of this 'rim city ring', rather than the individual cities of Amsterdam, Rotterdam or The Hague, was not only driven by his appreciation of the Dutch polycentric urban planning practice of the time, but also by the economic realities of this urbanised region. To Hall, it was the sophistication of the commercial enterprise of the city of Amsterdam, in combination with the port of Rotterdam's mighty industrial complex and The Hague's public administration that rightfully gave the Randstad a status of 'world city'. In their turn, Dutch planners have subsequently hailed the Randstad concept, in conjunction with the 'Green Heart', as the defining concepts of national spatial planning and urban development policy (Faludi, 1989; Faludi and Van der Valk, 1994; Korthals Altes, 1995).

In the following decades however, policymakers and planners failed to convert these two concepts into more formalised territorial structures of polycentric metropolitan governance (De Boelens, 1994, 1996; De Boer, 1996; Salet *et al.*, 2003). After the aforementioned trio of cities (Amsterdam-Rotterdam-The Hague), the Randstad was soon extended towards a quartet or even quintet of cities (respectively including Utrecht and subsequently

Almere). Moreover by the 1990s, the Randstad idea was challenged by new and alternative planning concepts involving clusters of cities, including the Central Netherlands Urban Ring (which included five Brabant cities and the Arnhem-Nijmegen region), or the rather randomly chosen 13 national and regional urban nodes of the national *Fourth Report* (Ministerie van VROM, 1988; Ministerie van VROM, 1991) to be followed up by the 13 national and regional urban networks of the *Fifth Report*, which included in total no less than 65 cities and towns (Ministerie van VROM, 2001). Public attention and funds were subsequently divided amongst all. However, the municipalities involved failed to deliver a coordinated strategy towards a more or less complementary, efficient and coherent polycentric urban system.

Something similar happened with the idea of the Green Heart of the Randstad. Although in the early 1990s national government and the three Green Heart provinces agreed on a spatial strategy (Stuurgroep Groene Hart, 1992), a major controversy quickly emerged between the minister of spatial planning and the minister of infrastructure with regard to the routing of a proposed high-speed rail line between Amsterdam and Rotterdam, with the latter favouring a route through the Green Heart. This obviously shows the softness of the planning concept. After controversial decisions to expand (new) towns and horticultural complexes in the area, by 2012 national government dropped the Green Heart as a designated national landscape (Ministerie van I&M, 2012). This was despite the opposition of more than 100 civil society organisations with a million members, who joined forces in that year to save a national Green Heart policy. The policy has since been devolved to the three involved provincial authorities and their particular whims and fancies. The result is that the highly praised Green Heart policy and its hegemonic discourse have finally dissolved, despite wider support from agricultural and environmental lobbies and a broad range of policy actors in and outside the area (Hajer, 1995; Hajer and Versteeg, 2005).

The demise of the national Green Heart 'doctrine', leaves the mainport idea as the last and only hegemonic discourse for the Randstad. It has encouraged not only public, but also private funds to invest in, around and towards the main (logistic) nodes of the Randstad. Debates and policy on the effects of ongoing globalisation and further European integration are almost exclusively directed to the Randstad and the perceived virtues of its two mainports (Van der Cammen and De Klerk, 2012: 390, 398). Moreover, the discourse got support from a wide range of stakeholders and shareholders, mainly organised under the Holland Distribution Council (*Nederland Distributieland*). This coalition boosted the arrival of European headquarters and European distribution centres in and around both the Amsterdam Schiphol Airport and Port of Rotterdam areas (BCI, 1997). Furthermore, the concept of the mainport was invoked to gain political and financial support for major infrastructure projects, such as the aforementioned high speed rail line and the *Betuwe* rail freight route to Germany, a new runway for Schiphol airport and the expansion of the Rotterdam *Maasvlakte* (port facilities) into the

North Sea. After almost three decades of policy and billions of euros of investment, we can conclude that the mainport doctrine has shaped the spatial, economic and discursive contours of the Randstad and beyond like no other spatial concept has done throughout history. In many ways, the mainport as a policy construct became a 'hegemonic discourse' particularly throughout the 'roaring nineties', an era characterised by intense globalisation and Castells' recognition and influential views on the 'spaces of flows' in a networked society (1996).

However, in the 2010s and in particular since 2013, the mainport as a policy discourse and academic frame of reference has come under increased criticism (see Jacobs, 2007; Van Gils *et al.*, 2009; Kuipers and Manshanden, 2010; Huijs, 2011). For one thing, the world in which the mainport was designed to internationally compete had changed considerably. For example, when the policy was conceived ICT and the world wide web were still in their embryonic phase, and they have become to dominate the global economy. Another matter is how, also beyond the control of Dutch planners, the economic landscape of actors involved in the globalised distribution of freight and passengers has changed. In the early 1990s container handling in the port of Rotterdam was still dominated by the locally based Europe Container Terminals (ECT), the shipping line Nedlloyd (also Dutch) was still going strong, and within the aviation industry KLM alone pioneered the hub and spoke system from their home base of Amsterdam Schiphol Airport. Through mergers and acquisition and horizontal integration this local (or national) embeddedness of transport firms and logistics industries has changed drastically at the close of the century. ECT became part of the Hutchison Whampoa conglomerate, Nedlloyd merged with P&O which was then purchased by Maersk Line while, finally, KLM became part of the Air France group. Along with a further internationalisation of the Dutch champions of transport and logistics, the perception of the benefits of the notion of the mainport, in what was essentially a discursive frame to justify large scale infrastructure investments, also changed. For example, in 2016, the government Advisory Council for the Environment and Infrastructure published a report highly critical of the mainport discourse as guiding principle for the future (RLI, 2016).

In this chapter we first trace the political history of the notion of the mainport, from its conception into discourse and how it relates to our understanding of the Randstad. We embed this discussion in an understanding of the relational constitution of policy agendas and (social) networks on the one hand (see Boelens and De Roo, 2016), and on the other, literature about the positioning of ports within globalised and urbanised systems of flows and supply chains (for instance Jacobs and Lagendijk, 2014). The central question of this chapter is: *how can we understand the evolution of the mainport policy and what are the prospects for its renewal?* The second part of this question is more open, but we want to place the 'mainport' in a more normative policy discussion about the position of the Dutch economy and what its main infrastructure assets should be in a volatile, complex and uncertain world.

The origins of the mainport: from conception to evolving discourse(s)

Since the 1980s the national spatial-economic planning policy with regard to Randstad Holland has been very much interlinked with a so-called 'mainport' or 'gateway strategy'. Due to the oil crises of the 1970s, as elsewhere, Dutch businesses and policymakers were confronted with an acute need to transform the very foundations of the post-war industrial economy and welfare state. At the same time reflections on emerging post-industrial conditions on the impact of the ongoing 'globalisation of markets' became more significant (Touraine, 1969; Fröbel *et al.*, 1980; Levitt, 1983; Piore and Sabel, 1984; Massey, 1984). It became clear that the domestic-market of the Netherlands was too small to perform a dominant role in the growth of its economy. Dutch economies had to reinvent themselves more strategically within larger, cross-border networks. As such, the port of Rotterdam – the busiest in the world at the time – was regarded as a major asset in a networked spatial-economic strategy (Kreukels and Wever, 1998). In addition, Amsterdam Airport Schiphol was assigned to become a potential 'Gateway to Europe', to target above all trans-Atlantic and Japanese transfer passengers travelling to and from other destinations in Europe. The national airline (KLM) needed to expand its corporate business model in this respect, introducing long-haul flights connected to feeders for domestic and short-haul services. Its famous 'hub and spoke' operations entered the scene. Furthermore, the urban agglomerations of Amsterdam and Rotterdam, and later on the Randstad as a whole, needed to refocus their economic-spatial policies on the spin-off of these so-called hubs; specifically providing space for European headquarters and European distribution centres of Asian and US transnational corporations. The goal was to regain the prime trading position of both Amsterdam and Rotterdam in the advent of a single European Market. For its part, the national government needed to invest in so-called 'main hinterland connections' like the high-speed rail links towards London, Paris and Frankfurt and dedicated rail freight lines from the port of Rotterdam towards its German hinterland. This modal shift from road to rail traffic would also be congruent with a preliminary sustainability (or now we might call climate) agenda.

This programme was strongly outlined in the report *'Schiphol towards 2000'* (in translation) compiled by a high-level government advisory committee (*Commissie van der Zwan*, 1986) and a study by the National Spatial Planning Agency called (also in translation) *'Spatial Explorations of the Main Infrastructure'* (RPD, 1986). At about the same time, the emerging policy strategy resulted in the creation of a powerful public-private lobby: the 'Holland International Distribution Council'. This council included administrations at various levels of scale as well as representatives of the Dutch transport industry. It opted to 'reinforce the internationally competitive position of the Netherlands by revitalising the age-old Dutch trade competence to the needs of present-day society'. (NDL, 1987; authors' translation). The mainport policy was from the beginning essentially logistical and infrastructural by nature, although time and again some stressed the growing importance of a much wider approach by promoting planning concepts like the Airport City (De Jong, 2012: 65), Harbour City (Projectbureau Rotterdam Stadshavens, 2008), or Airport Corridor (Schaafsma *et al.*, 2008). This critical bias stemmed from the fact that the mainport policy was (financially) largely dependent on, and eventually became the prime responsibility of the Ministry of Transport, Public Works and Water Management (currently: Ministry of Infrastructure and Water Management) and not the ministry responsible for spatial planning or the Ministry of Economic Affairs.

However, Dutch (public) support for the hub and transit functions of the mainports continued to weaken, more so since 2010. The fifth runway of Airport Schiphol, inaugurated in 2003, did not result in less noise pollution, as was originally expected. It provoked an ongoing, but largely unsatisfactory discussion with local residents about such issues as landing and take-off procedures, fly zones, metrics related to the number of flights and compensatory measures (Huijs, 2011; De Jong, 2012). Moreover, despite major investments such as the high speed rail link to Brussels and beyond, a dedicated rail freight line to Germany and multimodal projects, road congestion accompanied by environmental pollution, has increased massively (see for instance CE Delft, 2009). On the other hand, the growth in benefits (in terms of the number of jobs and added value) did not meet these increased (environmental) burdens (Atzema *et al.*, 2009). Moreover, the tight socio-economic link between air and seaports and urban economic growth weakened. Economic benefits have often spilled over to other regions, whereas negative impacts are still localised in port areas (Notteboom and Rodrigue, 2005; OECD, 2014). Furthermore, Dutch transport and logistical companies lost ground to those from eastern Europe and other low wage countries (NEA, 2009). Although the trade of goods still contributes some 7% to the GDP of the Netherlands, the added value of import and exports steadily decreased from 13% to 11% during the first decade of the twenty-first century (Statistics Netherlands, 2012). In the meantime, the so-called 'brainports' seemed to perform more smartly and with greater economic returns (ICF, 2011). Against this backdrop, there arose an ongoing new discussion in Dutch policymaking asking if the focus on mainports should be maintained or if a change of focus towards the digital agenda or brainports was required (DINL, 2015; RLI, 2016).[1] Mainport protagonists responded to stress their importance for the Dutch economy (VNO-NCW, 2016), although acknowledging the changing context, there seems to be recognition of a need to adapt focus. One of the proposed innovations is to no longer focus exclusively on the impact of the air or seaports as such, but to include the greater sea or airport region (Kuipers, 2018). Accordingly, one does no longer speak about mainports or gateways as such, but about 'the Amsterdam effect', 'the Rotterdam-effect' or even the 'Antwerp effect' on Dutch economies. However, the main focus is still on (derived) port economics, or at least about logistics as an important component of the Dutch economy. Because data about direct and indirect employment or added value are 'black boxed' and hard to grasp, there is some uncertainty in evolving from a discussion about matters of fact, towards matters of concern (Latour, 2005). Therefore, in order to move beyond an unfruitful normative discussion about mainports or brainports or other planning concepts, we propose to return to the origin of the (at one time) hegemonic mainport discourse, with help from new academic insights and propositions.

Beyond fixed concepts

Hajer and Versteeg (2005) define a discourse as 'an ensemble of ideas, concepts and categories through which meaning is given to social and physical phenomena, and which is produced and reproduced through an identifiable set of practices'. A hegemonic discourse would therefore relate to an at one time dominant set of ideas, which could penetrate other discourses and mould them so these match the prime discourse, therefore influencing real and multiple (investment) decisions. These decisions are as such the outcome of hegemonic discourses and thus regarded as socially constructed phenomena. In this sense, the mainport discourse indeed started with major deliberations of prominent Dutch transnational corporations (KLM, Philips, amongst others). This coincided with a neoliberal government agenda of 'work, work, work' at the time (the 1982–1986 Administration of Lubbers), which resulted in the establishment of a public-private think-tank, the *Van der Zwan* Committee introduced above. This coincided with new strategic and conceptually driven investment programmes by the ministries responsible for spatial planning (RPD, 1986) and infrastructure including the Dutch railways (the Rail 21 programme from 1987). This kind of thinking and acting was laid down in the 1988 Fourth Report on Spatial Planning (Ministerie van VROM, 1988) and in the 1988 Second Report on Traffic and Transport (Ministerie van V&W, 1988). All these interrelated actions established a discourse, which developed its own argumentative rationality, and remained dominant over a number of decades through, amongst others, a very effective lobby by the Holland Distribution Council and a number of newly established university spin offs, which reproduced and enlarged the discourse time and again.

This hegemonic policy discourse represents a highly relational, co-evolutionary understanding of planning and governance (Foucault, 1980; Massey, 1992; Gutting, 2003; Doel, 1999). For relational theorists planning concepts are not so much related to an exclusive, classical (Euclidean or Cartesian) topographical approach of planning, rather with a topological one (Murdoch, 2006). Whilst topography would focus on detailed analyses or descriptions of particular places to mark them as different from other places, topology would focus on the relations between these places (the 'hardware'), their specific uses over time (the 'software') and how they are organised (the 'orgware') in order to say something useful about their quality or efficiency.

This is particularly the case for logistical hubs and industrial districts or clusters, that are expected to enhance a so-called local buzz in global pipelines (Bathelt and Glückler, 2002; Markussen, 1996). More in general, relational theorists regard 'space' not just as a pre-given platform for action, but as a multiply combined feature, which is shaped and reproduced by multiple actors and entities, who are 'reshaped' in return (Belsey 2002, Massey, 2005). In topology therefore, volatile and changing interactions define the identity of a place and therefore enable the study of processes of spatial emergence and the arrival of new planning concepts, possibly to be regarded as hegemonic discourse. Spaces would be shaped by discourse, in the sense that discursive conventions become 'enshrined' in hegemonic and/or micro spaces (Foucault, 1972). Crucial for relational theorists is the idea that we should try to move beyond (what they call) 'contained spaces', which are pre-given, absolute and seen as a platform for action or confined for specific or predetermined purposes (as in zoning). Instead, there is a need to conceptualise space as 'socially produced sets of manifolds' (Crang and Thrift, 2000) to include not only the topography of space itself, but also the specific soft- and orgware evolutions over time. Planning concepts must be seen as indefinite; 'they must be open, adaptive and fluid, and their main purpose would be to *resonate* to changing circumstances, ideas and needs, instead of *represent* a specific purpose or interest' (Thrift, 1998).

According to this relational understanding of governance and planning, the mainport or gateway idea became not only driven by leading and conscious (human) actors over time, but was also sustained by factors of importance (such as reports, statistics, earnings and economic progress) and institutional innovations, like policies, investment programmes and specific organisations. Here leading actors, factors of importance and (formal or informal) institutional settings co-evolve within a specific discursive system, if possible (inter)mediated by planning concepts, which would resonate in return (see Figure 8.1). Throughout history mainport actors, factors and institutions in evolving spatio-temporal situations have indeed (re)constituted each other towards an interactive, affirmative hegemonic discourse. In the beginning such a discourse is essentially horizontal or flat; whilst structure and power relations evolve in an (inter)relational way over time. A flat relational approach would also mean that the hegemonic discourse is never finished but always (co-)evolving in volatile and changing settings, actors and/or institutional innovations alike. It could even go into the opposite or various directions, depending on the multiple and changing actors, factors or institutional innovations involved.

Against this backdrop, it is of main importance to 'track and trace' the relational networks of (socio-) economic assemblages, in order to get a better understanding of the future socio-economic policies. In reference to our present plural, complex and volatile world, without any centre or apex, these policies are fuzzy and may go in many directions. To remain with the old ideas of mainports or the Randstad as such (see for instance Ministerie van

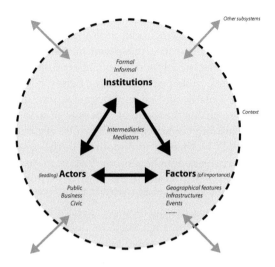

Figure 8.1 Scheme actor-relational approach of planning.
Source: Own illustration.

I&M *et al*, 2011), or to have them countervailed by concepts such as brain-ports (RLI, 2016) does not seem to be very fruitful in this respect, since there is also a lot of interaction between mainports and brainports, as we shall argue below. Therefore, we have to refocus instead on the core, that is emergent actor–networks, in order to understand whether they could or would become hegemonic or not. Although in these affairs planners could also take a medi-ating (moving information from one to the other) or intermediate (bringing partners together in old or new crossovers) role, only in this way we can achieve effective and fruitful planning in volatile and plural worlds. We will analyse some of these possible 'directions in the making', in order to return to what that could mean for the concepts of mainport and the Randstad.

The Metropolitan Region Amsterdam 'on the move'

Schiphol's aviation, which also includes Rotterdam The Hague and Eind-hoven airports (owned by the Schiphol group) has grown to some 80 million passengers, nearly 550,000 aircraft movements and more than 325 destina-tions. However, the operational results of Schiphol's logistic services have remained more or less constant, and even turned into a loss in recent years (see Figure 8.2). In its place, the returns from exploitation of Schiphol's con-sumers, real estate and participation businesses have almost tripled, from €146 million in 2010 to €406 million in 2018. Consumers and real estate account for almost 100% of the operational results of the Schiphol Group.[2] In terms of profit, Schiphol's spin-offs have therefore become far more important than its logistical core-business. Although some would claim that these spin-offs

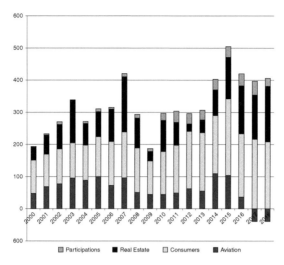

Figure 8.2 Operational results of the Schiphol Group 2000–2018.
Source: Own illustration based upon data from annual reports of the (Royal) Schiphol Group.

would not be possible without massive logistic operations, like a gas station would not sell consumer products without any petrol (Schaafsma *et al.*, 2008), these developments also make clear that the old mainport-discourse has seen its day. At the end of the 1980s the Schiphol Group, as one of the first across the globe, moved towards an Airport City concept (De Wijn, 2013). This means that the Group would not only focus on its hub position and airside connections, but also on its potential for socio-economic interaction and urban development, driven by a strategy to increase non-aviation revenues and the spin offs from its land side accessibility. By the 2000s, due to landside restrictions and other constraints, the Group moved even further towards a discourse of a so-called Metropolitan Airport Region (Schaafsma, 2012). It proposed to integrate its airport strategy into the regional-economic strategy of the so-called Metropolitan Region Amsterdam (MRA).[3] This was backed up by new (sub)concepts like airport corridor, smart accessibility, business clusters and 'borrowed size', the latter in relation to other booming areas in the Netherlands (Raspe, 2014; De Groot *et al.*, 2017). It would also be congruent with the ideas mentioned before, in particular the Amsterdam-effect on Dutch economic welfare. By the end of the 2010s, these ideas even stretched over to the whole of western Europe, towards London, Paris and Frankfurt, in order to secure the prime 'springboard location' of Schiphol within this European urban network, the strategy of *Enter NL* (Kernteam Kerncorridor Schiphol-Amsterdam, 2017, see Figure 8.3).

The main question is whether all these ideas would or could serve as a new hegemonic discourse: a so-called Mainport 2.0 discourse? To cut a long story short: the pace, variation and most importantly, one-dimensional message in which all these ideas operate, suggests that all these ideas remain just what

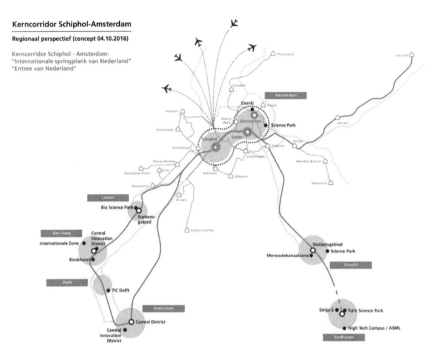

Figure 8.3 New operational concept for Schiphol.
Source: MUST.

they are: ideas. The ideas represent a specific interest – aviation economics – and do not resonate towards a self-organising and re-affirmative discourse that could lead civic, public and business actors, and which would be highly important for genuine institutional innovation. Moreover, the final result so far – the so-called prime 'springboard location' of Schiphol – implies that we have moved back almost 35 years ago when the gateway prefix of Schiphol was invented.

Nevertheless, when we analyse the debates about all these ideas more profoundly, we can also discover some (fragile) 'seeds' indicating a kind of novel discourse, beyond just a gateway or mainport prefix. The first one is that the largest governing political party in the municipal council of Amsterdam (GroenLinks or GreenLeft) could agree to an extension of the new north-south metro-line towards Schiphol – and subsequent business development along this corridor – in exchange for a massive reduction of aircraft movements.[4] Another seed is the request of leading firms in the Brainport Eindhoven region (ASML, and VDL for a part) to invest in a new high-speed rail link from Schiphol to the Rhein-Ruhr Area through Eindhoven; not only to enlarge the catchment area of Schiphol itself, but also to enhance the accessibility of the Eindhoven region and therefore enlarge its area to recruit high-skilled workers. This however should go hand in hand with a reduction of short-haul flights and thus, climate mitigation.[5] A third seed is the plea to avoid an overall concentration of promising business clusters in one major airport corridor (one can think of multimodal nodes, central business districts, innovation quarters and creative neighbourhoods for example), but instead to have a more open eye for the wide variation of related businesses and the surroundings in which they flourish (Atzema *et al.* 2011). Regarded from this angle, even Rotterdam could become an integrated part of the Metropolitan Region Amsterdam as indicated by recent spillover effects of the Dutch capital (StartupBlink, 2019). Additionally, national government and local administrations could make real progress with the various roundtables involving citizens in the wider Schiphol area and environmental interest groups, rather than selective redistribution of non-mainport aviation to other airports in order to meet opportunities for growth: still growing but now with a lesser pace (Royal Schiphol Group, 2016).

Until now each of these seeds has not rooted. Leading actors themselves or even possible intermediaries (like designers, planners or academics) seem reluctant or inactive at best. Seeds seem to be thrown out and blown away, without any real endeavour to back them up with additional research, focussed roundtables or proposals for institutional innovations, which, in turn, could attract new stakeholders and so on. In terms of actor-network-theory the more open and inviting seeds (than those introduced above) stay within the phase of problematisation, without moving towards mutual 'intéressement' or organisational enrolment. What is more, even if those 'translations' happen and planners would indeed mediate towards that effect, it would make no sense to mould each of these ideas again into one new mainport discourse. Rather it would be more effective to focus on more specified and multifarious discourses in order to stay in pace with the plural, dynamic and volatile interests in that respect and deliver assemblages and investment strategies that could work. Therefore, we could even wonder if there would still be a need for a quest towards a new mainport concept, or that we need to strive to various more open and resonating discourses with focused interrelational actors-factors-institutions in question.

A new conceptualisation of mainport Rotterdam

The planning and construction of Maasvlakte II (2008–2013), next to the construction of the dedicated freight (Betuwe) rail line (1997–2007), are probably the final outcomes of the traditional Rotterdam mainport discourse. In this discourse, competition with the ports of Antwerp and Hamburg was always deliberately invoked to address a sense of urgency in a world of ever-increasing flow of containerised transport primarily from Asia carried on ever larger vessels in need of equally sized port facilities. The required investments were justified by many studies on the direct and indirect economic impact of the Rotterdam port in terms of added value and employment for the Netherlands.

However, with the formal planning decision to build the Maasvlakte II, paradoxically the need to narrate the mainport story in policy circles became less: the goal was achieved so to speak. Perhaps more importantly, the global economic crisis of 2008 also generated a momentum that infrastructure planning purely based upon forecasts of throughputs has its limitations and re-orientation on resilience, scenario planning and complexity is required. Even the Port of Rotterdam Authority itself has stopped referring to mainport, even before the publication in 2016 of the critical report from the government advisory Council for the Environment and Infrastructure mentioned above. By 2011, *Port Compass*, the 2030 vision of the Port of Rotterdam Authority (2011) makes little reference to the idea of mainport. Rather, the port is defined at that moment as an industrial cluster and a global hub, referring to its still massively important oil refining and petrochemical industry, and its position as a major hub in containerised global supply chains. However, the business environment continued to change, rapidly, and with it the mainport discourse in a traditional sense lost appeal even among its former protagonists.

A key example of changing positions is the Rotterdam Port Authority. With the appointment of the new CEO, former vice president of Environment of Royal Dutch Shell, Allard Castelein, the port authority has shifted its attention away from port expansion and infrastructure planning towards *transition*. As one of the largest CO^2 emitters in Europe and a port economy largely driven by fossil fuels, the sustainable future of the port in the medium and long-term is seriously at stake. Managing the energy transition is a formidable task, but which also creates equal opportunities for innovation. At the end of the 2010s attention seems to be predominantly focussed on climate mitigation and the required contribution to the 2015 Paris Agreement (Wuppertal Institute, 2016). Moreover, large parts of the port area (almost one-third of the total) are still occupied by traditional oil refineries, petrochemical installations and coal-fired power plants. In addition, the Port Authority also sees itself confronted with the digitalisation of supply chains. Disruptive tech-giants Amazon and Alibaba are now calling the shots in the world of logistics with more traditional players in ocean-based freight such as Maersk, MSC, Hutchison-Whampoa struggling to keep up with change.

In such a dynamic context driven by innovation, digitalisation and energy transition, the presence nearby of a post-urbanised economy becomes a blessing in disguise (Hall and Jacobs, 2012), as it will allow for dynamic urbanisation externalities to unfold (Jacobs, 1969; Glaeser et al, 1992; Glaeser, 2011). It is through a diverse, but related set of industries within urbanised regions that 'new combinations' will emerge and generate prospects for renewal, adaptation and transformation of the economy. After years of functional, spatial, institutional and discursive separation of the port and city, there is again a prospect, and indeed a necessity, to realign ports with their host cities beyond mere planning and real estate led waterfront transformations (Hall, 2007; Hesse, 2010; Hall & Jacobs, 2012; Van den Berghe *et al*, 2018). This also implies that urban, regional and port stakeholders and the economic interests connected with globalised networks of flows and production (global terminal operators, shipping lines, refining and storage companies) have a direct stake and gain in sustainable, technologically driven transitions of the port and therefore need to strategically couple agendas, investment strategies and assets across territorial scales and along various networks.

After the corporatisation of the port authority in 2006, the city government for its part struggled for a number of years to develop a significant and coherent policy on the port economy beyond the often conflicting claims with the port authority on waterfront redevelopment in the area known as Cityports or *Stadshavens* (see for example Daamen, 2010). Although waterfront development continues to be a planning concern and still remains often a source of conflict between the port authority and the city (the latter the majority shareholder in the Port of Rotterdam Authority), more strategic and relational thinking emerged that focuses more on the urban dimension of port economies. Two prime examples can be given.

First, a series of studies demonstrates how Rotterdam is at the top of the international league as a *world port city* (Jacobs, 2009; Jacobs, Ducruet and De Langen, 2010; OECD, 2014), as an *international shipping centre* (various annual Baltic-Xinhua shipping reports) and as one of the *leading maritime capitals of the word* (Menon, 2015). This resulted in an increased awareness among city policymakers that Rotterdam does offer unique location factors for port-related businesses and foreign direct investment, beyond the pure operational ones offered in the port itself. Maritime business services, such as ship finance, marine insurance and specific international trade related law and customs practices are well represented in Rotterdam. These maritime business services play an important role in the wider economic ecosystem through their customisation and commodification of business solutions and their diffusion among operational clients locally as well as internationally (Jacobs, 2009). Moreover, the presence of these types of services is foundational to attracting European headquarters specialised in shipping and logistics, rather than pure European distribution centres that tend to locate in hinterlands. Indeed, as suggested by Hall and Jacobs (2012), policymakers in port cities should focus on this dynamic interplay between locally present port logistic operations, maritime business services and start-up communities. From this perspective transactions with a local, urbanised, but international orientated maritime business ecosystem needs to be recognised as one of the core foci of the port authority's vision and ambition (Kuipers, 2018; Port of Rotterdam Authority, 2011).

Second, in terms of energy transition and digitalisation, the municipality together with the wider metropolitan region and stakeholders (most notably, the port authority itself) offered a *Roadmap for the Next Economy* in a report presented by TIR Consulting Group led by Jeremy Rifkin (TIR Consulting Group, 2016). This report makes a plea for digital innovation and entrepreneurial activities related to sustainable shipping, maritime-based logistics and the transition of the port-industrial complex embedded within the wider metropolitan region. Rotterdam is not Amsterdam, Silicon Valley, Berlin or Tel Aviv but, it does host one of the world's largest concentrations of logistics operations. In this respect, in 2015 the Port Authority and the city government took the initiative to launch *PortXL*, an incubator for start-ups in the maritime and port logistics industries (Witte *et al.*, 2018). Numerous other initiatives have been taken, such as *Blocklab*, *YesDelft!*, *iTanks*, and *Smartport*, driven by an ecosystem approach and a 'coalition of the willing'. These initiatives are all directed towards a renewed thinking about how urban-based, maritime-based port economies function in the creation of smart, sustainable added-value in specialised but often highly internationalised logistics networks.

The various initiatives have already culminated in a mutual *Maritime Capital of Europe Agenda* endorsed by the Rotterdam Maritime Board that represents executives from the wider port community in order to create momentum for Rotterdam as a dynamic port-city ecosystem. By 2019, this had not resulted into a new hegemonic discourse for actions and investments. Much like the case of Schiphol Amsterdam and looking at the diversity of the initiatives mentioned above, we could question whether that would be at all possible. Given the comprehensiveness of the transition, digitalisation and innovation mentioned above, and given the heterogeneity of actors involved it would already be an enormous task to develop meaningful and decisive differential discourses, each with their own (socio-economic) conceptual focus and organisation. Furthermore, as Atzema *et al.* (2009) have pointed out, the new challenges would need a novel institutional layout and revenue models for the port authority, beyond the present landlord business model with its revenues based upon the number of port calls (tariffs) and land rents (Van der Lugt *et al.*, 2015). In order to effectively enhance co-evolutionary transitions from industrial clusters towards innovative socio-economic networks, there is a need for specific co-siting (physically), co-sourcing (materially) and co-flowing (networked) strategies, with each having its own institutional layout. These cannot be moulded into one single hegemonic discourse; but at best may lead to several heterogeneous ones under the umbrella of a mutual, but highly open agenda.

Conclusion: beyond the Randstad

In the context of contemporary challenges of networked economies, there is a real need for a rearrangement of existing planning discourses in a conceptual, actor-relational and institutional sense. Given the widespread opposition against mainports and its fuzzy and heterogeneous impact, the (global) 'stretched actors' involved and added to this the new ICT and plural socio-economic (institutional) settings, the concept of mainports as pure logistics turntables run by the Ministry of Infrastructure and Water Management has no longer any meaning. In the foreseeable future there will not be any new (third) extension of the Rotterdam port area in the sea, nor a sixth runway of Schiphol or an extensive (and expensive) transnational European hinterland connection, even if this would be worth pursuing in a post-climate world. At the end growth is indeed constrained, re-use is the future mantra as underlined in a string of reports by the Club of Rome from the seventies onwards. What is more, the debate about mainports is going in various directions, and the opportunities of these debates are hardly sufficiently supported by leading stakeholders and shareholders. There are new strands emerging, but they need further elaboration. Moreover, what has become clear is that we can no longer speak of one old or even a new hegemonic mainport discourse, on one or two locations, but that there are possibly many in various constellations and in several (connected) places. Furthermore, it suggests that the mainport (or even the Randstad as such) is not so much upheld anymore by one central ideology or planning concept, but rather by subtler horizontal assemblages of reciprocal actors, factors and institutions in the making, which are constituted by specific (co)evolving networks, rather than by specific actors or strategic concepts. If we would agree on this, that would mean a major reorientation and concentration of attention of not only the leading stakeholders themselves, but also of planners and contributing organisations such as universities, research institutes and interest groups. Instead of defending one or another great idea, it would need a refocus on the real issues at hand.

This kind of reorientation does not restrict itself to the mainports as such, but touches also upon the Randstad discourse and the need for a reinvention of spatial planning altogether. Confronted with the fuzzy, fragmented, cross-scaling and hardly predictable firm- or actor-network constellations, the Randstad concept has become redundant or even hopelessly out-dated. Although its geographic boundaries have never been fixed and its core idea fuzzy from the start (with the drawing of Van Lohuizen in 1927), the Randstad as a planning model is still too Cartesian to cope with the global or continental deliberations of the (sea/air) port operators on the one hand, or the more precise co-evolutionary deliberations of new innovative firm networks on the other. Instead, there is every reason to develop a fundamentally new kind of planning strategy, which would be more open to the dynamic, volatile and networked challenges of the co-evolutionary economic strategies mentioned before. In the words of relational theorists like Thrift (1998) there is a need for a Randstad concept that would be open, fluid and adaptive to changing circumstances and thereby probably plural and provisional in its content. Although that might sound too vague for decisive and straightforward politicians and policymakers, in fact that has always been the case in delta areas such as the Rhine, Meuse and Scheldt Delta ('Eurodelta'). This is because traditionally in deltas there is always a subtle interaction between prominent actors and the changing circumstances of tide, flood, geographical conditions and cyclical changes (Schuyt and Taverne, 2004; see Brand as well as Meyer elsewhere in this volume). Moreover, for survival urban dwellers in deltas (like the Eurodelta) have relied not so much on sovereigns or on central authorities, but on cooperation between peers, both in projects to strengthen dikes and the coast, and to construct land- and waterways, and in the organisation and maintenance of military defence, social and religious questions and economic welfare. This was the source for continuous, dynamic and resilient prosperity through the ages (Boelens and Taverne, 2011).

Referring to the persistent lock-ins discussed above, there is every reason to reorientate the age-old adaptive delta-culture in a modern way. Conceptually that would mean moving beyond generic concepts and planning models as such, and to orientate more precisely towards the multifaceted and multilayered mainport challenges of related variety, which are sometimes embedded, but mostly networked in a more open and dynamic sense, breaking with the constraint of one single kind of planning concept. Actor-relationally that would mean that we would have to concentrate on promising and resilient alliances between various stakeholders (businesses, governments, research institutions and the like) on specific themes and interests. Factor-wise it would mean enhancing new ideas beyond growth towards adaptive re-use and reinventing prosperity. Institutionally there is a need to re-discover the age-old governance of common pool resources, with its focus on specific goals and ambitions, whereby the outcomes are highly dependent on the actions of all resource users. Those more open, thematic and cross-border common pool resources would not fit in the classic mainport landlord-model. Instead, it would need highly dynamic and adaptive associative rules, laws, norms and sets of action, within an overall multi-fractured, but relational idea of metropolitan delta-regions.

Notes

1 See also Steltman, spokesman of the DiNL, the foundation which supports the notions of The Netherlands as a digital mainport (https://dutchitchannel. nl/611201/michiel-steltman-lsquo-we-hebben-impact-maar-zoeken-meer-slagkracht-rsquo.html, accessed 1 July 2020).
2 Annual Reports Schiphol Group 2000–2018.
3 MRA is a self-organised informal cooperation body of local and regional authorities in the northern part of the Randstad. Participants are 32 municipalities, the provinces of North Holland and Flevoland and Transport Authority Amsterdam (see Chapter 12).
4 Het Parool, 18 October 2018.
5 Computable 19 March 2018; De Telegraaf 18 January 2017.

References

Atzema, O., Boelens, L. and Veldman, B. (2009). *Voorbij de Lock-In [Beyond lock-in];* Een economisch institutionele herpositionering van de Rotterdamse haven. Universiteit Utrecht/ Strategem Group, Utrecht/The Hague.

Atzema, O., Goorts, A. and De Groot, C. (2011). *The Amsterdam family of clusters*; Economisch geografische relaties van elf bedrijvenclusters in de Metropoolregio Amsterdam, in opdracht van Bestuursforum Schiphol. Utrecht University Repository, Utrecht.

Bathelt, H. and Glückler, J. (2002). *Wirtschaftsgeographie [Economic geography]*; Ökonomische Beziehungen in räumlicher Perspektive, 2. korrigierte Auflage. Verlag Eugen Ulmer, Stuttgart.

BCI, Buck Consultants International (1997). *Europese distributie en waardetoevoeging door buitenlandse bedrijven [European distribution and added value by foreign companies]*. BCI, Nijmegen.

Belsey, C. (2002). *Poststructuralism; A very short introduction*. Oxford University Press, Oxford.

Boelens, L. (1994). 'De patroonloosheid van de Randstad; het probleem van de gespleten werelden'. In: Agricola, E. (Ed.) *Archipolis, over de grenzen van architectuur [Archipolis, about the borders of architecture]*. Delft, Eburon, 121–140.

Boelens, L. (1996). 'Randstad Holland: zijn nieuwe opgave en nieuwe onoverzichtelijkheid', *Archis*, 1, 66–80.

Boelens, L. and De Roo, G. (2016). 'Planning of undefined becoming: First encounters of planners beyond the plan', *Planning Theory*, 15(1), 42–67.

Boelens, L. and Taverne, E. (2011). 'A tale of two metropoles – In search of the historic DNA of the Eurodelta'. In: Lucassen, L. and Willems, W. (Eds.) *Why people want to live in cities*. Routledge, London/New York, 192–215.

Castells, M. (1996). *The rise of the network society*. Blackwell, Cambridge MA.

CE Delft (2009). *Are trucks taking their toll? The environmental, safety and congestion impacts of lorries in the EU*. CE Delft, Delft.

Commissie van der Zwan (1986). *Schiphol naar het jaar 2000 [Schiphol towards the year 2000]*. Commissie van der Zwan, Amsterdam.

Crang, M. and Thrift, N. (Eds.) (2000). *Thinking space*. Routledge, London.

Daamen, T. (2010). *Strategy as force; Towards effective strategies for urban development projects – The case of Rotterdam Cityports*, PhD thesis TU Delft. IOS Press, Amsterdam.

De Boer, N. (1996). *De Randstad bestaat niet: De onmacht tot grootstedelijk beleid [The Randstad does not exist: The failure to pursue a metropolitan policy']*. NAi Uitgevers, Rotterdam.

De Groot, H., Van Oort, F. and Smit, M.J. (2017). *Synergies between metropolitan, agglomeration, infrastructure and network policies in urban Europe: The case of the Lower Rhine Region*. Utrecht University Repository, Utrecht.

De Jong, B. (2012). *The Airport assembled*; Rethinking planning and policy making of Amsterdam Airport Schiphol by using the Actor-Network Theory, PhD thesis Utrecht University. Eburon, Delft.

De Wijn, J.W. (2013). 'City centre led to airport city. Jan Benthem architect at Schiphol, interviewed by Jan Willem de Wijn'. In: Bosma, K. (Ed.) *Megastructure Schiphol; Design in spectacular simplicity*. NAi010 Publishers, Rotterdam, 130–131.

DINL, Stichting Digitale Infrastructuur Nederland (2015). *Nederland als digitale mainport [The Netherlands as digital mainport]*; Position paper. DINL, Leidschendam.

Doel, M. (1999). *Poststructuralist geographies; The diabolical art of spatial science*. Edinburgh University Press, Edinburgh.

Ministerie van I&M (Infrastructuur en Milieu), Ministerie van Economische Zaken, Landbouw en Innovatie, Provincie Noord-Brabant, Provincie Zeeland, Provincie Zuid-Holland, Regio West-Brabant, Stadsregio Rotterdam, Drechtsteden (2011). *Dynamische Delta 2020–2040 [Dynamic delta 2020–2040]*; Visie en Afsprakenkader

MIRT-VAR, Meerjarenprogramma Infrastructuur, Ruimte & Transport (MIRT), Verkenning Antwerpen Rotterdam (VAR). Ministerie van I&M *et al*, s.l.

Faludi, A. (Ed.) (1989). 'Theme: Keeping the Netherlands in shape', *Built Environment*, 15(3), 5–64.

Faludi, A. and Van der Valk, A. (1994). *Rule and order – Dutch planning doctrine in the twentieth century*. Kluwer Academic Publishers, Dordrecht/Boston/London.

Foucault, M. (1972). *The archaeology of knowledge*. Pantheon Books, New York.

Foucault, M. (1980). *Power/knowledge; Selected interviews and other writings 1972–1977*. Pantheon Books, New York.

Fröbel, F., Heinrichs, J. and Kreye, O. (1980). *The new international division of labour; Structural unemployment in industrialised countries and industrialisation in developing countries*. Cambridge University Press, Cambridge.

Glaeser, E.L. (2011). *Triumph of the city; How are greatest invention makes us richer, smarter, greener, healthier and happier*. Macmillan, London.

Glaeser E.L., Kallal, H.D., Scheinkman, J.A. and Shleifer, A. (1992). 'Growth in cities', *Journal of Political Economy*, 100(6), 1126–1152.

Gutting, G. (Ed.) (2003). *The Cambridge companion to Foucault*. Cambridge University Press, Cambridge.

Hajer, M. (1995). *The politics of environmental discourse; Ecological modernization and the policy process*. Clarendon Press, Oxford.

Hajer, M. and Versteeg, W. (2005). 'A decade of discourse analysis of environmental politics: Achievements, challenges, perspectives', *Journal of Environmental Policy & Planning*, 7(3), 175–184.

Hall. P. (1966). *The world cities*. Weidenfeld & Nicolson, London.

Hall, P.V. (2007). 'Seaports, urban sustainability, and paradigm shift', *Journal of Urban Technology* 14(2), 87–101.

Hall, P.V. and Jacobs, W. (2012). 'Why are maritime ports (still) urban and why should policymakers care?' *Maritime Policy & Management*, 39(2), 189–206.

Hesse, M. (2010). 'Cities, material flows and the geography of spatial interaction: Urban places in the system of chains', *Global Networks*, 10(1), 75–91.

Huijs, M. (2011). *Building castles in the (Dutch) air: Understanding the policy deadlock of Amsterdam Airport Schiphol 1989–2009*, PhD thesis TU Delft. TU Delft repository, Delft.

ICF, Intelligent Communication Forum (2011). 'Brainport is the smartest region of the world', *Digital Dingle Market*, news article 3 June 2011.

Jacobs, J. (1969). *The economy of cities*. Vintage Books, New York.

Jacobs, W. (2007). *The political economy of Port competition. Institutional analyses of Rotterdam, Southern California and Dubai*. PhD thesis, Radboud University, Nijmegen. Academic Press Europe, Nijmegen.

Jacobs, W. (2009). *World Port city networks. Exploring the geography of advanced services in the global shipping industry*. Erasmus University, Rotterdam.

Jacobs, W., Ducruet, C. and De Langen, P. (2010). 'Integrating world cities into production networks, the case of port cities', *Global Networks*, 10(1), 92–113.

Jacobs, W. and Lagendijk, A. (2014). 'Strategic coupling as capacity. How seaports connect to global flows of containerized transport', *Global Networks*, 14(1), 44–62.

Kernteam Kerncorridor Schiphol-Amsterdam (2017). *Enter [NL] – Internationale Entree van Nederland [Enter NL; International entry of the Netherlands]*. Gemeente Amsterdam, Amsterdam.

Korthals Altes, W. (1995). *De Nederlandse planning doctrine in het fin de siècle [The Dutch planning doctrine at the turn of the century]*; Voorbereiding en doorwerking van de Vierde nota over de ruimtelijke ordening (extra), PhD thesis University of Amsterdam. Van Gorcum, Assen.

Kreukels, A. and Wever, E. (Eds) (1998). *North sea ports in transition: Changing tides.* Van Gorcum, Assen.

Kuipers, B. and Manshanden, W. (2010). *Van mainport naar wereldstadhaven [From mainport to world city port]*; Belang en betekenis van mainports in 2040 voor de Nederlandse economie, Onderzoek in opdracht van het Ministerie van Verkeer& Waterstaat. Erasmus Universiteit Rotterdam/ TNO, Rotterdam/ Delft.

Kuipers, B. (2018). *Het Rotterdam effect [The Rotterdam effect];* De impact van mainport Rotterdam op de Nederlandse Economie (with the cooperation of Van der Lugt, L., Jacobs, W., Streng, M., Jansen, M. and Van Haaren, J). Erasmus Centre for Urban, Port and Transport Economics (Erasmus UPT), Erasmus Universiteit, Rotterdam.

Latour, B. (2005). *Reassembling the social; An introduction to actor-network-theory.* Oxford University Press, Oxford.

Levitt, T. (1983). 'The globalization of markets', *Harvard Business Review*, 61, 307–318.

Markussen, A. (1996). 'Sticky places in slippery space: A typology of industrial districts', *Economic Geography*, 72(3), 293–313.

Massey, D. (1984). *Spatial division of labor; Social structures and the geography of production.* Methuen, New York.

Massey, D. (1992). 'Politics and space/time', *New Left Review*, 196, 65–84.

Massey, D. (2005). *For space.* Sage, London.

Menon Economics (2015). *The leading maritime capitals of Europe.* Menon Economics, Oslo [updated 2019].

Ministerie van I&M (Infrastructuur en Milieu) (2012). *Structuurvisie Infrastructuur en Ruimte [National spatial strategy for infrastructure and planning]; Nederland concurrerend, bereikbaar, leefbaar en veilig.* Ministerie van I&M, The Hague.

Ministerie van V&W (Verkeer en Waterstaat) (1988). *Tweede Structuurschema Verkeer en Vervoer [Second report on traffic and transport]*; Deel a: Beleidsvoornemen. Ministerie van V&W, The Hague.

Ministerie van VROM (Volkshuisvesting, Ruimtelijke Ordening en Milieubeheer) (1988). *Vierde nota over de ruimtelijke ordening; Deel a: Beleidsvoornemen [Fourth report on spatial planning; Green paper].* Ministerie van VROM, The Hague.

Ministerie van VROM (Volkshuisvesting, Ruimtelijke Ordening en Milieubeheer) (1991). *Vierde nota over de ruimtelijke ordening Extra [Fourth report on spatial planning extra].* Ministerie van VROM, The Hague.

Ministerie van VROM (Volkshuisvesting, Ruimtelijke Ordening en Milieubeheer) (2001). *Vijfde Nota over de Ruimtelijke Ordening 2000/2020 [Fifth report on spatial planning].* Ministerie van VROM, The Hague.

Murdoch, J. (2006). *Post-structuralist geography; A guide to relational space.* Sage, London.

NDL, Nederland Distributieland (1987). *Oprichtingsakte [Memorandum of Association].* NDL, The Hague.

NEA (2009). *Rentabiliteit van het wegvervoer op weg naar een nieuw dieptepunt, persbericht zomer 2009 [Productivity of road transport towards a new low point, press release Summer 2009].* NEA, Rijswijk.

Notteboom, T. and Rodrigue, J.-P. (2005). 'Port regionalization: Towards a new phase in port development', *Maritime Policy and Management*, 32(3), 297–313.

Notteboom, T., De Langen, P. and Jacobs, W. (2013). 'Institutional plasticity and path dependence in seaports; Interactions between institutions, port governance reforms and port authority routines', *Journal of Transport Geography*, 27, 26–35.

OECD (2014). *The competitiveness of global port-cities; Synthesis report.* OECD, Paris.

Piore, M.J. and Sabel, C.F. (1984). *The second industrial divide; Possibilities for prosperity.* Basic Books, New York.

Port of Rotterdam Authority (2011). *Port compass.* Havenvisie 2030. Port of Rotterdam Authority, Rotterdam.

Raspe, O. (2014). *Trends in de regionale economie [Regional economic trends];* Input voor de VNG-commissie Stedelijk Perspectief. Planbureau voor de Leefomgeving, The Hague.

RLI, Raad voor de Leefomgeving en Infrastructuur (2016). *Mainports voorbij [Beyond mainports].* RLI, The Hague

Projectbureau Rotterdam Stadshavens (2008). *Creating on the edge; Vijf strategieën voor duurzame gebiedsontwikkeling.* Projectbureau Stadshavens Rotterdam, Rotterdam

Royal Schiphol Group (2016). *Annual report 2016.* Royal Schiphol Group, Schiphol.

RPD, Rijksplanologische Dienst (1986). *Ruimtelijke Verkenningen Hoofdinfrastructuur (RUVEIN) [Spatial explorations of the main infrastructure].* Rijksplanologische Dienst, The Hague.

Salet, W., Thornley, A. and Kreukels, A (Eds) (2003). *Metropolitan governance and spatial planning; Comparative case studies of European city-regions.* Spon Press, London.

Schaafsma, M. (2012). 'Airports and cities in networks', *disP* 39(154), 28–36.

Schaafsma, M., Amkreutz, J. and Güller, M. (2008). *Airport and city – airport corridors;* Drivers of Economic Development. Schiphol Real Estate, Haarlemmermeer.

Schuyt, K. and Taverne, E. (2004). *Dutch culture in a European Perspective;* Volume 4. 1950: Prosperity and welfare. Royal Van Gorcum/Palgrave Macmillan, Assen/Basingstoke.

StartupBlink (2019). *Startup ecosystems rankings 2019.* StartupBlink, s.l.

Statistics Netherlands (CBS) (2012). *Annual report for 2012.* Statistics Netherlands, The Hague.

Stuurgroep Groene Hart (1992). *Groene Hart [Green heart];* Nadere uitwerking Vierde nota/Plan van aanpak ROM-beleid. Rijksplanologische Dienst/Provincie Zuid-Holland, The Hague.

Thrift, N. (1998). *Spatial formations.* Sage, London.

TIR Consulting Group (2016). *The third industrial revolution: Roadmap for the next economy for the metropolitan Region of Rotterdam and The Hague;* Research commissioned by the MRDH. Metropoolregio Rotterdam-The Hague, s.l.

Touraine, A. (1969). *Postindustrial society; Tomorrow's social history: Classes, conflicts and culture in the programmed society.* Random House, New York.

Van den Berghe, K., Jacobs, W. and Boelens, L. (2018). 'The relational geometry of the port-city interface: Case studies of Amsterdam, the Netherlands, and Ghent, Belgium', *Journal of Transport Geography*, 70, 55–63.

Van der Cammen, H. and De Klerk, L. (2012). *The selfmade land; Culture and evolution of urban and regional planning in the Netherlands.* Spectrum, Houten/Antwerpen.

Van der Lugt, L, De Langen, P. and Hagdorn, L. (2015). 'Beyond the landlord, worldwide empirical analyses of port authority strategies', *International Journal of Shipping and Transport Logistics*, 7(5), 570–596.

Van Gils, M., Huys, M. and De Jong, B. (Eds) (2009). *De Nederlandse Mainports onder druk [The Dutch mainports under pressure]; Speuren naar ontwikkelkracht.* Spectrum, Houten/Antwerpen.

Van Lohuizen, Th.K. (1927). 'Bevolkingsgroei van dorpen en steden in Holland en Utrecht tussen 1896 en 1920' [Population growth of villages and towns in Holland and Utrecht 1896–1920]. Woningdienst Rotterdam, Rotterdam.

VNO-NCW (2016). *Nederland voor altijd hét knooppunt van de wereld [The Netherlands forever the node at the global level].* VNO-NCW, The Hague.

Witte, P., Slack, B., Keesman, M., Jugie, J.-H. and Wiegmans, B. (2018). 'Facilitating start-ups in port-city innovation ecosystems: A case study of Montreal and Rotterdam', *Journal of Transport Geography*, 71, 224–234.

Wuppertal Institute (2016). *Decarbonization pathways for the industrial cluster of the Port of Rotterdam.* Final Report on behalf of Port of Rotterdam. Wuppertal Institute, Wuppertal.

9 Impact of social housing on the social structure of the Randstad

Marja Elsinga, Harry van der Heijden and Rosa Donoso Gomez

Introduction

The Randstad metropolitan region in the Netherlands is regarded worldwide as a model of a 'successful' polycentric metropolis. In terms of strategic spatial planning, actors in the housing market and housing policies are of major interest. Many different policies are possible, but this contribution focuses on the role of social rental housing in urban policies in the Randstad.

In 2019, about 30% of the Dutch housing stock consisted of social rental housing, and that makes the Dutch housing system different from most other housing systems. In the Randstad, the share of social rental dwellings is even higher, at 45%. This social rental sector provides affordable rental dwellings for a wide target group and explicitly aims to contribute to enhancing the quality of neighbourhoods. The housing associations that own and manage social rental housing play a key role in urban renewal and part of their remit is to ensure that there are mixed neighbourhoods. Moreover, social housing in the Netherlands is not public housing, as such, because it is provided by housing associations which are private non-profit organisations with social objectives. These private organisations with a public role became financially independent in 1995. In 2015 a new Housing Act came into force that implied some fundamental changes for urban policy: more targeting of lower-income groups and less emphasis on the urban dimension.

This chapter evaluates the Dutch social housing model and its impact on the quality of neighbourhoods. We describe the theoretical debate on the link between affordable housing and planning and the different models for social rental housing. We then describe the history of the Dutch social housing model, how the goals and characteristics of this model have changed over time, and how the current debate and the new Housing Act can be explained. Then we will look at the changing link between social housing and urban renewal and how social housing has changed from being a solution into being a problem. We then focus on the outcome of the Dutch social rental model by looking at the composition of the population of the large cities in the Randstad. Finally, we will reflect on the consequences of the 2015 Housing Act and whether there is any alternative to the policy direction implied by the new Act, a targeted sector at a market price.

Affordable housing and urban policies: different policy models

Urban policies and affordable housing

Many housing researchers have identified the link between land use policy and the provision of affordable housing (Priemus, 1998; Oxley, 2008; Mueller and Steiner, 2010). Whitehead (2007: 27) explains that the effective provision of affordable housing depends 'on the specifics of the legislative framework and the resultant property rights as well as on political will'. The spatial planning system is in many ways interrelated with the provision of affordable housing. For instance, affordable housing policy is generally defined at the national level as part of wider welfare policy, although it is at the local level where affordable dwellings are actually provided. Property rights, whether those of owners or of tenants, will directly affect the institutions of land development. The chosen property system will be an outcome of the implied welfare system. In the Netherlands, as in other parts of the world, municipalities play a key role in the provision of social housing by providing the space for it. Although their role has evolved throughout the twentieth century and right up until the present day, municipal land policy and management have competences that guarantee land for providers of social housing (Taşan-Kok *et al.*, 2011). Land management and provision in the Netherlands is closely related to the social rental system, in particular when it comes to the 30% of social rental dwellings that exist in the housing market.

Land policies that incentivise the provision of affordable housing can take a variety of forms. Depending on the context, the key question is how to enable the provision of housing for social rent and ownership both at an affordable price and a market price. Planning for residential uses and densities according to the demand for housing is one way to accomplish this, as is done in the United Kingdom (Crook and Whitehead, 2002). In the United States, something similar occurs on the basis of a mandate granted by the federal government to state-level governments. Each state prepares a consolidated plan which includes housing needs assessments, a market analysis and a strategic plan; and involves the participation of a range of not-for-profit corporations and municipal housing departments such as affordable housing providers. Another way to ensure the provision of affordable housing is through inclusionary zoning. These are municipal ordinances, which are sometimes mandatory, as in the case of California, with the purpose of facilitating the provision of housing for low-income homeownership (Schuetz *et al.*, 2011). Inclusionary zoning involves setting a percentage of units in each new or renovated building that must be sold as affordable housing. In exchange, developers receive a 'density bonus' or access to land in lieu of other incentives. Although inclusionary zoning seeks to promote mixed-income communities and equitable growth for all residents, research shows that inclusionary zoning can push up house prices and reduce the provision of dwellings, depending on the housing market in the local area (Schuetz *et al.*, 2011: 321). Both these examples of land policies from the United States and the United Kingdom focus on low-income home-ownership. The United States also has low-income rental housing, and there are additional programmes organised by the federal government that require collaboration at the planning and local level in order to be applied. To promote the well-being of neighbourhoods that include public housing, cities and housing authorities can join the *Choice Neighbourhoods Initiative*. The goal of this initiative is to bring economic opportunities to areas that already have a high concentration of public housing, to create mixed-income communities that have access to public transport (Been *et al.*, 2010).

Another example that demonstrates the link between planning policy and affordable housing policy can currently be seen in some Latin American countries. Apart from the self-help settlements, which are another way in which lower-income groups solve their housing needs, the main government policy is a subsidised scheme for low-income homeownership. Low-cost dwellings are provided by the private sector, but the municipalities play a crucial role as providers of serviced land (land with utilities, ready for construction) at an affordable price. The challenge is to coordinate the construction of housing development in the centre of the city and not only in the urban periphery where land is cheaper. In the case of low-income homeownership strategies, the price and management of land becomes a critical factor in the price of housing units. Government decentralisation and the modernisation of planning systems are important factors that influence the adoption of land policy instruments and regularisation (Smolka and Furtado, 2014). The focus on financial mechanisms to promote homeownership and investment in infrastructure pushes up land prices due to speculation, thereby transferring economic benefits to existing land owners (Fernandez and Maldonado Copello, 2009). Value capturing strategies are therefore now being implemented under constitutional mandates such as the 'social function of property'. Land policy and land regularisation are today in the centre of a portfolio of strategies to address both housing and urban challenges (Donoso and Elsinga, 2018).

In comparison to other regions in the world, the Dutch experience is therefore remarkable in terms of the results of a century of social rental policy. The history of land development and cooperation between municipalities and housing associations has helped to produce integrated and less segregated cities compared with many other countries (Tammaru *et al.*, 2016). Social housing is not found mainly in the urban periphery as in Latin America, and neither is it concentrated in certain districts as occurs in some US cities. However, although social housing is well integrated in Dutch cities, social mixing including inter-ethnic contact is still not evident (Boschman, 2012). Flourishing urban areas such as the Randstad attract many people, resulting in a high demand for housing, high land prices and high house prices. In Randstad cities, making space for affordable housing is, by definition, an issue, and therefore the resilience of an existing and already integrated social rental sector is important. The model of the social rental sector in the Netherlands is finding its way into the local planning system.

Broad social rental housing as a goal of urban policy

There is an ongoing debate in housing studies on the sustainability of such a 'unitary rental sector'. This means a social rental sector for a broad target group that is in competition with the commercial rental sector. According to Harloe (1995), such a model is not sustainable, while according to Kemeny (1995), it can be. Since the Netherlands is mentioned as a typical example of such a broad-based social rental sector, we will elaborate on this debate (see also Elsinga *et al.*, 2008).

Harloe's theory of the development of social rental housing in advanced capitalist countries is based on the proposition that in capitalist societies there tends to be an inverse relationship between the degree to which there are major opportunities for private accumulation in various aspects of providing for human needs, and the extent to which such provision may, at certain historical junctures, become wholly or partly decommodified (Harloe, 1995). When applied to housing, this means that housing will normally be provided as a commodity in capitalist societies. Only when adequate provision in a commodified form is not possible and when this situation has some broader significance for the dominant social and economic order, recourse is made to large-scale, partially decommodified, state-subsidised and politically controlled social rented housing (Harloe, 1995).

Harloe distinguishes two main models for social rental housing in Western industrialised countries: the mass model and the residual model. The characteristics of the mass model are extensive programmes for social rental dwellings, which are not specifically directed at housing the lowest income groups. Consequently, social housing tends not to become stigmatised under this model. These large-scale programmes are supported by production subsidies; income-dependent subsidies play a relatively unimportant part. Small-scale new construction programmes that are intended to house only the lowest-income groups characterise the residual model. Under the residual model, social housing tends to become more stigmatised, since it is used to accommodate politically, economically or socially marginalised groups. The mass model came to fruition in Western Europe after the Second World War. Starting in the mid-1970s, according to Harloe (1995), the situation in the United Kingdom moved towards the residual model. Harloe argues that (mass) social rental models naturally progress towards residual models. A reversion to mass provision is only likely to occur if the emergent phase of capitalist development gives rise to a new rationale for social rented housing production that targets sectors of the population which are part of the economic and political mainstream rather than at the margins (Harloe, 1995).

According to Kemeny (1995), Harloe's 'unilinear' theory is typically based on the Anglo-Saxon situation. As an alternative, Kemeny – a British researcher living in Sweden – has developed a theory of the dynamics of rental systems in which he distinguishes two rental housing models that may arise simultaneously in different countries.

Kemeny's theory is based on the proposition that the interaction between the economic development of rental housing stocks (maturation) and their long-term policy structuring can lead to different development trajectories for (rental) housing systems. The key dimension in this process is whether renting becomes compartmentalised into segregated markets or not (Kemeny, 1995). The concept of maturation is central to Kemeny's theory. The point of departure here is that non-profit organisations, unlike for-profit organisations, work on a cost-price basis: since non-profit providers generally do not require a market return on their equity, their financial costs are lower when debt represents a smaller proportion of the market value of the property, i.e. when the ratio of equity to market value is higher (Kemeny *et al.*, 2005). According to Kemeny *et al.* (2005), this ratio is a measure of the solidity of the rental organisation. The maturation process means that solidity increases over time, both through the amortisation of debt and the appreciation of market values.

Table 9.1 Main features of rental market models.

	Dual/residual rental market	Unitary rental market
Objective of social housing policy	Separate non-profit from market: no direct competition between non-profit and for-profit rental sectors	Integrated rental market, with direct competition between profit and non-profit rental sectors
Function of non-profit rental sector	Safety net function	Provision of housing to large segments of the population
Regulation	Non-profit rental sector closely regulated and subsidised	Regulation and subsidies for non-profit sector are phased out to allow direct competition with commercial providers
Rent levels	Social rent levels	Market-dependent rent level but lower than market rents
Segmentation of sector	Strong market segmentation Owner-occupied sector dominant (it is 'normal' to buy one's own house)	Limited market segmentation Sectors compete for households (tenure neutrality)
Households in non-profit rental sector	Strong concentration of low-income groups	Less strong concentration of low-income groups; medium- and high-income groups also included
Neighbourhoods	Marginalised	Implicit idea of mixed neighbourhoods

Source: Authors.

Kemeny terms the rental system that results from this 'dualist' since its distinguishing characteristic is the existence of parallel public and private rental systems that are subject to increasingly divergent forms of provision and conditions of tenure. Because access to the public rental sector is restricted to households on a low income and many households are not attracted by the private rental sector with its high rents and limited rental protection, demand is steered strongly towards the owner-occupied sector. As mentioned above, the dual rental market model bears a close resemblance to Harloe's residual housing model (Elsinga *et al.*, 2008). The main features of a unitary rental market model are summarised in Table 9.1, with those of the dual rental market model also included by way of comparison.

Kemeny focuses on the emergence and sustainability of unitary rental markets. There are, however, severe threats to the unitary rental model (Elsinga *et al*, 2008). First, the model is threatened by widespread support for homeownership policies. All governments in Europe support homeownership and try to encourage middle-income groups in particular to buy their own home. Moreover, competition between non-profit and for-profit housing is considered a problem by some policymakers. The Dutch, Swedish and French models have all been criticised by the European Commission because they distort competition. Since non-profit organisations receive 'state aid', their competition with for-profit organisations is deemed unfair. Second, the *raison d'être* of non-profit housing in a unitary rental market has been questioned. What exactly is their social aim and why should non-profit housing serve social aims? However, the urban dimension has often been neglected in this debate (Elsinga and Lind, 2013) which is of particular concern in this chapter. Regarding the urban dimension there seems to be an implicit assumption that a broad social rental sector implies mixed neighbourhoods. We now turn to this below in the next section after an overview of how the Dutch social housing system came about and changed over the course of years.

The Dutch social housing model

History and present situation

Social housing in the Netherlands has its roots in the civil society of the nineteenth century, when social housing emerged from private initiatives. The emergence of housing associations was consistent with the pillarised nature of Dutch society at a time when a wide range of institutions, such as trade unions, banks, insurance companies and farmers' cooperatives, were organised along protestant, catholic, liberal or socialist lines (Lijphart and Crepaz, 1991). But regardless of their background, housing associations focused mainly on healthy housing for working class families and were never intended only for the most vulnerable households, thus not meant as a residual model.

Housing associations became the subject of an increasing degree of government influence with the passing of the Housing Act in 1901. It was intended to regulate social housing providers and set up a framework for the provision of low-interest government loans to private non-profit organisations. Government influence grew gradually stronger during the twentieth century. After the Second World War, the social housing sector became a crucial tool in tackling housing shortages. From 1945 until 1990, the Dutch government remained closely involved in the activities and funding of housing associations and the social rental sector became a key element in the Dutch welfare state. As a result, housing associations were gradually transformed into semi-public institutions with strong financial and hierarchical ties with government. Parallel to the private housing associations, many municipalities set up their own housing departments that provided housing for those that were not served by housing associations: often the most vulnerable groups (Van der Schaar, 1987).

State control over housing associations was valued by social democratic politicians, while their private and non-public character was important for the support of the Christian Democrats and the Liberals. Christian Democrats in particular, who were part of almost all the post-war administrations in the Netherlands, valued the strong position of civil society organisations in providing affordable housing and sought to shield these from direct political involvement. The societal position of housing associations in the Netherlands was therefore the carefully balanced outcome of the distribution of political power.

Since the late 1980s, there has been growing pressure to transform the social housing system into a more marketised one. This implied encouraging homeownership and deregulating the social rental sector. Step by step, more freedom and responsibility were accorded to the social housing associations. In the 1990s, this process led to major deregulation and financial autonomy (Houard, 2011).

Housing associations have been financially independent from the government since the 'grossing and balancing operation' of 1995, when government loans as well as supply-side subsidies for building new dwellings and renovating existing ones, were abolished. The only remaining form of central government support is the guarantee for social housing loans. This is provided by the Guarantee Fund for Social Housing (WSW or *Waarborgfonds Sociale Woningbouw* in Dutch), which was set up in the 1980s, initially to fund housing improvements but later for all social housing loans. The WSW is funded by the associations themselves and backed by the government, which delivers a favourable rating. It enables non-profit associations to guarantee their loans, thus ensuring access to the capital market and low interest rates. The result is that housing associations now work as a revolving fund: they sell off a proportion of their dwellings and use the revenues for new investment. This has become a core component of their business. Moreover, housing associations manage their own financial resources and increasingly they use derivatives to limit the interest risk on their loans. For tenants on low incomes, a housing allowance is available, both in the social and private rented sector (Elsinga and Wassenberg, 2014).

Finally, almost all municipal housing companies have been 'privatised' to become housing associations. This means that housing associations are *de facto* the only providers of social housing in the Netherlands, blurring the informal separation between housing for low- to medium-income households, which was previously provided by housing associations, and housing for the most vulnerable, which was provided by municipal housing departments (Houard, 2011).

Governance

The provision of affordable housing in the Netherlands is characterised by the close involvement of local authorities and non-profit housing associations. In general, Dutch municipalities have a relatively high degree of autonomy in public affairs and the delivery of public services. *Co-governance* is a principle that is deeply rooted in Dutch public and administrative law and this enables local authorities to be involved in executing and implementing national policies. Since the 1980s, the delivery of public services in the Netherlands has been subject to strategic decentralisation in specific areas of public policy. Social housing was one of the first policy fields to be decentralised in the 1980s and 1990s. This shift was triggered by a policy document published by the State Secretary for Housing in 1989 and it ushered in a new era for the social housing sector, continuing the trend towards more autonomy that had started in the 1960s. The document stressed the importance of private initiative. It went on to state that housing associations had an important part to play in providing adequate housing for all, as laid down in the Dutch constitution. It also provided guidelines for enhancing the financial independence of the housing associations, with the Central Housing Fund (CFV or *Centraal Fonds Volkshuisvesting* in Dutch) and the Guarantee Fund for Social Housing Construction (WSW) being the main policy instruments (Elsinga and Van Bortel, 2011).

The Central Housing Fund is a government agency which supervises the financial viability of housing associations. It can order remedial action on the part of housing associations if they run into financial difficulties. If necessary, the CFV can provide additional financial support to housing associations while they implement these remedial actions. The WSW was set up in the 1980s initially to guarantee loans for housing improvements, and later to guarantee all housing loans. This guarantee fund is backed by the government, resulting in a triple A credit rating from the financial rating agencies. The fund enables non-profit organisations to guarantee their capital market loans, guaranteeing them access to the capital market and low interest rates. This check-and-balance double system provides a robust safety net for housing associations.

The financial and operational autonomy of social landlords and the absence of government subsidies imply that the Dutch government's ability to influence the behaviour of housing associations has become highly limited compared with the past. Legally, the government still provides official supervision, but the state entrusts the monitoring of performance by social housing associations mainly to the self-regulating capacity of the sector and to performance agreements between local governments and social housing associations, as described in the Social Housing Management Order (*Besluit Beheer Sociale Huursector*). Central government does not want to act as a micro-managing regulator for the social housing sector. Rather, it prefers to operate more like a systems manager, making sure that the necessary instruments, checks and balances, such as independent performance audits and internal supervisory boards, are in place to safeguard high-quality performance and good governance.

Some self-regulating instruments have been developed by Aedes, the national umbrella organisation for housing associations, and others have been set up by (groups of) housing associations. Members of Aedes are required to abide to a code of governance that is based on a corporate code used in the private sector. In addition, independent performance assessments every four years are compulsory for Aedes members. The regulations to guide the activities of housing associations (the Social Housing Management Act) are intentionally vague when it comes to the results expected from social landlords. This was based on the notion that performance should be negotiated at the local level by local performance agreements between housing associations and local authorities. Market discipline and competition between local social landlords were seen as the main performance incentives. Central government focuses primarily on supervising the financial viability of housing associations and only intervenes in cases of gross mismanagement and fraud. Supervision on performance is almost absent. Under the terms of the Housing Act, the responsibilities and operating conditions of housing associations are laid down in the Social Housing Management Order (abbreviated to BBSH in Dutch).

Since the 1990s, the public remit of the housing associations has been extended. Two policy areas have been included in revised editions of the BBSH. In 1997, the quality of neighbourhoods (*leefbaarheid*, meaning 'liveability') was added to the list of performance areas. In 2001, the responsibility for providing housing for households that require extra care and support was included in the BBSH. This performance field is often translated as the task of providing housing for the elderly, but in fact it also includes housing for other vulnerable groups such as disabled persons, drug users, homeless people or those in danger of losing their homes. Housing associations have an important degree of freedom with regard to their activities in this field (Houard, 2011).

This degree of freedom, in combination with the growing wealth of housing associations, has led to an unclear picture of the role of housing associations. Recently, some associations have invested in projects such as tunnels and boats while others have become the victims of fraud and mismanagement. Furthermore, the largest housing association in the Netherlands speculated with financial derivatives and almost bankrupted the whole social rental sector when the interest rates went down. This caused substantial societal distrust and resulted in a parliamentary inquiry. The conclusion of the parliamentary committee was that the social rental system failed due to a lack of regulation; there was weak government supervision and the self-regulation completely failed. The results of the inquiry are included in the new housing act that was enacted in March 2015.

The changing relationship between social housing and urban policy

In the seven decades since the end of the Second World War, roughly four distinct periods can be discerned with regard to the role of social housing in urban policy in the Netherlands. The first two periods fit within Harloe's mass housing model and the development of Kemeny's unitary model discussed above. In the third period, the mass housing model came to an end, but the unitary model flourished, because of the mature and (financially) independent position of housing associations. In the most recent fourth period, a development in the direction of a residual or dual model appears to have started (also see the next sub-section).

In the first period that immediately followed the Second World War, housing policy focused primarily on *solving the housing shortage* by building new homes as rapidly as possible with the aid of government funding and supply-side subsidies. Because of budgetary constraints, there was a tendency for the construction of cheap, austere dwellings in large-scale housing projects. The social housing sector was regarded as better able to execute and manage these projects than the private rental sector (Haffner *et al.*, 2009: 214). In the larger cities, especially in Amsterdam and Rotterdam, municipal housing companies played an important role in producing and managing new social rental housing. The persistent housing shortage meant that in the 1950s and 1960s, housing policy in the Netherlands focused on adding new dwellings to the housing stock and in particular social rental dwellings, mainly built on greenfield locations just outside existing cities.

In the 1970s and 1980s, the emphasis shifted to *improving housing conditions* (Boelhouwer *et al.*, 1996). With regard to urban renewal, this meant a shift from demolishing dwellings as part of 'urban reconstruction' (with dwellings usually being replaced by offices, shopping malls and motorways) to improving the existing housing stock (Schuiling *et al*, 1990). Housing quality problems in larger cities were, by now, concentrated in the pre-war privately owned housing stock, which was primarily made up of private rental and owner-occupied dwellings. Urban renewal concentrated on improving or replacing this stock. First, owners could apply for renovation subsidies. Second, municipalities or housing associations could buy neglected private properties, renovate them and add the improved dwelling to the housing stock of housing associations. Subsidies were available for buying as well as improving and managing these dwellings (Van der Heijden and Westra, 1988). Third, private dwellings were bought by municipalities and replaced by new-build dwellings. Often, these new dwellings were managed by housing associations.

Under the flag of 'building for the neighbourhood', housing policy in the cities aimed to provide better quality housing for the existing population, especially low-income groups (Schuiling, 2007). This was often accompanied by a process where private owner-occupied or private rented dwellings were converted into or replaced by social rented dwellings. In summary, social housing was considered the solution to the problem of urban decay during the 1970s and 1980s.

In the 1990s, housing policy and housing production in the Netherlands became more and more influenced by *market forces* and the phasing out of supply-side subsidies. The figures relating to new build homes changed radically: 70% of the production of government-designated new-building sites now had to be realised by market players without the aid of subsidies, whereas prior to that period, over 50% of production was still being realised through subsidy schemes (Boelhouwer *et al.*, 2006). At the same time, the focus of urban renewal changed from curative to preventive (Schuiling, 2007; Heijkers *et al.*, 2012). Ever more urban renewal projects were situated in neighbourhoods where social housing predominated, much of which had been built during the early post-war period; dwellings that were 30–40 years old. Urban renewal was no longer only about the quality of the housing stock or the living environment, but also about social and economic problems in neighbourhoods, such as the concentration in particular areas of low-income groups, the unemployed or ethnic minorities. This means that from being considered the solution to urban problems, social housing itself was regarded as the problem. In a 1997 white paper on urban renewal, housing associations were seen as key players in the urban renewal process since many of the problems were concentrated in areas where social rented housing predominated (Ministerie van VROM, 1997). Creating mixed neighbourhoods became an important policy goal. Social engineering was one of the instruments used to realise this (Schuiling, 2007). As a means of creating mixed neighbourhoods, part of the housing stock of housing associations was sold to the owner-occupied sector, either by selling off existing dwellings or by replacing demolished social rented dwellings with owner-occupied dwellings in order to improve the social quality of neighbourhoods, which had been part of the housing associations' new remit since 1997. At the neighbourhood level, housing associations often provided play facilities for children, neighbourhood wardens, environmental maintenance and community centres, particularly where local authorities had failed in these areas. They justified this investment as a way of improving the quality of life in their neighbourhoods and maintaining the value of their properties. Thus, housing associations had come to initiate and dominate the urban renewal process as the largest property owners. This reflects both the growing power of the associations and the diminishing capacity and financial resources of the local government.

Over the past 15 years, the position of housing associations and their role in urban renewal has come under pressure. This process started in 2005 when the European Commission, as part of the European Union's competition policy, advised the Dutch government to take measures to prevent state aid from straying into areas that should be subject to free competition. This state aid concerned the value of loans for housing associations, guaranteed under the public-sector backstop of the Dutch Social Housing Guarantee Fund. At the end of 2009, the Dutch government and the European Commission reached an agreement on the measures to be taken, under which a minimum of 90% of rent-controlled dwellings due to fall vacant must be allocated to lower-income households (Priemus and Gruis, 2011). The remaining maximum 10% can be allocated to middle-income groups. At the same time, the associations increasingly became the subject of political discussions. In addition to the question about whether they were using their capital sufficiently and efficiently, there have been a series of incidents involving gold-plating, fraud and financial incompetence (Van der Heijden, 2013; Hoekstra, 2017). As a result, housing associations are being forced to focus more on low-income groups and financial resources are being withdrawn by government. In the last 15 years, not only has social housing itself been regarded as a problem, but more and more the social landlords themselves became to be seen as part of that problem.

Since 2008, economic circumstances have changed and as a result, housing associations have had to focus more on their annual revenue, while their 'soft' goals such as enhancing their tenants' quality of life or well-being have become less of a priority (Elsinga and Wassenberg, 2014). Until the economic crisis, selling off dwellings to cover the losses incurred by renovation work and constructing new dwellings seemed to be an adequate financial model. However, the difficulties in the wider economy in the period 2009–2013 have meant that people were more reluctant to buy houses, including those offered by housing associations. Consequently, housing sales in these years were much lower than expected and this has undermined the housing associations' business model for urban renewal. Renewal activities had to be postponed or delayed all across the country, not just in the Randstad. Activities in the areas of demolition, refurbishment and new construction decreased, while cheap and simple maintenance measures prevailed. The demand for social rented dwellings has also changed as turnover rates have dropped and waiting times for even rather low-quality apartments have grown substantially. In this context, the urgency for renewal dropped (Elsinga and Wassenberg, 2014). Since 2014 the housing market in the Netherlands has recovered and housing shortages in the Randstad cities have increased. Renewal activities of housing associations have not increased much due to a deteriorated financial situation, caused especially by a new landlord levy, introduced in 2013.

Private renting as solution for the middle-income group

At its core, the debate is about who has the power to decide about the social housing stock: who owns the property, who makes decisions on refurbishments, new construction of social property, and who decides on rent levels or sales? This has been the debate since the housing association became a financially independent private organisation with social objectives. For many decades as we have seen, there was reliance on self-regulation by the social rental sector, by means of a governance code and social assessments for example. The parliamentary inquiry committee mentioned above concluded that self-regulation had failed, and the 2015 Housing Act therefore includes a stronger role for local government and closer supervision by central government. Moreover, the 2015 legislation also seeks to bring about a stronger position for tenants.

The discussion about creating a level playing field resulted in more targeting of social rental dwelling on lower-income groups. An income limit and a rent limit were introduced and regulations introduced in 2011 implied that 90% of social dwellings must be allocated to households with an income below the limit (€34,000). Moreover, an income-dependent rent policy was introduced in 2012 which implies extra yearly rent increases for households on an income above the limit. The assumption is that this extra rent increase will encourage middle-income groups to leave the social rental sector.

Housing associations not only have to pay corporation tax, but also a new landlord levy per dwelling, which was introduced in 2013. In this way, central government encourages housing associations to sell dwellings or increase rents beyond the limit of 'social housing'. For the 'non-social dwellings' housing associations do not have to pay the landlord levy. In other words, the central government provides incentives to housing associations to reduce their stock and to move towards the residual model. In addition, there is a new policy for housing allocation implying the lowest-income households only qualify for the most affordable dwellings. This results in increasing spatial concentration of the lower-income households.

For many decades the support for social housing and home ownership went hand in hand at the cost of the private rental sector. The implementation of the 2015 Housing Act is a clear demonstration of a move away from the unitary rental model. The support for homeownership is sustained. What is new is the ambition to increase the private rental sector. There is room for investment since the middle- and higher-income households are not able to access the social rental sector while many cannot afford to buy a house. Private investors are supposed to fill this gap called the middle segment of the housing market. The Housing Minister is explicitly addressing foreign investors.[1]

The impact of the Dutch model on the social fabric

In this section we analyse the consequences of post-war housing policy and urban policy on the social fabric of the largest cities in the Netherlands (the Randstad cities Amsterdam, Rotterdam, The Hague and Utrecht), using figures from the National Housing Survey. The main question here is whether changes in policy during the 1970s and 1980s (which were based on social housing as the solution to urban problems) and again from the mid-1990s (which were based on social housing and housing associations as a major part of urban problems) have led to changes in the social fabric of cities. We will focus on the income distribution and the position of different income groups within the urban housing market.

We begin our analysis by looking at the development of the different forms of tenure in the four largest cities. To put this development in perspective, we first present the development of tenures in the Netherlands as a whole (Figure 9.1). In the Netherlands since the Second World War, owner-occupied housing has increased as a share of the total housing stock, while private rented housing has decreased steadily. The proportion of social rented housing increased until the end of the 1980s and then started to decrease. With regard to the social rented sector, this development is in line with the policy changes that we described in the previous section.

In the four largest cities of the Netherlands which makes up the main part of the Randstad, the development of tenures is roughly comparable with the national picture, although there are significant differences with the national figures regarding the size of tenures (see Figure 9.2). In the largest cities, the share of the owner-occupied sector in the housing stock is much smaller and the proportion of both forms of rental is larger. Also, the expansion of social housing lasted rather longer in the large cities. In the early 1990s, over 50% of the housing stock in the largest cities was social rented housing. However, from the mid-1990s onwards, the importance of social housing in the cities started to decline as a consequence of the change in policy with regard to new production as well as urban renewal.

What did this rise and fall in the social rented sector mean for the representation of different income groups within the social rental sector? Figure 9.3 shows

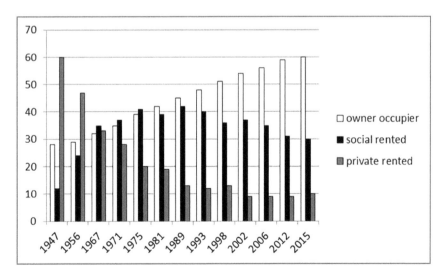

Figure 9.1 Housing stock according to tenure in the Netherlands, 1947–2015.
Source: Dutch National Housing Survey, several years.

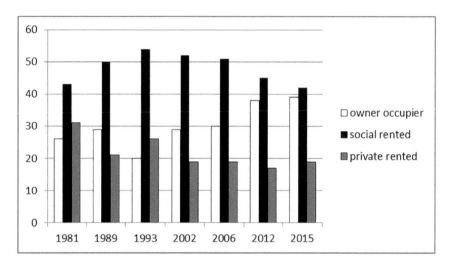

Figure 9.2 Housing stock according to tenure in the four largest cities of the Netherlands, 1981–2015.

Source: Dutch National Housing Survey, several years.

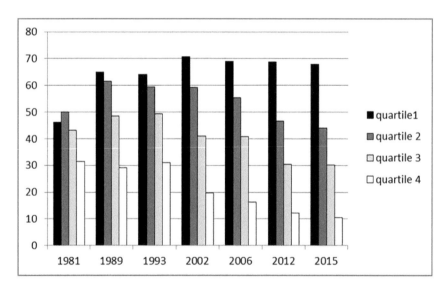

Figure 9.3 The share of households in social rented housing per income quartile in the four largest cities of the Netherlands, 1981–2015.

Source: Dutch National Housing Survey, several years.

that until 2002 the proportion of low-income households (quartile 1) living in social rental housing increased. After 2002, this stabilised at about 70%. But it also becomes clear that until 1993 the proportion of middle and higher-income groups living in social rented housing also increased; in 1993 over 30% of people in the highest-income group (quartile 4) in the large cities were

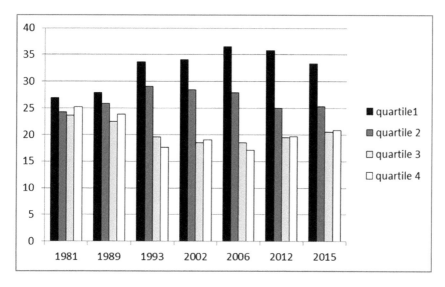

Figure 9.4 Households living in the four largest cities of the Netherlands by income quartile, 1981–2015.
Source: Dutch National Housing Survey, several years.

living in social rented housing. Housing associations were indeed providing housing for broad sections of the population. But in the second half of the 1990s, the proportion of middle and high-income groups living in social housing began to decrease and the concentration of low-income groups increased.

What have been the consequences of the decreasing proportion of social housing in the urban housing stock and the increased concentration of low-income groups within the social rented sector, in terms of the position of low-income groups on the urban housing market? Are low-income groups being pushed out of urban housing markets? Figure 9.4 shows that between 1981 and 2006 the concentration of households in the first two income quartiles living in the four largest cities increased continuously. Since 2006, the share of low-and lower middle-income households (income quartiles 1 and 2) has decreased while the proportion of medium-high and high-income groups (income quartiles 3 and 4) has increased. It seems that households in the first and the second income quartile have been the 'victims' of the marketisation of housing production and the obligation to target the decreasing social rented sector towards the lowest-income groups.

Conclusions

Social housing: solution or problem?

The housing model in the Randstad is something of an exception due to its huge social rental housing sector. Since more than 40% of the housing stock is social rental housing, the sector plays a key role in planning for housing in the Randstad. The role of social housing has changed substantially over recent decades, however. In the 1950s, social housing formed the main solution for the post-war housing shortage. In the 1970s, the renovation of deteriorating private housing stock and its conversion into social housing was a typical solution for the worsening of urban neighbourhoods. All this led to rapid growth of the sector which reached a peak of 54% in 1993 in the four large Randstad cities. Subsequently, social housing changed from being a solution to being part of the problem. The 1997 White Paper on Urban Renewal concludes that 'problem neighbourhoods' are mainly neighbourhoods where social rental housing predominates. The solution presented here is to remove social rental dwellings, either through demolition or sale, in order to create more mixed neighbourhoods. Moreover, social housing providers also became financially independent and the sale of social rental housing became a key element in their portfolio management. In 2005, social housing was considered an issue in the context of fair competition in Europe. State aid for social housing for a broad target group including not just lower-income households was deemed to be false competition with commercial landlords. This was the reason for ending open access to this sector and targeting social rental dwellings at just lower-income households. The figures presented in this chapter show that recently the number of high-income households in the four main cities of the Randstad has increased substantially, to the detriment of low and lower-middle income households.

The 2015 Housing Act is forcing housing associations to adopt a new role in urban renewal. The question is what exactly this role will be, what the role of the local government will be and whether local government will apply other planning instruments to affordable housing. Another interesting point for discussion is the extent to which municipalities are willing and able to take on the work that housing associations have been forced to abandon. Although cities like Amsterdam and Utrecht are trying to increase the production of private rental housing for middle-income groups, the results are limited because housing shortages in these cities lead to rents that are not affordable for these households.

Towards a dual or residual model?

Dutch social housing is often cited as an example of the unitary rental model: a broad model with 'market-like' rents. Currently, the 2015 Housing Act is pushing housing associations towards a different model: a new role for social rental housing. Does this mean that social housing in the Netherlands is moving towards a dual or residual housing model? This would be social housing as a safety net, associated with marginalisation and stigmatisation, and yet let at near-market rents. This may be the impossible compromise between the two extremes of Kemeny's model. It would also seem to incentivise all those who are able to buy to leave the social rental sector as soon as possible. It is obvious that there is no longer support for a unitary rental sector. The sector is clearly moving towards the dual or residual mode.

This raises the question of whether social landlords and municipalities have a vision on the spatial distribution of the social housing stock. For the time being, it looks like it is heading towards a marginalised sector active in the worst urban neighbourhoods, offering homes at near-market rents. A new vision could imply the ambition to create a smaller sector that is spread fairly evenly across the city, providing affordable housing for lower-income groups.

Note

1 See for example https://www.investingindutchhousing.nl/ (accessed July 2019).

References

Been, V., Cunningham, M., Adam, I.G., Gordon, A., Parilla, J., Turner, M.A., Whitney, S.V., Yowell, A. and Zimmerman, K. (2010). *Building Environmentally Sustainable Communities: A Framework for Inclusivity. What Works Collaborative*, New York and Washington DC.

Boelhouwer, P.J., Boumeester, H. and Van der Heijden, H. (2006). 'Stagnation in Dutch housing production and suggestions for a way forward', *Journal of Housing and the Built Environment*, 21(3), 299–314.

Boschman, S. (2012). 'Residential segregation and interethnic contact in the Netherlands', *Urban Studies*, 49(2), 353–367.

Crook, A.T.D.H. and Whitehead, C.M.E. (2002). 'Social housing and planning gain: Is this an appropriate way of providing affordable housing?', *Environment and Planning A: Economy and Space*, 34(7), 1259–1279.

Donoso, R.E. and Elsinga, M. (2018). 'Management of low-income condominiums in Bogota and Quito: The balance between property law and self-organization', *International Journal of Housing Policy*, 18(2), 312–334.

Elsinga, M., Haffner, M. and Van der Heijden, H. (2008). 'Threats for the Dutch unitary model', *European Journal of Housing Policy*, 8(1), 21–37.

Elsinga, M. and Lind, H. (2013). 'The effect of EU-Legislation on rental systems in Sweden and the Netherlands', *Housing Studies* 28(7), 960–970.

Elsinga, M. and Van Bortel, G. (2011). 'The future of social housing in the Netherlands'. In: Houard, N. (Ed.) *Social Housing across Europe*. La documentation Française, Paris, 98–115.

Elsinga, M. and Wassenberg, F. (2014). 'Social housing in the Netherlands'. In: Scanlon, K., C.M.E. Whitehead and Fernandez Arrigoitia, M. (Eds) *Social Housing in Europe*. Wiley, London.

Fernandez, E. and Maldonado Copello, M.M. (2009). 'Law and land policy in Latin America; Shifting paradigms and possibilities for action', *Land Lines*, 21(3), 14–19.

Haffner, M., Hoekstra, J., Oxley, M. and Van der Heijden, H. (2009). *Bridging the Gap Between Social and Market Rental Housing in Six European Countries*. IOS Press, Amsterdam.

Harloe, M. (1995). *The People's Home? Social Rented Housing in Europe & America*. Blackwell, Oxford/Cambridge.

Heijkers, B., Van der Velden, J. and Wassenberg, F. (2012). *Toekomst Stedelijke Vernieuwing na 2014 [The Future of Urban Renewal after 2014]*. KEI/Nicis, The Hague.

Hoekstra, J. (2017). 'Reregulation and residualization in Dutch social housing: A critical evaluation of new policies', *Critical Housing Analysis*, 4(1), 31–39.

Houard, N. (Ed.) (2011). *Social Housing across Europe*. La documentation Française, Paris.

Kemeny, J. (1995). *From Public Housing to the Social Market; Rental Policy Strategies in Comparative Perspective*. Routledge, London/New York.

Kemeny, J., Kersloot, J. and Thalmann, P. (2005). 'Non-profit housing influencing, leading and dominating the unitary rental market: Three case studies', *Housing Studies* 20(6), 855–872.

Lijphart, A. and Crepaz, M.M.L. (1991). 'Corporatism and consensus democracy in eighteen countries: Conceptual and empirical linkages', *British Journal of Political Science*, 21(2), 235–246.

Ministerie van VROM (Volkshuisvesting, Ruimtelijke Ordening en Milieubeheer) (1997). *Nota Stedelijke Vernieuwing [White Paper on Urban Renewal]*, Ministerie van VROM, The Hague.

Mueller, E. J. and Steiner, F. (2010). 'Integrating equity and environmental goals in local housing policy', *Housing Policy Debate*, 21(1), 93–98.

Oxley, M. (2008). 'Implicit land taxation and affordable housing provision in England', *Housing Studies*, 23(4), 661–671.

Priemus, H. (1998). 'Redifferentiation of the urban housing stock in the Netherlands: A strategy to prevent spatial segregation?', *Housing Studies*, 13(3), 301–310.

Priemus, H. and Gruis, V. (2011). 'Social housing and illegal state aid: The agreement between European Commission and Dutch Government', *International Journal of Housing Policy*, 11(1), 89–104.

Schuetz, J., Meltzer, R. and Been, V. (2011). 'Silver bullet or Trojan Horse? The effects of inclusionary zoning on local housing markets in the United States', *Urban Studies*, 48(2), 297–329.

Schuiling, D. (2007). 'Stadsvernieuwing door de jaren heen' [Urban renewal throughout time], *Rooilijn*, 40(3), 158–165.

Schuiling, D., Pflug, M. and Straub, J. (1990). *Functionele vernieuwing van binnensteden 1960–1990 [Functional renewal of inner cities 1960–1990]*; Lessen uit het reconstructieverleden, PDI-verkenningen nr. 58. Planologisch Demografisch Instituut Universiteit van Amsterdam, Amsterdam.

Smolka, M. and Furtado, F. (Eds) (2014). *Instrumentos notables de políticas de suelo en América Latina [Notable Instruments of Land Policy in Latin America]*. Cambridge MA, Lincoln Institute of Land Policy.

Tammaru, T., Marcińczak, S., Van Ham, M. and Musterd, S. (Eds) (2016). *Socioeconomic Segregation in European Capital Cities; East Meets West*. Routledge, London.

Taşan-Kok, T., Groetelaers, D., Haffner, M., Van der Heijden, H. and Korthals Altes, W. (2011). 'Providing cheap land for social housing: Breaching the state aid regulations of the single European Market?' *Regional Studies*, 47(4), 628–642.

Van der Heijden, H. (2013). *West European Housing Systems in a Comparative Perspective*, PhD thesis TU Delft. IOS Press, Amsterdam.

Van der Heijden, H. and Westra, H. (1988). *De aankoop van particuliere woningen door toegelaten instellingen en gemeenten [The Purchase of Private Dwellings by Housing Associations and Municipalities]*, Working paper 25. Delftse Universitaire Pers, Delft.

Van der Schaar, J. (1987). *Groei en bloei van het Nederlandse volkshuisvestingsbeleid [Growth and Prosperity of Dutch Housing Policy]*. Delftse Universitaire Pers, Delft.

Whitehead, C.M.E. (2007). 'Planning policies and affordable housing: England as a successful case study?' *Housing Studies*, 22(1), 25–44.

10 Interaction in the Delta

Culture, convention and knowledge clusters in the Randstad

Maurits de Hoog

Introduction: metropolis and interaction

The yearly Lowlands Festival in Biddinghuizen is a fine metaphor for the Dutch Metropolis. The thousands of small tents stand for the extremely diffuse urbanization pattern; the big tents, at the other extreme, for the strongly concentrated interaction environments.[1] Traditionally, the interaction environments of the logistics centres including the seaports, Schiphol Airport and the flower and vegetable auctions have been among the 'big tents'. They are main parts of the economic foundation for the Dutch Metropolis. Over many years the physical conditions which accompany a delta city region like the Randstad have been used to develop a strong and multifaceted complex of logistics centres. The transport sector in the Randstad is the strongest in Europe. In recent years a sizeable number of big tents have been added in other economic sectors. Against the main current of government policies in the past to promote the diffusion of economic activities across the territory, it is primarily in the largest cities where all sorts of new interaction environments have been realized. The Dutch Metropolis has become more diverse and raised to a higher level of quality.

In this chapter, the term metropolis, used twice already, does not refer to the size of the region's population or economy or home to work distances, but to the significance of *metropolitan functions* across wide territories or even across entire continents or the globe. In academic literature this has been accepted wisdom for some time (see for example, Pred, 1977) and has gained momentum through the discourse on global cities (Sassen, 1991; Simmonds and Hack, 2000; Scott, 2001).

In European policy-related discussions during the 1990s, the concept of metropolitan regions emerged, very much influenced by Germany where the concept of *Metropolregionen* had been enshrined in a 1993 policy document (BRBS, 1993) and which has been reconfirmed several times since then (BmVBS, 2006; BMVI, 2016). Publications of the Federal Institute for Research on Building, Urban Affairs and Spatial Development known by its German acronym as BBSR (*Bundesinstitut für Bau-, Stadt – und Raumforschung*), have been very influential in this respect in and outside Germany.

They include the 2011 study *Metropolitan Areas in Europe* (Federal Institute for Research on Building, Urban Affairs and Spatial Development, 2011) which emphasized that *metropolitan* functions transcend the level of the daily urban system. These functions have a different rhythm of use as well as a different spatial scope compared with many other (economic) functions which play a key role in distance to work approaches like the concept of functional urban regions or FURs (Cheshire and Hay, 1989; ESPON, 2005, 2007; OECD, 2013). This kind of thinking is extremely relevant for understanding the Randstad as it is not the total population, but the extent and significance of the metropolitan functions that determine the strength of a metropolitan region. A radius of 50 kilometres is regarded as typical for such regions. For the Netherlands this means that the focus should not be on Amsterdam, Rotterdam, The Hague or Utrecht individually, but the Randstad as a whole.

In the 2011 comparative study by the BBSR, five spatial domains of metropolitan functions (*Metropolfunktionsbereiche*) are distinguished: political, economic, academic-scientific, transport and culture. Indicators for the academic-scientific field are, for example, the number of top 500 universities and the number of international scientific institutions, journals and patents. Among the indicators for transport is the tonnage of goods transhipped through sea and airports. In the BBSR research, the Randstad emerges as one of the strongest metropolitan areas in Europe, with widely differentiated metropolitan functions across the five domains. These metropolitan functions are distributed over seven locations: the four largest cities, the two university cities of Leiden and Delft, and around Schiphol Airport.

Metropolitan functions are the 'hubs' in the flows of persons, goods, capital and information, and their strength determines the international position of cities and regions. In this chapter it is assumed that, in addition to their number and extent, the way they *cluster* also matters in the international context. Not only the facilities themselves, but also their location and context contribute to the attractiveness of a city or region as a prospective business location or travel destination. Therefore, it is important to examine the spatial and functional structure of clusters of facilities – *interaction environments* – at their location in cities and the relations between them.

An interaction environment is to be understood as a spatial environment with facilities for personal encounters and for the exchange of persons, goods, capital and/or information. This definition includes functions that are normally not regarded as metropolitan. However, the Randstad can be characterized as a delta city region. Horticulture and transport often form prime functions within delta economies, and that is particularly true for the Dutch Delta (see for instance Meyer in this volume, Meyer *et al.*, 2012; Boelens, 2014). Dutch sea and airports, along with the interaction environments around prime horticultural auctions, form extensive complexes. If the transhipment at auctions had been included in the German research mentioned above, the position of the Randstad would have been even stronger. The contrast between these logistics interaction environments and the new urban interaction environments in Amsterdam, Leiden, The Hague, Delft, Rotterdam and Utrecht is considerable, in both size and nature. The four largest cities have a mixed profile. Leiden and Delft have a more specialized profile.

This chapter focuses on the four largest cities in the sectors of culture, conventions and knowledge (the full analysis can be found in De Hoog, 2013)[2]. The next section presents a range of prime examples of interaction environments in the Randstad, leaving out interaction environments related to trade and logistics. The section thereafter presents a typology. The following section discusses some main challenges regarding interaction environments and their integration in the urban fabric. The chapter rounds off by discussing the relationship between interaction environments and the structure of the Randstad, and comes to the conclusion that the Randstad can indeed be called a metropolis.

The Randstad metropolitan interaction environments

In 1966, in the 'block map' in the Second Report on Physical Planning, Eo Wijers, the main urban designer behind the map, sketched a striking, modernist perspective for environmental differentiation in the Netherlands (Ministerie van VRO, 1966a). Yellow, orange, red and brown blocks indicate four types of urban environments, A, B, C and D, of varying size and with corresponding density, transport systems and facilities in a strict hierarchical order. The block map (see Figure 10.1) is now part of the canon of Dutch physical planning (Ministry of Infrastructure and the Environment, 2012).

The 'D urban environment' represented the largest urban cores, of about 250,000 residents, with, among other things, specialized shops such as furriers and what in those days were called 'pants palaces' (*broekenpaleizen*). In Wijers's vision, the Netherlands accommodates at least nine of these D environments, which include the centres of the four largest Randstad cities plus Groningen, Eindhoven, Arnhem, Enschede and Dordrecht. The vision was closely connected with the policy of national dispersal of people and economic activities which also is part of the Second Report. So there is no 'E environment' which, building logically on Wijers's types, would be an internationally oriented urban environment with, hypothetically, a million residents in a density of 100 dwellings per hectare, a metro network, and a corresponding package of facilities including museums, top institutes, hotels and conference centres. In the mid-1970s the E environment was rejected because it was said not to fit within the structure of Dutch cities as the reconstruction and extension of city cores would lead to massive destruction of older inner city neighbourhoods.

Despite several decades of dispersal policy (the policy ended in the 1980s during a period of recession) (Zonneveld in this volume; Wagenaar, 2011), precisely such a metropolitan E environment has arisen in and around Amsterdam since the 1990s. Amsterdam functions as the nucleus of the Dutch Metropolis. That is true particularly for the heart of the city, with urban

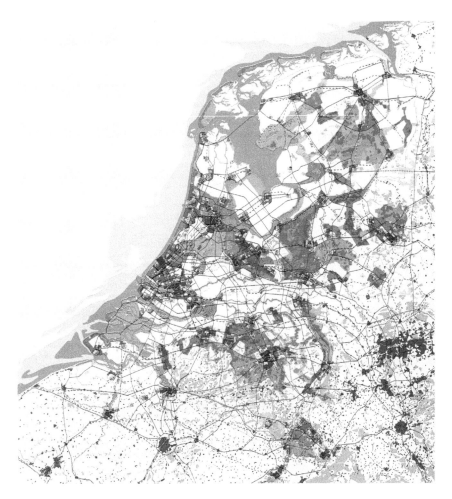

Figure 10.1 The block map of the 1966 national Second Report on spatial planning.
Source: Ministerie van VRO, 1966b.

interaction environments including the shopping district, university clusters and a whole series of entertainment and cultural quarters. In addition, the south flank of the Amsterdam region, in conjunction with the airport, has developed a second set of interaction environments around the business quarter known as the South Axis.

Some of the interaction environment clusters in the city centre and on the south flank of Amsterdam are developing rapidly and are on the brink of a leap forward in quality and size (Savini *et al.*, 2016). That is also true for the mixed and more diffuse coastal cluster around The Hague, with its seaside resorts, the R&D clusters in Leiden, and the collection of clusters in and around The Hague itself. This coastal cluster can be characterized as an up-and-coming E environment. More precisely formulated, in the four largest cities we encounter metropolitan interaction environments in the sectors of culture, conventions and knowledge, as explained in the following section.

Amsterdam

Of the largest cities, Amsterdam's E environment has a reach from the local to the international level of scale. There are in total at least eighteen interaction environments in the city – ten cultural clusters, two conference clusters and six knowledge clusters. Most of the clusters lie in and around the large, historic city centre. The central element is the Dam, a classic culture square. It is in the midst of a mixed district, with cultural facilities, hotels and conference facilities in addition to a large number of non-food stores. It is adjoined by culture and entertainment clusters such as the 1012 entertainment quarter which got its name from the postal code and includes the red-light district (Neuts *et al.*, 2014), Leidseplein and Rembrandtplein. Around this central district, but still within easy walking distance lie a series of other clusters: Museumplein, university centres and various culture quarters. The waterfront along the IJ is also being redeveloped.

The programme and the quality of the interaction environments in the city centre have developed at lightning speed into a situation in which there is now one large and differentiated inner city district and two rising cultural districts, Leidseplein-Museumplein and the East City Centre. At some distance lie the much smaller, rising clusters of Overhoeks (see Figure 10.2), the NDSM culture wharf and the Westergasfabriek culture park, the latter the former nineteenth-century gasworks of Amsterdam. A second concentration of interaction environments lies around the South Axis, with the RAI fair and conference centre, the VU (*Vrije Universteit*) and its Medical Centre, and

Figure 10.2 New Amsterdam cluster opposite the historical centre across the IJ.
Source: Editors.

the business quarter around Amsterdam's South Station. Together these clusters form a rising, mixed business district. Several other knowledge clusters – the Amsterdam Medical Centre or AMC,[3] Science Park, Slotervaart and Shell – and the leisure quarter around the ArenA Boulevard are spread around outside these two concentrations.

The Hague

The Hague excels in the political and administrative niche, counting seven interaction environments, with its three culture clusters, three conference clusters and one knowledge cluster. The clusters are developing rapidly, the offerings are broader, and as a result there is in fact the prospect of a metropolitan E environment here. Some of the interaction environments lie within walking distance of one another in the composite city centre district: the shopping quarter around the Lange Poten and Grote Marktstraat, the cultural clusters around the Binnenhof and the Spuiplein, and the knowledge quarter of the government ministries in the Wijnhaven quarter.

The International Zone is a rising district around the World Forum conference centre and the Kunstmuseum Den Haag cluster. A large number of hotels and a whole series of institutions, such as the Peace Palace and the European Criminal Court also lie in this district. A second emerging district is taking shape around the Scheveningen beach resort. With the addition of all kinds of cultural and conference facilities this long, narrow entertainment and hotel cluster along the seafront is taking on an increasingly mixed character. The recent reconstruction of the seaside promenade supports this new quality to the environment.

Rotterdam

Rotterdam excels in water transport due to its mainport function, but it also has eight interaction environments, with four culture clusters, two conference clusters and two knowledge clusters. Three of the four culture clusters (Schouwburgplein, Binnenrotte and Museumpark) lie around the central, highly specialized Lijnbaan shopping quarter. In recent years, as a consequence of intensification, blending of the programme and the redesign of public spaces, a more mixed and composite city centre district has emerged. The rising Leuvehaven cluster could also become a part of this district. The waterfront development on the Kop van Zuid and the two knowledge clusters connected to Erasmus University, Hoboken and Woudestein, lie at some distance from the city centre. Blijdorp Zoo, the RDM campus and the Heart of the South, with the Zuidplein shopping centre and the fair and sports centre Ahoy (used for the 2020 Eurovision Song Contest but postponed until a later date due to the Corona crisis), are still more peripheral.

Utrecht

The six Utrecht interaction environments are distinguished in the areas of science and culture, with two culture clusters, two conference clusters and two knowledge clusters. Most of the clusters lie in and around the relatively small, historic city centre, and are part of a developing, composite city centre district. With the radical reconstruction of the Hoog Catharijne shopping complex, the mixed shopping quarter around Vredenburg, the Museum quarter and the Jaarbeurs fair and entertainment centre will be more strongly integrated. Outside the city lies the extensive and successful Uithof knowledge district. Since December 2019 it is connected to the city centre by a new tram line.

The Holland Cluster

Together, the metropolitan interaction environments of the Dutch Metropolis yield a different image on a map from the familiar picture of the Randstad: the 'Holland Cluster'. The centres of the four largest cities play an important role, but they are part of a multi-coloured network with a whole series of more peripheral districts, such as the South Axis (Amsterdam), the International Zone (The Hague), the University of Technology (TU) district in Delft, the Uithof (Utrecht) and Scheveningen (The Hague), and a cloud of attractions, auctions and R&D centres. Aside from the logistics interaction environments of the large sea and airport sites, and the horticulture auctions, the following eleven districts are the largest and most powerful urban interaction environments in the Dutch Metropolis:

- three city centre districts: the mixed district around the Dam and the cultural district around Leidseplein-Museumplein in Amsterdam, and the composite district in the centre of The Hague;
- two specialized knowledge districts in Delft and Utrecht;
- six rising districts: the Rotterdam central city with its adjoining Museumpark and Leuvehaven clusters, the 'expanded heart of the city' in Utrecht, the rising cultural district in the eastern part of the inner city in Amsterdam, the mixed Amsterdam South Axis business district, the International Zone in The Hague, and the seafront at Scheveningen.

A typology of interaction environments

In the above analysis of the culture, conference and knowledge clusters, considerable attention was devoted to the diverse types of interaction environments. That permits us to now sharpen the comparison between logistics and metropolitan interaction environments. It appears that there are all sorts of parallel types that can be distinguished in different sectors. For example, it appears that there are all sorts of different centres: shopping centres, culture centres, conference centres, medical centres and university centres. Comparable examples can be found among squares, quarters and parks. It is striking that for the description of logistics interaction environments in particular, there are no similar precise terms. We have to make do with general terms, such as sites and areas. At the largest scale we find a parallel between region and 'valley'. The various interaction environments can be grouped under four main types: built, urban, green and neutral interaction environments.

Built interaction environments: centres – court complexes – terminals

The Randstad has a large number of *centres*. The criteria which apply to all centres are that they are compact, including built facilities with robust programming, and are owned and managed by one organization. The various spaces are not accessed via public spaces, but connected 'indoors' by a system of corridors, passages, interior streets or courts. Often there are set opening hours, and only a few entrances. Frequently, supporting programmes do not lie around the centre, but are included 'in house'. The *court complex* and the *terminal* are variants of this type.

The most famous centre in the Netherlands is Hoog Catharijne. It contains 160 stores, with a total floor area of 42,000 m². Because of its vast size, Hoog Catharijne could perhaps better be termed a super mall, comparable with examples like the CentrO in Oberhausen Germany, the Bluewater complex in south east England or the planned EuropaCity near Roissy airport in France. The discussion which has rumbled on for years about the integration of Hoog Catharijne into the city is indicative of a general problem with centres of this sort. Hoog Catharijne was supposed to be the connector between Utrecht Central Station and the historical core of the city. But centres are cities turned in on itself. That is also true for many trade fair and conference centres, and for university centres. The sites of the Amsterdam RAI Convention Centre and Utrecht Jaarbeurs are even somewhat larger than Hoog Catharijne. They are major barriers in the urban fabric. Efforts are sometimes made to make the centre more permeable by connecting the separate sections of the buildings not at ground level, but at the first or second level. The larger the centre, however, the more difficult successful integration will be.

The University of Amsterdam centre on Roeterseiland occupies a relatively small area and was recently better integrated into the city. Cultural centres such as the Muziekgebouw in Amsterdam and Tivoli Vredenburg Utrecht are even more compact. These centres fit easily into their surroundings.

The R&D centres of businesses and institutions like Shell in Amsterdam, the European Space Agency (ESA) in Noordwijk, the ECN (Energy Research Centre of the Netherlands) in Petten and the RIVM (National Institute for Public Health and the Environment) in Bilthoven, also cover several hectares, and in terms of built volume are comparable with university centres. However, they often are on large sites outside the city and integration into their surroundings is not an issue. The new Shell Research Centre in

Amsterdam is relatively compact. With the move of RIVM to the Utrecht Uithof, the institute will fit into the public nature of this knowledge district.

The *court* type also looks like a centre. It is compact, and the various parts are often connected internally, but unlike the centre the courts are open to the public. Despite this quality, it is a type of interaction environment rarely found in the Netherlands. For instance, one does not find a self-standing series of public courtyards with shops in Dutch city centres, like the Häckische Höfe in Berlin. There are a few examples of other sorts. The most beautiful is the ensemble of the Buitenhof, Binnenhof, Hofvijver and Plein in The Hague, with the parliament buildings and the Ridderzaal (Knights' Hall) and their supporting programme of cafés, restaurants and meeting facilities around them. The Binnenhof complex itself has a radius of 100 metres. The court complex with university functions on the Amsterdam Binnengasthuis site (a former, large inner city hospital) is the only example of this type in the knowledge sector. It has a radius of 175 metres. There are other smaller – and usually historic – examples of court complexes spread around the cities, such as the Oostindisch Huis in Amsterdam. They are often remnants of monasteries.

Large facilities for logistics interaction environments are often called *terminals*. The terminal at Schiphol is comprised of a whole series of spatial elements: arrival and departure halls, parking garages, check-in windows, offices, shops and restaurants, and a whole circuit of piers, baggage belts, gates and platforms. Compared with centres, these complexes have a more composite form, the elements are linked in a series, and are often accessible without leaving the building. Efficient management of the logistics process is the central concern.

Stations are also increasingly often called terminals. Various public transit modes intersect with one another in one building complex, in which all the accompanying facilities are included. In recent years all four main stations in the Holland Cluster have been redesigned and opened much more to their surroundings. This adds a lot of quality to these terminals. One also encounters terminals in sea ports. A cruise terminal is oriented to passengers, but sometimes cargo piers and loading and unloading facilities are also called terminals, as in the case of container terminals. However, one rarely encounters buildings in such terminals.

Urban interaction environments: squares, streets, fronts, quarters and districts

Urban interaction environments are characterized by their combination of public spaces and buildings, which are owned and managed by multiple persons, organizations or institutions. The buildings are oriented to, and accessible from, public spaces. There is often a repetition of built units of comparable size: stores, cafés, theatres, departmental buildings and museums in a more or less mixed form.

Considered in terms of the area they occupy, the types found here arrange themselves into a series from small to large. In European cities, *squares* have traditionally been the most concentrated public spaces for people encountering one another and exchanges of all sorts. It was there that markets were held, and townsmen built their churches, city halls and financial exchanges around them. Presently they come in all shapes and sizes like shopping squares, entertainment squares, classic and modern culture squares. Most squares in The Netherlands are relatively small. The radius of most entertainment and culture squares, including the built facilities around them, does not exceed 175 metres. Only the Amsterdam Museumplein and Arena Boulevard are larger. The Museumplein stands apart for the extreme dimensions of its open space, the Arena Boulevard for the massive size of the venues around it – the Arena itself (recently rechristened as the Johan Cruijff Arena), but also the Pathé Arena cinema, the AFAS Live (formerly known as Heineken Music Hall), Villa Arena and the Ziggo Dome.

Many *streets* are mixed interaction environments par excellence. Only in a limited number of cases they are dominated by one specific function. Shopping streets are distinguished by the predominant presence of stores. Over recent decades most shopping streets with non-food stores in city centres have been redesigned as pedestrian areas, modelled on the successful concept of Rotterdam's Lijnbaan, established from the 1950s. Another specialized case is the entertainment street. Amsterdam's Reguliersdwarsstraat hosts 20 cafés and discos, the Zeedijk 12. The Nes, in Amsterdam, is the only culture street in the Netherlands, with three major theatres: Frascati, the Brakke Grond and the Comedy Theatre.

The *river or seafront* with its characteristic public space of a promenade is a mixed form of square and street. The promenade, in the form of a beach boulevard (Scheveningen) or quay (Rotterdam), is built up on only one side, giving it a strong orientation.

Most *quarters* have a radius of 350 to 400 metres. The relatively strong specialization of quarters in the 'Dutch Metropolis' is striking – for instance, the shopping quarters in the city centres of The Hague and Rotterdam, the culture and entertainment quarters in Amsterdam, the knowledge quarter in Leiden and the business quarter of the Amsterdam South Axis.

In Amsterdam Nieuwendijk, Kalverstraat and Leidsestraat, together with the nine Straatjes, the Haarlemmerdijk/Haarlemmerstraat (see Figure 10.3) and the Jordaan, form a complete shopping district with 1000 stores and a radius of almost 750 metres. It is a relatively mixed district, including the classic culture square of the Dam in the middle, and a whole series of culture and entertainment squares and quarters around it. Its commercial success has led to sometimes massive rent increases which caused some homogenization (shops owned by chains) in main streets and dispersal of independent shops in side streets and nearby areas.

In addition to this city centre district, there are two other specialized districts in the 'Dutch Metropolis', the Utrecht Uithof and the TU Delft district.

Figure 10.3 The Haarlemmerstraat/Haarlemmerdijk.
Source: Editors.

Amsterdam's cultural districts are presently emerging. With the integration of the various quarters of the South Axis, this area will also grow to the size of a district. The TU Delft district is an extremely large knowledge district with a radius of 1,500 metres, and it is therefore perhaps better to term this interaction environment a super-district. Its sheer size and dispersed character make it one of the least attractive university campuses of the Netherlands.

Green interaction environments: gardens, wharves, parks and campuses

In the interaction environments of the Holland Cluster, the term 'park' is to be found with various meanings. In addition to public culture and science parks, such as the Museumpark in Rotterdam, the Amsterdam based Westergasfabriek and the Bio Science Park in Leiden, there are countless amusement parks and attractions such as Madurodam in the Hague and zoos spread through the Holland Cluster, and the more closed R&D campuses that are also termed 'research parks'. The 'culture wharf' is a more unpolished version of the culture park.

It is striking that businesses and institutions also play an important role in the development, ownership and management of the publicly accessible culture and science parks. The Westergasfabriek was developed by MAB Project Developers and is managed by Westergasfabriek Ltd., and the NDSM wharf by Kinetisch Noord, legally a (nonprofit) trust. Universities play a central role in many science parks, and also in the commercial exploitation of the sites for non-university functions. Rotterdam's Museumpark is an exception, being managed by the city.

Enclosed green space is a characteristic of all these interaction environments. Garden and park are thus – just as was the case for urban interaction environments like quarters and districts – indications of their size. They can lie both in, and outside, cities. The classic botanical and zoological gardens, and playgrounds, are the smallest. Amsterdam's Hortus for instance measures 1.2 ha. The largest attraction park in the Holland Cluster is Walibi Biddinghuizen, with an area of 120 hectare (40 hectare of theme park, 20 ha of vacation bungalow park, and a 60 ha event site), and is comparable with Leiden's Bio Science Park in extent.

Neutral interaction environments: site, field, area and region

In everyday speech, various neutral terms such as site, field, area and region are used for a number of interaction environments. They can lie in cities, or outside them. A region transcends the scale of the city. A site, such as an industrial site for storage, industrial production or energy plants, is a sizeable piece of land. The word is also used for event sites, and sports fields reflect a similar usage. Compared with the other interaction environments that were discussed above, a site has a less distinct form. It is suitable for various uses, and there is often just a simple fence around it. A field is distinguished by the presence of grass, such as on a landing field or sports field. The term area indicates the whole of the sites used for a specific function, such as a greenhouse or harbour area.

The term region indicates a large area with common topographic characteristics, such as a coastal region or flower bulb region. As a reflection from Silicon Valley, in recent years the term valley has been used for a region associated with specific products or facilities, as in the case of FoodValley (primarily the host town of Wageningen University and Research Centre plus seven other municipalities) or Health Valley Netherlands in Nijmegen (a label chosen by various, obviously competing initiatives).

Some main challenges

Series and mix

Interaction environments fall into series based on their size. Most centres, courtyard complexes, squares and gardens have a radius of 175–200 metres and an area of 10–12 ha. Quarters, campuses and parks have a radius of 350–400 metres and an area of 40–50 ha; districts have a radius of 700–800 metres, and an area of 150–200 ha: always a doubling of the radius, and a quadrupling of the area. On the other hand, it remains difficult to formulate a generally valid principle. There are just too many exceptions. More research seems necessary.

Some urban interaction environments are, by definition, more mixed than others, if only as a result of the combination of public space and private buildings. In many other interaction environments the public space is limited, or at least there are limits on access to it. That is also the snag; the limited access makes encounters and exchanges less open and more strongly programmed and controlled. Therefore, many universities are carrying out radical operations to open up their strongly inwardly oriented centres to the city. It is precisely this open interaction in an urban environment that is seen as the advantage of being located in the city.

Nevertheless, it is striking to note how little mixture there is in most urban interaction environments. In most cases, a mixed environment is to be understood as one with several other functions in addition to public space and dwellings. Many shopping and entertainment clusters – be they streets, squares or complete quarters – are pretty much limited to that one function. Here and there, projects like 'homes over shops', or adjusted night open hours, are being used to encourage mixing. The 1012 entertainment quarter in Amsterdam is probably the most extreme example of a specialized urban interaction environment.

On the other hand, a certain degree of specialization is precisely the strong point of many urban interaction environments. The combination with other, similar functions, sectors or even atmospheres, draws specific target audiences and therefore encourages diversity and quality. Between 'extremely specialized' and 'fully integrated' there are 'composite' and 'mixed' environments – two interesting categories deserving further study.

The strolling city

At the core of interaction environments are halls where people watch and listen to performances, speeches or competitions, or wander around looking at new products or unusual objects. Impressions and experiences get shared, deepened and interpreted in conversations around the halls, in corridors, foyers and cafeterias in the buildings, but also on the streets, in the cafés, lunchrooms, coffee shops and restaurants along them. This 'supporting programme' in the immediate vicinity plays an important role. The greater anonymity of the public places, as compared with university cafeterias or theatre foyers, guarantees a greater intensity of contacts, and can facilitate unexpected stimuli and encounters. That is one reason that many universities seek to break open their centres and campuses and better integrate them into the city.

Interaction and the city are however natural allies to one another at many more points. Markets and concentrated forms of interaction such as events and festivals thrive in cities. Increasing numbers of visitors combine an afternoon of shopping with an evening out, or stay overnight and make a Sunday morning stroll. Many tourists succumb to the temptation to wander around a city and let it surprise them. In many cases, the culture, shopping and cuisine will be decisive factors in the choice of a host city for a convention.

The famous Dutch architect Aldo van Eyck summed up the magic of the city in his design for the pavilion for the Sonsbeek exhibition in the summer of 1966. The pavilion was built as an exhibition space for sculptures. They do not stand in a large space, or in a park, but in a structure with six tall, parallel walls, with niches and apertures.[4] You can only experience the sculptures by wandering through this small city: 'Bump! – Sorry – What's this? Oh hello!'[5] That is, in essence, the quality of the city.

The design of public space

The design of its public space – the 'floor' of the city – is of paramount importance for strolling. The Dutch norm for this was set in 1988 with the plans for a complete make-over for the centre of The Hague, *De Kern Gezond* ('The Healthy Core'). The plan – or better, the programme – was commissioned by the municipal authorities in The Hague, and drawn up by the landscape architect Alle Hosper. It is characterized by the choice to use only one type of paving brick and kerb, and for a family of lighting fixtures, sewer grates and street furniture. These create a restful street scene and provide continuity. Within this there are five areas distinguished, each with its own atmosphere and spatial identity, such as wide and narrow shopping streets, and the series of urban and green squares. These areas are all organized around parallel 'lines', built on former barrier islands in the coastal zone. These long lines, and the 'heart line' which crosses them and ties them together, are carefully detailed.

In the course of the 1990s, almost all the streets and squares of the centre of The Hague were re-designed. Grote Marktstraat and Rijnstraat were tunnelled for the tram. It has been an unusually successful project. The various shopping and culture clusters have come to form a single district, in a natural manner. Only the supporting line from the Spuiplein to Central Station has not lived up to its promise, and the integration of the culture clusters around the Spuiplein and the Wijnhaven quarter, with the government ministries, has remained problematic. Redesigns are under construction now.

The design of public space is crucial for the success of almost all emerging districts. Many of the combinations we have discussed will stand or fall with better integration of car traffic into the urban fabric. For the International Zone in The Hague the central factor is the ability to cross the western ring road conveniently, and in Rotterdam it is the success in making the area around the Westblaak a continuous urban fabric. For the 'expanded heart' of Utrecht the redesign of the Catharijnesingel and the Stationsplein will be the proof of the pudding.[6]

Conclusion: a Dutch metropolis

The definition of the metropolis used here, with its strong emphasis on metropolitan functions, is related to the manner in which Niek de Boer, professor of City and Region at Delft University of Technology from 1969 to 1989, looked at environments in big cities. In 1996, in his polemic book (in translation) 'The Randstad does not exist: The failure to pursue a metropolitan policy' (De Boer, 1996) he dissected the spatial policy that the Netherlands had maintained since the 1966 Second Report on Spatial Planning (Ministerie VRO, 1966a), He noted that not only the national government, but also the large cities, fell shamefully short in their vision of the development of metropolitan qualities and an attractive, large-scale urban environment focused on interaction. In De Boer's view, that was a serious denial of metropolitan quality. De Boer also noted that the Netherlands had no attractive metropolitan environment that counted internationally. Amsterdam scored the best, and The Hague trailed at a distance; Rotterdam and Utrecht did not count at all in 1996, according to de Boer.

What is the state of affairs a quarter of a century later? According to many including the OECD (2007, 2014) the Randstad stands high in the rankings, but when examined more closely, the picture is more mixed. The power of attraction exerted by the Dutch Metropolis is defined by a multiplicity of factors. In addition to its accessible location via Schiphol Airport, many studies also cite the still relatively easy accessibility of its residential market, the level of prices and taxes, its hospitality, facilities for overnight stays and international orientation.

In line with international trends the number of visitors to the main Dutch cities has grown strongly since 2000, be it international tourists, shoppers, participants in conventions or youngsters visiting festivals. In Amsterdam the number of overnight hotel stays doubled from 8 million in 2003 to near 17 million in 2018, Airbnb and other bed & breakfast facilities not included.[7] The crowds congregating at the weekends on the busiest streets and squares has caused a controversial debate in local media and politics. New policies were introduced like 'balancing' or 'spreading' tourism.

Over the last decade, substantial investment has taken place, and all kinds of new interaction environments have been introduced spread around the cities in the Netherlands: culture parks, waterfronts, arenas, convention centres, science parks, leisure boulevards, etc. These have expanded the offerings greatly. Nevertheless, most of the visitors want to go to the inner cities. Dealing with more visitors and improving quality, safety and accessibility of the existing interaction environments seems now the main assignment for urban planning and design.

In this respect, a main difference occurs between the northern and the southern part of the Randstad. In the north, in the Metropolitan Region Amsterdam (MRA), the seventeenth-century inner city of Amsterdam is becoming the busiest cluster of interaction environments, indeed it is becoming a 'super district', combining the smaller interaction environments into one large cluster with a radius of 1.5 kilometres and easily accessible by bike and foot. A good example of the integration process is the construction of the 'Red Carpet'. This project is a redesign of the central backbone of the city along Amstel River: the Stationsplein, Damrak, Rokin and Munt. Connected with the realization of the North/South Metro line which is in use since Summer 2018, the previously fragmented public space is once again becoming a whole, barriers are being removed, and car traffic is being rerouted. The effect of the redesign is that the adjoining 1012 entertainment quarter and the university quarter around the Binnengasthuis site connect now with the shopping district around the Nieuwendijk, Dam and Kalverstraat in a natural manner. The areas become more easily accessible for various groups of pedestrians. This encourages a better mix. The same process of integrating clusters is on its way on the southern and eastern side of the inner city, integrating the Museumplein-cluster, with the Van Gogh and Rijksmuseum, and the Oosterdok-cluster, with the Maritime and Science museum, in the super district. At the time of writing the redesign and reconstruction of the Central Station has been finalized after a 20-year construction period. Now it has become possible to establish a new connection with the River IJ and the upcoming cultural cluster on the northern bank of the IJ (see Figure 10.2). New parks, a quay and bike bridges over the water will give access to the currently poorly accessible banks of the river. The focus on connections, accessibility and attractive public space helps to spread visitors within the new super district in Amsterdam. The reduction of car traffic and redesign of public space is a crucial condition for success.

The structure of interaction environments in the southern part of the Randstad is quite different. The Metropolitan Region Rotterdam The Hague (MRDH) is a more composite and deconcentrated region. Interaction is already spread out from the Scheveningen and International Zone clusters along the coast in the north to Rotterdam Zuidplein with the big Ahoy exhibition, sport and music complex in the south. Since 2006 the different interaction clusters, including the inner cities of The Hague and Rotterdam, are connected via *RandstadRail*. Former separate train, metro and tram networks have become better integrated. Train services are to some extent replaced by metro and the new network makes the clusters more easily accessible.

The Amsterdam super district contrasts sharply with the Rotterdam-The Hague network of clusters, with bikes and pedestrian space versus metro as the main connector. The super district is an international attractor comparable to the central districts of Berlin and Rome and an important motor for economic growth, for start-ups and scale-ups in the new service and tech economy. But this quality also means extreme pressure on and conflicts on public space. Many inhabitants of the city of Amsterdam prefer the periphery over the inner city. Daily life in the network metropolis of Rotterdam-The Hague seems to be the more sophisticated and pleasant one. Nevertheless, the amount, diversity and combinations of interaction environments in both the Amsterdam and Rotterdam-The Hague regions give the Randstad a unique metropolitan character, combining a deconcentrated urban pattern with high quality public facilities.

Notes

1 For some amazing images see: https://lowlands.nl/ (accessed 7 April 2020).
2 As the interaction environments discussed in this chapter exhibit rapid changes (in particular enlargement and mergers) this analysis has been updated until the end of 2019. The 2020 Corona crisis resulted in an abrupt change in many interaction environments as 'interaction' itself became an issue. The resulting

economic effects may have lasting effects on some interaction environments due to the possible bankruptcy of many businesses.

3 The medical faculties of the two Amsterdam universities (University of Amsterdam and Free University) are strongly cooperating since mid-2018. This resulted in the merger of both academic hospitals into one single giant hospital, the Amsterdam University Medical Centre or UMC. The two formerly separated hospitals kept their locations: Location AMC and Location VUmc.

4 Today the pavilion can be found in the garden of the Kröller-Müller Museum. See https://krollermuller.nl/en/aldo-van-eyck-aldo-van-eyck-pavilion (accessed 7 April 2020).

5 Aldo van Eyck (1918–1999) was a Dutch architect and co-founder of Team X, the group of young, post-war architects, criticizing pre-war modern architects for their limited 'functional' approach of city life. During the sixties and seventies Van Eyck was strongly involved in the debate on renewing inner cities in the Netherlands (see also: Lefaivre and Tzonis, 1999).

6 See: https://cu2030.nl/page/english (accessed 7 April 2020).

7 At the time of writing the figures for 2019 were not known yet. See: https://data.amsterdam.nl/artikelen/artikel/toerisme-in-amsterdam/5df34c3d-06be-40ca-ac8f-b0f8c05c2499/ (accessed 7 April 2020).

References

BmVBS, Bundesministerium für Verkehr, Bauwesen und Stadsentwicklung (2006). *Leitbilder und Handlungsstrategien für die Raumentwicklung in Deutschland [Leitbilder and Operational Strategies for the Spatial Development of Germany]*; Verabschiedet von der Ministerkonferenz für Raumordnung am 30.06.2006. BmVBS, Berlin.

BMVI, Bundesministerium für Verkehr und digitale Infrastruktur (2016). *Leitbilder und Handlungsstrategien für die Raumentwicklung in Deutschland [Leitbilder and Operational Strategies for the Spatial Development of Germany]*; Verabschiedet von der Ministerkonferenz für Raumordnung am 9. März 2016. BMVI, Berlin.

Boelens, L. (2014). 'Delta Governance: The DNA of a specific kind of urbanization', *Built Environment*, 40(2), 169–183.

BRBS, Bundesministerium für Raumordnung, Bauwesen und Städtebau (1993). *Raumordnungspolitischer Orientierungsrahmen: Leitbilder für die räumliche Entwicklung der Bundesrepublik Deutschland [Spatial Policy Framework: Leitbilder for the Spatial Development of the Federal Republic of Germany]*. BRBS, Bonn.

Cheshire, P.C. and Hay, D.G. (Eds) (1989). *Urban Problems in Western Europe; An Economic Analysis*. Unwin Hyman, London.

De Boer, N. (1996). *De Randstad bestaat niet: De onmacht tot grootstedelijk beleid [The Randstad Does Not Exist: The Failure to Pursue a Metropolitan Policy]*. NAi Uitgevers, Rotterdam.

De Hoog, M. (2013). *The Dutch Metropolis: Designing Quality Interaction Environments*. THOTH, Bussum.

ESPON (2005). *ESPON 1.1.1: Potentials for Polycentric Development in Europe*; Project report, Revised version 5 March 2005. ESPON, Esch-sur-Alzette.

ESPON (2007). *ESPON Project 1.4.3: Study on Urban Functions*; Final Report March 2007. ESPON, Esch-sur-Alzette.

Federal Institute for Research on Building, Urban Affairs and Spatial Development (2011). *Metropolitan Areas in Europe*, BBSR-Online-Publikation, Nr. 01/2011. BBSR, Bonn.

Lefaivre, L. and Tzonis, A. (1999). *Aldo van Eyck: Humanist Rebel – Inbetweening in a Postwar World*. 010 Publishers, Rotterdam.

Meyer, H., Nillisen, A.L. and Zonneveld, W. (2012). 'Rotterdam: A city and a Mainport on the edge of a delta', *European Planning Studies*, 20(1), 71–94.

Ministerie van VRO (Volkshuisvesting en Ruimtelijke Ordening) (1966a). *Tweede nota over de ruimtelijke ordening [Second Report on Spatial Planning]*. Staatsuitgeverij, The Hague.

Ministerie van VRO (Volkshuisvesting en Ruimtelijke Ordening) (1966b). *Tweede nota over de ruimtelijke ordening [Second Report on Spatial Planning]*; Kaartenbijlage [Map appendix]. Staatsuitgeverij, The Hague.

Ministry of Infrastructure and the Environment (2012). *35 Icons of Dutch Spatial Planning/35 iconen van ruimtelijke ordening in Nederland*. Ministry of Infrastructure and the Environment, The Hague.

Neuts, B., Devos, T. and Dirckx, T. (2014). 'Turning off the red lights: Entrepreneurial urban strategies in 'De Wallen' Amsterdam', *Applied Geography*, 49, 37–44.

OECD (2007). *OECD Territorial Reviews: Randstad Holland, Netherlands*. OECD, Paris.

OECD (2013). *Definition of Functional Urban Areas (FUA) for the OECD metropolitan database*. OECD, Paris.

OECD (2014). *OECD Territorial Reviews: Netherlands*. OECD, Paris.

Pred, A. (1977). *City-Systems in Advanced Economies; Past Growth, Present Processes, and Future Development Options*. Hutchinson University Library, London.

Sassen, S. (1991). *The Global City: New York, London, Tokyo*. Princeton University Press, Princeton.

Savini, F., Boterman, W.R, Van Gent, W.P.C. and Majoor, S. (2016). 'Amsterdam in the 21st century: Geography, housing, spatial development and politics', *Cities*, 52, 103–113.

Scott, A.J. (Ed.) (2001). *Global City-Regions; Trends, Theory, Policy*. Oxford University Press, Oxford.

Simmonds, R. and Hack, G. (Eds) (2000). *Global City Regions: Their Emerging Forms*. Spon Press, London/New York.

Wagenaar, C. (2011). *Town Planning in the Netherlands since 1800; Responses to Enlightenment Ideas and Geopolitical Realities*. 010 Publishers, Rotterdam.

Part IV

Governance, planning and design

11 Randstad

From a spatial planning concept to a place name

Wil Zonneveld

Introduction

There are not many polynuclear urban regions with a name as widely known as the Randstad. 'Randstad' though is an entirely artificial concept: a deliberately chosen metaphor relating to urban form at a roughly 80km x 80km scale which does not go back to any pre-existing geographical name. It is a genuine planners' concept, invented with the sole purpose of defining spatial planning issues and to formulate strategies to deal with them. The Randstad became internationally widely known – at least amongst planning professionals and academics – through two books both published in 1966: *Greenheart Metropolis* by Gerald L. Burke and *The World Cities* by Peter Hall. Peter Hall's book in particular became famous and was updated in 1977 and 1984. The first edition included two polynuclear regions: 'Randstad Holland' and the 'Rhine-Ruhr'. In the third edition Rhine-Ruhr was dropped 'for reasons of space' (Hall, 1984: 3); while the verdict on the planning approach towards metropolitan growth of the Randstad was even more positively compared with the original 1966 version, albeit with one reservation: what about implementation of all the paper plans? (Hall, 1984).

It is most likely that Peter Hall (he died in 2014 at the age of 82) would have been very disappointed about the present situation. In the Netherlands today Randstad has become a rather neutral place name. In the sense of place identity, Randstad does not mean a lot to most people, the area is simply too large (Musterd and Van Zelm, 2001). As a *planning* concept, a term used to express public norms and aspirations towards a desired territorial structure, it no longer has a distinct flavour, neither as the object of *national* spatial planning (one may even doubt whether currently there is still such thing as national spatial planning) nor as a region in which there is strong cooperation between local and regional administrations. The idea of an integrated spatial planning approach, advocated by many planners over the course of decades, has evaporated as we will see in this chapter. The same has happened to the ambition to create a governmental authority at this level which over a period of three-quarters of a century was conceived several times, but has at each stage died more or less peacefully (this will be discussed in next chapter).

This chapter seeks to unravel the history of the Randstad planning concept. Our focus is primarily on the national level as a lot of the thinking about the Randstad has been carried out within national planning organisations (although not exclusively as we move towards the present) and trickled down to provincial and municipal planning. Our story starts with a short section about the very first visualisation of the Randstad which was created in the early 1920s. The metaphor of Randstad was not yet invented and planning on this large scale, let alone national planning, was far beyond the horizon.

The 1950s saw the genuine birth of the Randstad concept which was soon amended within less than a decade due to developments *outside* the planning system, in particular population and urban growth, together with a rising trend towards suburbanisation. Conceptual innovation *within* the planning profession included the arrival of novel geographical notions emphasising a trend towards decentralisation and deconcentration of cities and towns. This inspired planners to think in terms of multiscalar urban structures and an ever-larger Randstad.

We then turn to the 1970s and 1980s by which time there was a reversal in thinking towards a downscaling of the Randstad, which eventually led to a heavy emphasis on the fortunes and misfortunes of the individual Randstad cities. From the late 1980s efforts were directed towards conceptual innovation and new interpretations of the Randstad were introduced in two waves. Novel Randstad conceptualisations sought to move away from classic *location* issues towards the question of how Randstad cities and urban functions within them relate to each other and to (supra)regional urban structures and networks. We will see that these innovations eventually fail for various reasons. We then explain the gradual marginalisation of national spatial planning from the 2000s when comprehensive spatial planning gave way to project-based planning in which there was less interest in spatial concepts like the Randstad. We end the chapter with a discussion of critical issues arising from the various Randstad conceptualisations.

Early images of the Randstad

Early traces of the Randstad concept go back as far as the 1920s and 1930s. Planning at the regional level did not exist, at least not in statutory planning. Scattered development was taking place which went against the ideas of 'systematic urbanization' (Faludi and Van der Valk, 1994: 54) advocated by professionals who we now would call 'spatial planners'. On the occasion of the 1924 Amsterdam Conference of the International Garden Cities and Town Planning Association (the forerunner of the present International Federation for Housing and Planning), one planner presented a map which is generally considered as the very first visualisation of the Randstad, although the term as such was not yet in use. This vintage GIS map prepared by Van Lohuizen (the original is lost, just a photograph is left of it) presents population growth of municipalities in the west of the country during the 1869–1920 period

(Van der Valk, 1990). The map clearly shows a ring of cities and towns with high growth figures surrounding an area with hardly any growth (see Figure 11.1). The map was used to call for statutory regional planning. Politically this fell on deaf ears. About three decades later Van Lohuizen became involved in the preparation of the report 'The Development of the West of the Country' report (Ahsmann, 1990) which we discuss below.

In 1938 the actual Randstad metaphor was born but interestingly not as part of a town planning agenda but as part of a transport logic. In a letter to the Dutch government, KLM (then and now the main Dutch airline) advocated a new location for an airport far more central than the existing airport which was near Amsterdam. KLM said the new airport should be located right in the middle of the 'Randstad Holland' east of the city of Leiden. It was the particular configuration of the Randstad which led to these thoughts. (Van der Valk, 1990: 60; translation by author, emphasis added)

> [A] large horseshoe shaped *city* with over 3 million inhabitants, (…) the population centres Utrecht, Het Gooi, Amsterdam, Haarlem, the Bulb Area, Leiden, Wassenaar, the Hague, Delft, Schiedam, Rotterdam and Dordrecht forming one *contiguous* area.

In the national airport debate other terms were used which, according to Meijers (2019), gives a clear indication of uncertainty in finding an appropriate territorial concept (translation author): *metropool Holland* (metropolis Holland), *zoom-metropolis Holland* (edge-metropolis Holland) or *wereldstad*

Figure 11.1 The very first visualisation of the Randstad *avant la lettre* by Th.K. van Lohuizen.
Source: Van der Valk, 1990.

Holland (world city Holland). The idea of a single metropolis in which one has to find the most logical, central location was far beyond the horizon of the involved municipalities. Amsterdam, Rotterdam and The Hague advocated three different locations with one shared characteristic: proximity to these three cities. In 1938 the government decided that the national airport should stay in the same location: at Schiphol near Amsterdam. Although some sort of regional approach towards territorial issues was beginning to emerge within several provincial administrations (Van der Cammen and De Klerk, 2012), the Randstad concept nevertheless looked stillborn close to the outbreak of the Second World War and the German occupation of the country in 1940.

The arrival of the Randstad as a comprehensive spatial concept

The start of national planning

Under the German occupation from 1941, a rather centralised planning system was introduced, a somewhat contested beginning for Dutch national (and regional) spatial planning (Van Dam and Vuijsje, 2011). This created the basis for establishing the *Rijksdienst voor het Nationale Plan* (RNP), or Government Service for the National Plan (referred to as Government Service from here). The National Plan itself would give broad outlines of development which were to be detailed in mandatory provincial structure plans and municipal zoning plans. Room for discretion would be limited as the content of the National Plan would be binding.

During wartime one of the key issues addressed by the Government Service was industrial dispersal. Although the ports in the west of the country offered good locations for industry and employment, it was a question whether continuous concentration in the West (in these days often written with a capital letter) was desirable (Faludi and Van der Valk, 1994: 79). To reverse migration trends *'geleide industrievestiging'* (guided industrial development) would be needed. A prime motivation was the maintenance of the structure of the Randstad and its 'dispersed pattern' (Faludi and Van der Valk, 1994): there are no cities with more than one million inhabitants while the Randstad at large should remain a 'garland of [...] towns arranged around a more or less unspoiled agricultural area' (Faludi and Van der Valk, 1994: 79). So, the future of the Randstad implied an ordering of the main spatial structure of the entire country and a very wide and strong mandate for national planning. This normative position could not be maintained in the immediate post-war period as this would imply a trespassing of the boundaries of other ministries and a violation of the principle of the Netherlands as a decentralised unitary state where provinces and municipalities play a strong role in policy development and implementation (Toonen, 1987, 1990).

Attention to the West

In spite of the sensitive relationships with sectoral departments, it was the West which became the focus of national planning at the end of the 1940s and early 1950s. Its development became a matter of great political concern as the built-up area of the Randstad was expected to double in size over the following 30 years or so. In the political discussions several problems were identified. For instance: the vast greenhouse complex called the Westland would be threatened by urbanisation as the nearby city of The Hague, thanks to its coastal location, could not grow in any other direction. With fresh memories of the 1944 winter of starvation the – partial – loss of such an important centre of food production was highly sensitive. The expansion of the steel works in the north-western corner of the Randstad, a prime objective of industrialisation policy, would require an entire new city. In the north-eastern Randstad corner of The Gooij the constellation of mid-sized towns surrounded by forests and heath was already turning into an area where pockets of nature were encircled by urban areas.

In 1950 the Minister of Reconstruction and Housing, responsible for national spatial planning, invited the executives of the three western provinces and the three largest cities (Utrecht evidently was not considered relevant at this stage) to discuss the future of the West. His worries were shared and for him this was enough to invite the so-called Permanent Commission on Spatial Planning, one of the bodies created during the wartime period, to study the development of the West. This request was a sensible move: the idea was that advice on planning should not come from spatial planners directly but from and through a body in which all relevant government departments were represented by senior officials (Faludi and Van der Valk, 1994). Planners could play their game, so to speak, in a Technical (sic) Working Commission, formed by specialists from various government departments and agencies, as well as from the three western provinces and the three largest cities. This cross-sectoral as well as multi-level approach towards policy making would become a rather strong characteristic of Dutch national planning.

The Advisory Report was published in 1958: '*De Ontwikkeling van het Westen des Lands*' (in literature the common translation is: The Development of the West of the Country). It presented a comprehensive vision of the Randstad (WWDL, 1958a), supported by an intricate and extensive empirical ('technical') analysis in a separate volume (WWDL, 1958b). The Report opens in the style of a geography textbook (including images) to explain the spatial structure of the Randstad and why the sum of the urban agglomerations of the West should be called Randstad (WWDL, 1958a): two large conurbations with a segmented structure, each shaped like a bow located around a large, relatively empty agricultural area: the Green Heart. It argues that the structure of this 'Dutch metropole' (WWDL, 1958a) is such that there is a 'healthy interplay' (WWDL, 1958b) between the city and the countryside. This is absent in many other multi-million 'metropoles' across the Western world as these tend to grow from one single centre. The structure is under pressure though from 'multiple concentration' largely due to a favourable location of the Randstad in the Rhine delta: it is in fact the 'port function' which drives development in the West.

In just over one and a half pages the quintessence of the advice is presented: the 1980 Development Scheme is based on three 'basic principles':

1   a clear delineation of areas for agriculture and areas within the urban sphere meaning: concentration on the urban ring while preserving an agricultural middle area;
2   preservation of the main agglomerations as spatially identifiable elements of 'sound habitable' size, and where needed growth is rounded off; and
3   expansion of the Randstad in an outward direction through an overspill to adjacent areas north, east and south of the Randstad (WWDL, 1958a: 32–33).

These principles '...will make it possible that the Randstad can develop into a decentralised *world city* of true Dutch nature, while the spectre of some foreign metropoles is avoided.' (WWDL, 1958a: 33; translation author, emphasis added). How this could be achieved is elaborated in a set of highly connected spatial concepts. The first principle leads to the Green Heart as we have already seen. The second one leads to the almost military metaphor of buffer zones which should be at least 4km wide to separate cities visually as well as 'virtually' (WWDL, 1958b). The third principle is simply called (outward) radiation through the creation of new towns, the Dutch term (*nieuwe steden*) being a direct translation of the British term. The two conurbations also get a metaphorical label: north and south 'wing'. Most metaphors were rather expressive and plastic as they were primarily about urban morphology (Figure 11.2).

Compared with this bold vision the governance philosophy is quite shallow (WWDL, 1958a). There is a general call for cooperation between government, trade and industry and civil society. Provinces are summoned to elaborate regional plans (under post-war provisional law they acquired the necessary competences) or modify the existing ones, while municipalities should provide proper extension plans. The Advisory Committee also emphasised a need for 'administrative provisions' like 'inter-municipal bodies'. It argued that these should acquire all critical competences from municipalities, an idea which would in fact lead to an administrative, fourth layer between municipalities and the three provinces. In subsequent decades the idea of such a fourth administrative layer emerged several times but was always strongly opposed from all sides (as explained in the following chapter).

Interestingly, the Advisory Report contained a minority report from the representative of the transport ministry, Le Cosquino de Bussy, who was fully against the idea of a Green Heart and outward growth. With the exception of the South Wing, where urban pressure was particularly strong,

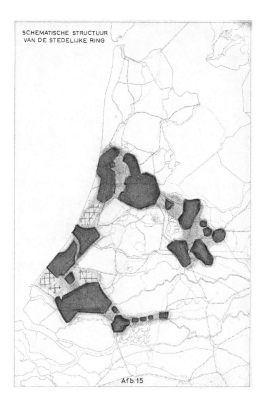

Figure 11.2 Visualisation of the desired morphological structure of the Randstad. Source: WWDL, 1958a.

he proposed an inward growth of the Randstad. He did not agree that the Randstad was already a 'world city'. Instead he argued that if the Randstad would like to play its future role as one of the large centres of Western Europe, 'concentration is of fundamental importance' (WWDL, 1958a: 41–42; translation author); that trade and industry would not be helped by geographical dispersal and long distances and travel times; and that cultural facilities and citizens would benefit from concentration from employment opportunities that could be reached much more easily. He also argued that the Green Heart could accommodate growth of some of the existing centres, provided it was done carefully. Altogether, he was of the view that the principles on which the advisory report is based 'are too much postulated as axioms and need to be reconsidered' (WWDL, 1958a: 42, translation author).

Obviously, this forms a full-blown attack on the empirical as well as normative base of the Randstad vision. However, in 1960 the government accepted the majority vision in the very first national report (*nota*) on spatial planning (Ministerie van Bouwnijverheid, 1960: 89–91). This report combined national dispersal policy as laid down in a 1958 report on indus-trialisation (Ministerie van EZ, 1958) with the Randstad vision. The Report rounds off with a 20-page chapter on implementation. A key role is given to a new spatial planning act being prepared at that stage. This act would give the provinces a major role in regional planning. Proper coordination between government departments is also emphasised. No overhaul of the country's administrative system is foreseen, although there are many small municipali-ties that faced the challenge of adequate administrative power and the capac-ity to prepare sound spatial plans, the solution has nevertheless to come from municipal cooperation and, if that is not sufficient, through amalgamation. Only for the largest agglomerations was government willing to introduce new bills to create special 'administrative solutions', but what this could mean apart from the annexation of smaller municipalities by the larger cities is not explained (Ministerie van Bouwnijverheid, 1960: 136).

Enlargement of the Randstad concept

A novel institutional base for spatial planning

In 1965 the planning armamentarium changes quite drastically. Finally, after years of discussion the new Spatial Planning Act comes into force, clearly describing planning competences at all three administrative levels. The new law closely follows the principle of the Netherlands as a decentralised unitary state. This means that the only plan which binds citizens is the municipal zoning plan. Relationships between the three administrative levels and their statutory plans are subtle. For instance, although the municipal land-use plan needs approval from the provincial executive, its content is not prescribed in the provincial regional plan. The province can issue a directive, so can the national government. However, due to the deliberative nature of Dutch plan-ning culture the use of this 'nuclear' option is not used very often (Needham, 2007; see also Needham, 2014).

The 1965 law established the National Spatial Planning Agency. This gives a new zeal to policy making and plan-making. Important to note is that the Dutch name of the new agency no longer makes any reference to a (national) plan, just to 'planology' (*Rijksplanologische Dienst* or RPD from here). The law takes effect in a period of rapid spatial changes. After years of austerity there is a steep rise in income. This makes it possible for many to buy a car as well as to move from a city apartment in an old neighbourhood to a new, semi-detached house outside the city. Above all there is a population boom. The 1960 planning report already assumed 15 million inhabitants in 2000 (the actual figure in 1960 was about 11.5 million), forecasts in the mid-1960s are a couple of millions more.

It is in that context that the 1966 Second Report on Spatial Planning is published. Yet again a new vocabulary is introduced. New terms and visuals may give the impression (for this view see Schuyt and Taverne, 2000: 141) that the report abandons the 1958/1960 scheme of Randstad, Green Heart and buffer zones. What the Second Report in fact does is an enlargement of the territorial scope of the Randstad concept. Both Randstad wings are expected to evolve in giant urban zones, especially the North Wing: from Alkmaar in the north-west of the country to Arnhem/Nijmegen in the east; an area about 140 km wide. Other urban zones (*stedelijke zones*; the foreign loan word 'conurbation' is dropped) in the south and south-east of the country will also emerge, while similar processes in the east and the north of the country are regarded as highly likely. As a consequence, the Green Heart has to become bigger. The new, rather tedious technical name is *Centrale Open Ruimte* ('Central Open Space'), formed by the Green Heart, the adjoining river area in the centre of the country and a large offshoot in a south-western direction: the Middle Delta as the Delta flood works turn estuaries into recreational lakes. Next to the Green Heart also the buffer zone concept is rolled out to other parts of the country.

Novel relational planning concepts

The real innovation of the Second Report regards the regional level. Clearly inspired by international as well as novel domestic literature on so-called *stadsgewesten* (city regions) and the rising trend towards suburbanisation, the notion of self-contained cities and (new) towns, highly characteristic of the 1958 Randstad report as well as the 1960 government report, is abandoned. 'The almost total motorization of society' (Ministerie van VRO, 1966: 77; translation author) will inevitably lead to a 'spread fabric' of large urban centres surrounded by a range of small centres which through their mutual relations form a 'functional whole' (Ministerie van VRO, 1966). The makers of the report do not expect any territorial limitations to this process as individual city regions would eventually merge into the already mentioned urban zones. Infographics are used to elucidate these developments (see Figure 11.3). Altogether this means that key principles of the 1958 report on morphology and zoning are combined with a more relational understanding of urbanisation. This regionalisation of urban structures is supposed to affect the administrative structure of the country, especially in its most urbanised parts. In a lengthy exposé (Ministerie van VRO, 1966), which amongst others emphasises that a fourth administrative layer is highly undesirable, government concludes that in these parts of the country (the city regions in the Randstad and a number of city regions elsewhere) a genuine regional administration needs to be established. In these regions municipalities will remain but planning competences of the provinces are to be transferred. Although this would cut big chunks out of provincial territories, especially in the three western provinces, no grand changes are anticipated at this level.

Clearly, the Second Report is a product of research and urban design, the latter more strongly than the former. A strong indication of this is the concept of environment differentiation (there is no ideal translation of the Dutch original *milieudifferentiatie*). City regions in the future form a mosaic of four

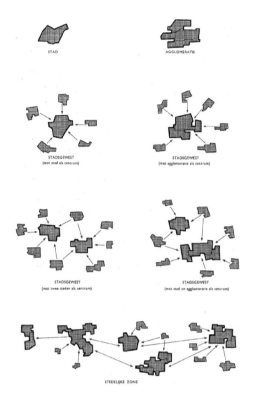

Figure 11.3 The historical development from freestanding cities to large, complex
         urban zones.
Source: Ministerie van VRO, 1966.

different types, simply called A, B, C and D. These types range from small
villages and towns of about 5.000 inhabitants plus services (the A type) to the
D type, central units of about 250.000 inhabitants with high-level services
like a concert hall, shopping malls and high-capacity public transport facilities. The numerical relation between the four types follows rather closely
central place theory as there are many units of the A type but far less of the
D type. It is assumed there will only be 9 D environments in the year 2000,
the time horizon of the report: 5 in the Randstad (Amsterdam, Rotterdam,
The Hague, Utrecht and Dordrecht) and 4 elsewhere. A highly detailed map
of the entire country was made which showed the exact location of all A-B-
C-D environments. As these were all visualised as squares and rectangles
this map became known as the *blokjeskaart* (block map). National planners
even dared to cross the borders with Belgium and Germany, as the future
2,000 structure of the Antwerp-Ghent, Liège and Aachen city regions was
'designed' in the same way.

The most well-known concept of the Second Report without doubt is *ge-bundelde deconcentratie* (generally translated as 'concentrated deconcentration'). This oxymoron is a brilliant invention as it seeks to join up a societal trend with a planning ambition. The former is the ever-stronger trend (at least in the 1960s) to live outside cities in a neatly organised suburban environment, the latter is the planning objective to steer development in such a way that open spaces, with their agricultural economy and valuable landscapes, are safeguarded. According to Peter Hall, this is '[…] a model well worth study by other nations' (1984: 115).

The bold vision and spatial concepts of Second Report are well regarded today but have received some serious criticism in their time (Faludi and Van der Valk, 1994; Siraa *et al.*, 1995), in particular, the empirical base, and the consideration of alternatives as well as implementation were thought to be weak. Interestingly, the Amsterdam spatial planning professor Steigena commented that nobody seems to be responsible for the Randstad (Faludi and Van der Valk, 1994). A critical issue was that government did not specify how overspill centres would be realised, although, unlike its 1960 predecessor, locations for some of these centres were identified (Ministerie van VRO, 1966).

In the early 1970s a debate took place around the question of whether the Randstad is a metropole. The discussion was centred around the idea of an 'E-environment', which '…is equal to (and which can compete with) that of metropoles elsewhere in northwest Europe' (RARO, 1972: 6; translation author). In this debate the general conclusion was that in the Netherlands only the Randstad offers the necessary condition for 'metropole formation'. But this would only possible if the functional coherence within the Randstad was increased: entailing more functional specialisation within and between cities, and better transport connections between them (especially between the 'big four') and other European 'core areas' (Zonneveld, 1992). However, many questions were raised. Is the E-environment a spatial entity having a concrete location? Does the competition between Randstad cities allow for shared metropole status? Is the creation of an E-environment dependent on urban growth and to what extent is decentralisation of the Randstad through outward radiation and overspill centres undermining the necessary critical mass? Is The Netherlands not too small to carry an E-environment? (BSPO, 1975).

The debate gradually fizzled out. A main reason was that the development of the E-environment became associated with the reconstruction (opponents in those days would say: destruction) of inner city areas and the replacement of houses by offices and urban highways. This became highly contested, especially in Amsterdam. The debated ended in 1976 as government concluded that 'metropolitan development' would have an adverse effect on the quality of life in inner cities because the loss of houses and their replacement elsewhere could threaten the Green Heart.

Downscaling the Randstad

A change of spatial concepts in a relatively short period of time is often caused by what can be called 'explosive issues' (Zonneveld, 1991). In the early 1970s such issues made a revision of the Second Report necessary. It was argued that, suburbanisation was not 'bundled' but rather, haphazard and that migration out of cities was hollowing out the demographic and economic base of the cities. The grand reconstruction of inner-city areas was meeting ever-greater opposition. The oil crisis of 1973 demonstrated the vulnerability of urban structures based on car use. Also the demographic forecasts of the mid-1960s proved to be false.

The new creed of the 1970s expressed in a massive Third Report became the 'bundling of urban development'. While the makers of the Second Report foresaw an expanding urban region, the Third Report proposed clear perimeters based on travel time by public transport. The notion of the Randstad then became a constellation of the four large and contained city regions (Amsterdam, Rotterdam, The Hague and Utrecht) with an outer perimeter based on 35 minutes travel time by public transport, and for the smaller cities 25 minutes. *Groeikernen* (growth centres; *overloopkernen* or overspill centres acquired a rather negative connotation) should be located within these perimeters.

The Third Report is not entirely consistent since not all the proposed growth centres met the new criteria. The location of some was based on the rationale of the makers of the 1958 Advisory Report discussed above: further away from the Randstad and expected to become economically self-sufficient. This counts specifically for Alkmaar, Hoorn and Lelystad and to a certain extent also for Almere. The realisation of a new railway line in the 1980s makes the location of this latter town consistent with the urban region perimeter. By the mid-1970s the tools and financial arrangements were set in place for 'bundled urbanisation' and what was to become one of the largest projects in the history of Dutch spatial planning but what some would call a thinning out or depletion of the Randstad (Frieling, 1983, 1997).

The Third Report is made up of sub-reports. The main one for our discussion is the *Verstedelijkingsnota* (Urbanisation Report) first published in 1976 and revised in 1979. By 1983, the politically binding part was revised again. The perimeters around the urban regions were tightened so as to avoid expansion resulting from faster public transport. Boundaries using travel time were replaced by fixed distances: 12km from the centre of the four largest cities and 8km for other cities. The notion of *bundeling* (bundling) was replaced by *concentratie* (concentration). Growth centres located outside urban regions were to end their tasks by 1990.

There are two main reasons for this change. First, the fall of the population of many cities, partly caused by spatial planning overspill and the creation of new towns, put critical urban services under pressure. Second, the growth centre policy became highly expensive for government in the context of a serious economic recession kicked-off by the 1979 oil crisis. The Randstad concept continues in use but to a large extent reduced to a place name only with emphasis now on the individual urban regions and cities. The 25-year objective for outward migration from the Randstad was dropped. In translation: 'Regions on their own force' and not 'Randstad force' is the new creed, with again, a close relationship between Randstad policies and national spatial-economic policy.

Reconceptualising the Randstad: from West Wing to Deltametropolis

The rise and fall of the Randstad West Wing

Efforts to plan the development of the Randstad were seemingly over with the finalisation of the growth centre policy in sight. National planning, and with it the RPD, was heavily criticised for overly technocratic planning and inward-looking negotiative processes guided by 'administrative centrism' (Den Hoed *et al.*, 1983; Kickert, 1996). In parliament, spokespeople from various political parties called for a less elaborate, more forward-looking sort of planning far less focused on housing given the recession. This required a less procedural and more appealing and visionary planning which was delivered in a Fourth Report, with an apparently radical relational vision on the Randstad.

For the RPD the making of a new planning vision putting planning high on the political agenda was an urgent task in the light of rumours of possible abolition of the agency after the 1986 general election. The new vision would need a radical approach both in process and content, employing new spatial imaginaries (Neefjes, 1988). If the economy is suffering, what planning has to do is to integrate economy in its spatial concepts, something which had not happened before (Waterhout *et al.*, 2013). In 1986, the RPD published a spatial planning Memorandum on its own account, eschewing the norms of interdepartmental negotiation which might have diluted its visionary and spatial design content.

This Memorandum almost exclusively focuses on the Randstad, meeting the call for selective instead of comprehensive planning. The rationale is above all spatial-economic, arguing that the Randstad is the most important area for the establishment of competitive companies and by far has the best international and global connections. Inspiration is taken from the 'Europe 1992' project leading to the finalisation of the dismantling of trade barriers with the then European Community and the expectation that a new phase in European integration would expose regions and cities and not countries as a whole to growing international competition.

After conferences in various parts of the country, in itself an indication of a more open, outward looking plan-making philosophy, the RPD concluded that the classic Randstad concept is no longer valid, as the economic core also involves places outside the Randstad which made the scale of the traditional Randstad concept 'too small'. On the other hand, the Randstad is 'too big': the best conditions for the establishment of international companies in the most competitive economic sectors (above all business services) are offered in an area much smaller than the classic Randstad. The RPD draws the conclusion that Utrecht does not belong to the Randstad but instead to the so-called *Stedenring Centraal Nederland* (Central Netherlands Urban Ring) (Zonneveld, 1992; Faludi and Van der Valk, 1994; Van Duinen, 2004; see also Van Duinen, 2015). The remaining part of the Randstad acquires a new name: *Westvleugel* (West Wing).

The first official draft of the Fourth Report was not even printed when this reconceptualisation of the Randstad met with serious opposition. The Ring concept is readily accepted, but the Ministry of Economic Affairs was against the idea of a West Wing. It rejected both the sectoral emphasis on business services as well as the spatial emphasis on just three Randstad cities. The ministry claimed: there is no empirical ground for such 'discrimination' (Zonneveld, 1992). The trespassing of another ministerial domain, that of the Ministry of Economic Affairs is also a bone of contention.

Not surprisingly, there was widespread opposition to the Fourth Report from the city and province of Utrecht about the 'relegation' to the Central Netherlands Urban Ring, and, among others, from the other three Randstad cities and provinces. In 1995 these bodies formed a cooperation body known as the *Randstad Overleg Ruimtelijke Ordening* or RORO (Randstad Platform on Spatial Planning) (Quist, 1993: 49). The idea of the West Wing was roundly criticised because it threatened the presentation of the Randstad as a whole to the international audience while it also undermined genuine cooperation within the Randstad. Opponents also argued that the RPD used out-of-date empirical evidence and that the proposals threatened the Green Heart and the green belt between the North and South Wings.

The outcome was that on empirical as well as normative grounds the West Wing idea was rejected. Interestingly the metaphor gives some reason to expect urbanisation in areas which so far are regarded as open spaces. This can be explained by the fact that the Wing concept in the sense of North and South Wing has been used over the course of years as a label to describe areas of intense urbanisation and urban growth. That the West Wing is not about urbanisation but, following the RPD, about three cities regarded as best positioned in the international, economic competition, did not come across (Korthals Altes, 1995). From the perspective of conceptualisation as communication the decision to choose the Wing as the preferred metaphor is therefore quite a blunder. In the first official 1988 version of the Fourth Report 'West Wing' is replaced by the *Westelijk deel Randstad* (Western Part Randstad), on the assumption that this would neutralise opposition. However, Utrecht was still not regarded as belonging to this 'part'. In the event, parliament rejected the idea and the four Randstad cities received equal status with the same symbol used for all on the statutory policy map.

In 1989 the coalition government shifted from centre-right to centre-left and a social-democrat became minister for spatial planning, which according to Waterhout *et al.* (2013) set a novel neo-liberal course for planning. The international position of the country moved to the background and planning returned to 'its roots' (Faludi and Van der Valk, 1994). Growth management and the location of new housing again became central themes, together with environmental quality, and another round of plan-making resulted in the *Vierde Nota Extra* or VINEX (Fourth Report Extra). The Randstad is defined as a 'horseshoe' of nine city regions (four big and five smaller) with no clear outer perimeter. A set of criteria is given for the location of new urban areas according to the principle of bundling, and the perimeters of the Green Heart are mapped with the provinces required to detail them precisely.

Some attention to the international position of the Randstad remains, although somewhat hidden in text and images. In light of the fierce discussion just a few years earlier, it is rather surprising that the VINEX states that the best chances to attract international companies can be found in Amsterdam, Rotterdam and The Hague (Ministerie van VROM, 1993: 38). In the years up to about the 2000s, main political attention is given to the second large urbanisation project in the history of Dutch national planning: the realisation of the so-called VINEX areas which were to absorb over 50 per cent of new housing growth. The Fourth Report starts out as a conceptual revolution by introducing a new Randstad concept based on the economic competitiveness of just three main cities instead of focussing on the urban form of the classic Randstad 'ring' and measures to preserve open spaces. In the end, the latter prevails in planning politics.

From Randstad to Deltametropolis

From the perspective of planning the 1990s form a decade with different faces. While national planning embarked yet again on a gigantic national housing project, criticism of national spatial planning grew again, with great concerns about the role of national government, vis-à-vis other levels of administration and society at large. There was also criticism about government's perception of spatial structures and consequences for intervention strategies. Underlying the critique the idea of a network society was highly influential. It suggests that, organisationally, national government should become far more selective and focus on issues and territories which are of genuine national importance (NSCGP, 1998; Hajer and Zonneveld, 2000; Van der Cammen and De Klerk, 2012). Conceptually, government should drop the idea that cities are morphologically as well as functionally demarcated particularly regarding the west of the country.

Sectoral policy departments questioned the monopoly of the ministry responsible for spatial planning by introducing alternative planning concepts and strategies (NSGCP, 1998; Priemus, 1999). The Ministry of Economic Affairs was most challenging, taking the metaphor of network society in a rather extreme way by pleading for economic development along the network of motorways in the shape of corridors and business sites at motorway junctions. In this context of conceptual turmoil, in 1996 a group of professors from the Universities of Delft and Amsterdam launched an initiative called *Het Metropolitane Debat* or HMD (The Metropolitan Debate) (Van Duinen, 2004). They demonstrated that a high level of dispersal of population and jobs and therefore a further thinning out of the Randstad is inevitable unless planning is willing to change. In collaboration with the four Randstad cities, in 1998 they published what was to become a highly influential document: the *Verklaring Deltametropool* (The Deltametropolis Declaration). A new concept was born: the Deltametropolis.

The Declaration can be read as a straightforward attempt to breathe new life into the old idea of the western part of The Netherlands constituting the country's most important production and consumption environment, the future of which should be put expressly in a European perspective (Lambregts and Zonneveld, 2004). It argued that the Randstad and the Green Heart should not be conceived as an accidental collection of cities with rural zones between them, but rather as a coherent polynucleated metropolitan region which should be encouraged – through spatial policy – in its competitive struggle with other European metropolitan regions. The declaration opposes the idea that the Randstad was overpopulated, so strong formerly. Instead, the area was a rather thinly populated metropolis with ample opportunity for improving the spatial quality through better coordination of policies and more daring spatial design.

Initially, it seemed that the claims of the councils of the four Randstad cities would fall on deaf ears. 'Deltametropolis' was not mentioned once in the Starting Memorandum issued in preparation of the fifth policy document on spatial planning (Ministerie van VROM *et al.*, 1999). The Randstad was not even considered to be a coherent spatial entity, but rather to consist of three smaller entities (Lambregts and Zonneveld, 2004). In the first edition of the fifth policy document on spatial planning this was 'corrected' (Ministerie van VROM, 2001: 226; translation author) (Figure 11.4).

> The image of the spatial main structure of the western part of the country, based on the development of two independent mainports, nine city regions, a range of regional overspill areas and buffer zones is to be exchanged for one single spatial concept. The Deltametropolis becomes [...] one national urban network.

The designation of the Deltametropolis was controversial though. Some, like the Deltametropolis Association, thought that the government did not take the idea far enough, while others considered it too great a move up the ladder of spatial scales (Lambregts and Zonneveld, 2004). In the end, central government followed the path of the Working Commission for the Western

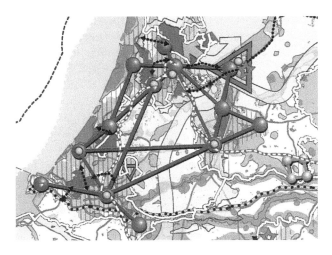

Figure 11.4 Detail of the statutory Fifth Report map 'National Spatial Policy'.
Source: Ministerie van VROM, 2002.

Netherlands 45 years before, to single out the level of the Randstad/Deltametropolis as the most relevant for policy making in the west of the country. Strong emphasis was also put on the international ambitions attached to the concept. Deltametropolis is explicitly presented as a 'national urban network of international magnitude' (Ministerie van VROM, 2002: 34, translation author), the development of which is the country's 'best bet' for future success (Lambregts and Zonneveld, 2004).

Reconceptualising the Randstad once more: towards project-based planning

Spatial and economic concepts

April 2002 saw the collapse of the coalition government responsible for the Fifth Report. By then the document was about three-quarters of its way through the formal adoption procedure. In the Netherlands a fallen government usually rounds off any current business, but the finalisation of the Fifth Report was on the parliamentary list of politically controversial issues that should be rolled over to the next administration. This was in stark contrast to the technical view of planning dominant in earlier decades. Parliament deferred the reading of the Fifth Report and, in effect, sounded its death knell (Zonneveld, 2005).

The follow-up document in Dutch still carried the word *Nota* or Report in its title (*Nota Ruimte*), although the English title better reflects its real ambitions: 'National Spatial Strategy'. While a report suggests a pile of paper, strategy suggests making things happen. Also, the Strategy has a meaning-ful subtitle: 'Creating Space for Development', development clearly meaning here, economic development. The prime motto became 'decentralize when possible, centralize when necessary' (Ministeries van VROM *et al.*, 2004a: 24, translation author; see also: Waterhout *et al.*, 2013; Zonneveld and Evers, 2014). Compared with the Fifth Report there was far less emphasis on spatial quality and a less restrictive attitude to the location of urban development. Also, while all preceding planning reports have been prepared within the ministry responsible for spatial planning, the Strategy has a new powerful co-author: the Ministry of Economic Affairs (officially the strategy bears the signature of four departments). This clearly had a decisive effect on its content in general and how it considered the Randstad in particular as we will see.

Legally, the National Spatial Strategy is the final version of the Fifth Report (the full, official title in English is: National Policy Strategy for Infrastructure and Spatial Planning). To avoid going through the oblig-atory national planning report procedure again, the Strategy partly fol-lows the approach of the preceding Fifth Report while at the same time clearly following a different path in terms of content. For example, it neatly adopts the definition of urban networks from the Fifth Report, but retains only six of 13 networks (Ministeries van VROM, LNV, VenW en EZ, 2004b). Furthermore, the Strategy is less strict about the composition of the six national urban networks and apart from the core cities, leaves it up to local government to decide. The Strategy only shows schematically the areas where urbanisation will be 'bundled'. Nowhere is the concept of Deltametropolis used. Instead, the Strategy returns to Randstad, adding 'Holland' to its name.

The Strategy introduces a second urban concept clearly showing the signa-ture of the Ministry of Economic Affairs: economic core areas. Thirteen are identified, located partly in and partly outside the urban networks with three situated in the Randstad (see Figure 11.5). The Strategy accords more or less equal importance to the concepts of urban network and economic core area, but the relationship between the two is rather obscure. The urban networks form a policy layer from the VROM Ministry, while the Ministry of Eco-nomic Affairs adds the policy layer formed by the economic core areas. This discretionary approach encouraged municipalities to work together so that they received available subsidies for economic core areas for the realisation of large, complex business estates, a.k.a. 'top projects' (Ministeries van VROM, LNV, VenW en EZ, 2004b). The latter points to a key characteristic of the Strategy: a third policy layer above the other two of nationally supported project spaces, most of these located in the Randstad Holland. Probably the most important ones are the mainports Rotterdam and Schiphol (the squares in Figure 11.5). There are other 'ports' as well: Brainport Eindhoven and five Greenports, (the triangles in Figure 11.5) large agricultural complexes, four out five located in the Randstad. Finally, there are the so-called 'New Key Projects': the makeover of five main railway stations, with again four out of

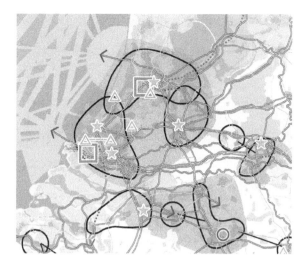

Figure 11.5 Detail of the statutory 2004 Spatial Strategy map 'National Spatial Main Structure'.
Source: Ministerie van VROM *et al.*, 2004b.

five located in the Randstad (Spaans *et al.*, 2013) (see the stars in Figure 11.5). This project-oriented, pragmatic instead of visionary approach (Balz, 2018) to national spatial planning was to become the main characteristic of the 2012 successor.

From yet again two Randstad wings to a place name

In 2005, in the middle of finalisation of the National Spatial Strategy, parliament raised concerns about weakly underpinned investments decisions and called for improved justification through long-term strategic planning (Balz and Zonneveld, 2018). Apparently, the Strategy itself, in which projects became to overshadow spatial concepts, was not regarded as sufficient. By July 2006 the centre-right government collapsed, followed by elections and extensive coalition talks. It was not until February 2007 that a new government, again led by Christian-Democrats announced first a reform of the process protocol for the allocation of infrastructure funds, and second, a new planning framework confined spatially to the Randstad region.

The manner in which the second issue was taken up needs some explanation. The ministry responsible for infrastructure was struggling with delays in the implementation of projects, supposedly due to administrative fragmentation, which was particularly problematic for the Randstad as the country's most important economic region. To counteract fragmentation, the ministry started the so-called Randstad Urgency programme. Its main intention was to prioritise projects from the many proposals that crowded the ministry's agenda. The Ministry of VROM managed to insert a special project into the programme: the *Structural Vision Randstad 2040*. Randstad 2040 was to establish guiding principles for long-term spatial planning and in this way influence future (infrastructure) project decisions (Balz and Zonneveld, 2018). As Waterhout *et al.* (2013) point out, under 'old style' planning (roughly up to the Fifth Report) a vision like Randstad 2040 would have been developed *beforehand* as a framework for identifying and justifying projects. As the Randstad Urgency program fell under the authority of the ministry responsible for infrastructure, the ministry of VROM obviously feared being sidetracked. Therefore, the making of a planning report was a project intended to influence all other projects.

The most striking element of the Randstad 2040 report published in 2008 is that it returns once more to the structure and composition of the Randstad. On the basis of an array of figures and what is regarded as factual evidence on daily urban systems, it reached the conclusion that the Randstad is not a single network but two distinctive regions: Northern and Southern Randstad (see Figure 6 in chapter 14). They are not 'closed' but have important physical and economic connections with other urban regions. Gone is the use of striking metaphors, in language or in visuals: the two Randstad areas are simply visualised as rectangles avoiding any suggestion of boundaries. The spatial development perspective shown in Figure 14.6 has an under layer of highly stylised symbols (lines, arrows and dots) and an upper layer of projects (the small black circles) which are ongoing or under discussion, most of which are not led by VROM. The obvious suggestion is that this development perspective should form the framework guiding the decision-making processes on the myriad of Randstad urgency projects.

Randstad 2040 was published exactly half a century after *The Development of the West of the Country*. While the 1958 report was an advisory report, Randstad 2040 is a policy report, in fact the very first to be dedicated to only the Randstad. With hindsight we can say it is also the *last* genuine spatial planning strategy at the national level. It was seeking to integrate the objectives and actions of various interests, in particular between spatial quality and economic development and competitiveness. It clearly bears the signature of social-democratic thinking about spatial planning because the responsible minister was from this political group which traditionally takes interest in trying to steer spatial development.

The year of publication, 2008, is ominous. It was the beginning of the most severe economic recession since the 1930s. In the same way that the recession of 1980 led to the introduction of competitiveness in national spatial planning, the recession of 2008 led to an overall dominance of economic objectives in national spatial planning. The political composition of the government coalition clearly contributed to that. In 2010 a new coalition took office, positioned more strongly to the right compared with the coalition responsible for the 2006 strategy and even more compared with the coalition responsible for Randstad 2040. The new minister was from the centre-right liberal party and an outspoken adherent of neo-liberal thinking.

The new coalition was highly energetic on spatial planning. As part of a wider reorganisation of the public sector it immediately started to dismantle the ministry of VROM (RO stands for *Ruimtelijke Ordening*). Spatial planning is moved to a ministry called Infrastructure and Environment. This means that for the first time since 1965 there is no ministry with RO in its name: obviously a case of *nomen est omen*.

On taking office, the coalition government immediately began work on a new planning policy, and Randstad 2040 was abandoned. Although the new planning report aimed to replace eight other policy documents and while such an endeavour in the past would have taken several years, the new (draft) National Spatial Strategy for Infrastructure and Planning (SVIR: *Structuurvisie Infrastructuur en Ruimte*) took only a few months to prepare (Zonneveld and Evers, 2014). The 2006 approach to 'decentralize when possible, centralize when necessary' went further: government will only act if national interests are at stake. Consequently, the number of national interests was brought down from 39 to 13 and only one was loosely connected to urbanisation: 'cautious consideration and transparent decision-making in relation to all spatial and infrastructural decisions' (Ministerie van IenM, 2012: 60; translation author). In essence this is a procedural statement which replaces the former national interest 'bundling of urbanization and economic activities' (Ministerie van IenM, 2012: 108; translation author). The spatial concept of bundling was terminated and likewise: urban networks, national buffer zones, and even the Green Heart. 'Spatial quality' was only used in a descriptive way (see: Ministerie van IenM, 2012: 13) because every statement which includes 'strengthening of spatial quality' was also deleted.

None of the descriptions of the 13 national interests mentions Randstad. The 'National Spatial Main Structure' map (see Figure 11.6) pictures the (former) Randstad in a way which is entirely different compared with all preceding policy reports. What we see is a layer of projects which is almost the same when compared with Randstad 2040, although the symbol for metropolitan parks is gone. The red lines encircle 'urban regions with a concentration of top sectors'. The concept of urban regions is only descriptive: the policies are in the projects. The red lines were simply called 'elastics' in the hallways of the ministry of I&M (Balz and Zonneveld, 2018). For the Randstad there are two elastics which connect to the classic understanding of the Randstad formed by a northern and a southern wing. They do not have any meaning in terms of policy. The Randstad, if used at all, has become only a place name. The same counts for the successor of the SVIR: the 2019 (Draft) National Strategy on Spatial Planning and the Environment (Ministry of the Interior and Kingdom Relations, 2019).

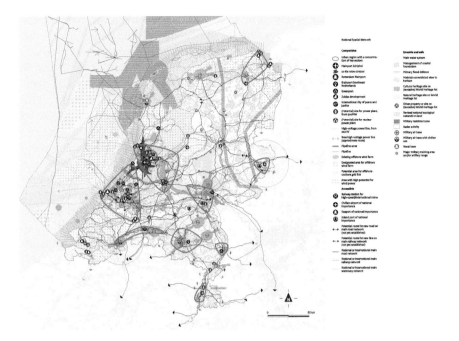

Figure 11.6 The National Spatial Main Structure according to the 2012 National
         Policy Strategy.
Source: Ministry of IandE, 2011.

Discussion and conclusion

The Randstad as a planning concept has been around for more than 60 years,
if one recognises the 1958 advisory report about the 'West of the Country' as
the starting point. There are grounds to argue that the concept is much older,
about a century. Although the metaphor 'Randstad' was not invented at the
time, the 1924 map made by Van Lohuizen obviously showed the emergence
of a supra-regional scale in need of government intervention to avoid endless,
contiguous urban areas.

If one overlooks the entire period discussed in this chapter, whether this
period is sixty years or (nearly) one hundred years, the continuity in the efforts to conceptualise and re-conceptualise the nature of the Randstad supra-
region is striking. This is evident in the almost constant change between levels
of scale at which spatial planning should act, and expressed by a bewildering
variety of terms, metaphors and visuals. Briefly, Randstad planning began
with an emphasis on the independent nature of cities (late 1950s and early
1960s); followed by perceptions of boundless city regions and urban zones
(late 1960s); and a very long period of ever-restricted visions of well-defined
city regions; then promotion of the compact city idea (late 1980s and 1990s);
and more recently, with the notion of urban networks. Today the Randstad
(Holland) is just a place name.

Conceptualisations of the Randstad move back and forth between an emphasis on urban *form* or morphology as expressed by the distinction made between built-up and open areas or 'green' and 'red', and an emphasis on urban *structure*, which is primarily about relationships between different parts of the Randstad, as expressed by flows and complementarities between cities. The latter is a relational interpretation of the structure of the Randstad, which was a feature of the 1966 Second Planning Report, the controversial concept of the Randstad West Wing of the late 1980s (which was almost paradoxically combined with a very strong emphasis on compact cities and severe restrictions on building programmes outside main cities), and the Deltametropolis concept of the 2001 Fifth Planning Report. The urban network concept is probably the most 'relational' of all Randstad concepts as it looked beyond commuting patterns, inspired by the seminal work on the network society by Manuel Castells as well as European discussions on urban patterns across the continent (NSPA, 2000).

This brings us to the following question: does the constant revision of interpretations of the geography of the Randstad matter? If geographies in the 'real' world change, should planning not change as well and adopt a new 'concept'? We think that there are a few dangers. First of all, the changes in the vocabulary of planning have taken place with time intervals of about 5 to 10 years. This is obviously much faster than the actual change of the Randstad geography and points in the direction of a policy domain which is highly internalised and parochial in the way it functions in the political world. It is exactly why national spatial planning has been criticised over the course of years, in particular during the late 1990s (NSCGP, 1999). This clearly has contributed to the discontinuance of the Spatial Planning Agency in 2001 to be followed by the abolition of the ministry of VROM in 2010.

Second, while recognising that planning and planners should always be prepared to learn from spatial and societal changes: the continuous adoption of new planning concepts does not favour continuity in policy. Before implementation measures are put in place, the conceptual basis of planning might have changed already. The most important example highlighted in this chapter concerns new town policies. We have seen that the idea of new towns as an alternative to the continuous growth of cities was introduced in the late 1950s. It took almost 15 years to reach full agreement between administrative levels and policy sectors on how and where to create these new towns (which had even acquired a new name). By then perceptions of critical urban problems had changed which meant that the location of some of these new towns was no longer reasonable. The other side of the story is nevertheless that over the course of several decades hundreds of thousands of houses in the Randstad (but also elsewhere) have been built on locations selected by and through spatial planning. This may be called a success as do Faludi and Van der Valk (1994) and Korthals Altes (2006).

Next to success there is failure. Possibly the grandest failure of Randstad planning is its incapacity to arrive at a proper integration on the question of where to locate new urban development and how that could or should relate to infrastructure planning, especially in the domain of public transport. As Schrijnen points out in Chapter 15 the main public transport structure at the Randstad level is offered by the national railways (NS: *Nederlandse Spoorwegen*). One level down, at the level of the Haarlem-Schiphol-Amsterdam-Utrecht and Leiden-The Hague-Rotterdam-Dordrecht 'wings' there is nothing which could be compared with, for example, the German S-bahn systems or the RER system to be found in the Paris region. There is currently one single regional rail link between Rotterdam and The Hague, somewhat deceptively called Randstad Rail. All other rail systems in this southern Randstad wing, apart from the NS system, are local although one former NS local line from Rotterdam to the coastal town of Hoek van Holland has been re-opened as a light rail link in 2019. The multibillion Amsterdam North/South line with its length of just under 10 km is just a local line: opened in 2018 it does not go beyond the municipal border. Preliminary discussions have started for an extension to Schiphol Airport which would add another 14km of rail track. Whether this will materialise and on what time scale remains to be seen.

One may speculate about the causes of the lack of integration between urban and infrastructure planning. Obviously, policy departments often behave like the proverbial policy silos. Nevertheless, we would also like to suggest that a major cause is situated in the domain of *spatial* planning which deliberately aimed for a segmented Randstad morphology preventing the arrival of critical population mass needed for high quality public transport links at the regional 'wing' level. The uncertainty and ongoing discussions across several decades about the level of *functional* integration of the Randstad did not help either. The decision taken in the 2008 Randstad 2040 planning report that the Randstad is in fact a constellation of two regions, put an end to all pleas to develop a new orbital public transport system connecting all four Randstad cities. Whether such a highly centralised system with a limited number of stops would fit the strongly polynuclear structure of the Randstad is a moot point though.

A final conclusion we would like to draw here is that the sheer scale of the Randstad, an area of approximately 80 by 80km, is probably too large to handle as a single spatial planning region. Currently, the national government is no longer willing to take the lead in terms of visioning and policy making. The next chapter seeks to make clear whether the so-called metropolitan regions of Amsterdam and Rotterdam The Hague are capable of taking a leading role.

References

Ahsmann, R. (1990). *De Werkcommissie Westen des Lands [The Working Commission for the Western Netherlands]; Een historisch onderzoek naar de Werkcommissie voor het onderzoek naar de ontwikkeling van het Westen des Lands (1951–1958)*, PSVA-publicatie no. 10. Nederlands Instituut voor Ruimtelijke Ordening en Volkshuisvesting, The Hague.

Balz, V. (2018). 'Regional design: Discretionary approaches to regional planning in The Netherlands', *Planning Theory*, 17(3), 332–354.

Balz, V. and Zonneveld, W. (2018). 'Transformations of planning rationales: Changing spaces for governance in recent Dutch national planning', *Planning Theory & Practice*, 19(3), 363–384.

BSPO, Bestuur van de Sectie Planologisch Onderzoekers (1975). 'Het E-milieu onder de loep' [Scrutinizing the E-environment], *Stedebouw & Volkshuisvesting*, 56(6), 218–227.

Burke, G.L. (1966). *Greenheart Metropolis; Planning the Western Netherlands*. MacMillan, London.

Den Hoed, P., Salet, W.G.M. and Van der Sluijs, H. (1983). *Planning als onderneming [Planning as an Undertaking]*, Voorstudies en achtergronden nr.V34, Wetenschappelijke Raad voor het Regeringsbeleid. Staatsuitgeverij, The Hague.

Faludi, A. and Van der Valk, A. (1994). *Rule and Order: Dutch Planning Doctrine in the Twentieth Century*. Kluwer Academic Publishers, Dordrecht/Boston/London.

Frieling, D.H. (1983). 'Concepties en hun gevolgen' [Conceptions and their consequences], *Stedebouw & Volkshuisvesting*, 64(6), 258–269.

Frieling, D.H. (1997). 'Verstedelijking als politieke opgave' [Urbanization as a political challenge], *Stedebouw en Ruimtelijke Ordening*, 78(5), 4–8.

Hajer, M.A. and Zonneveld, W. (2000). 'Spatial planning in the network society – Rethinking the principles of planning in the Netherlands', *European Planning Studies*, 8(3), 337–355.

Hall, P. (1966). *The World Cities*. Weidenfeld and Nicolson, London.

Hall, P. (1984). *The World Cities*; Third edition. Weidenfeld and Nicolson, London.

Kickert, W.J.M. (1996). 'Expansion and diversification of public administration in the post-war welfare state: The case of the Netherlands', *Public Administration Review*, 56(1), 88–94.

Korthals Altes, W. K. (1995). *De Nederlandse planningdoctrine in het fin de siècle [Dutch Planning Doctrine at the Turn of the Century]; Ervaringen met* voorbereiding en doorwerking van de Vierde nota (Extra), PhD Thesis University of Amsterdam. Van Gorcum, Assen.

Korthals Altes, W. K. (2006). 'Stagnation in housing production: Another success in the Dutch 'planner's paradise?', *Environment and Planning B: Urban Analytics and City Science*, 33(1), 97–114.

Lambregts, B. and Zonneveld, W. (2004). 'From Randstad to Deltametropolis: Changing attitudes towards the scattered metropolis', *European Planning Studies*, 12(3), 299–322.

Meijers, E. (2019). 'Herkomst van het concept Randstad [The origin of the Randstad concept]; De strijd om de locatie van de nationale luchthaven', *Geografie*, 27(1), 32–33.

Ministerie van Bouwnijverheid (1960). *Nota inzake de ruimtelijke ordening in Nederland [Report Concerning the Spatial Organization of The Netherlands]*. Staatsuitgeverij, The Hague.

Ministerie van EZ (Economische Zaken) (1958). *Zesde nota inzake de industrialisatie van Nederland [Sixth Report about the Industrialisation of the Netherlands]*. Staatsuitgeverij, The Hague.

Ministerie van IenM (Infrastructuur en Milieu) (2012). *Structuurvisie Infrastructuur en Ruimte [National Policy Strategy for Infrastructure and Spatial Planning]*. Ministerie van IenM, The Hague

Ministerie van VRO (Volkshuisvesting en Ruimtelijke Ordening) (1966). *Tweede nota over de ruimtelijke ordening [Second Report on Spatial Planning]*. Staatsuitgeverij, The Hague.

Ministerie van VROM (Volkshuisvesting, Ruimtelijke Ordening en Milieubeheer) (1993). *Vierde nota over de ruimtelijke ordening Extra [VINEX: Fourth Report on Spatial Planning Extra]*; Deel 4: Planologische Kernbeslissing Nationaal Ruimtelijk Beleid. Ministerie van VROM, The Hague.

Ministerie van VROM (Volkshuisvesting, Ruimtelijke Ordening en Milieubeheer) (2001). *Ruimte maken, ruimte delen: Vijfde Nota over de Ruimtelijke Ordening 2000/2020 [Creating Space, Sharing Space: Fifth Report on Spatial Planning 2000/2020]*; Vastgesteld door de ministerraad op 20 December 2000 [PKB Deel 1]. Ministerie van VROM/Rijksplanologische Dienst, The Hague.

Ministerie van VROM (Volkshuisvesting, Ruimtelijke Ordening en Milieubeheer) (2002). *Ruimte maken, ruimte delen: Vijfde Nota over de Ruimtelijke Ordening 2000/2020 [Creating Space, Sharing Space: Fifth Report on Spatial Planning 2000/2020]; PKB Deel 3, Kabinetsstandpunt – PKB Deel 2, Resultaten van inspraak, bestuurlijk overleg en advies*. Ministerie van VROM/Rijksplanologische Dienst, The Hague.

Ministerie van VROM (Volkshuisvesting, Ruimtelijke Ordening en Milieubeheer), Ministerie van Economische Zaken, Ministerie van Landbouw, Natuurbeheer en Visserij and Ministerie van Verkeer en Waterstaat (1999). *De ruimte van Nederland: Startnota ruimtelijke ordening 1999 [The Territory of The Netherlands: Starting Memorandum Spatial Planning 1999]*. Sdu Uitgevers, The Hague.

Ministeries van VROM, LNV, VenW en EZ (2004a). *Nota Ruimte: Ruimte voor ontwikkeling [National Spatial Strategy]*. Ministerie van VROM, The Hague.

Ministeries van VROM, LNV, VenW en EZ (2004b). *Nota Ruimte: Ruimte voor ontwikkeling [National Spatial Strategy]*; Deel 4: tekst van parlementaire instemming. Ministerie van VROM, The Hague.

Ministry of IandE (Infrastructure and the Environment) (2011). Summary National Policy Strategy for Infrastructure and Spatial Planning; Making the Netherlands competitive, accessible, liveable and safe. Ministry of IandE, The Hague.

Ministry of the Interior and Kingdom Relations (2019). *Draft National Strategy on Spatial Planning and the Environment*; A sustainable perspective for our living environment. Ministry of the Interior and Kingdom Relations, The Hague.

Musterd, S. and Van Zelm, I. (2001). 'Polycentricity, households and the identity of places', *Urban Studies*, 38(4), 679– 696.

Needham, B. (2007). *Dutch Land Use Planning; Planning and Managing Land Use in the Netherlands, the Principles and the Practice*. Sdu Uitgevers, The Hague.

Needham, B. (2014). *Dutch Land-use Planning; The Principles and the Practice*. Ashgate, Surrey.

Neefjes, M.C.M. (1988). *Beleidslevenscyclus: Perspectief voor nationale ruimtelijke planning [The Policy Cycle: A Perspective for National Spatial Planning]*, MSc thesis. Planologisch en Demografisch Instituut Universiteit van Amsterdam, Amsterdam.

NSCGP, Netherlands Scientific Council for Government Policy (1999). *Spatial Development Policy*; Summary of the 53rd report, Reports to the Government No. 53. Sdu Publishers, The Hague.

NSPA, National Spatial Planning Agency (2000). *Spatial Perspectives in Europe; Spatial Reconnaissances 1999*. Ministry of Housing, Spatial Planning and the Environment, The Hague.

Priemus, H. (1999). 'Four ministries, four spatial planning perspectives? Dutch evidence on the persistent problem of horizontal coordination', *European Planning Studies*, 7(5), 563–585.

Quist, L. (1993). *Randstad Overleg Ruimtelijke Ordening, een onderzoek naar interprovinciale samenwerking [The Randstad Consultation Platform for Spatial Planning: A Study into Interregional Co-operation].* Delft University Press, Delft.

RARO, Raad van Advies voor de Ruimtelijke Ordening (1972). *Advies over de elementen van een aanvullende regeringsnota op de Tweede nota ruimtelijke ordening [Advice about the Components of a Supplementary Report to the Second Report on Spatial Planning].* RARO, The Hague.

Schuyt, K. and Taverne, E. (2000). *1950. Welvaart in zwart-wit [Contrasts in Prosperity: The Netherlands in the 1950s].* SDU, The Hague.

Siraa, T., Van der Valk, A. and Wissink, W.L. (1995). *Met het oog op de omgeving: Een geschiedenis van de zorg voor de kwaliteit van de leefomgeving [Focusing on the Environment: A History of Caring about the Quality of the Living Environment]; Het ministerie van Volkshuisvesting, Ruimtelijke Ordening en Milieubeheer (1965–1995).* SDU-Uitgevers, The Hague.

Spaans, M., Trip, J.J. and Van der Wouden, R. (2013). 'Evaluating the impact of national government involvement in local development projects in the Netherlands', *Cities*, 31, 29–36.

Toonen, Th.J. (1987). 'The Netherlands: A decentralised unitary state in a welfare society', *West European Politics*, 10(4), 108–129.

Toonen, Th.J. (1990). 'The unitary state as a system of co-governance: The case of the Netherlands', *Public Administration*, 68(3), 281–296.

Van Dam, H. and Vuijsje, H. (2011). *Plannenmakers in oorlogstijd [Planners in Wartime]; Het omstreden begin van de Nederlandse ruimtelijke ordening.* De Vrije Uitgevers, Amersfoort.

Van der Cammen, H. and De Klerk, L. (2012). *The Selfmade Land. Culture and Evolution of Urban and Regional Planning in the Netherlands.* Unieboek/Het Spectrum, Houten/Antwerpen

Van der Valk, A. (1990). *Het levenswerk van Th.K. van Lohuizen 1890–1956 [The Lifework of Th. K van Lohuizen 1890–1956];* De eenheid van het stedebouwkundige werk. Delft University Press, Delft.

Van Duinen, L. (2004). *Planning Imagery: The Emergence and Development of New Planning Concepts in Dutch National Spatial Policy,* PhD thesis University of Amsterdam.

Van Duinen, L. (2015). 'New spatial concepts between innovation and lock-in: The case of the Dutch Deltametropolis', *Planning Practice & Research*, 30(5), 548–596.

Waterhout, B., Othengrafen, F. and Sykes, O. (2013). 'Neo-liberalization processes and spatial planning in France, Germany and the Netherlands: an exploration', *Planning Practice & Research*, 28(1), 141–159.

WWDL, Werkcommissie Westen des Lands (1958a). *De ontwikkeling van het Westen des lands: Rapport [The Development of the West of the Country: Advisory Report].* Staatsdrukkerij, The Hague.

WWDL, Werkcommissie Westen des Lands (1958b). *De ontwikkeling van het Westen des lands: Toelichting [The Development of the West of the Country: Explanatory Report].* Staatsdrukkerij, The Hague.

Zonneveld, W. (1991). *Conceptvorming in de ruimtelijke planning [Conceptualisation in Spatial Planning];* Patronen en processen, Planologische Studies nr.9a, PhD thesis

University of Amsterdam. Planologisch en Demografisch Instituut Universiteit van Amsterdam, Amsterdam.

Zonneveld, W. (1992). *Naar een beter gebruik van ruimtelijke planconcepten [Towards a Better Use of Spatial Concepts]*, Planologische Verkenningen 64. Planologisch Demografisch Instituut Universiteit van Amsterdam, Amsterdam.

Zonneveld, W. (2005). 'In search of conceptual modernization: The new Dutch "national spatial strategy"', *Journal of Housing and the Built Environment*, 20(4), 425–443.

Zonneveld, W. and Evers, D. (2014). 'Dutch national spatial planning at the end of an era'. In: Reimer, M., Getimis, P. and Blotevogel, H. (Eds) *Spatial Planning Systems and Practices in Europe; A Comparative Perspective on Continuity and Changes*. Routledge, New York/Oxon, 61–82.

12 Governance and power in the metropolitan regions of the Randstad

Marjolein Spaans, Wil Zonneveld and Dominic Stead

Introduction

Trends in decentralisation and globalisation are increasingly testing the capacity of regional economies to adapt and exploit their competitive advantages while also offering new opportunities for regional development. All levels of government are rethinking their strategies for building competitive, sustainable and inclusive urban territories (OECD, 2016). Effective relations between different levels of government, as well as greater participation by citizens, firms, education and research institutions, and other non-state actors, are required in order to improve the delivery and quality of public services (OECD, 2016).

In practice there has been a rapid development of consultation and coordination structures in response to growing spatial interaction and integration at the supra-local level, including metropolitan regions (as well as other types of regions). The private sector and voluntary actors are increasingly participating in the management of territories. Government itself has become a multi-actor system as policy sectors (the proverbial silos) have their own agendas while the range of semi-autonomous governmental agencies add to administrative complexity (e.g. airport and port authorities, public transport providers and their managing authorities).

This has resulted in the pursuit of new governance arrangements for metropolitan areas. The OECD (2015) distinguishes between four broad categories of metropolitan governance arrangements that can be found around the world. The first is informal or soft co-ordination and is often found in instances of polycentric urban development. Lightly institutionalised platforms for information sharing and consultation are relatively easy both to implement and to undo. They typically lack enforcement tools, and their relationship with citizens and other levels of government tends to remain rather minimal.

Inter-municipal authorities form the second category. There are two sub-categories. When established for a single purpose such as waste collection, such authorities seek to share costs and responsibilities across their members (in the Netherlands literally hundreds of these authorities can be found, often with overlapping boundaries).[1] The second sub-category is formed by multi-purpose authorities which embrace a defined range of key policies for urban development such as land use, transport and infrastructure.

The third category are supra-municipal authorities. The difference with the previous category is that this arrangement brings with it the creation of an additional layer of government *above* municipalities either by creating a directly elected metropolitan government, or with the upper governments (in the Netherlands that would be national government) establishing a non-elected metropolitan structure. The extent of municipal involvement and financial capacity often determine the effectiveness of a supra-municipal authority (OECD, 2015).

The fourth and final category is formed by so-called metropolitan cities with a special status. Cities that, for instance, exceed a legally defined population threshold can be upgraded by national government. Sometimes only capital cities acquire such a status which puts them on the same footing as the next upper level of government and gives them broader competencies.

According to the OECD these categories are not mutually exclusive: different arrangements may coexist in the same country, and even within the same metropolitan area (OECD, 2015). For example, a metropolitan area may adopt one arrangement for a specific public service but another arrangement for other services. According to the OECD more than half of the metropolitan governance bodies across the world rely on informal or soft coordination arrangements. The prime explanation is that they are relatively easy to create (and to dismantle), they do not break into a country's administrative system and, for that reason, do not require any legal provision from upper levels of government.

As we will see, every category identified above appeared as an option in decades of discussions about the improvement of governance capacity in urban regions, especially in the Randstad area. This chapter concentrates on the nature and powers of governance arrangements in two Dutch metropolitan areas, both situated in the Randstad: the Metropolitan Region Amsterdam (*Metropoolregio Amsterdam* or MRA) and the Metropolitan Region Rotterdam The Hague (*Metropoolregio Rotterdam Den Haag* or MRDH). To do so, it draws on the work of Healey (2006) and Haran (2010). Both Healey and Haran identify a triad of similar (but differing) factors influencing the decision environment. Healey draws on the work of Giddens (1984) in her analysis of institutional adaptation and change, identifying three key flows which shape the materialities and identities of actors and create the structural forces that they experience: 'material resources', 'authoritative resources' and 'ideas and frames of reference'. Meanwhile, Haran draws on the work of Lukes (1974) and distinguishes three dimensions to explain the way power is used to organise the relationships between the actors involved in regional governance: 'resources', 'process' and 'meaning'. In this chapter, the powers derived from 'resources', 'process' and 'meaning' are used to structure the analysis and comparison of governance arrangements in the two Dutch metropolitan areas.

The *power of resources* has close ties to Healey's dimension of 'material resources'. For Healey, material resources refer to goods and assets, technologies, finance and labour power. Under the power of resources, Haran refers to information, knowledge and expertise, political access, control of money, rewards and sanctions, including the mechanisms for their distribution like laws and regulations. In this chapter, legal competences for different activities (e.g. spatial, transport and economic development) are also included under this form of power.

The *power of process* is related to Healey's flow of authoritative resources, which includes regulatory power, and the power to regulate the behaviour of others through formal and informal norms, codes and laws (Healey, 2006). Haran (2010) refers to the power of process as the power of actors to prevent certain issues from reaching collective decision-making agendas. This chapter considers the power of process by analysing the actor network and relations.

The *power of meaning* is closely linked to Healey's flow of ideas and frames of reference, the power to generate new imaginations and shape identities and values (Healey, 2006). According to Haran (2010), this power relates to the capacity to shape perceptions and beliefs. In spatial planning this is closely related to visioning, the creation of 'images of the future' (see also Shipley, 2002), which is often intrinsically linked to visualisation and map-making or 'framing with images' (Faludi, 1996; Zonneveld, 2005). This power is about how the structure of metropolitan regions is perceived.

The analysis presented is based on a mixture of primary and secondary sources, building on earlier related work by the authors (including Zonneveld and Spaans, 2014; Spaans and Zonneveld, 2015, 2016; Spaans and Stead, 2016). The chapter is divided into six main parts. It continues with an overview of recent international trends in metropolitan governance. It then presents a summary of trends in sub-national governance in the Netherlands. This is followed by analyses of power in the MRDH and MRA. It concludes with a reflection on the extent to which the powers of metropolitan governance in the two cases coincide and have experienced similar changes.

Trends in regional and metropolitan governance in an international perspective

Trends in regional governance

Building on the work of Lidström (2007) and Fürst (2009), a number of closely interlinked contemporary trends in regional governance can be identified across Europe and beyond (Stead and Pálné Kovács, 2016). These trends can be summarised under five headings: (1) redefining of the role of the nation-state; (2) the strengthening of lower levels of self-government; (3) increasing diversity, variation and even asymmetry of governance; (4) increasing marketisation of the public domain and (5) shifting rationales for intervention.

The establishment and gradual expansion of the EU has changed the role of national borders and has contributed to the transfer of decision-making powers both upwards and downwards: to the supranational and sub-national levels. European regional policy, primarily through the Structural Funds and Cohesion Funds, has contributed to the establishment of new regional bodies (or the strengthening of existing bodies) to administer European regional policy resources. At the same time, territorial management and planning approaches in member states are being increasingly shaped by European policies and initiatives (e.g. structural fund rules, environmental management and nature protection directives). Meanwhile, the role of the nation-state has been challenged from inside in some cases where demands for separatism or self-government have been made, motivated by regional culture or identity arguments.

In many European countries, examples can be found where functions have been decentralised from central government to local and regional levels of government. In some, this has happened as a result of the reorganisation of sub-national government, either by amalgamating municipalities or regions or by creating new regional levels of self-government. Reforms in sub-national government have been enacted in various countries where comprehensive reforms of the whole structure of local and regional government have taken place, including amalgamations of municipalities and regions, and the transfer of functions between different levels of government (see for example Galland and Enemark, 2013). In some cases, however, reforms to government structures and competences have not always been accompanied by corresponding shifts in funding allocations for a variety of reasons, including the political difficulties or complexities of fiscal reforms (Maier, 1998; OECD, 2001).

This tendency towards diversity can be seen as the result of the empowerment of lower levels of government. Not only is the scope for variation between sub-national units greater, some units are also permitted to follow their own paths that may differ from the general national pattern. Various types of asymmetry can be distinguished: political, administrative and fiscal (Loughlin, 2007).[2]

The increased involvement of non-state actors (including the private sector) is one of the central dimensions of the shifts from government to governance (see for example Kooiman, 1993). Many functions that were seen as typical public responsibilities during the peak of the welfare state era when government rather than governance prevailed, have more recently either been privatised or are run jointly by public and private providers. Public organisations are increasingly taking an 'enabling' role where other actors are the providers of public services. In many countries, the welfare state has been reconfigured in ways that makes it less centralised and less redistributive, and more oriented to promoting the role of the market. Outsourcing is one of the ways in which non-state actors (including private and non-profit) are increasingly involved in delivering goods and/or services, a trend closely associated with the emergence of 'new public management'. Governments can outsource the delivery of services in two ways: providing technical support (e.g. consultancy or back-office functions for government); and/or delivering goods or services directly to the end user on behalf of the government (e.g. public transport or waste disposal services).

Territorial governance is being redefined in the light of important societal challenges, new powers and responsibilities and new attempts to increase the societal relevance of planning. Across Europe, territorial governance is being recast as a way of managing the increasing interdependencies of actors involved in territorial development (Stead and Meijers, 2009). Because the competition for various goods and services often extends well beyond national boundaries, the pressure to introduce governance reforms to respond to these challenges has increased. Moreover, the internationalisation of trade, education and communication is also contributing to shifts in the way in which territorial governance is practised and conceptualised.

Trends in metropolitan governance

Metropolitan governance bodies – bodies aiming at organising responsibilities among public authorities in metropolitan areas – are extremely common in most OECD countries. Very few countries have no metropolitan governance body at all, although rarely are all metropolitan areas in a country covered by a metropolitan governance body. Since the 1990s, there has been renewed momentum in the creation of metropolitan governance bodies (or in the reform of existing ones). According to the OECD Metropolitan Survey held in 2013 (Ahrend *et al.*, 2014), more than two-thirds of OECD metropolitan areas currently have some kind of body or agency responsible for metropolitan governance (Figure 12.1). However, not all these bodies have many, or even any, legal powers.

A majority of metropolitan governance bodies work on regional development, spatial planning and transport. However, considerable diversity exists in their legal status, composition, power, budget and staff, and consequently in their impact on policy design and implementation. Within OECD countries, around 80% of metropolitan governance bodies work on regional development, over 70% on transport and over 60% on spatial planning. More than half of metropolitan governance bodies are active in these three fields at the same time (OECD, 2015).

Metropolitan-wide planning can be achieved by either formal and informal institutions or a mix thereof, depending on how sectoral competencies are divided. The effectiveness of either institutional approach depends to a large extent on the types of issues that a territory faces, the relationships among the actors, the resources at their disposal and, in general, the capacity to implement a common agenda. The policies of upper level governments, regional or national, have a major impact on the adoption of inter-municipal or metropolitan planning frameworks. (OECD, 2017) The majority of metropolitan governance bodies in the OECD tend to involve forms of informal

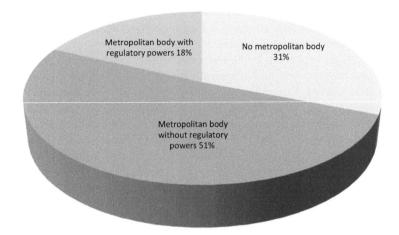

Figure 12.1 Share of OECD metropolitan areas with a body responsible for metro-
        politan governance.
Source: Own illustration based on Ahrend *et al.,* 2014.

or soft co-ordination; less than a quarter of OECD metropolitan areas have
governance bodies that impose regulations.

Links to political authority are directly tied to an entity's capacity to raise
funds independently and to establish binding regulation (the 'power of resources'). Informal forms of metropolitan governance can struggle to implement a common agenda where major trade-offs are required and have weaker
connections to the citizens they govern in terms of democratic legitimacy
and accountability. Despite these drawbacks, there are many reasons why
metropolitan areas have chosen to adopt more informal approaches to metropolitan collaboration, including the critical role they play in establishing a
common metropolitan agenda (OECD, 2017).

Intergovernmental transfers are highly instrumental across OECD countries in establishing metropolitan forms of governance. In the Netherlands,
however, such mechanisms are not currently employed. Here, the national
government funds large projects of metropolitan importance directly in the
domain of transport and infrastructure, rather than being funded by metropolitan regions as these regions lack taxation competences.

Searching for regional governance in the Netherlands

Many of the general trends discussed above are also visible in the Netherlands. Here too, the 1990s marked an important point in the search for new
forms of metropolitan governance. Indeed, the quest to find regional and
metropolitan governance structures had started a few decades earlier while
becoming highly frenetic in the years after 1990. Quite typical for the Dutch

case is that more than one spatial scale was involved: the level of the entire Randstad as well as the level of its two constituting 'wings' and the urban regions within these wings.

First efforts to find 'suitable' regional governance arrangements

The present administrative structure of the Netherlands goes back to the 1848 constitution which defines two levels below the national level: provinces and municipalities. In those days there were 11 provinces and more than 1,200 municipalities. Today, by comparison, there are 12 provinces and 355 municipalities. Not surprisingly whether municipalities could effectively deal with spatial development became an issue in the following years. Discussions gained momentum during the first decades of the twentieth century as urbanisation started to become a regional phenomenon through suburbanisation and rapid urbanisation, in particular in industrial and mining areas and in the west of the country. From the 1910s onwards, strong pleas for regional spatial planning were made, in particular after 1924 when a large international conference on this subject took place in Amsterdam. At that stage there were still more than 1,000 municipalities. Planners called for giving planning competences to the provinces. However, national government regarded this as far too centralising (Faludi and Van der Valk, 1994) arguing instead that regional planning issues should be dealt with by (voluntary) cooperation between municipalities.

After the Second World War the Netherlands embarked on a long quest to find suitable governance arrangements, most specifically for metropolitan regions (Needham, 2014). For example, the national so-called Second Planning Report of 1966 proposed a fourth administrative layer in selected urban regions. This asymmetric solution (only applicable in a part of the country) was eight years later followed by a proposal to create a fourth level across the entire country through 44 districts (*rayons*) with planning and implementation competences. This idea was soon abandoned as in 1976 a new coalition government proposed continuation of the three levels of administration but to regionalise the middle – provincial – layer: from 11 to 26 provinces. In follow-up proposals the number went down to 24 and 17, respectively. Massive opposition from politicians, administrators, academics and civil society at large eventually led to the withdrawal of all legislative proposals in 1983. Regional governance had to be achieved through municipal cooperation and the capacity to do so had to come from the application of the so-called Joint Regulations Act (WGR: *Wet Gemeenschappelijke Regelingen*) of which a first version dates from 1950. This act opens up the possibility of cooperation between provinces, municipalities and water boards, but without directly elected councils: the watershed with a full-blown administrative layer. After the collapse of the plans to establish 'new style' provinces, a new WGR came into force on January 1, 1985. A principal objective was that all the present cooperation provisions had to be bundled and integrated to foster effectiveness and transparency, with the provinces in a kind of supervisory role. This 'conclusion' (i.e. intermunicipal cooperation) would only hold for a few years.

Opening Pandora's box once more

The economic recession of the 1980s particularly affected the four largest cities of the Randstad. In 1988 the government decided to install a heavy-weight advisory committee to evaluate policies with an effect on the socio-economic position of these cities, the so-called Montijn Committee. One area this committee specifically looked at was local governance. The main conclusion was that voluntary municipal cooperation based on the WGR was insufficient. The advice on what to do was twofold and essentially multi-scalar: (1) create four regional municipalities in the Randstad; and (2) create an Administrative Platform Randstad. How the second proposal was taken up we will discuss in the next section.

On the basis of this advice and a range of other studies and advisory reports, government decided in 1993 for the top-down creation of so-called city-provinces in seven regions, including Amsterdam, Rotterdam and The Hague (the other regions were Utrecht, Arnhem-Nijmegen, Eindhoven and the Twente region in the east of the country). This would have to be achieved in a processual sort of way, instead of one single step. The route was laid down in the 1994 'Framework Law Administration in Change' stipulating the establishment of *mandatory* municipal cooperation bodies in the seven regions in preparation of full-blown city-provinces. The temporary regional constructs acquired the rather unattractive name of 'framework law areas' (*kaderwetgebieden*).

The form of cooperation was clarified in a 1995 legislative proposal concerning the Rotterdam region: the new Rotterdam city-province would be formed by existing municipalities and the creation of new municipalities by splitting up Rotterdam. A similar trajectory was foreseen for Amsterdam. The idea that both Rotterdam and Amsterdam would 'vanish' led to a massive civil society opposition. Making use of local regulations a referendum was organised in both cities. The liquidation of the Rotterdam and Amsterdam municipalities was rejected by a vast majority (Lambregts *et al.*, 2008). Initially government wanted to push through the idea of city-provinces but this idea had to be abandoned as parliamentary support in the end proved to be lacking, even in the government coalition.

In retrospect it did not come as a surprise that government changed to the trajectory of intermunicipal cooperation once more. By January 1, 2006, the Framework Law was withdrawn and a new Joint Regulations Act came into force. This version of the act provided additional competences in the field of spatial planning and public transport for the seven areas mentioned above plus one region in the south of the Limburg province. They acquired a highly bureaucratic, technical name: 'WGR plus' regions. The new competences for the public bodies created by WGR plus included the making of mandatory regional structure plans (*structuurplannen*). However, this latter competence did not last very long. In 2008 a new Spatial Planning Act came into force which took away the plan-making competences of the WGR plus regions (Janssen-Jansen, 2011). Parliament considered the democratic legitimisation of WGR plus decision-making as rather poor.[3]

This story shows the vulnerable political basis of asymmetric solutions which sit somewhere between the standard, countrywide administrative layers, and it should not come as a surprise that just after eight years in existence all WGR plus regions were abolished in January 2015. A major reason for giving back competences to provinces and municipalities was the perceived lack of democratic legitimacy of the WGR plus regions (OECD, 2017) although this was not a dominant issue when they were created. Responsibilities for transport and related funding from national government were returned to the provinces, except for the provinces of South-Holland and North-Holland, where they had officially lost competences since the 2005 WGR plus Act. In South-Holland the areas of the two WGR plus regions were combined to form the Rotterdam-The Hague Transport Authority (see below). The Amsterdam WGR plus region, without any change in its boundaries, became the Transport Authority Amsterdam (TAA). Both transport authorities are mandatory forms of cooperation sharing the same legal basis. Both form the commissioning authority for public transport by bus, tram and underground railway (excluding the services of the national railway company). They also finance improvements to the regional infrastructure for goods vehicles, cars, bicycles and public transport, so investments in physical infrastructure. Both entities are strictly briefed to limit their activities to transport and in no way expand their actions to other areas. We explain below how issues outside (public) transport are addressed to network-type arrangements called metropolitan regions (Figure 12.2).

The emergence and downfall of Randstad cooperation bodies

Since the Randstad concept was invented as a planning concept at the end of the 1950s it was national government that was responsible for spatial strategy in this area. However, in the early 1970s some sort of cooperation between the provinces of North-Holland, South-Holland and Utrecht started under an acronym which only civil servants can invent: Dripo (a Dutch acronym for 'three provinces'). In 1975 the South-Holland executive took the initiative to broaden and deepen the cooperation by suggesting that also the four main Randstad cities should participate. However, the other two provinces feared that these cities would dominate. North-Holland was anxious that Amsterdam would reach out to the Green Heart (Quist, 1993). This proposal and 'Dripo' in general faded into oblivion shortly afterwards.

Amidst the economic recession of the 1980s cooperation between the three Randstad provinces picked up again in various domains from 1985

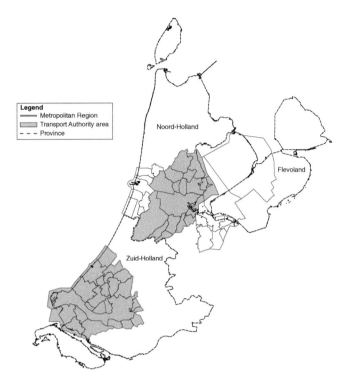

Figure 12.2 Location and perimeters of the two Randstad metropolitan regions and
      their transport authorities.

Source: Own illustration.

onwards, including spatial planning (Quist, 1993). The province of Flevoland
started to participate as an observer as its main city, the new town Almere,
played a key role for the northern part of the Randstad. In 1994 this province
became a full member of *Regio Randstad*, since 1991 the official name for cooperation in the domain of planning (Lambregts and Zonneveld, 2004). As
an expression of a desire to deepen relations, the Randstad provinces decided
to base their cooperation under this banner. Cooperation in the Randstad
seemed to intensify even more when as of September 2002 not only the four
main Randstad cities but also the WGR plus city-regions around these cities
joined Regio Randstad. The joint provisions arrangement was adapted and
from that moment cooperation was not only multi-actor but also multi-level,
involving 12 actors. Cooperation had a twin objective: (1) to strengthen the
international competitive position of the Randstad and (2) to improve quality
of life (Lambregts *et al.*, 2008).

This expansion from 4 to 12 Regio Randstad actors could be regarded as
a logical consequence of yet another Randstad organisation: the Administrative Committee for the Randstad (BCR: *Bestuurlijke Commissie Randstad*).

This rather giant negotiation platform included the 12 Randstad authorities and no less than five ministries. It was created in 1997 to renew the covenants between national government, provinces, urban regions and municipalities on housing allocation and production (Dijkink *et al.*, 2001). Later on, its tasks became much wider: not only the coordination of central government's spatial investments in the Randstad but also to manage Randstad-input for the fifth national planning report to be published in 2001 (Lambregts and Zonneveld, 2004).

Changes in government coalitions, in nearly all cases preceded by national elections, played an important role in the changing perceptions of how to (re) organise regional governance as discussed above. Likewise, changing perceptions about the importance of the Randstad for the country as a whole and the boundaries and internal structure of the Randstad had similar repercussions. In mid-2002 a new coalition government took office which was less convinced of the need to put the level of the Randstad centre stage (Lambregts *et al.*, 2008). The Randstad was divided into four programme areas, and concrete policies and investment strategies were coordinated with the authorities in each of these four regions (Amsterdam; Utrecht; Rotterdam The Hague; and the Green Heart). However, a later coalition government again attached greater importance to the Randstad. Warned by ever-lower rankings of the Randstad in international comparisons, it established a high-level committee which was asked to advise on its administrative structure. The assumption was that administrative bustle (*'bestuurlijke drukte'*) was seriously undermining all efforts to improve the competitive position of the Randstad. Early in 2007, the committee issued the daring advice to create one single metropolitan government for the entire Randstad that would take over a range of (mainly planning) competences of the provinces and the four WGR plus regions.

Another coalition than the one which established the Randstad advisory committee set aside this strongly formulated advice. Weary of governmental reform in general, support for this negative decision came from several research and advisory bodies. In 2006 the Netherlands Institute for Spatial Research published an elaborate report showing that the Randstad is not a single, integrated urban region but on the whole is formed by two sub-regions (Ritsema van Eck *et al.*, 2006). About a year later the OECD acknowledged that although the Randstad may represent a relevant scale in relation to certain issues, it did not consider the introduction of a Randstad authority a necessity and instead favoured the strengthening of the governance capacity of city-regions (OECD, 2007 as discussed by Lambregts *et al.*, 2008). Moreover, at the request of parliament, the Netherlands Institute for Spatial Research (De Vries and Evers, 2008; see also Evers and De Vries, 2013) made a comparison between the organisation of governance within the Randstad and a (small) sample of other urban regions. The general assumption was that the situation in the Randstad was far worse when compared with examples abroad. The assessment agency concluded that this was definitely not the case. In 2008 the government advisory council on spatial planning recommended that the creation of coalitions around strategic projects is far more effective than an overall restructuring of the administrative system (VROM-Raad, 2008).

By the time this latter advice was published the 12 partners of Region Randstad had already taken the decision to terminate their cooperation body by January 2008. Two dominant reasons are named in a frank letter by its chairman, the Crown's Commissioner of the province of South-Holland (Franssen, 2007): (1) Randstad Region partners were becoming ever less prepared to prioritise the Randstad scale; and (2) the organisation was too heavy and too 'administrative' while the shared ambitions were too weak. The letter also points out that there was no match between how the Region Randstad works and how government organises programmes which seek to support the economy of the Randstad. Under the so-called Randstad Urgent Programme which started in 2007 all (35) projects became supervised by high-level administrative teams: one administrator from national government and one from local government, a sort of implicit reply to the VROM-Raad advice.

Since the disappearance of Region Randstad in 2008 there is no longer a cooperation body at this level. However, 'Region Randstad' is still used as a label for various joint lobbying and promotion activities by the four Randstad provinces in Brussels.[4]

Metropolitan Region Rotterdam The Hague

Introduction

In the early 2000s, the southern Randstad or South Wing became conceptualised as one of the urban networks in the Netherlands. This new national planning concept meant that groups of cities could form networks tied together by functional relations, physical infrastructure and connected government. When the director of the Department of Spatial Planning and Transport in the province of South-Holland assumed office in 2002, he set up the South Wing Studio (*Atelier Zuidvleugel*). His opinion was that the South Wing was suffering from an abundance of plans, strategies and fierce competition between local planning actors and municipalities and that an institution which would be independent from daily political routine and which would have time to reflect would help the province as well as other planning actors to develop a regional frame of reference for decision-making (Balz and Zonneveld, 2015: 877). The focus of this Studio was design-oriented and helpful in bringing relevant stakeholders informally together and introducing them to the level of scale of the southern Randstad.

Around the same time, in 1997, an informal multi-level government cooperation platform in the southern Randstad was set up (Dijkink *et al.*, 2001). Members included the province, the two main cities, the two WGR plus city-regions and three WGR regions. This Administrative Platform South Wing (*Bestuurlijk Platform Zuidvleugel*) covered the city-regions of Rotterdam and The Hague with extensions towards Leiden to the north and Dordrecht to the south with the task to improve the coordination of urban development in the area. Its aim was to undertake preparatory work for a new covenant between the regional and national governments regarding investments in infrastructure and other spatial projects in the southern Randstad (Dijkink *et al.*, 2001). In 2000 the decision was taken to make the platform a permanent structure supported by a small secretariat located in the House of the Province of South-Holland in The Hague. It did not have decision-making or executive tasks, but formed the setting for negotiations with central government about investments in which the province had the strongest agenda-setting role (Spaans and Zonneveld, 2016).

The Metropolitan Region Rotterdam The Hague or MRDH was formed in 2010 when national government announced the abolition of the WGR plus city-regions. As the WGR plus city-regions were also the transport authorities for their territory and as such received considerable national budget for public transport, the announced abolition initiated a quest for these budgets and intensified the power play between municipalities and province. A new arrangement had to be set up to replace the city-regions. One option was that the infrastructure tasks would go to the province. The mayors of both Rotterdam and The Hague chose to block off this route as this meant that a large central government budget would find its way annually to the province. The metropolitan region placed itself at the forefront. In the law regarding the abolishment of the WGR plus regions, national government indicated that because of the complexity in the Randstad wings the new transport authority would cover the geographical area of the MRDH. But the exact elaboration was left to municipalities and provinces. This resulted in the metropolitan region becoming the transport authority and a formal arrangement: fixed boundaries and formal duties (which go hand in hand) but, like the city-regions before that, without an elected council. In December 2014 a joint provision was signed for the transport authority. On 1 January 2015, all eight Dutch city-regions were abolished and the MRDH was formally appointed by central government as the transport authority.

As MRDH gained in power, the informal cooperation for the larger area in the southern Randstad – the Administrative Platform South Wing – repositioned itself in 2016 as Network Southern Randstad focussing on strategic spatial-economic issues and cooperation with national government on national public investments in the field (Zuidvleugel, 2015).

As mentioned, the MRDH was formed by the integration of the two former WGR plus city-regions of Rotterdam and The Hague. The MRDH cuts a large chunk out of the territory of the province of South-Holland as it houses more than 60% of the population and 36% of the land area. The geographical area spans 23 municipalities which vary considerably in population size and nature. It covers a metropolitan authority tasked with transport and economic development responsibilities for this territory. One of the core ambitions of the MRDH authority is to bring the economies of Rotterdam and The Hague closer together while generating growth and well-being (OECD, 2016).

The power of resources

The previous section explained that the MRDH emerged as a new metropolitan-scale institution with the ambition of becoming the transport authority but at the same time it also embraced additional ambitions. While emerging, the MRDH envisaged an even broader scope which was narrowed to a twofold focus: transport and economic development. The broader scope at the start covered three coherent strategies (1) to exploit the potential of being a single daily urban system by improving internal connectivity; (2) to make better use of, and invest in the knowledge and innovation potential of the region; and (3) to fully exploit the wide diversity in amenities, services and landscape assets of the region (Meijers *et al.*, 2013).

When we compare the two pillars of the MRDH, the Transport Authority (TA) is much more formalised and with a considerably higher budget than the economic development pillar. The MRDH's budget is composed of public transport subsidies from national government[5] and contributions from the participating municipalities for the economic development pillar. It is important to stress that MRDH has only limited possibilities to broaden its financial resources as it is not allowed to levy taxes or impose other fees or charges. In the Netherlands, most taxes are collected at the national level and then redistributed to the local and provincial levels. Municipalities collect approximately one-sixth of their budget by levying local taxes.

In 2019 the budget in the field of public transport was 0.74 billion euro (the budget is not indexed which means that its value is going down due to inflation), which is used both for the operation of public transport and investment in new infrastructure. The Transport Authority pillar employs 56 full-time staff in 2019.[6] Legal competences and financial resources in the field of economic development are much more limited, which is also reflected in a more limited staffing: 12 full-time staff members in 2019. For this task the MRDH does not possess any 'hard tools' as its responsibilities are based on a voluntary agreement among member municipalities without any enforcement mechanisms. The annual budget of about 4.8 million euro (for 2019) comes primarily from the municipal authorities, in the form of a fixed amount per resident from each member municipality: 2.58 euro in 2019. According to the OECD (2016), such a funding arrangement for the economic pillar of the MRDH is common across the OECD, and its per capita budget is comparable to other informal metropolitan associations without regulatory powers. In terms of staffing, the MRDH has a smaller secretariat compared to other OECD metropolitan governance bodies that oversee a similar population size, but the MRDH has a more limited set of responsibilities.

The power of process

Shifts in leadership form an important underlying reason for the emergence of the MRDH. For a long time there have been tensions between the three major appointed administrators – the mayors of the two main cities of Rotterdam and The Hague and the Crown's Commissioner of the province of South-Holland.[7] This did not help the body to function as a cohesive policy network (Spaans and Zonneveld, 2015). When in 2008 in both Rotterdam and The Hague new mayors were appointed the politics changed drastically. Although they were from two different political parties they got on very well unlike their predecessors. It is because of them that the MRDH performs as a genuine politically approved informal governance arrangement (Spaans and Zonneveld, 2016). Although the MRDH and the province of South-Holland had a problematic relationship at the start, their cooperation has improved (OECD, 2016). As both governance bodies each have their own responsibilities in a partly overlapping geographical area they simply have to cooperate in economic and transport planning. After the abolition of the WGR plus city-regions in 2015, the Province of South-Holland and the MRDH signed a management agreement in 2016 and renewed and refined this in 2018, which focuses on the common fields of traffic and transport and economic business climate. The Network Southern Randstad complements this cooperation.

The MRDH has been established in a formal joint arrangement under the Joint Regulations Act of 2016 (MRDH, 2018a). The voluntary bottom-up collaboration among municipalities is a positive, distinctive feature of the MRDH compared to other OECD metropolitan regions built around two large cities (OECD, 2016). The organisation mirrors how provinces and municipalities are organised: a General Board and an Executive Board which cover both pillars of the MRDH. The current organisation of the MRDH reflects the balance between the two major cities on the one hand and the smaller municipalities on the other. The Executive Board includes the mayors of Rotterdam and The Hague (who act as chair and vice-chair) and representatives from three other municipalities.

The mayors of the two major cities rotate every two years as the chair of the General Board which is the highest decision-making body of the MRDH. This body comprises 27 members and meets four or five times a year. Representatives in the General Board have a varying number of votes, depending on the population size of the municipality they represent.[8] Decisions within the general management require an absolute majority of votes, but given the Dutch culture of political consensus, it is generally expected that most decisions will be taken unanimously. It is interesting that the two major cities together do not have the majority of votes although they represent more than half of the inhabitants of the MRDH (OECD, 2016). Some of the smaller municipalities hesitated to join the MRDH due to their fear of being overruled by the two cities but this was resolved by the sharing of votes.

Although the MRDH as a governance body is not directly elected, it has indirect legitimacy: bottom-up from the local level. Residents of the MRDH are given the right to speak at MRDH meetings. Participation is possible if the resident has an interest in a topic that is on the agenda of the meeting.[9]

The power of meaning

The MRDH deliberately restricted itself to the policy fields of transport and economic development. Responsibilities of the Transport Authority MRDH relate to public transport in its territory, while the province has competences (and related budgets) for provincial infrastructure (roads and waterways). As OECD (2016: 125) puts it: economic development is a competency of the province but it is also a field of work of the MRDH. The responsibilities for spatial planning however have remained a function of the province. The initial sensitivities between the province and MRDH have probably had as a result that the MRDH does not develop any development visions on maps (rather than text and figures) for its territory that might fuel any antagonisms.

Publications on the website of the MRDH hardly include visualisations and those included refer to visual analyses in the MRDH Atlas (MRDH, 2014). Thus, meaning in the sense of 'framing with images' is not employed by MRDH. The aim of the MRDH to increase economic growth by fostering economic integration of the region needs spatial planning policies formulated by the province to contribute to this goal by providing sufficient space for the economy to grow (OECD, 2016). Achieving these ambitions requires that policy areas of both MRDH and province are well co-ordinated. Figure 12.3 shows an attempt by the MRDH to stress the importance of such integration by relating economic clusters to each other. But this type of visualisation is *ad hoc* and is not used in external framing of the MRDH area.

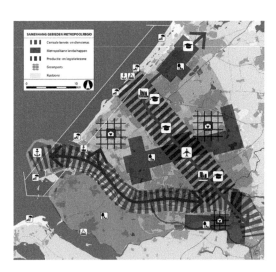

Figure 12.3 An attempt to visualise the spatial structure of the MRDH as a system of axes, zones and clusters.
Source: MRDH, 2014.

Metropolitan Region Amsterdam and Transport Authority Amsterdam

Introduction

Cooperation in metropolitan regions is often multi-scalar as we have ex-plained above. The Amsterdam region is an obvious example as there are two cooperation structures which cut different slices out of the wider area spatially connected to Amsterdam while they also have different 'powers'. First, there is the region covered by the Transport Authority Amsterdam (TAA). Legally it is the successor of the WGR plus city-region Amsterdam, terminated on December 31, 2016. The new entity grounded on the Joint Regulations Act took over. The boundaries did not change: the area includes 15 municipalities, all within the province of North-Holland. The land area is 38% of the territory of this province and it houses roughly 54% of its pop-ulation (about 1.5 million), percentages which are comparable with those of the MRDH.

The second, much larger entity is the Metropolitan Region Amsterdam or MRA. Having a population of about 2.5 million it is located in two provinces: North-Holland and Flevoland. Based on a covenant signed in March 2017, its membership includes 32 municipalities, the authorities of the two provinces, as well as, interestingly, the Transport Authority Amsterdam. The MRA covers a large area: 59% of the geographical area of North-Holland falls within the MRA and no less than 77% of its popula-tion. The figures for Flevoland are 42% (area) and 69% (population). As in the MRDH, the Transport Authority Amsterdam falls within the OECD category known as 'inter-municipal authorities' while the MRA is informal or soft co-ordination.

The MRA and even more the TAA has a track record in cooperation going back in time. The MRA cooperation started in the late 1990s under the banner of North Wing Consultation (*Noordvleugeloverleg*). After seven high-level conferences joined by administrators from the entire area, the structure was consolidated in its present elaborate form. The smaller-scale Informal Agglomeration Amsterdam Consultation (*Informeel Agglomeratie Overleg Amsterdam*) started about 30 years earlier in 1969 (Van der Lans, 2006). It went through successive periods of ever stronger cooperation, each phase indicated by a slightly different name, eventually leading to the present legally based stage of Transport Authority (see Lambregts *et al.*, 2008; Haran, 2010; Janssen-Jansen, 2011; Levelt and Janssen-Jansen, 2013; OECD, 2016, 2017).

The power of resources

If we compare MRA with the TAA then obviously the first one is lighter in the sense of not having a statutory basis. In theory, the cooperation within MRA could also be based on the Joint Regulations Act, but politically this was not acceptable to its membership (Stadsregio Amsterdam, 2016). In essence, the MRA is a network although one could argue like the OECD does (OECD, 2017: 153) that it is also a political body as it is based on a political agreement, discussed and accepted amongst all its members, meaning 32 municipalities and two provincial councils. Although 'light' the predecessor of the MRA, the North Wing Consultation was considerably lighter as there was no written agreement at all. Its main resource was based on *process*: meetings between administrators on a regular basis leading to several political agreements (we will come back to this below). The fact that this kind of co-operation has continued for nearly two decades and is politically formalised in a covenant means that although MRA lacks the 'power to implement' (OECD 2017: 157) it has created a valuable resource, namely trust.

Having no power to implement means MRA cooperation is 'cheap' in financial terms. Organisationally the cooperation is based on annual contributions from its members. As specified in the 2017 covenant the municipal members contribute €1.5 per inhabitant. While in the MRDH this is 72% more, in the MRA also the provinces contribute. North-Holland pays the same as Amsterdam, and Flevoland the same as its biggest town, Almere. Both North-Holland and Amsterdam also contribute extra to one of the three 'platforms': Economy (see below). For 2019 this leads to a budget of about €8.25 million (MRA, 2018). About a quarter of this budget is needed for running the MRA bureau. The number of staff is small: about 12 fte (MRA, 2016, 2018). As the MRA is not a legal entity all staff members work on the basis of secondment from municipalities, especially Amsterdam. There is a strong multiplier effect in terms of staffing. According to a rough estimate (MRA, 2016), about 60 to 80 fte across all MRA members are working on the implementation of the so-called MRA agenda, plus the cooperation itself like the preparation of meetings.

The transport authorities in the Amsterdam region and the Rotterdam-The Hague region have similar competences, but the budgets vary. Annually the TAA receives about €390 million from national government, which is much less compared with the MRDH as the latter region has a far more complex urban structure. Every year there is about €4.5 million available for research while the TAA bureau (mainly staff) costs about €7.5 million (VA, 2018) which is about four times more compared with the MRA. This means that about 3% of the annual budget is not directly spent on (public) transport and infrastructure.

Both the MRA and the TAA spend some of their budget on research. The MRA focuses on the analysis of the housing market, the state and structure of the MRA economy and the energy transition. The TAA has a much larger research budget and the focus is primarily on accessibility studies. One particular project is about the modelling of (future) transport called VENOM: Traffic Model Metropolitan Region Amsterdam (VENOM, 2016). Interestingly the research area is not the TAA region but the MRA area. The spatial logic is obvious: the TAA area does not cover the functional urban area of Amsterdam while the MRA area does to a much higher degree. This is reflected in the VENOM partnership which at the time of writing is in its third period (2017–2020). In addition, to the TAA, partners include the two provinces, the Ministry of Infrastructure and the municipality of Amsterdam plus ten other local, regional and national partners.

The power of process

This particular power or capacity is about how shared policy agendas come about and how the TAA, as well as the MRA, creates authoritative capacity within their constituencies as well as within their broader political context. As both entities are situated between constitutionally defined administrative levels with directly elected councils, a rather crucial issue concerns how legitimacy and accountability is organised, while at the same time dominance of Amsterdam is mitigated. The latter is a more sensitive issue compared with the MRDH as Amsterdam in terms of population and economy heavily dominates the MRA and even more the TAA.

In parallel with the MRDH, the TAA has a General Board (called Regional Council) as well as an Executive Board. The Regional Council has 51 members. Although the number of seats a municipality has is related to population size the Joint Provision uses a sliding scale. While more than half the population of the TAA lives in Amsterdam, the number of seats in the Council is less than a quarter. Members are appointed by the municipalities through their councils and the majority is recruited from these councils. The Council decides on the distribution of the financial funds across (four) programmes and projects. The Daily Board is rather small, with four members. The chair is an alderman of Amsterdam, holding a portfolio which includes transport and mobility.

The MRA has what the OECD calls a 'flexible geometry' (OECD, 2016: 177). Concrete activities and work processes rest on platforms. Of the three platforms, the Transport Platform works is exceptional: most MRA municipalities do not participate in this platform (but are represented by the provinces) and the membership is limited to those parties that participate in the TAA. The MRA Mobility Platform functions as a kind of interface between the MRA and the TAA. Some projects falling under this platform are not even limited to the boundaries of the MRA, in particular a project called MRA-E which seeks to stimulate electric transport in all municipalities not only in North-Holland and Flevoland, but also neighbouring Utrecht.

The Economy Platform focuses on employment and competitiveness. One of its main achievements it inherited from the period of the North Wing Conferences which preceded the MRA cooperation, namely the decision made at the fourth, 2005 North Wing conference to establish a platform to create a joint policy on the development of locations for offices and trade and industry: PLABEKA (*Platform Bedrijven en Kantoren*). As municipalities in the

Netherlands tend to compete with each other in this area (Needham, 2007: 74–75), this is no mean achievement. Connected to the Platform Economy albeit not a genuine MRA 'institute' is the Amsterdam Economic Board. The composition follows the classic triple helix formula. It has an advisory role both for the Amsterdam municipality as well as the MRA.

Most MRA municipalities are represented only indirectly in the Platform Economy as nearly all municipality members participate on behalf of one of the seven MRA *sub-regions*. This implies not only that MRA cooperation is characterised by a flexible geometry, but is also multi-scalar. Sub-regions play a crucial role in the Territory Platform which of all three platforms has the broadest focus. However, the platform does not call itself (in translation) Spatial Planning (see for this interpretation OECD, 2017: 149). The Dutch equivalent (*ruimtelijke ordening*) has the connotation of defining land-use through zoning plans. As this is a statutory competence this could not be dealt with by a network organisation such as the MRA. However, within the Territory Platform municipalities in MRA seek to coordinate house building programmes on the level of the sub-regions as well as on the level of the entire MRA. This is roughly the housing equivalent of PLABEKA. Both arrangements obviously have spatial implications, but the legally binding decisions on land-use are taken by the individual municipal councils according to the credo to be found on many MRA webpages and in published material: no competences are transferred from the participating authorities to the MRA.

There are connections between the three platforms. These are dealt with by four so-called portfolio consultations, their members are recruited from the ranks of municipal aldermen as well as the two provincial executives. The domains covered are sustainability; building and housing; landscape; and art, culture and heritage.

The power of meaning

What capacity do the TAA and the MRA have to shape perceptions and beliefs, both within the partnerships as well as the outside world? In its publicity material the TAA emphasises its *functional* relevance: 'working for a region in which people can quickly and easily reach their destination' (TAA, n.d.: 1). Interestingly, if one visits the website and clicks on 'area' the menu does not only show the municipal members but also the MRA which suggests that the TAA is not just active within the boundary of the area formed by its 15 municipal members but in a much wider area, forming an integrated mobility system.

As the TAA is a mandatory form of cooperation, there is less need to work on its profile and relevance. In contrast, the MRA is a voluntary partnership with a much wider focus and a much bigger area compared with the TAA. There is, therefore, much more need to show relevance, particularly to keep its membership together. In such a context, framing becomes particularly important: creating perspectives on how to understand or perceive a particular, complex situation (Rein and Schön, 1993), in this case a territory. This can be done through words and images.

In its use of language, two particular concepts are important. First, there is a particular emphasis on the Metropolitan Region as a *daily urban system*, a space forming a coherent area for its inhabitants.[10] This obviously suggests it is only 'natural' to regard this area as a logical object of policy cooperation. Second, the area is no longer conceived as the North Wing of the Randstad but as Metropolitan Region Amsterdam. At the 7th North Wing Conference, December 2007 the decision for the name change was taken, only two months after the decision to abolish the Randstad Region. Both events were connected to each other. North Wing obviously is linked to Randstad as the concept originates from a discussion about its structure and morphology. Doing away with the Randstad paved the way for another much more attractive 'label' due to the connotation of the area being a metropolis: a world-class regional city based on Amsterdam. Also, images played a role in the perception of the MRA. In early 2008, after a year of intense debates, conferences and design studios, a 138 pages vision document was published (MRA, 2008). Its key image served as a kind of logo for the following years (Förster *et al.*, 2016) (see Figure 12.4).

In 2016 a new policy map was created. This time it is not called a development vision but an action map (*actiekaart*). It is part of a glossy publication of 60 pages bearing the names of dozens of authors, under the auspices of the Platform Territory (MRA, 2016). It is not a replacement of the development vision but an addition, showing all the projects that are carried out in the region over a period of four years (2016–2020), demonstrating that the MRA cooperation has drive, momentum and practical relevance.

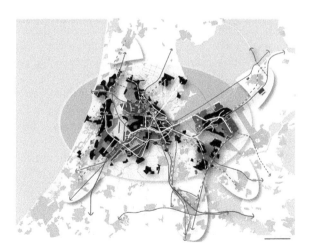

Figure 12.4 Image of spatial integration in the MRA area and the direction of main external relations.
Source: MRA, 2008.

Conclusions

The Netherlands is obviously no exception when it comes to the rescaling of governance. What is striking is the duration of the 'quest' and the many turns that have been taken over the course of time. The four broad categories of metropolitan governance arrangements as identified by the OECD have all been discussed at some stage. A fifth model was also considered: a new fourth layer of administration across the entire country, including elected councils. The fourth model involving special status of metropolitan cities (the proposal to create city-provinces) finally seemed to become the trajectory for seven regions, but resistance from civil society and eventually parliament led to the option of inter-municipal authorities (the WGR plus regions).

Government and parliament has changed its mind time and time again: the perceived lack of democratic legitimacy was the insurmountable stumble block. Since 2010, just two metropolitan regions exist in the country, both situated in the Randstad. In these two regions, there is currently a supra-local authority in the domain of (public) transport with some measures to safe-guard a form of legitimacy by giving elected members of local councils an advisory role. The two authorities are almost exclusively dependent upon government funding as municipalities (and provinces) have a very slim tax base. Clearly, the abolition of the multi-purpose city-regions in the Nether-lands runs counter to trends in metropolitan governance as observed by the OECD.

For a large-scale Randstad authority, governance complexity simply proved to be too great while the level of functional integration between the various parts of the Randstad as expressed, for example, by commuting pat-terns, is lacking. Alongside the two statutory Randstad transport authorities soft-coordination takes place under the banner of 'metropolitan regions'. The MRDH is more focused on economic development while the area is the same as that of the transport authority. The MRA is much more comprehensive in its ambitions and is 'working' for an area almost twice as big compared with the Transport Authority.

Looking at the MRDH and MRA in more detail, we arrive at the fol-lowing conclusions in relation to the three categories of power on which our analysis is based. When it comes to the *power of resources* both regions are almost exclusively dependent on national government funding, at least in the transport domain as already stated. Outside this domain there are (very) limited resources for staff and projects, although especially in the MRA there seems to be a large multiplier effect in relation to staff due to the comprehen-siveness and multi-scalarity of the cooperation.

From the perspective of the *power of process* we conclude that the two met-ropolitan regions seem to slowly converge in the way in which they are or-ganised. Both have, for example, a daily board and a supervisory board, the latter mostly recruited from municipal councils. Nevertheless, they also show two major differences: the province (i.e. North-Holland and Flevoland) is a prominent participant in the MRA and joined at the beginning. At the phase of emergence of the MRDH, the province was even foreclosed. Currently, the province participates in some of the MRDH committees.

The second major difference is geographical in nature: even though there might surely still be discussion about the precise external borders, it is the intention of the MRA to be inclusive and cover the whole daily urban system of Amsterdam in its metropolitan governance arrangement. In the MRDH two urban agglomerations (Leiden and Dordrecht) which are functionally part of the daily urban system are not represented in the metropolitan governance arrangement. From this perspective there seems to be a fundamental flaw in the arrangement. This may have an impact on the degree to which policy integration in the focus policy areas can be reached.

With respect to the *power of meaning* we observe a major difference in the fact that the MRA is actively using visions, maps and spatial images as a way of bringing coherence in the issues at the table between the actors involved and, in the projects, and programmes at stake in the region. Accessibility, economy and spatial planning seemed to be much more aligned than in the MRDH where spatial images are almost non-existent and spatial planning is not a policy field with which it wants to relate. Rather, economic development is the integrating frame here.

Notes

1 In the Netherlands the steering bodies are usually recruited from the ranks of municipal aldermen or (elected) municipal councillors.
2 The 'special' and 'ordinary' regions in Italy provide one example of political asymmetry and diversity within a state. Different forms of territorial administration within the UK provide one example of administrative and fiscal asymmetries, where the three territorial offices representing Scotland, Wales and Northern Ireland have distinct relations and arrangements with London. Meanwhile, in Spain, the Basque Country and Navarre have more financial (and legal) autonomy than the rest of the country, and exhibit fiscal asymmetry.
3 https://www.denederlandsegrondwet.nl/id/vilqfxp1clz9/intergemeentelijke_samenwerking; accessed 7 August 2019.
4 See: https://www.nl-prov.eu/regional-offices/randstad-region/?lang=en (accessed 11 February 2020).
5 Largely based on the Broad goal-oriented grant for transport (BDU or *Brede Doeluitkering* in Dutch) which is a financing programme for regional traffic and transport projects funded by central government.
6 Data from: Metropoolregio Rotterdam Den Haag (2018) Begroting 2019 en meerjarenbeeld 2020–2022 Metropoolregio Rotterdam Den Haag, Rotterdam: MRDH.
7 Mayors and Crown's Commissioners are appointed by national government and not elected.
8 Each representative of Rotterdam has 15 votes, each representative of The Hague has 13 votes, the representatives of Delft, Zoetermeer and Westland have 9 votes and so on, up to the smallest municipalities, whose representatives have 2 votes each (OECD, 2016: 145).
9 https://mrdh.nl/bestuur; accessed 11 February 2020).
10 See for instance: https://www.amsterdam.nl/bestuur-organisatie/volg-beleid/ontwikkeling/metropoolregio/; accessed 11 February 2020.

References

Ahrend, R., Gamper, C. and Schumann, A. (2014). *The OECD Metropolitan Governance Survey: A Quantitative Description of Governance Structures in Large Urban Agglomerations*, OECD Regional Development Working Papers, 2014/04. OECD Publishing, Paris.

Balz, V. and Zonneveld, W. (2015). 'Regional Design in the Context of Fragmented Territorial Governance: South Wing Studio', *European Planning Studies*, 23(5), 871–891.

De Vries, J. and Evers, D. (2008). *Bestuur en ruimte: de Randstad in internationaal perspectief [Governance and Territory: An International Perspective on the Randstad]*, Beleidsadviezen 07. Ruimtelijk Planbureau, Den Haag.

Dijkink, G., Hajer, M., De Jong, M. and Salet, W. (2001). 'De Zuidvleugel van de Randstad: Instituties en Discoursen' [The South Wing of the Randstad: Institutions and Discourses]. In: WRR Stuurgroep Toekomstonderzoek en Strategisch Omgevingsbeleid, *Zijlicht op Toekomstonderzoek; Vier cases [Shedding Light on Research about the Future]*. WRR Stuurgroep Toekomstonderzoek en Strategisch Omgevingsbeleid, Den Haag, 17–112.

Evers, D. and De Vries, J. (2013). 'Explaining Governance in Five Mega-City Regions: Rethinking the Role of Hierarchy and Government', *European Planning Studies*, 21(4), 536–555.

Faludi, A. (1996). 'Framing with Images', *Environment and Planning B: Planning and Design*, 23(1), 93–108.

Faludi, A. and Van der Valk, A. (1994). *Rule and Order: Dutch Planning Doctrine in the Twentieth Century*. Kluwer Academic Publishers, Dordrecht/Boston/London.

Förster, A., Balz, V., Thierstein, A. and Zonneveld, W. (2016). *The Conference 'Shaping Regional Futures: Mapping, Designing, Transforming!' A Documentation*. Technische Universität München/Delft University of Technology, Munich/Delft.

Franssen, J. (2007). *Voorstel tot opheffing van gemeenschappelijke regeling Samenwerkingsverband Randstad [Proposal to End Joint Provision Randstad Cooperation]*. Regio Randstad, Utrecht.

Fürst, D. (2009). 'Planning Cultures en Route to a Better Comprehension of "Planning Processes"?' In: Knieling, J. and Othengrafen, F. (Eds) *Planning Cultures in Europe: Decoding Cultural Phenomena in Urban and Regional Planning*. Ashgate, Farnham, 23–38.

Galland, D. and Enemark, S. (2013). 'Impact of Structural Reforms on Planning Systems and Policies: Loss of Spatial Consciousness?' *European Journal of Spatial Development*, Refereed article No. 52, 1–23.

Giddens, A. (1984). *The Constitution of Society*. Policy Press, Cambridge.

Haran, N. (2010). *The Power to Collaborate: How Judicious Use of Power Accelerates the Strategic Capacity of Regions in the Netherlands*, PhD Thesis, University of Amsterdam. Eburon, Delft.

Healey, P. (2006). 'Transforming Governance: Challenges of Institutional Adaptation and a New Politics of Space', *European Planning Studies*, 14(3), 299–320.

Janssen-Jansen, L. (2011). 'From Amsterdam to Amsterdam Metropolitan Area: A Paradigm Shift', *International Planning Studies*, 16(3), 257–272.

Kooiman, J. (Ed.) (1993). *Modern Governance; New Government-Society Interactions*. Sage Publishing, London.

Lambregts, B., Janssen-Jansen, L. and Haran, N. (2008). 'Effective Governance for Competitive Regions in Europe: The Difficult Case of the Randstad', *GeoJournal*, 72(1–2), 45–57.

Lambregts, B. and Zonneveld, W. (2004). 'From Randstad to Deltametropolis: Changing Attitudes towards the Scattered Metropolis', *European Planning Studies*, 12(3), 299–322.

Levelt, M. and Janssen-Jansen, L. (2013). 'The Amsterdam Metropolitan Area Challenge: Opportunities for Inclusive Coproduction in City-region Governance', *Environment and Planning C: Government & Policy*, 31(3), 540–555.

Lidström, A. (2007). 'Territorial Governance in Transition', *Regional and Federal Studies*, 17(4), 499–508.

Loughlin, J. (2007). 'Reconfiguring the State: Trends in Territorial Governance in European States', *Regional and Federal Studies*, 17(4), 385–403.

Lukes, S. (1974). *Power: A Radical View.* Palgrave Macmillan, Basingstoke.

Maier, K. (1998). 'Czech Planning in Transition: Assets and Deficiencies', *International Planning Studies*, 3(3), 351–365.

Meijers, E., Hollander, K. and Hoogerbrugge, M. (2013). *A Strategic Knowledge and Research Agenda on Polycentric Metropolitan Areas.* European Metropolitan Network Institute, The Hague.

MRA, Metropoolregio Amsterdam (2008). *Ontwikkelingsbeeld 2040 [Development Vision 2040].* MRA, Amsterdam.

MRA, Metropoolregio Amsterdam (2016). *Opzet MRA-bureau [Organisation MRA Bureau];* Internal note 19 October 2016. MRA, Amsterdam.

MRA, Metropoolregio Amsterdam (2018). *MRA Werkplan en Begroting 2019 [MRA Plan of Work and Budget 2019]; Concept versie: ter vaststelling door de Regiegroep van de MRA Oktober 2018.* MRA, Amsterdam.

MRDH, Metropoolregio Rotterdam Den Haag (2014). *Atlas Metropoolregio Rotterdam Den Haag [Atlas Metropolitan Region Rotterdam The Hague].* MRDH, Rotterdam.

MRDH, Metropoolregio Rotterdam Den Haag (2018a). *Werkwijzer Metropoolregio Rotterdam Den Haag [Method of Working Metropolitan Region Rotterdam The Hague].* MRDH, Rotterdam.

MRDH, Metropoolregio Rotterdam Den Haag (2018b). *Partnerships Have Power.* MRDH, Rotterdam.

Needham, B. (2007). *Dutch Land Use Planning; Planning and Managing Land Use in the Netherlands, the Principles and the Practice,* Reeks Planologie nr. 9. Sdu Uitgevers, Den Haag.

Needham, B. (2014). *Dutch Land-use Planning; The Principles and the Practice.* Ashgate, Surrey.

OECD (2001). *OECD Territorial Outlook,* 2001 Edition. OECD Publishing, Paris.

OECD (2007). *Territorial Reviews: Randstad Holland, The Netherlands.* OECD Publishing, Paris.

OECD (2015). *Governing the City.* OECD Publishing, Paris.

OECD (2016). *OECD Territorial Reviews: The Metropolitan Region of Rotterdam The Hague, Netherlands.* OECD Publishing, Paris.

OECD (2017). *The Governance of Land Use in the Netherlands: The Case of Amsterdam.* OECD Publishing, Paris.

Quist, H.J. (1993). *Randstad Overleg Ruimtelijke Ordening [Randstad Platform on Spatial Planning];* Een onderzoek naar interprovinciale samenwerking, Stedelijke en Regionale Verkenningen 2. Delftse Universitaire Pers, Delft.

Rein, M. and Schön, D. (1993). 'Reframing Policy Discourse'. In: Fischer, F. and Forester, J. (Eds) *The Argumentative Turn in Policy Analysis and Planning.* UCL Press, London, 145–166.

Ritsema van Eck, J., Van Oort, F., Raspe, O., Daalhuizen, F. and Van Brussel, J. (2006). *Vele steden maken nog geen Randstad [Many Cities Do Not Make a Single Randstad]*. Ruimtelijk Planbureau/ NAi Uitgevers, Den Haag/Rotterdam.

Shipley, R. (2002). 'Visioning in Planning: Is the Practice Based on Sound Theory?' *Environment and Planning A: Economy and Space*, 34(1), 7–22.

Spaans, M. and Stead, D. (2016). 'Integrating Public Transport and Urban Development in the Southern Randstad'. In: Schmitt, P. and Van Well, L. (Eds) *Territorial Governance across Europe; Pathways, Practices and Prospects*. Routledge, London/New York, 126–140.

Spaans, M. and Zonneveld, W. (2015). 'Evolving Regional Spaces: Shifting Levels in the Southern Part of the Randstad'. Allmendinger, P., Haughton, G., Knieling, J. and Othengrafen, F. (Eds) *Soft Spaces in Europe; Re-negotiating Governance, Boundaries and Borders*. Routledge, London/New York, 95–128.

Spaans, M. and Zonneveld, W. (2016). 'Informal Governance Arrangements in the Southern Randstad: Understanding the Dynamics in a Polycentric Region', *TESG: Tijdschrift voor Economische en Sociale Geografie*, 107(1), 115–125.

Stead, D. and Meijers, E. (2009). 'Spatial Planning and Sectoral Policy Integration: Concepts, Facilitators and Inhibitors', *Planning Theory and Practice*, 10(3), 317–332.

Stead, D. and Pálné Kovács, I. (2016). 'Shifts in Governance and Government across Europe'. In: Schmitt, P. and Van Well, L. (Eds) *Territorial Governance across Europe; Pathways, Practices and Prospects*. Routledge, London/New York, 21–35.

TAA, Transport Authority Amsterdam (n.d.). *Profile of the Transport Authority Amsterdam*. Vervoerregio Amsterdam, Amsterdam.

VA, Vervoerregio Amsterdam (2018). *Programmabegroting 2019–2022 [Programme Budget 2019–2022]*; Vastgesteld door de Regioraad op 16 oktober 2018. Vervoerregio Amsterdam, Amsterdam.

Van der Lans, J. (2006). *Kleine geschiedenis van de stadsregio Amsterdam [Short History of the Amsterdam City Region]; Standvastig x lichtvoetig x zwaarmoedig*. Inmerc, Wormer.

VENOM (2016). *Samenwerkingsovereenkomst 2017–2020 [Cooperation Agreement 2017–2020]*. Stadsregio, Amsterdam.

VROM-Raad (2008). *Wisselende coalities: naar een effectief regionaal ruimtelijk beleid [Variable Coalitions: Towards Effective Regional Spatial Policy]*. VROM-Raad, The Hague.

Zonneveld, W. (2005). 'Multiple visioning: New ways of constructing transnational spatial visions', *Environment & Planning C: Government and Policy*, 23(1), 41–62.

Zonneveld, W. and Spaans, M. (2014). 'Meta-governance and Developing Integrated Territorial Strategies: The Case Study of MIRT Territorial Agendas in the Randstad (Netherlands)', *Planning Theory and Practice*, 15(4), 543–562.

Zuidvleugel (2015). *Naar een network Zuidelijke Randstad [Towards a Southern Randstad Network]*; Een eerste stap in het veranderen van de overheidssamenwerking op het niveau van de Zuidvleugel van de Randstad. https://staten.zuid-holland. nl/DMS_Import/Statencommissie_Ruimte_en_Leefomgeving_RenL/2016/ Ruimte_en_Leefomgeving_31_augustus_2016/Bespreekstukken/Regionaal_ economisch_beleid/Toekomst_samenwerking_Zuidvleugel.org (accessed 11 February 2020).

13 In control of urban sprawl?

Examining the effectiveness of national spatial planning in the Randstad, 1958–2018

Ries van der Wouden

Introduction

Urban sprawl has been a part of the urbanisation process in the Netherlands for a long time. Because of a growing population in seventeenth century in Amsterdam, some industries were placed outside the city borders (Abrahamse, 2010: 227–248). Poor immigrants moved from the countryside to the outskirts of the city, whereas members of the urban elite bought land at some distance from the city to build their summer residences in the more pleasant parts of the Dutch countryside. The construction of railways during the nineteenth century gave a new impulse to this process. However, it took another century before urban sprawl became an issue for national spatial planning in European countries. In the United Kingdom, this happened just after the Second World War although some planning concepts had been formulated decades before. The Town and Country Planning Act of 1947 led to a new land-use policy, the Green Belt with containment around London and other large cities, and the construction of new towns' (Hall, 1988; Bruegmann, 2005). The Netherlands followed during the 1950s when planners and politicians feared the uncontrolled urbanisation of the Randstad, the polycentric conurbation in the West of the Netherlands (Faludi and Van der Valk, 1994; Van der Cammen and De Klerk, 2012). Controlling urban sprawl was the first and foremost issue of national spatial planning, and became even more urgent during the 1960s when the suburbanisation process speeded up and became a mass phenomenon. Sprawl kept its prominent place into the twenty-first century, despite the many changes in spatial planning itself.

Spatial planning in the Netherlands has established a strong reputation, not only for being comprehensive but also for being effective (Faludi and Van der Valk, 1994; Bontje, 2003; Hall, 2014). This reputation may be justified for the Dutch struggle against the sea, but not for the containment of urban sprawl, as this chapter will show. The results of the analysis of 60 years of urban sprawl in relation to spatial planning and its institutions cast serious doubts on the effectiveness of spatial planning in the Netherlands.

The chapter is structured as follows. The next section discusses the central theoretical concepts of urban sprawl, spatial policy and institutional change.

Following this, a section is devoted to policy debates and research on the Randstad polycentric urban area, then urban sprawl in the Randstad area of Netherlands is analysed using data on population change and land use. The findings are related to national spatial policy and institutional change. The long period of time the analysis covers allows for examination of the influence of planning and institutional changes. This assessment will be summarised in the last section of this chapter, which concludes with the debate on the future of urbanisation policy.

Defining urban sprawl and its relation to spatial planning

Urban sprawl is hardly a neutral concept. In the debate amongst urban planners and politicians, a lot of negative connotations are attributed to urban sprawl: it is considered to unnecessarily consume land, to promote car use leading to segregation, to be unattractive or visually intrusive, to be unsustainable and above all it is unplanned (Bruegmann, 2005; Couch *et al.*, 2007). But urban sprawl cannot be inherently negative, because many families have gained more living space by moving to a suburban environment. Rather it is a matter of balancing individual gains against collective costs. Nor are planning systems unequivocally 'anti-sprawl'. As this chapter shows, some planning decisions may facilitate urban sprawl rather than containing it. In order to analyse urban sprawl, we need to take distance from the normative emotions it evokes, and consider it as a part of the urbanisation process, with both negative and positive consequences.

First, how should we define urban sprawl? In their attempt of 'wrestling sprawl to the ground' in order to make it measurable, Galster and his co-authors focus correctly on urban form and land use. They distinguish eight dimensions of sprawl: density, continuity, concentration, clustering, centrality, nuclearity, mixed uses and proximity. Sprawl has low scores on one or more of these dimensions of land use (Galster *et al.*, 2001; see also Dieleman and Wegener, 2004). Others have tried to summarise sprawl in one or two indices of land use (Jaeger and Schwick, 2014; Oueslati *et al.*, 2015; Aurambout *et al.*, 2018). However, these empirical definitions have serious limitations for the analysis of 60 years of urban sprawl in the Netherlands. In the first place, these definitions ask for far more data than are available over such a long period of time. Time series on these aspects of land use simply are not there, the only available source is demographic data. Furthermore, the methods are fit to analyse sprawl in monocentric urban areas, but far less suitable for polycentric urban regions like the Randstad urban area in the Netherlands. For these reasons, this chapter draws from Bruegmann's pragmatic definition of urban sprawl: low-density, scattered urban development without systematic large-scale or regional public land-use planning (Bruegmann, 2005: 18).

Second, how can we connect urban sprawl with spatial planning and institutions? Here, the distinction between the 'moving actors' (households, retailers, companies) and the 'non-moving actors' (national and municipal governments, private developers, housing corporations etc.) is essential in the process of urban sprawl (Lüdeke *et al.*, 2007: 184). While the first category actually 'makes' the urban sprawl by moving to another place, the second category influences urban sprawl by decisions on regulations, investments and other policy instruments. The two sets of actors can act in coordination or not, but together the actors of the second category form the governance of the urbanisation process, and therefore of urban sprawl. The actions of both categories are enabled or restricted by institutions: planning organisations, government structures, laws and rules, available policy instruments, but also discourse coalitions and informal routines and cultures (Buitelaar *et al.*, 2007; Schmidt, 2010). Following Giddens (1984), we accept that institutions change over time because of the actions of the people involved, rather than being fixed structures. Many of the changes, though not all, are incremental. Therefore, path-dependency is very important also in spatial planning and its institutions (Couch *et al.*, 2011; Sorensen, 2015).

This is not the first case study on the interaction between spatial planning, institutions and urban sprawl. From a similar point of view, although covering a shorter period of time, Pagliarin analysed urban sprawl in the Barcelona and Milan regions. She concludes that institutional differences regarding the authority of both regional governments were a key factor in the containment of urban sprawl (Pagliarin, 2018). In his evaluation of sprawl in the Tokyo region, Sorensen states that the failure to contain sprawl in this region was due to the lack of policy instruments, as compared to the situation in most western countries. Instead of the 'low-scale' land readjustment policy instrument, more general land-use regulations would have been more effective (Sorensen, 1999). The European-wide analysis of cases of urban sprawl by Couch *et al.* shows the influence of economic, demographic and cultural factors. In Stockholm, for example, urban sprawl was exacerbated by a combination of wealth and lifestyle. Second homes around the city were often turned into permanent homes; they were the blind spot of spatial planning. In Liverpool, there was a combination of decline and urban sprawl. However, since the 1980s, this sprawl has been contained by a combination of green belt policy and the municipality's commitment to urban regeneration. But the declining city of Leipzig shows a massive amount of urban sprawl, partly due to a lack of planning. And in Vienna, new arrangements between regional and municipal authorities were made in order to contain sprawl (Couch *et al.*, 2007). These studies, therefore, conclude that planning and institutions can make a difference.

These are the theoretical elements for the analysis of the relationships between urban sprawl, spatial policy and institutional change in the Randstad area. This analysis treats the motives and individual actions of the 'moving actors' as a given. The aggregate results of their efforts will be visible in the presented data on population change and land use. The chapter concentrates on the effects of spatial planning on urban sprawl. In a qualitative assessment, the effects of planning are evaluated as well as the influence of external factors (like economic development and changing urban cultures). Because of its scale, the Randstad became a national planning issue, and the chapter therefore focuses on national spatial planning. National spatial planning, in turn, is facilitated or restricted by institutions. During the six decades of this analysis, major institutional changes have influenced national spatial planning and its results, as this chapter will show.

The Randstad in the 1950s and beyond: a new issue in planning and research

The polycentric Randstad area includes the urban ring (containing the four largest cities of the Netherlands) as well as the central open space, known as 'the Green Heart'. It became a central issue in national spatial planning after the Second World War. The population boom during the post-war years and the internal migration to the Randstad, made containing urban growth in the Randstad area a priority of spatial planning. Since the Randstad covers large areas of three provinces, the role of the national government was more or less self-evident. A committee for the western Netherlands advised the Dutch Government on this issue (see also Chapter 11). The committee published its final report in 1958 (Werkcommissie Westen des Lands, 1958). The report recommends that the government should allow urban growth outside the Randstad urban ring to prevent urban sprawl into the Green Heart. This recommendation became part of national spatial planning. For this reason, 1958 may be considered as the year in which the planning concept of the Randstad was conceived.

The Randstad area has been studied frequently since 1958 (e.g. Dieleman and Musterd, 1992; Dieleman *et al.*, 1999; Lambregts, 2009). Some studies analysed the relationship between spatial planning and urban sprawl. Geurs and Van Wee compared existing spatial planning with two model scenarios on land use (2006). Both scenarios are more liberal than the real planning system; one has no restrictions on the use of land for urbanisation, and the other in addition assumes a large degree of interregional migration. Because of the methodology used, the outcome is not surprising: without spatial planning, urban sprawl would have been more rampant. Bontje uses a different method. He compared the planned distribution of population with actual developments, and concluded that spatial planning might have had some positive effects, but did not manage to change the overall trend of urban sprawl (Bontje, 2003). The method used in this chapter's analysis of urban sprawl and spatial planning is closest to that of Bontje. It differs from both studies in two respects. First, the two studies span three decades, whereas this one covers six decades. This enables a more in-depth study of the relationships between urban sprawl, spatial planning and institutional changes. Second, this study combines demographic data with land-use statistics. Although the land-use statistics only cover the last two decades, they add something very valuable; namely, they include not only residential land use, but also that of transport, infrastructure and business parks. Together, they provide a more complete view of urban sprawl.

In its 1958 report, the Committee for the Western Netherlands defined the municipalities that belonged to the Randstad urban ring (Werkcommissie Westen des Lands, 1958: 9). This definition was also adopted for this research on urban sprawl, with a few small adaptations because of changing municipal borders. Apart from the Randstad urban ring, the analysis in this chapter also includes two other zones in the western part of the Netherlands: the already mentioned Green Heart (municipalities within the central open space at the inside of the urban ring) and the outer ring (municipalities in a zone of approximately 20–40 kilometres around the Randstad urban ring). To compare developments in these three zones, over time, the zones were kept constant, despite changing planning definitions of the Green Heart (Pieterse *et al.*, 2005: 96–97). The results of the analysis of urban sprawl are discussed in the next section.

Patterns of urban sprawl in the Randstad area

Two types of demographic change were important for urban sprawl in the Randstad area. The first change was population growth and internal migration to the western part of the Netherlands. This development started in the years after the Second World War. The second change was the process of suburbanisation. Many households left the large cities and moved into suburban municipalities (explained in Chapter 7). The size of the population of the large Dutch cities declined rapidly after the early 1960s. Table 13.1 shows the relative population changes over the 1960–2017 period in and around the Randstad area in the spatial categories of the Randstad urban ring, the Green Heart, and the outer ring. Within these three categories, a subdivision is made between cities and smaller municipalities.

These changes brought about between 1960 and 1990 two types of urban sprawl. First, an almost classical pattern of monocentric urban sprawl within the Randstad urban ring. The largest cities lost a substantial amount of their population, whereas other municipalities grew. The smaller the municipality, the faster the population growth (with the exception of the middle-sized cities of the 1980s). During the last two decades, this process was reversed. The largest cities show the highest growth rates, higher than the average of the total area and of the entire Netherlands. This process of re-urbanisation fits into a global pattern, but Dutch spatial planning might have helped it along. This is discussed in the next section. Second, there was urban sprawl from the polycentric Randstad urban ring to the Green Heart and the outer ring, from the 1960s up to the new millennium. During the 1960s and 1970s, the relative population growth was highest in the Green Heart, followed by that in the outer ring. After that, their positions reversed. The national growth centre policy may have contributed to this change (see below). The general conclusion from the

Table 13.1 Population change 1960–2017 (in %)

	1960–1970 (%)	1970–1980 (%)	1980–1990 (%)	1990–2000 (%)	2000–2010 (%)	2010–2017 (%)	Population 2017
Randstad urban ring	4.8	−5.3	0.4	4.4	4.8	6.1	4,680,440
of which							
Cities > 250,000	−4.3	−15.0	−2.2	2.6	7.8	8.2	2,347,527
Cities 100,000–250,000	10.0	2.9	2.6	8.2	3.9	5.0	811,018
Cities 50,000–100,000	18.4	5.0	1.7	5.6	−0.5	4.2	776,920
Other	32.1	13.9	4.7	4.4	2.9	2.8	744,975
Green Heart	33.9	32.5	13.9	9.5	7.0	1.9	1,216,026
of which							
Cities > 50,000	31.1	58.5	27.8	13.8	14.0	2.8	470,031
Other	34.8	23.5	7.7	7.3	3.1	1.4	745,995
Outer ring	30.2	30.5	23.0	16.6	8.6	3.0	1,847,278
of which							
Cities > 50,000	68.7	66.4	63.9	25.7	13.2	5.7	730,612
Other	23.3	19.0	8.8	11.2	5.7	1.3	1,116,666
Total area	11.0	4.3	6.7	7.5	6.1	4.9	7,743,744
Netherlands	13.5	8.7	5.7	6.5	4.5	3.1	17,081,507

Source data: Statistics Netherlands (CBS).

population data is that into the new millennium, the process of urban sprawl slowed down substantially. How valid is this conclusion? Population data give indications about change in residential areas, but not about business parks and transport infrastructure. Land-use statistics include all urban categories, but, for the Netherlands, consistent data are only available for about the last two decades. Table 13.2 shows the changes in urban land use from 1996.

In general, the growth rates of urban land use were far higher during the first decade, compared to the second. This is explained by the economic crisis of 2008 and the ensuing years which caused a severe stagnation in the urbanisation process. And there are some remarkable differences compared to the population data in Table 13.1. The re-urbanisation process of the Randstad urban ring from the 1990s onward is clearly visible in the population data, whereas this is not the case for the land-use data. The growth rates were higher for the other two categories, with the exception of the outer ring between 2006 and 2015. This is at least partly explained by the higher density of land use within the urban ring, where population growth resulted in less land use than within the Green Heart and the outer ring. The relatively high growth rates of the largest cities within the Randstad urban ring are a sign of re-urbanisation (the slightly smaller percentage of urban land use in 2015 compared to 2006 was caused by an expansion of the total land area of some cities). More remarkable

Table 13.2 Urban land use as part of total land use, 1996–2015

	1996	2006	2015	Urban land 2015
	%	%	%	km^2
Randstad urban ring				
Urban land use	39.7	41.7	42.3	861
% Change		8.9	1.4	
of which				
Cities >250.000	53.3	55.4	54.4	380
% Change		13.9	1.6	
Green Heart				
Urban land use	13.0	15.4	16.4	337
% Change		18.0	11.0	
Outer ring				
Urban land use	10.9	12.5	12.7	495
% Change		12.4	0.3	
Total area				
Urban land use	18.5	20.7	21.2	1,694
% Change		11.5	2.8	
Netherlands				
Urban land use	12.2	13.6	14.1	5,264
% Change		11.3	3.9	

Source data: Statistics Netherlands (CBS).

are the high growth rates of urban land use within the Green Heart. Therefore, land-use data suggest that urban sprawl in the Green Heart continued during the later decades of the study. This was mainly caused by the increase in land use by business parks (55% between 1996 and 2015). This growth rate was far higher than those of residential areas within the Green Heart (21%) and of business parks within the Randstad urban ring (31%). This may be explained by the differing planning regimes for business parks and residential areas. In the following section, the roles of spatial planning and institutional change related to urban sprawl are evaluated. Because of a major policy change during the 1980s, the evaluation is divided into two parts: 1958–1988 and 1988–2018.

Spatial planning, institutional change and urban sprawl

1958–1988

During the post-war years, national spatial planning was coordinated by the Bureau for the National Plan (*Rijksdienst voor het Nationale Plan*). Following the advice of the 1958 report, the Bureau developed a spatial planning strategy: a combination of zoning (keeping the Green Heart and green zones between urban areas) and development. The development strategy aimed to concentrate suburbanisation in growth centres. Although urban growth centres were being considered as possibilities for housing the growing population as early as in the 1950s (Borchert *et al.*, 1981), they did not catch on until the start of the 'concentrated deconcentration' policy in the 1966 Second Report on Spatial Planning. A major institutional change had taken place: in 1965 the Spatial Planning Act (WRO: *Wet op de Ruimtelijke Ordening*) came into force. The Bureau for the National Plan was reorganised into the National Spatial Planning Agency (RPD: *Rijksplanologische Dienst*). The Dutch national spatial planning system started to unfold its specific characteristics, comprehensive and highly institutionalised (Alterman, 2001: 13; Van der Wouden *et al.*, 2011). Of course, spatial planning had to fit in the three-layered Dutch government system of national government, provinces and municipalities. The Spatial Planning Act provided municipalities with a relatively large amount of authority. Therefore, implementation of the urban growth centre policy meant regular negotiations with provinces and municipalities, and it sometimes took a long time before an agreement could be reached about the selection of the specific municipalities and the volume of houses to be built.

Urban growth centres was the central policy issue during the 1970s. Essential to this policy was the choice of the locations for the growth centres. Most of the 16 main growth centres were located in and around the Randstad area (Reijndorp *et al.*, 2012). Many of them were along the outer ring of the Randstad, but some were located within or adjacent to the Green Heart: Zoetermeer, Haarlemmermeer and Capelle aan den IJssel. This does not match the goal of keeping the Green Heart of the Randstad as open as possible. It explains part of the population growth within the Green Heart during the 1960s and 1970s, as shown in Table 13.1. For the decades that followed, this also created a path dependence, as is explained in the next section.

The implementation of the growth centre policy was based upon the collaboration between the spatial planning system and the public housing sector. Public housing provided the funds for the development, spatial planning the locations of the urban growth centres. In the early 1970s, following a number of failed attempts in the 1960s to liberalise the housing market, housing once again was considered an integral part of the Dutch welfare state, supported by large subsidies. Those were the 'golden chains' that bound municipalities and public housing companies to national policy. In addition, the urban growth centres received subsidies that lowered land prices. These combined subsidies amounted to an estimated 15% of total housing construction costs (Faludi and Van der Valk, 1994). Furthermore, these financial flows had to be in line with those from other ministries in infrastructure and public facilities. On a government level, the collaboration was made official in the interdepartmental committee on growth centres and urban expansion.

Growth centre policy accelerated the construction of new housing. But the economic crisis of 1973 caused major changes. The housing market for owner-occupiers collapsed and there was no job growth. However, the urban growth centre policy remained firmly based on government-funded public housing, which resulted in continuing growth. Therefore, many evaluations of the growth centre policy had remarkably positive conclusions: spatial planning had prevented further urban sprawl (Bloemberg and Van Zeijl, 1986; Faludi and van der Valk, 1990; RPD, 1990). But the unequivocally positive conclusion would only be justified if judged against the alternative of having no national spatial planning at all. Therefore, other authors have given a more balanced judgement of the positive and negative results of the growth centre policy (for instance Nozeman, 1990). Although the urban sprawl into the Green Heart was reduced, it did not stop, as can be concluded from the population data in Table 13.1. It was only from the 1980s onward that the relative urban sprawl to the outer ring surpassed that to the Green Heart. In addition, despite national spatial planning, there were also large building sites outside urban growth centres; Borchert *et al.* speak of 'illegal growth centres' (Borchert *et al.*, 1981: 146). Furthermore, some older cities within the Green Heart also grew faster than projected (RPD, 1990). Here, the influence can be seen of the decentralised institutional structure, with municipalities being able to pursue their own interests even if this would be counter to national policy.

More importantly, however, the growth centre policy did not slow urban decline. The suburbanisation of large numbers of families meant a loss for the large cities, both socially and economically. The economic crisis of the 1970s and 1980s accelerated the urban crisis. This led to a major change in the national spatial planning strategy in the 1983 national strategy on urban areas (Ministerie van VROM, 1983), replacing 'concentrated deconcentration' with 'concentration' and in a later stage a 'compact city' policy. The growth centre policy was gradually ended, as well as its subsidies.

1988–2018

During the 1980s, a new spatial planning agenda for the Netherlands emerged—a metropolitan agenda, with the compact city as its most important concept. It resulted in the 1988 Fourth National Report on Spatial Planning (Ministerie van VROM, 1988). This involved a reorientation of spatial policy away from public housing to economic development and infrastructure. There were two reasons for this change. First, international competition was on the increase, due to globalisation. For Europe, the effect was further enhanced by the 1992 Maastricht Treaty which reduced the economic impact of borders between countries within Europe. Urban regions, in particular, were believed to become affected. Second, the urban economy had been hit by the crisis. Industrial employment was declining rapidly, which resulted in the closure of many companies, among which were the shipyards around Amsterdam and Rotterdam. As before, containment of urban sprawl remained an important goal, now to be realised by redeveloping urban areas.

Although the Fourth Report meant a significant change in policy, initially, there was overall continuity in the national institutional context. The RPD, being the main policy agency, had taken a firm hold again of policy coordination. As before, there were no large spatial planning budgets to invest in spatial development. Therefore, the success of the Fourth National Report was primarily dependent on convincing other ministries to invest in the newly designed national spatial structure. This proved an effective coordination strategy. Many activities ensued within adjacent spatial policy fields. Within a few years, a number of new policy plans were formulated: on traffic and infrastructure, housing, nature, the environment, green areas, and regional economic development. All plans shared the same spatial focus (Van der Wouden, 2015; Van der Wouden, 2016). A new government subsequently published the 1990 'Vinex' policy document (Vinex is the Dutch acronym for Fourth National Report Extra as explained in Chapter 11), planning the development of new residential areas within or nearby urban areas ('Vinex locations'), thus translating the compact city concept into new housing projects (Ministerie van VROM, 1990).

The resulting urbanisation strategy combined inner-city redevelopment ('key projects') with new greenfield developments around the city. Major key projects are located in the port districts and the railway station areas (BSP and TU Delft, 2009; Spaans *et al.*, 2013). Both public and private investments played a central role in the policy's implementation. Policy agreements between national and local government initially covered the 1995–2005 period and were extended up to 2010. The resulting growth in urban housing stock caused a population increase in the large cities in the Randstad urban ring, from the 1990s onward (see Table 13.1).

The urban renaissance was not only influenced by national spatial policy, but also, first and foremost, by the urban municipalities themselves, who in turn profited from the positive economic development. At the local level, there were major institutional changes. A new spatial development model emerged, based on public-private collaborations between municipalities and market stakeholders. Because new housing production particularly focused on homeownership rather than rented social housing, this attracted the attention of new stakeholders such as urban development companies. Often, municipalities acquired land for development and cleared and prepared the land for construction. This land would subsequently be sold to market stakeholders, who then built and sold new housing. Municipalities made a profit from selling this prepared land, while market stakeholders profited from the sale of the houses (Van der Wouden, 2015).

The inner-city brownfield projects added new houses for middle- and higher-income groups to the urban housing stock, thus enabling further economic and demographic growth. Together with the greenfield residential locations close to the cities, they provided for more than 650,000 dwellings between 1995 and 2005 (RIGO, 2007). These are positive results, at least in quantitative terms. However, the emphasis on the quantitative objectives has led to a great deal of criticism throughout the Netherlands. 'A monomorphic sea of houses' and 'cities without character', were often-heard qualifications, which indicated that the new areas had a 'lack of variation and authenticity'. Most inhabitants, however, were positive about their homes and immediate environment, although less so about the price of their houses (Van der Wouden, 2015). And more importantly, the 'compact city' policy did not stop urban sprawl. Many large new residential areas were built close to or even within the Green Heart of the Randstad. Also, some of the former urban growth centres within the Randstad were allocated new Vinex locations. In this respect, the urban growth centre policy was being continued, as well as urban sprawl. Table 13.1 shows that, during the 1990s and 2000s, the relative population growth in the Green Heart was higher than in the Randstad urban ring. This pattern remained unchanged until the 2010s. And the land-use data in Table 13.2 show a continuing higher growth rate for the Green Heart, mainly caused by business parks. The policy regime of business parks has a strong local focus, and municipalities have been eager to develop business parks in order to attract employment.

In the meantime, the spatial planning system had changed. First of all, in 2001, the RPD, the national policy coordinating agency was divided into a policy department within the Ministry of Public Housing, Spatial Planning and the Environment and an independent knowledge institute, the Netherlands Institute for Spatial Research (RPB: *Ruimtelijk Planbureau*) (Van der Wouden *et al.*, 2006). The combination of policy-making and evaluation within one organisation was no longer considered effective, according to a report by a Dutch parliamentary committee (Werkgroep Vijfde Nota, 2000). Thus, the knowledge infrastructure was placed at some distance from the national policy coordination agency. Decentralisation of spatial planning from the national government to the municipalities followed (Zonneveld and Evers, 2014). As a result, national policy coordination weakened.

More institutional changes followed. In 2008, a new Spatial Planning Act came into force. But 2008 was also the year of the financial and real estate crisis. It resulted in vacant offices and retail buildings and in the stagnation of new housing construction. The effects of the real estate crisis also affected the land market. Municipalities, housing corporations and developers were left owning land without development prospects. A source of income turned into a loss (Buitelaar and Bregman, 2016). The local development model based on the cooperation of municipalities, large development companies and housing corporations ended, at least temporally. However, it did not end the process of re-urbanisation. Both population data (Table 13.1) and land-use data (Table 13.2) show continuing growth in the large cities.

Conclusion: in control of urban sprawl?

Did spatial planning change the process of urban sprawl, and if so, in what way? And what was the role of the institutional framework and its changes? This section summarises the conclusion of the analysis. Figure 13.1 gives an overview of major events during six decades covering spatial planning, institutional change, external factors and urban sprawl. Although causal relationships are difficult to disentangle, some conclusions can be drawn.

- Although containing urban sprawl in the Randstad area was already formulated as a policy issue during the 1950s, it took a long time before this became incorporated into a policy strategy. The development process of

	1960s	1970s	1980s	1990s	2000s	2010–2018
spatial planning						
national policy	sprawl on the agenda	urban growth management	metropolitan agenda	compact cities	decentralization	sustainability agenda
implementation		growth centres / public housing investments		Vinex policy / investment in infrastructure		climate policy
local policy	industrial development	public housing		inner city redevelopment / new suburban residential areas		energy transition
institutional change						
national	Spatial Planning Act (1966) / National spatial planning agency RPD (1966)				new Spatial Planning Act (2008) / division of RPD (2001)	
local	decentralization spatial planning / public cooperation			public-private cooperation	stagnation land-use policy	
external factors						
economical	growth	de-industrialization	crisis	growth	crisis (2008) / knowledge economy	recovery
social	migration to Randstad / start of suburbanization		urban crisis	new urban growth	popularity urban living / gentrification	
urban sprawl						
Randstad/polycentric	Green Heart		outer ring		land-use business parks / Green Heart	urban ring
cities/monocentric	from cities to smaller municipalities within urban ring			start re-urbanization		high growth cities

Figure 13.1 Timeline of urbanisation in the Randstad area.
Source: Own illustration.

growth centres started at the beginning of the 1970s. The idea was to direct urban sprawl more towards the outer ring rather than to the Green Heart, but the first policy results were not visible until the 1980s.

- As an urban sprawl containment strategy, growth centre policy was not consistent. Most of the growth centres were within the outer ring of the Randstad, but some were in or close to the Green Heart. This did not only facilitate the continuation of urban sprawl, but also created a path dependence for the future. During the 1990s, new suburban residential areas were also allocated to former growth centres within the Green Heart. Past spatial planning decisions thus facilitated further urban sprawl.
- The major institutional change during the 1960s—the Spatial Planning Act—also had an influence on urban sprawl. The planning system was decentralised. Therefore, municipalities in the Green Heart could develop new residential areas outside the growth centre programme, and thus grew faster than foreseen. This subverted the national strategy of containing sprawl.
- During its first decades, national spatial planning was directed at containing urban sprawl from the polycentric urban ring towards other areas, and less at containing monocentric sprawl within the urban ring. It lasted until the 1980s, before the developmental strategy of 'compact cities' directed the latter. This resulted in the re-urbanisation of the large cities.
- The slowing down of sprawl in the Green Heart during the last decades as indicated in the population data is not confirmed by the land-use data. In particular, the amount of land used by business parks increased rapidly. The local planning regime governing business park development may explain this phenomenon. In this way, urban sprawl in the Green Heart continued.
- Surprisingly, the decentralisation of spatial planning and the decrease in national policy coordination capacity did not result in an increase of urban sprawl. Re-urbanisation continued, helped by the growth in urban employment and the popularity of urban living. Most large cities rapidly recovered from the crisis of 2008. Obviously, the re-urbanisation process was strong enough to continue without national spatial planning.

In summary, national spatial planning did not prevent further urbanisation and sprawl within the Green Heart, despite the fact that it redirected some sprawl to the outer ring. The national 'compact city' development strategy of the 1990s seemed effective for the re-urbanisation of the large cities, but did not contain sprawl either. Institutional change helped national policy coordination in some cases (National Spatial Planning Agency in 1966, public-private cooperation at the local level in the 1990s), but not in others (the local focus of the Spatial Planning Act). The reputation of Dutch national spatial planning of being effective in containing urban sprawl is unwarranted, or at best only partly justified.

Sixty years of urbanisation and sprawl have changed the morphology of the Randstad thoroughly. During the 1950s, the Randstad consisted of densely populated cities in an open landscape. Nowadays, the Randstad is an urban network, with cities, growth centres, suburban areas, new business parks and extensive network infrastructure. And it still contains open space, but in smaller areas than before. Borders between urban and suburban areas are blurred, a reason for some authors to label the current phase of urbanisation as 'post-suburban' (Phelps and Wood, 2011). Furthermore, new urban 'species' came into existence such as the 'edge cities' like Schiphol airport (Garreau, 1991; Bontje and Burdack, 2005). There is no reason to believe that this process of urbanisation will end in the near future. On the contrary, the increasing pressures on the Dutch housing market urged the government to announce in 2018 that a million new houses should be built before 2030. Again, quantity threatens to prevail over quality, as was the case for the growth centre policy and the major part of the Vinex policy. It is important to learn from these experiences, and to add to the quality of urban living instead of just adding numbers of houses. It is the only road to a sustainable urban future, combining prosperity with social and ecological values.

References

Abrahamse, J.E. (2010). *De grote uitleg van Amsterdam: stadsontwikkeling in de zeventiende eeuw [The Grand Extension of Amsterdam, City Development and Urbanism in the Seventeenth Century].* Thoth, Bussum.

Alterman, R. (Ed.) (2001). *National-Level Planning in Democratic Countries.* Liverpool University Press, Liverpool.

Aurambout, J.-P., Barranco, R. and Lavalle, C. (2018). 'Towards a Simpler Characterization of Urban Sprawl across Urban Areas in Europe', *Land,* 7(1) 33: 1–18.

Bloemberg, J.T.M., and Van Zeijl, J.B. (1986). *De toekomst van de groeikernen, een verkennende studie [The Future of Growth Centres, an Outlook].* Rijksplanologische Dienst, The Hague.

Bontje, M. (2003). 'A "Planner's Paradise" Lost? Past, Present and Future of Dutch national Urbanization Policy', *European Urban and Regional Studies,* 10(2), 135–151.

Bontje, M. and Burdack, J. (2005). 'Edge Cities, European-style: Examples from Paris and the Randstad', *Cities,* 22(4), 317–330.

Borchert, J.G., Egbers, G.J.J. and De Smidt, M. (1981). *Ruimtelijk beleid in Nederland [Spatial Policy in the Netherlands].* Unieboek, Bussum.

Bruegmann, R. (2005). *Sprawl, a Compact History.* University of Chicago Press, Chicago.

BSP and TU Delft (2009). *Evaluatie sleutelprojecten [Evaluation National Key Projects].* Bureau Stedelijke Planning, Gouda.

Buitelaar, E. and Bregman, A. (2016). 'Dutch Land Development Institutions in the Face of Crisis: Trembling Pillars in the Planners' Paradise', *European Planning Studies,* 24(7), 1281–1294.

Buitelaar, E., Lagendijk, A. and Jacobs, W. (2007). 'A Theory of Institutional Change: Illustrated by Dutch City-provinces and Dutch Land Policy', *Environment and Planning A: Economy and Space,* 39(4), 891–908.

Couch, C., Leontidu, L. and Petschel-Held, G. (Eds) (2007). *Urban Sprawl in Europe: Landscapes, Land-use Change and Policy.* Blackwell, Oxford.

Couch, C., Sykes O. and Börstinghaus, W. (2011). 'Thirty Years of Urban Regeneration in Britain, Germany and France: The Importance of Context and Path Dependency', *Progress in Planning*, 75(1), 1–52.

Dieleman, F., Dijst, M. and Spit, T. (1999). 'Planning the Compact City: The Randstad Holland Experience', *European Planning Studies*, 7(5), 605–621

Dieleman, F. and Musterd, S. (Eds) (1992). *The Randstad: A Research and Policy Laboratory*. Kluwer Academic Publishers, Dordrecht/Boston/London.

Dieleman, F. and Wegener, M. (2004). 'Compact City and Urban Sprawl', *Built Environment*, 30(4), 308–323.

Faludi, A. and Van der Valk, A. (1990). *De groeikernen als hoekstenen van de Nederlandse ruimtelijke planningdoctrine [The Growth Centres as Corner Stones of Dutch Spatial Planning Doctrine]*. Van Gorcum, Assen.

Faludi, A. and Van der Valk, A. (1994). *Rule and Order: Dutch Planning Doctrine in the Twentieth Century*. Kluwer Academic Publishers, Dordrecht/Boston/London.

Galster, G., Hanson, R., Ratcliffe, M.R., Wolman, H., Coleman, S. and Freihage, J. (2001). 'Wrestling Sprawl to the Ground: Defining and Measuring an Elusive Concept', *Housing Policy Debate*, 12(40), 681–717.

Garreau, J. (1991). *Edge City: Life on the New Frontier*. Doubleday, New York.

Geurs, K.T. and Van Wee, B. (2006). 'Ex-post Evaluation of Thirty Years of Compact Urban Development in the Netherlands', *Urban Studies*, 43(1), 139–160.

Giddens, A. (1984). *The Constitution of Society*. The Polity Press, Cambridge.

Hall, P. (1988). *Cities of Tomorrow*. Blackwell, Oxford.

Hall, P. (2014). *Good Cities, Better Lives: How Europe Discovered the Lost Art of Urbanism*. Routledge, London.

Jaeger, J. and Schwick, C. (2014). 'Improving the Measurement of Urban Sprawl: Weighted Urban Proliferation (WUP) and Its Application to Switzerland', *Ecological Indicators*, 38, 294–308.

Lambregts, B. (2009). *The Polycentric Metropolis Unpacked: Concepts, Trends and Policy in the Randstad Holland,* PhD thesis, University of Amsterdam. Amsterdam Institute for Metropolitan and International Development Studies (AMIDSt), Amsterdam.

Lüdeke, M., Reckien, D. and Petschel-Held, G. (2007). 'Modelling Urban Sprawl: Actors and Mathematics'. In: Couch, C., Leontidu, L. and Petschel-Held, G. (Eds) *Urban Sprawl in Europe: Landscapes, Land-use Change and Policy*. Blackwell, Oxford, 181–215.

Ministerie van VROM (Volkshuisvesting, Ruimtelijke Ordening en Milieubeheer) (1983). *Structuurschets Stedelijke Gebieden 1983 Deel a: Beleidsvoornemen [National Policy Strategy on Urban Areas 1983: Green Paper]*. Ministerie van VROM, The Hague.

Ministerie van VROM (Volkshuisvesting, Ruimtelijke Ordening en Milieubeheer) (1988). *Vierde nota over de ruimtelijke ordening, Deel a: Beleidsvoornemen [Fourth Report on Spatial Planning: Green Paper]*. SDU Uitgeverij, The Hague.

Ministerie van VROM (Volkshuisvesting, Ruimtelijke Ordening en Milieubeheer) (1990). *Vierde nota over de Ruimtelijke Ordening Extra, Deel 1: ontwerp-planologische kernbeslissing [Fourth Report on Spatial Planning Extra: Green Paper]*. Ministerie van VROM, The Hague.

Nozeman, E.F. (1990). 'Dutch New Towns: Triumph or Disaster?' *TESG: Tijdschrift voor Economische en Sociale Geografie*, 81(2), 149–155.

Oueslati, W., Alvani, S. and Garrod, G. (2015). 'Determinants of Urban Sprawl in European Cities'. *Urban Studies*, 52(9), 1594–1614.

Pagliarin, S. (2018). 'Linking Processes and Patterns: Spatial Planning, Governance and Urban Sprawl in the Barcelona and Milan Metropolitan Regions', *Urban Studies*, 55(16), 3651–3668.

Phelps, N. and Wood, A. (2011). 'The New Post-suburban Politics?' *Urban Studies,* 48(12), 2591–2610.

Pieterse, N., Van der Wagt, M., Daalhuizen, F., Piek, M. Künzel, F., Aykaç, R. (2005). *Het gedeelde land van de Randstad [The Common Land of the Randstad]*; Ontwikkeling en toekomst van het Groene Hart. Ruimtelijk Planbureau/ NAi Uitgevers, The Hague/Rotterdam.

Reijndorp, A., Bijlsma, L., Nio, I. and Van der Wouden, R. (2012). *Nieuwe steden in de Randstad [New Towns in the Randstad]*. Planbureau voor de Leefomgeving, The Hague.

RIGO (2007). *Evaluatie verstedelijking VINEX 1995 tot 2005. Eindrapport [Evaluation of Urban Development VINEX 1994–2000. Final Report]*. Ministerie van VROM (Volkshuisvesting, Ruimtelijke Ordening en Milieubeheer), The Hague.

RPD (Rijksplanologische Dienst) (1990). *Ruimtelijke verkenningen 1990 [Spatial Reconnaissance 1990]*. RPD, The Hague.

Schmidt, V. (2010). 'Taking Ideas and Discourse Seriously: Explaining Change through Discursive Institutionalism as the Fourth 'new institutionalism', *European Political Science Review,* 2(1), 1–25.

Sorensen, A. (1999). 'Land Readjustment, Urban Planning and Urban Sprawl in the Tokyo Metropolitan Area', *Urban Studies,* 36(13), 2333–2360.

Sorensen, A. (2015). 'Taking Path Dependence Seriously: An Historical Institutionalist Research Agenda in Planning History', *Planning Perspectives,* 30(1), 17–38.

Spaans, M., Trip, J.J. and Van der Wouden, R. (2013). 'Evaluating the Impact of National Government Involvement in Local Development Projects in the Netherlands', *Cities,* 31, 29–36.

Van der Cammen, H., and De Klerk, L. (2012). *The Selfmade Land. Culture and Evolution of Urban and Regional Planning in the Netherlands.* Unieboek – Het Spectrum, Houten – Antwerpen.

Van der Wouden, R. (Ed.) (2015). *De ruimtelijke metamorfose van Nederland 1988– 2015. Het tijdperk van de Vierde Nota [The Spatial Metamorphosis of the Netherlands 1988–2015. The Fourth Report Era].* Planbureau voor de Leefomgeving/nai010 Publishers, The Hague/Rotterdam.

Van der Wouden, R. (2016). 'Succes of falen? Een halve eeuw verstedelijkingsbeleid in Nederland' [Succes or Failure? Fifty Years of Urbanization Policy in The Netherlands]. *Ruimte en Maatschappij,* 8(1), 6–26.

Van der Wouden, R., Dammers, E. and Van Ravesteijn, N. (2006). 'Knowledge and Policy in the Netherlands. The Role of the Netherlands Institute for Spatial Research', *disP,* 163(2), 34–42.

Van der Wouden, R., Evers, D. and Kuiper, R. (2011). 'De veranderende positie van de ruimtelijke ordening in Nederland' [The Changing Position of Spatial Planning in the Netherlands], *Ruimte en Maatschappij,* 2(3), 6–24.

Werkcommissie Westen des Lands (1958). *De ontwikkeling van het Westen des lands: Rapport [The Development of the West of the Country: Advisory Report].* Staatsdrukkerij, The Hague.

Werkgroep Vijfde nota Ruimtelijke Ordening (2000). *Notie van ruimte. Verslag van het onderzoek [Notion of Space. Proceedings of the Research]*, TK 27 210, no. 1–2. Sdu, The Hague.

Zonneveld, W. and Evers, D. (2014). 'Dutch National Spatial Planning at the End of an Era'. In: Reimer, M., Getimis, P. and Blotevogel, H. (Eds) *Spatial Planning Systems and Practices in Europe: A Comparative Perspective on Continuity and Change.* Routledge, New York/Oxon, 61–82.

14 Probing and planning the future of the Dutch Randstad

David Evers and Jan Vogelij

Introduction

Since the 'discovery' or social construction of the Randstad, Dutch spatial planners and policymakers have been preoccupied with its future development (e.g. van der Wusten and Faludi, 1992; Masser, 1993; De Boer, 1996; Ritsema van Eck *et al.*, 2006). Its complex and paradoxical nature – for example, as the nation's main concentration of people and economic activity, yet internally diffuse, as the nation's gateway to Europe, yet internally congested, as the nation's most valuable land, yet most threatened by climate change – has fuelled speculations of potential future trajectories for this urban region. Will the cities functionally coalesce to form a relatively coherent metropolitan area the likes of Paris and London? Or will the Randstad expand, either contiguously or along key transport corridors, into the intermediate zone, gradually absorbing and consuming cities such as Amersfoort, Dordrecht or even Eindhoven? Or will the Randstad eventually disappear as sea levels rise? And, most predominantly, as the perceived motor of the Dutch economy, how will the Randstad fare within the changing European and global marketplace, and what can it do to compete? Insight into these questions is essential for making strategic policy decisions.

Concerns about the Randstad's position now and in the future have spawned considerable performance-oriented research. This has ranged from simple benchmarking exercises to more sophisticated outlook studies on the structure of the Randstad's economy (OECD, 2007; Weterings *et al.*, 2011). Various future studies have also been carried out which shed light on different aspects of the Randstad's position in a wider national and global context, such as the scenarios produced on European regional policy (ESPON, 2007), spatial development (Ministerie van VROM, 1997; RPB, 2003), national macroeconomic environment (CPB *et al.*, 2006; CPB, 2011) sustainable development (Kuiper, 2010) and nature (PBL, 2011). Each of these exercises presents divergent – usually four – possible futures in which the Randstad could develop.

In the second half of the 2000s, a spatial strategy – tellingly called a 'vision' in Dutch[1] – for the Randstad was drawn up (Ministerie van VROM,

2008). The Randstad 2040 Strategy sketched out trends, translated these into four divergent developmental models, and subsequently synthesized the most promising or desirable aspects into a single future vision. It was the first time such an ambitious exercise was carried out at this level. The history of this process and its aftermath raises some pertinent questions: to what extent were the conclusions drawn in the various future studies relevant or valid for the development of Randstad 2040, and to what extent did the scenarios allow Dutch policymakers to make meaningful choices? And, finally, what was done with this strategy afterwards?

This chapter takes a critical look at how the future of the Randstad has been probed and planned. It begins with a general discussion of the strengths and limitations of future-oriented research for policymaking and identifies some common pitfalls. Afterwards, several future-oriented studies on the Randstad are discussed which appeared in the run-up to the production of the Randstad 2040 Strategy. This is followed up by an examination of how the acclaimed Dutch urban design approach was used to draw up the Randstad 2040 Strategy. The next section takes a critical look at the disappointing outcome of this process and offers some explanations for it. In the conclusions, we reflect on the utility of future-oriented research and design activities for spatial planning.

Anticipating and understanding the future

The future is, by definition, unknown and yet human beings have an insatiable need to attain some degree of certainty regarding future events and circumstances. This desire is especially acute among those responsible for making collective decisions, in whose hands the future of many is placed. In premodern times, foretelling the future was entrusted to shamans, soothsayers and priests. Today, science is expected to play a similar role, and a discipline of 'futures studies' has emerged to answer the call. Depending on the perception of the level of ambiguity, different methods are brought to bear such as outlooks, forecasts, projections, prognoses, and scenarios to support decision-making (Dammers *et al.*, 2019).

One of the most widely applied tools to support complex decision-making, and therefore get a handle on the future, is an outlook. Its method consists of an analysis of the current state-of-affairs, taking both internal and external factors into account, in order to suggest an appropriate course of action. One of the most common methods is the SWOT analysis that surveys endogenous (strengths and weaknesses) and exogenous (opportunities and threats) factors regarding an organization or entity, usually summarizing the outcomes in a simple matrix. The method originated to support strategic planning in the private sector, but it is also commonly applied by governmental agencies due to its conceptual simplicity. Because public-sector bodies such as municipalities have more diverse and ambiguous aims than private firms or NGOs, these SWOT applications are less straightforward. For example, a high percentage of public housing could be considered either a strength or a weakness, and an influx of new residents both an opportunity or a threat depending on the political climate. For this reason, governments sometimes prefer outlooks that identify crucial environmental factors, such as PEST (political, economic, social and technological) or PESTEL (PEST plus environmental and legal factors), rather than the implicitly normative SWOT.

Although an outlook does not address the content of the future explicitly, it often does so implicitly by means of its identification of long-term trends and developments and the elaboration of strategic recommendations, which may take a long time to take effect. When considering explicitly future-oriented research methods, it is useful to rank them according to the level of perceived uncertainty (see Figure 14.1). In general, one should be less confident about making statements about events in the distant future than the immediate future, although there are some important exceptions to this (e.g. when trends are very gradual like climate change, or when change is predictably cyclical like seasons). The level of certainty usually declines the more complex the environment is perceived to be; high complexity can make even short-term developments very hard to predict.

When the perceived level of certainty is high, *forecasting* is a viable option. This method identifies the most likely future within a given margin of error (bandwidth) and is usually based on an extrapolation of trends considered predictable and robust. This method is often favoured by decision-makers because it provides a clear basis for action. Forecasts are sometimes supplemented by brief reflections on what potential 'system shocks' (such as a technological breakthrough that revolutionizes social and economic life, a world war or epidemic) could have on the dominant trend. Forecasts can also be embellished with considerations of the effects of policy responses. Still, the primary function of a forecast is to describe the (that is, a single) future as accurately as possible. A normative variation of a forecast is a plan in its broadest

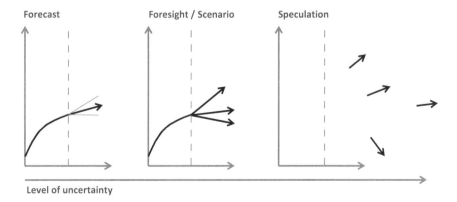

Figure 14.1 Level of uncertainty and research methods.
Source: Van Nieuwenhuijze *et al.*, 2015.

sense. In essence, a plan outlines the steps that need to be taken towards a particular desirable future.

When one is unsure about the result of an essential variable, it may become necessary to split up the possibilities and deal with them separately. A broad term for this method is *foresight*, of which the scenario method is one of the most well-known and applied (Van Asselt *et al.*, 2010). Scenarios are essentially narratives about the future, which 'do not need to be necessarily desirable or probable, but merely possible' (Salewski, 2012: 296). What is important is that each future-state can be described as resulting from a plausible causal chain of events and decision points (Kahn, 1965; Dammers *et al.*, 2019).

The different possible futures explored in scenario studies can vary according to environmental factors, namely those over which one has little or no control (e.g. level of economic growth, technological innovation) or according to a particular course of action (e.g. level of regulation or cooperation) which represents a genuine choice. Obviously, the number of possible futures that can be explored in scenario studies is virtually endless, and the number of futures increases exponentially when creating nested scenarios (i.e. variations within a particular future). The challenge then is to draw up a small number of scenarios that can be readily compared, discussed and understood. One method is to produce a reference scenario (sometimes called a baseline or trend scenario) and then generate a few alternatives with respect to this, usually by modifying a single variable. Another common method is the production of four possible futures using two distinct variables as axes. These kinds of scenarios fall into two basic types: normative, which vary policy choices (e.g. environmental protection and social welfare), and exploratory, which vary external variables (e.g. economic growth and geopolitics). The former is used to reflect on the long-term implications of policy decisions whereas the second is usually used to identify robust policy strategies (Avin and Goodspeed, 2020; Kahan, 2020).

Forecasting is relatively straightforward for devising an appropriate strategy, whereas the multiple futures in scenario studies might suggest divergent courses of action. For this reason, the relationship between foresight studies and policymaking is more complex than with forecasts. There is a danger that decision-makers will try to choose *between* scenarios in an early stage of the decision-making process, rather than formulating appropriate courses of action *within* scenarios. In the case of environmental scenarios, this misses the point of the scenario exercise altogether as these variables are intended to be exogenous. But even with respect to policy-oriented scenarios – where desirability between scenarios is obviously a matter for discussion – focus should be on understanding the dynamics and storylines within each of the scenarios. In this sense, scenario studies are different from ex-ante evaluations that attempt to measure the impacts of policy decisions.

Another danger is that decision-makers focus exclusively on certain scenarios because they are primarily interested in the consequences of a particular outcome. They may feel justified in doing this if the selected scenarios are perceived as the most problematic, assuming that the response in the other cases would just be a watered-down version of the extreme case. Excluding plausible futures from consideration can undermine the usefulness of the study however. In the case of less-popular low economic growth scenarios, depending on the storyline, not only can the substantive problems be quite different, but also the capacity of decision-makers to deal with them. Alternatively, when all attention is focussed on the baseline scenario, the foresight is reduced to a forecast, even though the level of uncertainty was deemed too high to warrant this. If, as time progresses, actual developments prove to resemble one of the excluded scenarios, the study might be blamed for being 'wrong'. For these reasons, creators of foresight studies should create awareness for the risks of misinterpreting the study.

Finally, we can consider *speculations*, sometimes referred to as wild cards or black swans. These are necessary in situations where uncertainty is so high that no meaningful storyline from the present can be constructed. Examples include revolutionary technologies (e.g. nanotechnology or nuclear fusion) or the aftermath of sudden, unexpected game-changing events like the fall of the Berlin Wall, the Twin Towers or Lehman Brothers. Utopic or dystopic visions generally fall into this category, such as 'smart cities', 'green cities' or 'sea of houses' (see below). Speculations can be useful in stimulating discussion and exploring plausibility. Speculative design can widen the range of possibilities by proposing unforeseen concepts. Because of their lack of direct connection to the present, speculations are often seen as less useful in the development of strategic policy and (quantitatively) informing decision-making, than forecasting and foresight. On the other hand, since extreme unexpected events can and do occur (e.g. the 2020 COVID-19 pandemic), speculation can be a valuable supplement to the other methods for studying the future.

Probing the future of the Randstad

The Randstad has been subjected, and continues to be subjected, to many of the prognosticative methods discussed above. It would be beyond the scope of this chapter to treat the fate of the Randstad in all of these. Some years ago an inventory of future studies in Europe found no less than 273 being produced by the Netherlands, 80% of which were commissioned by the public sector (Van Asselt *et al.*, 2010: 18). For this reason, attention will be focussed on a few key examples relevant to spatial planning. This section will touch on how these have been applied, and their strengths, weaknesses, advantages and pitfalls.

One of the most significant studies in the run-up to the Randstad 2040 Strategy is the *Territorial Review* of the Randstad (OECD, 2007). As the study identifies economic competitiveness as the main objective, this enabled the performance of a SWOT analysis of sorts, which focussed on the housing market, accessibility, the (skilled) labour market and governance. Via benchmarking, the report was able to formulate recommendations to strengthen the Randstad's position vis-à-vis its competitors. The main strengths of the Randstad identified in the report included its wealth, high levels of employment and economic openness and diversity. One of the most important structural weaknesses was its internal accessibility (OECD, 2007: 75). The report recommended a transport authority be set up at the Randstad level to improve coordination, something which was started soon afterwards, but later abandoned following a change in government. The report also lauded the plans to introduce road pricing by 2012, something which (also for political reasons) was discontinued but is gaining support again. Therefore, the outlook was informative and the position of the OECD as an international observer influential.

About a decade ago, the world-renowned planning scholar Peter Hall (2009) engaged in forecasting the state of cities half a century from now, on the basis of trends signalled in the POLYNET study on emerging 'mega-city regions', which included, for example, the Randstad, South East of England and Rhein-Ruhr (Hall and Pain, 2006). The study predicted urban concentration at the mega-city region level, but deconcentration within them. In Hall's view, the key economic sectors in these regions (finance and business, government and corporate headquarters and creative and cultural industries), and the activities (e.g. hotels, restaurants, art galleries, multimedia services) 'operating in the interstices of these sectors', would allow city centres to retain their position. The main technological influence on urban systems, Hall (2009) predicted, would be the completion of a pan-European high-speed rail network. Multimodal hubs such as Schiphol, Heathrow and Charles de Gaulle were in his view expected to become new centres powerful enough to compete with the cities they serve, while smaller-scale transit-oriented developments would produce clustered urbanization around nodes along a corridor. A relevant 'wild card' was the possible development of a zero-emissions vehicle, an innovation that would accelerate urban diffusion. Obviously, this view of the future is predominantly a singular forecast and exhibits little variation. The main message to policymakers was to develop strategies against this backdrop.

The ESPON programme has produced a multitude of spatial scenario exercises on the European territory. A project completed in 2006 contained no less than 30 thematic environmental and policy scenarios (e.g. economy, demography, enlargement, environment, transport). The study combined both qualitative (literature review, expert knowledge) and quantitative methods (demographic projections, econometric modelling) in the scenario development. The four integrated scenarios with a time horizon of 2030 modeled the performance of European policy packages against a baseline scenario, with population and GDP as the main output indicators. The study also contained a 'roll-back scenario' that explored which policy measures would be needed to achieve a set 'desirable' future, which is, in essence, a strategy or plan rather than a scenario (ESPON, 2007).

Some observations can be made regarding the performance of the Randstad within the two integrated scenarios which received by far the most policy attention: the competition-oriented scenario and the cohesion-oriented scenario, which can also be considered polar opposites. In the former, the European Union concentrates its efforts towards promoting the strongest regions in order to enhance its competitiveness in the global economy. In this scenario, the emphasis is on enlargement, free trade and reducing administrative burdens. For example, EU agricultural and cohesion policies are slashed in favour of innovation and R&D programmes, and investments in infrastructure are concentrated in top-regions. Conversely, in the cohesion oriented scenario, the EU focuses its policy efforts on promoting equal opportunities among citizens across the European territory: the budget of cohesion policy is increased and targeted to lagging regions while agricultural policy is adjusted to promote the modernization of production in these same areas. As the focus is on intensifying European integration, no EU enlargements take place within the cohesion-oriented scenario (ESPON, 2007; Evers, 2010).

Rhetorically, the write-up of the scenario project − both in the final report as well as the ESPON publication intended for a larger audience − places less emphasis on the scenario storylines and more on comparing the different outcomes. Taken to the extreme, one could argue that this style of presentation is more akin to an ex-ante policy evaluation that helps decision-makers choose between options than a forecasting study that helps them to devise coping strategies within alternative futures. The outcome of the scenario project was also illustrated by means of a multi-layered thematic map of Europe in 2030. The two maps quickly took centre stage in the subsequent political discussions (see Figure 14.2).

Despite the myriad differences between the two outcomes in this ESPON study, the Randstad remains squarely within the main economic core area of Europe in both. The most important territorial development is arguably the shape of this core economic area or, more generally, the 'area of concentration of flows and activities' (ESPON, 2007). In the 'competitiveness' scenario this has contracted (with respect to the baseline, not pictured) to a narrow corridor stretching from Manchester to Florence with offshoots to Copenhagen to the North, Marseille to the West and Budapest to the East. This outcome roughly conforms to the forecast by Hall (2009), although the EU has enlarged to include the Balkans and Turkey in the scenario. In general, 'competitiveness' can be considered as favourable for the Randstad: the overall economic growth of the EU is higher in absolute terms and that of the core area in relative terms. The main drawbacks of this scenario stem from the consequences of high economic growth such as housing shortages

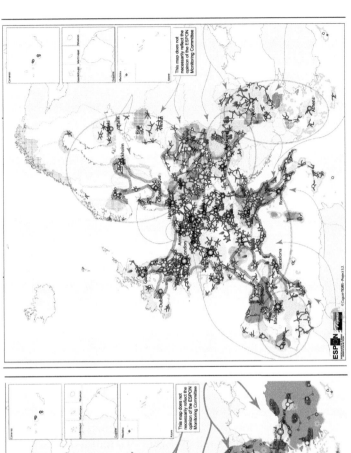

The final image 2030 of the cohesion-oriented scenario

The final image 2030 of the competitiveness-oriented scenario

Figure 14.2 The European territory in 2030.
Source: ESPON, 2007

due to high immigration, which may lead to social and ethnic polarization, and traffic congestion (ESPON, 2007).

The 'cohesion' scenario, by contrast, imagines a broadening of the core economic area of Europe to include all but the most peripheral regions of an EU which, except for the expected entry of Romania and Bulgaria, has not enlarged territorially. The function of the Randstad however remains the same: as a magnet for economic activity in the heart of Europe. Still, as the total growth level is lower and more evenly distributed across the European territory, this role will certainly be less prominent than in 'competitiveness', and consequently the associated urban problems less severe as well.

The main territorial problems signalled in the ESPON study are located well outside of the Randstad. The risk of industrial decline is high, for example, in large swaths of France, Germany and Denmark in 'competitiveness', and northern England and eastern Germany in 'cohesion'. The study also predicted severe ageing in northern Spain and Italy (with small variations in each scenario), eastern Germany and parts of Poland, and rural marginalization in most new member states. In this sense, the ESPON scenarios put the internal shortcomings of the Randstad and the external threats signalled by OECD (2007) into perspective.

A project which was equally ambitious in scope, but focussed exclusively on the Netherlands was the *Welfare, Prosperity and Quality of the Living Environment* (WLO) study produced by a collaboration of government think-tanks (CPB *et al.*, 2006). Whereas the integrated scenarios of the ESPON study represented policy variations relative to a trend scenario and the production of a 'desirable' alternative, the WLO created four separate scenarios using the typology international/national and public/private. Although the focus was on the Netherlands, the level of detail was little better than ESPON: the country was divided into three regions: Randstad, an intermediate zone and 'the rest' (see Figure 14.3). Employing complex quantitative modelling, the study attempted to draw conclusions regarding the future locations of residences, businesses as well as traffic, agriculture, energy, environment, nature and water. As far as spatial planning is concerned, the pressure for urbanization

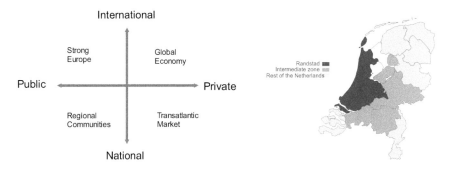

Figure 14.3 Scenario structure and spatial scope.
Source: CPB *et al.*, 2006.

(and therefore the competition between land-uses) is the greatest in the high-growth scenarios: 'transatlantic market' and 'global economy'.

The WLO scenarios are additionally significant because they have been used as a basis for a number of more detailed thematic scenario studies. For example, the report *Netherlands Later* used these global scenarios to measure the potential effects on the physical environment, such as environmental pollution, carbon emissions and land use (MNP, 2007). Regarding the latter, the report included a series of land-use maps illustrating the differences between scenarios. In this way, the scenario exercise was not just a way to posit and describe a possible future, but as an analytical tool. The comparison of futures can shed light on developments that are robust versus those that are more variable.[2]

Paraphrasing Marx, we can rightly now consider that all these studies have hitherto only interpreted the future of the Randstad in various ways, but the point is to change it. That is the realm of spatial planning. Indeed, a key feature of planning documents is to not only describe the existing spatial structure but also to make normative claims about it that suggest certain courses of policy action for its future development (Faludi and Van der Valk, 1994). The next section turns to the changing position of the Randstad in various national plans up to the decision to draw up the Randstad 2040 Strategy.

Planning the future of the Randstad

As a national planning concept, the Randstad has had vacillating support over its more than 50-year history. Specifically, the level of cohesion between its constituent parts has been a continual source of disagreement.[3] In 1956, even before the first national strategy had been drawn up, the national planner Jacob Thijsse created a dystopic vision of a sprawling 'sea of houses' (see Figure 14.4) to illustrate what could happen to the western Netherlands if urbanization was left unchecked (Van der Wusten and Faludi, 1992): the Randstad's unique structure would cease to exist, becoming instead a sprawling metropolis like any other. The first national spatial strategy (1960) argued that the Randstad, as a configuration of historically distinct cities in close proximity, had distinct advantages over large contiguous agglomerations such as Paris or London. It proposed a policy of urban diffusion away from the Randstad while preserving the Green Heart. Essentially, it was proposing a strategy for future spatial development on the basis of an outlook and supported by a speculation regarding inaction.

The approach taken by its successor, the second national spatial strategy (1966), was based on the outcome of a revised population prognosis. According to the new calculations, the Dutch population would swell to 20 million by 2000, placing more urbanization pressure on the Randstad than anticipated. Stronger containment policies would be needed to preserve the integrity of the Randstad's structure. It also advocated bundling suburban

Figure 14.4 A 'sea of houses'.
Source: De Ranitz, 1964.

development according to a principle of 'concentrated deconcentration', which led to the highly effective growth centres policy. To the extent that these policy actions had an effect on actual urbanization patterns, we can see the close interrelationship in spatial planning between thinking about the future (population prognoses) and taking specific actions to alter the future (urbanization strategies).

Soon thereafter, it was found that prognoses that gave rise to the diffusion and containment policies proved too extreme. As the growth centres policy was being implemented in the third spatial strategy, misgivings began to arise about the effects of the policy on the core cities. A 1984 report on urban areas indicated that urbanization should be bundled. In the period that followed, attention shifted from the Randstad as a whole to individual city regions. The tenor of the 1988 fourth spatial strategy reflects this: international competition took place between cities, and sufficient infrastructure, especially to important transport hubs or 'mainports'. The status of the Randstad concept in the fifth national spatial strategy (2001), never ratified due to a sudden electoral change, was equally as low: this document focussed instead on 'urban networks'. At the same time, a professional organization attempting to keep the concept alive rebranded it as the Deltametropolis.

It was not until the mid-2000s that the political discussion on the future of the Randstad resurfaced. Headlines that the region had slipped in rank as a business environment, the critical assessment of the Randstad's competitiveness by already discussed OECD outlook (2007), and calls for a Randstad province to ease the administrative burden (CVR, 2007) were contributing factors (Evers and De Vries, 2012). In 2006, member of parliament Wolter Lemstra, with unanimous support, called on the government to come up with a long-term vision for the Randstad (Vink and Wieringa, 2009). This would be the first and only time such a document would be produced.[4]

The Ministry of VROM answered the call by commissioning a series of outlooks on how the Randstad compared to similar metropolitan regions (Ministerie van VROM, 2008). In the Spring of 2007, it published a memorandum announcing that it would draw up a strategic vision for the Randstad in 2040. At the same time, and somewhat paradoxically, the intergovernmental agreement Randstad Urgent was signed, headed by the Ministry of Transport and Public Works. This had a narrower focus: namely to bring cohesion to infrastructure investments, partly by coordinating these with urbanization processes. In this sense, Randstad Urgent can be regarded as a direct response to the OECD outlook which was concerned about the accessibility of the Randstad. Although the official line was that both processes would be mutually enforcing (Randstad 2040 was formally part of Randstad Urgent), the fact that implementation (backroom political bargaining using technocratic methods) was occurring conterminously with strategic decision-making (open public consultation using design methods) is obviously problematic. The fact that the two processes were steered by competing ministries only served to underline this tension.

Towards Randstad 2040

The launch of the Randstad 2040 process was accompanied by series of activities according to the logic of the 'design-oriented planning' approach (see Figure 14.5).

As a first step, the Ministry of VROM initiated a broad debate on the future of the Randstad, involving professionals, policymakers and government officials. Participants were encouraged to provide input directly, and about 400 individuals engaged in four online discussions (Ministerie van VROM, 2008: 16). In addition, research institutes and advisory councils were asked to provide feedback on the memorandum, and preparations were put into motion on the strategic environmental assessment (SEA) as required by EU regulations.

Among the preliminary activities (step 2 in Figure 14.5) was a series of land-use modelling exercises that illustrated possible developmental pathways based on assumptions about economy, demography and the like. In their reflection on the use of land-use modelling for policy development in the Netherlands, Jacobs et al. (2011) note that, '[p]olicy-makers seem, in fact, averse to being confronted with uncertainty. They prefer a clear, singular reference point against which policy choices can be tested. Great confidence is therefore placed on the baseline conditions used for the 'what if?' simulations' (Jacobs et al., 2011: 146–147). Despite this, the models did not attempt

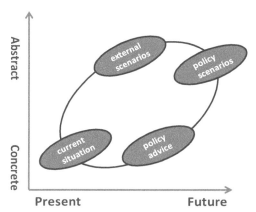

1. **Survey of conditions of study area (e.g. outlook)**
2. **Develop scenarios on basis of environmental factors that cannot be controlled**
3. **Develop scenarios where different policy actions will lead to different futures**
4. **Identify short-term and long-term actions.**

Figure 14.5 Design-oriented planning.
Source: Dammers *et al.*, 2013.

to predict future developments (e.g. a baseline or business-as-usual scenario) but provide input for the creation of scenarios. Still, significant choices were made regarding input that powerfully affected the outcomes.

> This long-term vision for the Randstad is based on trend-based and high-growth [WLO] scenarios (respectively Transatlantic Market and Global Economy). These scenarios were used because the government wishes to have the Randstad grow into a sustainable and competitive top-region in Europe. Because the future is uncertain, and trends can change, these two scenarios generate the most robust policy options.
>
> (Ministerie van VROM, 2008: 140; translation authors)

The rationale for omitting the less-dynamic scenarios assumed that the main planning challenge is to accommodate growth (Jacobs *et al.*, 2011). This decision was directly responsible for defining the subsequent planning challenge of finding space for approximately half a million new homes in the Randstad by 2040 (Ministerie van VROM, 2008).

The following spring, the vision-making process entered a new phase (step 3 in Figure 14.5). Teams of urban designers were hired to elaborate on the different ways in which the Randstad could physically develop. They were provided with three broad developmental pathways: centre city (consolidation in the capital Amsterdam), cities city (functional differentiation between Randstad cities) and park city (diffusion and interconnectedness), all of which were based on the high-growth WLO scenarios. The design challenge was then to accommodate the demand for functions according to the pathway logic.

The design workshops resulted in the production of three discrete developmental models for the Randstad: World City, Coast City and Country City (Hendriks, 2009a,b; see Text box 14.1). Whereas the pathways resembled scenarios, in the sense that they contained broad narratives about how future development could occur, the developmental models concentrated on the situation in 2040 and the policy packages necessary to achieve this. In this sense, they served as alternative visions or even plans.

A few observations can be made about the design process. One advantage of the three models is that they illustrated how certain decisions produce a path dependency that limits future decision-making. The Country City model, for example, implies car dependency – high-quality mass transit would be unfeasible in this urbanization pattern. In that sense, they do operate as scenarios rather than speculations.

> By presenting their ideas graphically, the project team demonstrated that the government could be frank about the differences between the cities [...] The maps thus helped clarify some complex policy issues. Visualization of the options also exposed their spatial consequences.
>
> (Vink and Wieringa, 2009: 23)

Looking back a few years later, the then head of the design department at the Ministry asserted that 'The design results were used, as were the outcomes of the other preparatory tracks, as input to the negotiations and discussions between politicians, local organizations and policymakers' (quoted in Hendriks, 2009a: 36–37). Here, the easy-to-digest developmental models were placed in the spotlight as the outcome of policy alternatives. Salewski (2012: 305) in a critical review of Dutch spatial design processes noted that, 'In the communication process the final image of an extreme future state is most powerful, while the underlying diachronic analysis is usually lost'. In this way, the developmental models – although produced in a different manner and for a different purpose – performed a very similar function to the ESPON integrated scenario maps.

During the next stage of transforming these insights into policy standpoints (step 4 in Figure 14.5), the discourse shifted to financial realities, short-term consequences and the administrative feasibility of each model. At this point, a mismatch seemed to emerge between the qualitative information presented (land-use patterns on maps) and the quantitative information demanded by policymakers (number of homes, kilometres of infrastructure and, above all, the amount of public investment needed for this). The models also became politicized (particularly World City which concentrated investment in Amsterdam), since '[p]oliticians find little of interest in models like these unless they happen to overlap with the objectives they have set for their own terms of office' (Hendriks, 2009b: 114). As attention increasingly focussed on the implementation of a specific model, the fundamental issue

Text Box 14.1: Three discrete developmental models for Randstad 2040

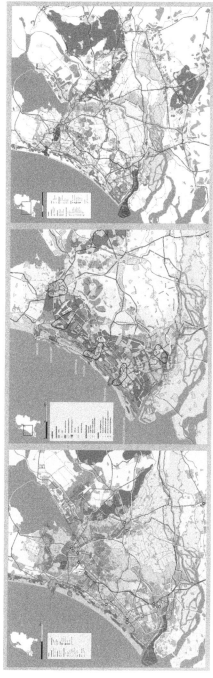

World City: this model links up to the notion of agglomeration tendencies in the global economy. It highlights the unique selling points of the Randstad such as its highly skilled labour force, attractiveness as a tourist destination and Schiphol Airport. It aims to enhance metropolitan qualities. The Amsterdam region is slated for growth, and investments focus on improving accessibility. The southern wing will receive investments in landscape, amenities, public transport and low-density housing.

Coast City: this model consists of a 'ladder' along the coast with transport infrastructure defining the stiles and rungs. It envisions compact development along the various nodes which fulfil a variety of functions. Different modalities connect the constituent parts, from light rail to motorways.

Country City: in this model, urbanization takes place where it is simplest to do so, and therefore reflects preferences of the free market. Suburban development is expected to rise in Brabant and Gelderland, entailing a dispersion from the Randstad and lower population densities overall.

Source images: Ministerie van VROM, 2008; Summary texts: Authors of trade-offs between the models in social costs and benefits receded into the background.

Like the 2007 ESPON study that immediately preceded it, one of the final challenges was to consolidate the three developmental pathways and models into a single vision or strategy. One method was to combine commonalities. For example, the underlying 'blue-green' structure of nature and water proved highly determinative of where future development should occur. This notion was taken on in the final document by identifying 'metropolitan parks' for the Randstad. In the end, the 'desirable' spatial development perspective seemed to combine elements mostly from the World City and Coastal City developmental models (see Figure 14.6).

The design process received accolades from foreign observers, including the OECD whose critical assessment was one of the motivators: 'There have been several good examples of forward-looking visions within the domain of place-based policies, such as the "Randstad 2040" vision and the preparation for an Olympic Bid' (OECD, 2010: 4). In September 2008, the government published Randstad 2040.

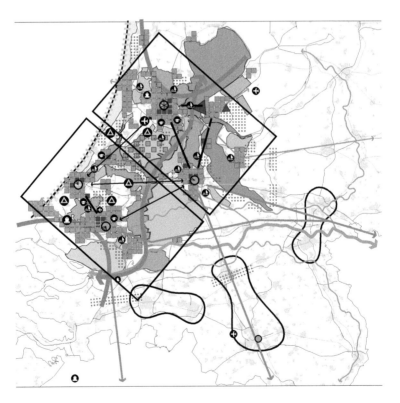

Figure 14.6 The 'Randstad 2040' spatial development perspective.
Source: Ministerie van VROM, 2008.

Performance of Randstad 2040

With the benefit of over a decade of hindsight, it is possible to reflect on the degree to which Randstad 2040 can be considered a success, and why. Still, it is no easy matter to evaluate broad-based strategic documents like this due to their long-term orientation and inherent fuzziness. Mastop and Faludi (1997) propose three criteria to assess the performance of strategic plans like Randstad 2040. First, are operational decisions sufficiently specified within the framework of the plan? Second, does the plan remain relevant if conditions change? Third, does the plan influence the decisions and actions of others? In the case of Randstad 2040, the verdict is clear. As we will elaborate below, the festivities surrounding the successful completion of the document in 2008 would be short-lived, as the economic crisis immediately eclipsed all other considerations. Two years later, the Ministry attempted to rekindle interest by means of a symposium (Lupi *et al.*, 2010), but after the 2010 elections, the new government opted instead to abolish national spatial policy almost entirely, and Randstad 2040 along with it. In the span of a few years, this vision for the future had become a relic of the past. Using Mastop and Faludi's terminology, it failed to provide a framework for decision-making, failed to remain relevant under changing conditions and, finally, failed to influence the decisions of others.

The extremely short lifespan of Randstad 2040 powerfully calls into question the value of the generating such vast amounts of studies and scenarios, consultation rounds and debate. Aside from the larger question of whether the Randstad is a suitable concept for understanding future spatial development in the first place, it is interesting to reflect on why this world-renowned planning concept failed to obtain an effective spatial plan, especially in a nation that prides itself on its strategic spatial planning. In other words, what caused the poor performance of this document?

In our analyses we posit that the performance of Randstad 2040 was hampered by problems of both probing and planning. On the one hand, deficiencies within the future-probing activities made it more vulnerable to substantive and political change. On the other hand, insufficient mobilization of political commitment (e.g. by establishing a clear framework for action) and wider societal engagement during the planning process made it less influential than envisioned.

Shortcomings regarding probing

Randstad 2040 built on a number of future-oriented studies. An outlook had identified internal weaknesses and external threats, which provided the impetus for generating a long-term strategy. In the design process, future images (speculations) were drawn up in the form of developmental models, underpinned by scenario studies such as the WLO. In theory, all the ingredients for success were present. What happened?

First, and perhaps most importantly, it can be argued that the Randstad 2040 process failed to account for uncertainty of external factors. By opting to consider only the high-growth Global Economy and Transatlantic Market scenarios, it misused the WLO scenario study. This decision committed a methodological sin of 'choosing' between environmental scenarios, which are supposed to be independent and exogenous. Scenario studies are best used to identify coping mechanisms that work well across possible futures as this produces robust potential policy interventions. Only considering one kind of future – in this case, economic prosperity – carries risks of irrelevance if reality proves otherwise.

This is precisely what happened. Despite all expectations that growth would continue, the nation was plunged, along with the majority of the global economy, into a severe recession shortly after the publication of Randstad 2040. Because it failed to account for the low-growth situation the Netherlands suddenly found itself in, its credibility as a framework to guide future decision-making diminished almost overnight. Randstad 2040 provided no real guidance on to deal with shrinkage and stagnation. Its main challenge of finding locations to build 500,000 new homes seemed anachronistic if not absurd as homeowners were increasingly faced with foreclosures and negative equity mortgages, and as construction ground to a halt throughout the Netherlands. Slogans such as 'making what's strong even stronger' rang hollow to politicians preoccupied with the economic and financial fallout of the crisis and, more concretely, how to deal with unbuilt development sites owned by municipalities in order to avoid bankruptcy. Randstad 2040 failed to account for this future and therefore lost the opportunity to make a meaningful contribution to the most important planning challenge facing the Randstad.

Secondly, Randstad 2040 failed to sufficiently account for political uncertainly. Institutional continuity cannot be taken for granted. In order to retain its relevance under changing political circumstances, a good strategy should be flexible, adaptive and contain contingency measures. One such measure is to secure commitment from a powerful, institutionally embedded organization headed by a politician of stature. Recent Dutch examples of this include the making of strategies on climate mitigation and energy transition (Klimaatberaad, 2018). This was not the case for Randstad 2040: it was supported by a weak organization coordinating various thematic 'implementation alliances' consisting of experts and civil servants delivering quite general suggestions for ongoing steps. Opting for a governance approach where the national government had assumed the role of a participant rather than a leader (Lupi *et al.*, 2010) may have undermined national-level commitment. Unsurprisingly, the follow-up process died a silent death.

Furthermore, following the 2010 elections, the Ministry of VROM, which had initiated the Randstad 2040 process, was dismantled. Its responsibilities were dispersed over other ministries, and spatial planning failed to return in name. As stated, the aim of the next government was to decentralize national spatial planning as much as possible. Only essential 'national interests' would be retained. By 2011, it announced that virtually all national planning would be abolished, including Randstad 2040. A well-known champion, together with a broad base of support for the achievements for the design process, might possibly have succeeded in arguing that Randstad 2040 was in the national interest.

Shortcomings regarding planning

The organization of the process was ambitious and aimed to quickly achieve a broad base of support. In so doing, it made some debatable choices with respect to theory. For example, several studies on complex decision-making processes in a network society suggest that effective decision-making requires full openness to society and decision-making in several rounds (Teisman, 2000). Ideally, each round is concluded when its participants are satisfied with the results, and every new round involves different participants with different considerations and institutional worldviews (De Bruijn *et al.*, 2008). In this way, content evolves and becomes more specific, locally differentiated as well as becoming more internalized as a result of co-authorship (Vogelij, 2015). Considered from this perspective, the activities of Randstad 2040 may have been too swift: the future storytelling, public consultation and professional debate, write-up and institutional embedding all happened in about a year. The process was very streamlined and efficient, but arguably too efficient to make a lasting impact on those who should carry it out. In retrospect, a slower process with more iterations and opportunities for feedback would have probably increased feelings of co-authorship, and with it, co-ownership of the outcomes (Vogelij, 2015).

A second point regards public engagement. Salewski (2012: 303) noted that scenarios are useful, even necessary, to bring planners, designers and decision-makers together, but not sufficient for the wider engagement to ensure performance. Looking back, we can observe that, despite all intentions, the work for Randstad 2040 was mainly done by the community of planning experts and civil servants and the number of participants became smaller, not larger, over time. The process began with approximately 400 people, representing a wide variety of interests and professions, but only about 60 were active in the last stage where 'implementation alliances' were supposed to take over. Rather than reaching out, the circle contracted. Rather than viewing the production of an integrated vision as an endpoint to be implemented, it should have been considered as an opening bid for a broad public debate. Since experts are not automatically trusted and often regarded as complicit political elites, consensus among the Randstad 2040 participants does not imply wide societal support. On the contrary, expert consensus – especially after such a rapid decision-making process – might enhance suspicion. On the other hand, disagreement among experts can be just as confusing: it is ironic that as this vision-making process for the Randstad was underway, opinion-makers such as Wim Derksen, Director of the Netherlands Institute for Spatial Research (RPB), argued that the Randstad does not exist (Ritsema van Eck *et al.*, 2006).

Reflection and epilogue

The Dutch are renowned for strategic spatial planning, especially at the regional and national level. Planning for future spatial development requires, as we have seen, exercises in probing the future by means of imaginative speculations, quantitative and qualitative scenarios, storytelling, and trend analyses and prognoses. All these methods are effective depending on the level of uncertainty and the public that needs to be engaged.

At first glance, the Randstad 2040 process seems exemplary. In less than two years, a vast amount of quantitative data was produced and analysed, developmental pathways identified by experts and these elaborated into alternative developmental models. The best aspects of each model were subsequently synthesized into an integrated vision for the Randstad, and teams of civil servants and experts were charged with carrying this out. It is not surprising that the OECD was impressed by the swiftness and elegance of the textbook design process.

Given this, the failure of this process on all counts of performance is astonishing. With the benefit of hindsight, some cracks in the edifice can be identified that can serve as warnings or lessons for future probing and strategic planning processes. First, it was not completely clear which policy actions the strategy was supposed to guide. Its status as a project within the coterminous operational program Randstad Urgent (rather than the other way around) is illustrative. Second, Randstad 2040 was not robust enough to adapt to changing circumstances. The decision to only consider high-growth options on the eve of an economic crisis prevented it from providing guidance within the new context of stagnation. Subsequently, the vision was quickly viewed as outdated and irrelevant. Finally, if the strategy had enjoyed popular support and secured political ownership, it would have been more difficult to abolish it so soon after its publication (Ministerie van IenM, 2012).

Aside from a small circle of professionals who may remember it, Randstad 2040 has faded into obscurity. National planning has become dismantled and more oriented to implementing sectoral objectives such as infrastructure and the energy transition rather than urbanization (Zonneveld and Evers, 2014). At the time of writing, a new national strategy is being drawn up as required by the upcoming Environment and Planning Act, which seeks to resolve competing land-use claims for energy, nature, agriculture, infrastructure, and urban development. Like Randstad 2040, the future is being probed using all the methods described above, resulting in an extensive body of information and stories about alternative futures. It is to be hoped that history will not repeat itself by restricting the scope to only those scenarios viewed as likely or interesting, or by failing to engage the wider public and mobilize political support before producing a single vision.

Notes

1 In this chapter, we recognize that these two terms are similar, but not identical. A vision presents an image of the future (or futures) and is rather vague about the underlying storyline, whereas a strategy is intended to coordinate specific actions required to reach a more general goal. Ideally, a future-oriented policy document would contain both elements.
2 More recently, the WLO scenarios provided the backdrop for perspectives on nature (*natuurverkenning*) and water. Some years later, they were elaborated at the regional level to provide insight on future demand for homes, business space and transport infrastructure (*ruimtelijke verkenningen*). These fall out of the scope of this chapter.
3 This was already apparent in the study leading up to the first national planning strategy (WWDL, 1958) that described the Randstad as a ring of urban agglomerations around a relatively open area that consisted, morphologically and functionally, of a northern and southern wing (De Boer, 1996).
4 One could argue that the 1958 report on the western part of the Netherlands (WWDL, 1958) fulfilled a similar role, but this would be mistaken as that document was drawn up by national civil servants rather than being a product of a wide political and societal debate. In addition, it was intended as advice rather than a statement of policy. In addition, thematic policy documents have been drafted at the Randstad level (e.g. green infrastructure in the 1990s), but – in addition to having limited scope – are less future-oriented. Chapter 11 discusses this report in more detail.

References

Avin, U. and Goodspeed, R. (2020). 'Using Exploratory Scenarios in Planning Practice: A Spectrum of Approaches', *Journal of the American Planning Association*, 86(4), 403–416.

CPB, Centraal Planbureau (2011). *Macro economische verkenning 2011 [Macro Economic Exploration]*. CPB, The Hague.

CPB, MNP and RPB, Centraal Planbureau, Milieu- en Natuurplanbureau and Ruimtelijk Planbureau (2006). *Welvaart en Leefomgeving [Welfare and the Living Environment]*; Een scenariostudie voor Nederland in 2040. CPB, MNP and RPB, The Hague.

CVR, Commissie Versterking Randstad (2007). *Advies Commissie Versterking Randstad [Advisory Report Committee Strengthening the Randstad]*. https://kennisopenbaarbestuur.nl/media/212235/Advies-Commissie-Versterking-Randstad.pdf (accessed 18 January 2020).

Dammers, E., Van 't Klooster, S., De Wit, B., Hilderink, H., Petersen, A. and Tuinstra, W. (2019). *Building Scenarios for Environmental, Nature and Spatial Planning policy: A Guidance Document*, PBL Netherlands Environmental Assessment Agency, The Hague.

De Boer, N. (1996). *De Randstad bestaat niet: De onmacht tot grootstedelijk beleid [The Randstad Does Not Exist: The Failure to Pursue a Metropolitan Policy]*. NAi Uitgevers, Rotterdam.

De Bruijn, H., Ten Heuvelhof, E. and In't Veld, R. (2008). *Procesmanagement [Process Management]; Over procesontwerp en besluitvorming*. Academic Service, The Hague.

De Ranitz, J. (1964). 'De distributie van ruimte' [The distribution of space]. In: Steigenga, W., De Ranitz, J. and Van Poelje, S.O. (Eds) *De stedelijke ontwikkeling in Nederland [Urban Developments in the Netherlands].* Nederlandsche Maatschappij voor Nijverheid en Handel, Haarlem, 77–166.

ESPON, European Observation Network for Territorial Development and Cohesion (2007). *Scenarios on the Territorial Future of Europe.* ESPON, Luxembourg.

Evers, D. (2010). 'Scenarios on the Spatial and Economic Development of Europe', *Futures*, 42(8), 804–816.

Evers, D. and De Vries, J. (2012). 'Explaining Governance in Five Mega-City Regions: Rethinking the Role of Hierarchy and Government', *European Planning Studies*, 21(4), 536–555.

Faludi, A. and Van der Valk, A. (1994). *Rule and Order: Dutch Planning Doctrine in the Twentieth Century.* Kluwer Academic Publishers, Dordrecht/Boston/London.

Hall, P. (2009). 'Looking Backward, Looking Forward: The City Region of the Mid-21st Century', *Regional Studies*, 43(6), 803–817.

Hall, P. and Pain, K. (Eds) (2006). *The Polycentric Metropolis; Learning from Mega-city Regions in Europe.* Earthscan, London.

Hendriks, M. (2009a). 'Designing Without Fear – In Conversation With Henk Ovink and Jan Brouwer'. In: Blank, H., Van Boheemen, Y., Bouw, M., Brouwer, J., Feddes, Y., Van Hees, J., Hendriks, M., Ovink, H., Petersen, J.W. and Wierenga, E. (Eds) *Designing Randstad 2040, Design and Politics #2.* 010 Publishers, Rotterdam, 27–37.

Hendriks, M. (2009b). 'Designing for a Future Randstad'. In: Blank, H., Van Boheemen, Y., Bouw, M., Brouwer, J., Feddes, Y., Van Hees, J., Hendriks, M., Ovink, H., Petersen, J.W. and Wierenga, E. (Eds) *Designing Randstad 2040, Design and Politics #2.* 010 Publishers, Rotterdam, 105–116.

Jacobs, C., Bouwman, A., Koomen, E. and Van der Burg, A. (2011). 'Lessons Learned from Using Land-Use Simulation in Regional Planning'. In: Koomen, E. and Borsboom-van Beurden, J. (Eds) *Land-use Modelling in Planning Practice.* Springer, Dordrecht, 131–149.

Kahan, J.P. (2020). Educating Researchers in the Metadiscipline of Foresight. *Foresight*, Vol. ahead-of-print, No. ahead-of-print (available at https://doi.org/10.1108/FS-03-2020-0022).

Kahn, H. (1965). *On Escalation, Metaphors and Scenarios.* Preager, New York.

Klimaatberaad (2018). *Ontwerp van het Klimaatakkoord [Draft Climate Agreement]*; Den Haag, 21 December 2018. Sociaal-Economische Raad, The Hague.

Kuiper, R. (2010). *The Netherlands in the Future. Second Sustainability Outlook, The Physical Living Environment in the Netherlands.* PBL Netherlands Environmental Assessment Agency, Bilthoven.

Lupi, T., Wassenberg, F. and Pen, C.-J. (2010). *Randstad 2040 is nu! [Randstad 2040 Is Now!].* Nicis Institute, The Hague.

Masser, I. (1993). 'The Randstad: A Central Concept in Dutch Planning?'. In: Faludi, A. (Ed.) *Dutch Strategic Planning in International Perspective*, SISWO Publication 372. Netherlands Institute for Advanced Study in the Humanities and Social Sciences, Amsterdam, 87–96.

Mastop, H. and Faludi, A. (1997). 'Evaluation of Strategic Plans: The Performance Principle', *Environment and Planning B: Urban Analytics and City Science*, 24(6), 815–832.

Ministerie van IenM (Infrastructuur en Milieu) (2012). *Structuurvisie Infrastructuur en Ruimte [National Policy Strategy for Infrastructure and Spatial Planning].* Ministerie van IenM, The Hague.

Ministerie van VROM (Volkshuisvesting, Ruimtelijke Ordening en Milieubeheer) (1997). *Nederland 2030 – Discussienota [Nederland 2030 – Discussion Report]*; Verkenning Ruimtelijke Perspectieven. Ministerie van VROM, The Hague.

Ministerie van VROM (Volkshuisvesting, Ruimtelijke Ordening en Milieubeheer) (2008). *Structuurvisie Randstad 2040: Naar een duurzame en concurrerende Europese topregio [Vision Randstad 2040: Towards a Sustainable and Competitive European Top Region]*. Ministerie van VROM, The Hague.

MNP, Milieu- en Natuurplanbureau (2007). *Milieubalans 2007 [Environmental Audit 2007]*. MNP, Bilthoven.

OECD (2007). *OECD Territorial Reviews: Randstad Holland, The Netherlands*. OECD Publishing, Paris.

OECD (2010). *National Place-based Policies in the Netherlands*. OECD Publishing, Paris.

PBL, Planbureau voor de Leefomgeving (2011). *Nederland in 2040: een land van regio's [The Netherlands in 2040: A Country of Regions]*, Ruimtelijke Verkenning 2011. Planbureau voor de Leefomgeving, The Hague.

Ritsema van Eck, J., Van Oort, F., Raspe, O., Daalhuizen, F. and Van Brussel, J. (2006). *Vele steden maken nog geen Randstad [Many Cities Do Not Make a Randstad]*. NAi Uitgevers/Ruimtelijk Planbureau, Rotterdam/The Hague.

RPB, Ruimtelijk Planbureau (2003). *Scene; een kwartet ruimtelijke scenario's voor Nederland [Scene: Four Spatial Scenarios for the Netherlands]*. RPB, The Hague.

Salewski, C. (2012). *Dutch New Worlds; Scenarios in Physical Planning and Design in the Netherlands: 1970–2000*. 010 Publishers, Rotterdam.

Teisman G. (2000). 'Models For Research Into Decision-making Processes: On Phases, Streams and Decision-making Rounds', *Public Administration*, 78(4), 937–956.

Van Asselt, M., Faas, A., Van der Molen, F. and Veenman, S. (2010). *Uit Zicht: toekomstverkennen met beleid [Foresight: Future Studies with Policy]*. Wetenschappelijke Raad voor het Regeringsbeleid, The Hague.

Van der Wusten, H. and Faludi, A. (1992). 'The Randstad: A Playground for Physical Planners'. In: Dieleman, F. and Musterd, S. (Eds) *The Randstad: A Research and Policy Laboratory*. Kluwer Academic Publishers, Dordrecht/Boston/London, 17–38.

Vink, B. and Wieringa, E. (2009). 'The Way Ahead to a Randstad 2040'. In: Blank, H., Van Boheemen, Y., Bouw, M., Brouwer, J., Feddes, Y., Van Hees, J., Hendriks, M., Ovink, H., Petersen, J.W. and Wierenga, E. (Eds) *Designing Randstad 2040, Design and Politics #2*, 010, Rotterdam, 18–23.

Vogelij, J. (2015). *Effective Strategy Making; Co-designing Scenarios as a Tool for Strategic Planning*, PhD Thesis TU Delft, Series A+BE Architecture and the Built Environment #07 2015. BK Books, TU Delft.

Weterings, A., Raspe, O. and Van den Berge, M. (2011). *The European Landscape of Knowledge-intensive Foreign-owned Firms and the Attractiveness of Dutch Regions*. PBL Netherlands Environmental Assessment Agency, The Hague.

WWDL, Werkcommissie Westen des Lands (1958). *De ontwikkeling van het Westen des lands: Rapport [The Development of the West of the Country: Advisory Report]*. Staatsdrukkerij, The Hague.

Zonneveld, W. and Evers, D. (2014). 'Dutch National Spatial Planning at the End of an Era'. In: Reimer, M., Getimis, P. and Blotevogel, H. (Eds) *Spatial Planning Systems and Practices in Europe; A Comparative Perspective on Continuity and Changes*. Routledge, New York/Oxon, 61–82.

15 The (im)possible design of the Randstad

Perspectives for the future

Joost Schrijnen

Introduction: metropolitan landscapes

The city is a constructed expression of the landscape on and in which it is built. Its location determines its economic character and forms its inhabitants; in turn, it is they who knead the landscape and the city into a place of human habitation. This is how landscape, people and economy grow to become a co-alescent culture. The Dutch cities all tell this story, albeit sometimes brutally interrupted by external circumstances such as floods or war. It is often recon-firmed by taxation systems and the governance of the city and its hinterland. The power of these individual urban stories is a cultural asset in itself but, in the Netherlands, they overshadow the development of a metropolis which is occurring autonomously and largely undirected in a movement towards a Dutch, or rather 'Holland' metropolis.

Many of the major European and North American metropolises are char-acterised by a unique individual relationship between their topographical and economic position at the scale of their metropolitan space, whereby a particu-lar metropolitan landscape can be experienced. This is often reinforced by structures and buildings that are the result of the administrative power and the money at work on such a grand metropolitan scale.

How such an entirety of landscape and metropolitan structure is spatially experienced partly determines the meaning it is given by residents and visi-tors. It is this factor which exposes the 'impossibility' (or perhaps the possi-bility) of the design of the Randstad conurbation, or of the as-yet not clearly defined 'Holland metropolis'. As a spatial concept, the Randstad can be 'read' from the air or on the map as a coherent whole. But on the ground, as you move through it, its internal connections are primarily functional and there are still few, if any, structure-defining spatial elements which are part of its daily metropolitan life (examples are given below). The visitor experi-ences no positive spatiality or identity imbuing the whole entity with a strong meaning of its own, transcending the autonomous identities of the individual cities within it.

This chapter describes a number of aspects of the power of the relation-ship between landscape, economy and city/metropolis. We discern within this a path dependency (North, 1990): the past steers the present, but also allows room for new choices for the existing cities. And we see the economic power of centrality (Tordoir, 2006). As well as presenting a few international comparisons, we look at the spatial position of some of the cities within the Randstad and at their metropolitan potential from the perspective of landscape, centrality and infrastructure networks. The common thread running through this discussion is the spatial form of the structures involved, the significance of their details, and the extent to which they can interpret city and landscape meaningfully for users and visitors. This chapter also identifies examples – bright spots – from which a feasible design for a recognisable metropolitan space could possibly be derived.

Metropolitan concepts and international comparisons

There is no clear definition of the modern term, metropolis. In Ancient Greek, the word originally referred to the 'mother city' of colonies. Today we interpret it as a very large city and its surrounding urban areas, a meaning which implies a certain centrality of the core city with respect to its periphery. Other terms are also sometimes used for metropolitan areas, contiguous or otherwise, such as conurbation and, in the Dutch context at least, urban agglomeration (see, for example, Salet, 2006). Administratively, we may speak of a metropolitan region. Then there is the term 'megalopolis', for a collection of metropolises (Gottmann, 1957; Hall, 1997; Hall and Pain, 2006). Another is 'network city', which is not the same as a 'city network'; it is the distance between the component cities or their centres which determines which of these two terms is most appropriate. The Randstad, with its polycentric structure, could be called a polycentric region or a city network. The lack of a dominant centre or unified central administration (De Boer, 1996) often results in the rejection of attempts to characterise it as a metropolis (Ritsema van Eck *et al.*, 2006). Relatively recently, 'metropolitan region' has been introduced as an overarching although loosely defined concept covering parts of the Randstad – around Amsterdam, quite unashamedly, with the creation of the Metropolitan Region Amsterdam (MRA) and, rather more hesitantly, around the Randstad's 'South Wing', the Metropolitan Region Rotterdam The Hague (MRDH) (see Chapter 12 for a discussion about the metropolitan regions). Amsterdam on its own could currently be labelled a metropolis – albeit a small one (Hemel, 2016).

In this chapter, a metropolis is understood to mean: *an urban agglomeration with many residents who generate facilities which are part of the daily urban system of the surrounding region and at the same time are also relevant to the global citizen.* This assumes a perfect access network that guarantees not only internal accessibility on a day-to-day basis but also perfect external accessibility in relation to other cities and metropolises across the continent and the rest of the globe. Such a region need not necessarily be monocentric, or contiguous, but it does require an airport with an extensive network of preferably direct connections and economic, cultural, administrative and sporting facilities of global stature.

The Randstad already satisfies these conditions to a reasonable extent, even though it makes no co-ordinated effort to do so, but it could do even better. We might try to imbue the Randstad with the image of a metropolis, but in reality, it still consists of separate cities with strong identities of their own. Of these, the MRA is the most metropolitan, with a huge number of facilities to match, such as interaction environments (De Hoog, 2013; see also Chapter 10). There is good reason why more than two-thirds of the tourists entering the Netherlands at Schiphol Airport have Amsterdam as their destination (Boonekamp *et al.*, 2014). The Randstad is neither experienced as a whole spatially nor governed as one administratively; it is an expanding but fragmented conurbation, rooted in municipal and district-based concepts of urbanisation which have started to touch or overlap as they grow. This history, in conjunction with the fact that the surrounding and interior countryside is regarded mainly as a space for agricultural production, does nothing to contribute to a possible future for the Randstad as a coherent Holland metropolis. Other urban agglomerations such as Arnhem-Nijmegen and Eindhoven (where officials are already using the 'metropolitan region' label) also confirm the centrality of Amsterdam through faster links which effectively bring them more firmly within its orbit.

For a number of the old, traditional metropolises elsewhere, things are different. Due to growth, the concentration of power and money and the spatial structure that can be experienced by residents and visitors, Paris, London, Berlin, New York, Los Angeles and San Francisco, to name a few, are recognisable entities at the metropolitan level. Even though they too sometimes have far from perfect forms of governance. That does not undermine their metropolitan identity and image however. Paris has the Seine, for instance, plus the strong axis of the Champs-Elysées, the Bois de Boulogne, the Haussmann buildings and the hills looking down on its urban maelstrom. London has the Thames, Oxford Street, the theatre and museum districts, the city parks, the Underground and its orbital routes. Berlin has the Brandenburg Gate and Tiergarten, Friedrichstraße, Potsdam and Lake Wannsee. San Francisco – the same size as the Randstad, with as many inhabitants plus a large number of universities – has the Bay, the Golden Gate Bridge, the ocean and the Bay Authority. Los Angeles has the ocean and Santa Monica, the view of Hollywood and the outlook from Hollywood of the metropolis with its grid-pattern streets. Last but not least, New York has Manhattan and the Hudson River, the Statue of Liberty, the bridges, a bewildering variety of neighbourhoods and the vistas of the city, as well as those from it to other metropolitan spaces such as New Jersey. This all involves the same principles: visibility and experience of a metropolitan scale stretching for miles, defined by major landscape features and, within them, urban design and architectural structures and objects. And, on top of that, they have all the functional features mentioned in the definition above, especially the everyday accessibility of outstanding amenities which also form part of a set of legal, financial, cultural, administrative and economic institutions of global standing.

Many cities, two metropolitan regions

Amsterdam and its Metropolitan Region (MRA)

Amsterdam originated in a delta wetland of the River Amstel and the *Zuiderzee* ('Southern Sea'), a bay of the North Sea (Feddes, 2012; see also Chapter 3). The mediaeval city and its seventeenth-century extension formed concentrically, oriented towards the IJ and the *IJmeer* (Lake IJ) in the east, bodies of water which connected its port to the Zuiderzee and the rest of the world. Inland, numerous waterways linked Amsterdam to other towns and markets in the hinterland. With the arrival of the railways in the nineteenth century and the emblematic positioning of their Central Station in the IJ, right in the middle of the old port in the heart of the city, Amsterdam emphatically reoriented itself towards this new mode of transport. At about the same time, the completion of the North Sea Canal in 1876 moved its focus westwards from the IJmeer in the east. Later, the construction of the Afsluitdijk enclosing dam transformed the open Zuiderzee into the *IJsselmeer* (Lake IJssel). Until well into the nineteenth century, Holland's natural water infrastructure shaped the city's economic and spatial structure. In the second half of the twentieth century, important new orientations emerged: to the north-east, the new town of Almere and the IJsselmeer polders, and to the south-west, Schiphol Airport as the hub of a yet another new mode of transport.

In 1992, the city council decided that these new orientations should be acknowledged with the development of the *Zuidas* (Southern Axis) as the Netherlands' principal business district and as the fulcrum of a broader Schiphol-Almere development corridor (Majoor, 2007; Trip, 2008). This triggered a dramatic reorientation of Amsterdam's economic focus away from the IJ and towards Schiphol, a shift which is still underway (see Chapter 8). At the same time, though, the rings of its orbital motorways and railways reconfirm the concentric structure of the old city, whilst Haarlem, Zandvoort, Purmerend, Zaanstad, the Hilversum region (Het Gooi) and Almere have all become part of Amsterdam's metropolitan centrality because of that structure. The concentration of employment and culture in Amsterdam, the existing regional infrastructure and Amsterdam's 'finger city' concept (as detailed in the 2012 Structure Plan), all re-emphasise the city's topographical beginnings on the IJ. This presents an opportunity to redefine the IJ and IJmeer as a central urban recreational area of the Metropolitan Region Amsterdam (a partnership of 32 local authorities, two provinces and the Amsterdam Transport Authority), as long as Almere and Amsterdam are prepared to focus more upon these 'blue structures'. In short, it is a small, compact metropolis rooted in natural landscapes. Amsterdam may possibly become the centre of the Holland metropolis if its connections with other urban regions and centres are accelerated. This is a spatial and economic path dependency which should be cherished and stimulated.

The Hague, Rotterdam and their Metropolitan Region (MRDH)

'Royal Residence City, The Hague on Sea' was founded and grew on coastal sand ridges bordering a large peat wetland. The Hague has traditionally been the seat of princes and government (see Meijers, *et al.*, 2014) in the decentralised unitary state that is the Netherlands (Toonen, 1987). Historically, the rich lived comfortably on the sandy ground and the poor on the peat bogs, with the centre of government in the transitional zone between the two landscapes. Due to the particular circumstances around the beginning of the twentieth century, the Peace Palace was built in this neutral, somewhat dull administrative city. Since then, by tenaciously extrapolating that one event into a form of path dependency (governance, public service, neutrality), The Hague has made itself the third city of the United Nations, the self-styled 'international city of peace and justice' and home to numerous NGOs, with a living environment to match and Schiphol Airport just a short distance away. Inclusion in a network of fast rail links to European capitals would also seem obvious, but in that respect, its position remains relatively poor.

Rotterdam has evolved from a port city into a riverside city (Meyer, 1999) with the world's tenth-largest port, and still the biggest in Europe by far. The development of the Rotterdam region parallel to the river is reflected in its diamond-shaped metro and motorway systems, with business parks and the airport shielded from the landscape on the north side, and on the south side the almost completely urbanised island of IJsselmonde. It would not be natural for Rotterdam to opt for an exclusive orientation, be that towards the Randstad, towards the Rhine-Meuse Delta and Antwerp, or towards Germany. Given its location, the city has to involve all these areas in its urban and economic performance. Internally, meanwhile, its reorientation towards the river is now leading to a recentralisation, clearly visible in the skyline, with the result that the importance of other centres is being reduced.

Rotterdam and The Hague are both too small to host a true metropolitan culture and the associated amenities. Because of their different but equally skewed demographics (young, not well-educated and relatively poor on the one hand, wealthy and ageing on the other), they lack the diversity needed to support complete metropolitan programmes in their own right, although both do have metropolitan facilities of importance to the Randstad, or the Holland metropolis, as a whole. The hypothesis implicit in their co-operation under the banner of a single metropolitan region, namely that together Rotterdam and The Hague form a genuine metropolis, has yet to be substantiated. They share no common centrality and no vision of unifying metropolitan services and amenities for the entire MRDH. Only through massive improvement of the regional infrastructure network to enable far greater mutual use of one another's facilities is there any chance of upscaling their metro-politan status. The current wide distribution of these facilities provides for no added potential or synergy in and of itself. There are powerful landscape foundations for the urban identities of both Rotterdam and The Hague in-dividually, but none as yet for the combined metropolitan region; these still need to be created and shaped, and then they have to be programmed to function effectively within the new entity. Possible candidates include the coast, the Rottemeren (the lakes north of Rotterdam), central Delfland (the large green area between Rotterdam, The Hague and Delft) and the river delta in the south-west. Rotterdam and The Hague are currently following their own paths in developing their metropolitan facilities, based upon their own defining activities: shipping and logistics for the one, law and peace for the other. They do not necessarily share an economic future. However, the various living environments in their two city regions are complementary and so interesting as possible foundations for the intensified use of existing facilities. That will, though, require a much better regional infrastructure network and urban concentration on the infrastructure nodes.

Networks: polycentricity without boundaries?

Accessibility measured in time is one of the fundaments of facilities at the metropolitan level. Theoretically, the car would be the ideal means of access because it allows one to reach any point freely. In practice, however, that is not the case. Road traffic disrupts spatial quality (due to noise and noise barriers, air pollution, congestion issues and heavy use of space). Vehicular mobility also results in unfettered distribution of facilities, whereas concen-tration and hence accessibility by very large groups are at the heart of func-tional specialisation, in terms of providing particular facilities which imbue the metropolis with its metropolitan character and level. Public transport is therefore indispensable. The inflexibility of rail systems, however, requires a strategy whereby all parts of the urban network are used and are connected to all modalities at all public transport intersections and stops. From this per-spective, we now look again at the metropolitan regions of the Randstad, but this time in reverse order.

The South Wing of the Randstad (Leiden, The Hague, Rotterdam, Dor-drecht) is a polycentric network city *'avant la lettre'*. Transcending the auton-omy of local and national public transport franchisees and spatial jurisdictions, a transit-network development strategy was introduced at the beginning of 2000, dubbed *Stedenbaan* (Cities Line). It entailed intensified use of the space around every public transport stop, with all transport modalities connected at them (Balz and Schrijnen, 2009). However, subsequent research (Atelier Zuidvleugel, 2006; see also Balz and Schrijnen, 2009; Balz and Zonneveld, 2015) has shown that there is still considerable unused spatial capacity around all the stations. It will be a long time before there really can be an inte-grated network in the South Wing. *Nederlandse Spoorwegen* (NS, the Dutch

Railways), a national operator, runs the network of local trains (known as 'Sprinters'), whilst Rotterdam and The Hague both have their own tram systems and Rotterdam its metro system. These networks are all still focused upon their own centrality. Only recently has joint operation of the first metro line between Rotterdam and The Hague, RandstadRail, begun (see Figure 15.1). The present transport authority for the MRDH, established in 2015, still has a lot to do to achieve full system integration.

Substantial expansion of the interregional road network is taking place in the South Wing. New motorways have been built, including an important stretch of the A4, or are under construction. Among the latter is a north-south connection between the east-west A15 and A20 motorways, via the Blankenburg Tunnel under the Nieuwe Waterweg, the main shipping channel to and from the Port of Rotterdam. These major investments are increasing inter-urban traffic capacity and accessibility, and in the process shifting the emphasis from infrastructure focused primarily upon individual cities to that on a regional and metropolitan scale. The bulk of their financing comes from central government, with modest regional contributions. And their design is largely anti-urban, with numerous tunnels and noise screens.

Ambitions to transform the South Wing into a true metropolitan region should therefore no longer be hindered by an absence of transport networks. Yet that is not confirmed by its overall design. The strategy of interlinking the various modalities is still relatively new. Whilst major new station projects with relevant integration of functions and transport modalities are being developed or have been completed (see Figure 15.2 for an example), a clear programming and an overarching landscape-based strategy on a metropolitan scale are still lacking.

Figure 15.1 The final stop of RandstadRail in The Hague.
Source: Editors.

Figure 15.2 The new The Hague Central Station, a major public transport hub.
Source: Editors.

The 'North Wing' of the Randstad, meanwhile, is witnessing a series of overlapping initiatives all based upon the centrality of Amsterdam and the development of intersections along its orbital railway lines and motorways, which in places run in close parallel. Inventories of public transport stops and nodes in this region reveal that, as in the South Wing, there is still substantial free capacity for new urban development (Ram *et al.*, 2013). Here, too, major expansions of the regional road network are underway or have recently been completed. These include the second Coen Tunnel under the North Sea Canal and major improvement works along the Schiphol-Amsterdam-Almere motorway corridor. The rail network has already been upgraded with the opening of the North-South Line metro connecting Amsterdam Noord with Central Station and the Zuidas, with a possible future extension to Schiphol. Amsterdam differs from Rotterdam and The Hague, though, in that the scale and reach of its metro system remains municipal. However, a development towards a metropolitan region situated around the IJmeer and along the North Sea Canal could be stimulated through the expansion of the existing networks, for instance by a dedicated bus corridor allowing fast and frequent services between Haarlem, Schiphol and south and south-east Amsterdam in combination with the already mentioned extension of Amsterdam's metro system towards the airport.

Every attempt so far to develop a pan-Randstad public transport system has failed. Due to all kinds of institutional constraints, none have succeeded in transcending the 'wing' level. This is largely because the systems concerned are either primarily national (the NS network) or primarily city-based. In only one case, under the auspices of the MRDH, is there a focus upon the metropolitan region. Given that the process of evolution from autonomous cities in an open landscape through urban regions with a dominant centre to metropolitan regions with multiple centres has been underway for only 30 years since the early 1990s, it is understandable that the transition is still underway but restrained by physical, institutional and cultural realities.

Conclusion: the Holland metropolis within reach?

The Randstad already functions as a metropolis in a number of respects, the centrality of Amsterdam, with its broad international programme being its most powerful urban element. One new and particular aspect to this is the crucial role now played by the IT and data sector in Amsterdam: the city is emerging as one of the world's leading data hubs, with data centres spreading throughout the northern Netherlands. In the light of such success, Amsterdam people are inclined to see their city as THE Dutch metropolis. Yet it has no control over the international Port of Rotterdam with its logistical services and companies or the increasingly prominent role played by The Hague on the world stage in terms of governance, peace and justice, never mind the globally important high-tech industry of Eindhoven. The international functioning of the Randstad as a whole and of the Dutch cities individually rests on their respective historical positions in terms of trade, access to Europe, culture, higher education, research and urbanity. Perhaps the most dominant aspect now, though, without which these international orientations could not have developed in their present form, is the dependence on Schiphol Airport with its impressive global network. Further growth of the aviation sector is currently encountering considerable public resistance, however, and for the time being the creation of a single network of airports, in which Schiphol, Eindhoven, Rotterdam and Lelystad are all controlled and programmed by one entity, is thwarted by European regulations. This is despite the fact that the Royal Schiphol Group owns all four airports. However, the future of air traffic and airports has suddenly become highly uncertain due to the Covid 19 crisis.

Expanding the user base needed to maintain top-class metropolitan facilities requires greater compactness in order to increase the intensity of interaction. This can be achieved through the concept of 'borrowed size', whereby smaller cities 'borrow' agglomeration benefits from larger ones nearby (Meijers and Burger, 2015). The main condition being that the quality of connections is outstanding. Such a 'borrowed-size' situation has already been created between Rotterdam and Amsterdam, which are now linked by high-speed intercity direct trains with journey times comparable to those of a metro line. Commuters can travel from one to the other within 45 minutes. This enhances central Rotterdam's appeal as an international place to live and work, just like Amsterdam.

Yet there is still no sense of urgency to develop a metropolis on the 'Holland scale'. There are no governance structures at this level, and no ambitions in this direction on the part of national government. Nor is there any guiding concept or pattern of facilities that speaks of any metropolitan aspiration. No Olympic Games, no World Expo, no football World Cup. Whilst studies are being undertaken into the kind of investments which might help strengthen spatial economic cohesion between the northern and southern Randstad (the wings) and Eindhoven in an international context (REOS, 2017), there is little public or administrative support for activities on this scale or for a strategy targeted at this level. Indeed, such notions are more likely to attract accusations of megalomania fuelled not least by a recent history of massive budget overspends on major rail infrastructure projects including the Betuwe Route, an international rail freight railway between Rotterdam and Germany, and the high-speed passenger line from Amsterdam to Brussels and beyond. There is no common urban or landscape identity that reflects a shared vision on a higher scale. The 'Green Heart' belongs to the farmers, not the city, the coast to Zandvoort or The Hague, the rivers to Nijmegen or Rotterdam, the IJ to Amsterdam.

Then there is the time-lag in national spatial planning. Both the Third Report on Spatial Planning in the 1970s and its successor, the Fourth Report (Extra) in the late 1980s and 1990s, sought to concentrate urban development at the level of city regions and deliberately not on the scale of the larger Holland metropolis, including its connections with the Arnhem-Nijmegen and Eindhoven regions. The 2019 Draft 'National Strategy on Spatial Planning and the Environment' does not have a clear spatial vision, let alone a strategy on this level. The spatial, administrative and mental impediments outlined above, plus the fact that the Dutch government has pulled out of financing major projects on this scale, and has not appointed any regional or metropolitan entity to do this in its place, will make it difficult to properly guide and facilitate the inevitable growth of the Holland metropolis in spatial terms. Nevertheless, that metropolis seems to be forming naturally.

References

Atelier Zuidvleugel (2006). *Werkboek 004: Stedenbaan [Work Book 004: Cities Line].* Atelier Zuidvleugel, Den Haag).

Balz, V.E. and Schrijnen, J. (2009). 'From Concept to Projects: Stedenbaan, The Netherlands'. In: Curtis, C., Renne, J.L. and Bertolini, L. (Eds) *Transit Oriented Development; Making it Happen.* Ashgate, Farnham, 71–90.

Balz, V. and Zonneveld, W. (2015). 'Regional Design in the Context of Fragmented Territorial Governance: South Wing Studio', *European Planning Studies*, 23(5), 871–891.

Boonekamp, T., Veldhuis, J. and Lieshout, R. (2014). *Korte- en middellange termijn prognosemodel luchthavens [Short and Midterm Prognosis Model for Airports], Vervoersprognose voor Nederlandse luchthavens.* SEO, Amsterdam.

De Boer, N. (1996). *De Randstad bestaat niet: De onmacht tot grootstedelijk beleid [The Randstad Does Not Exist: The Failure to Pursue a Metropolitan Policy].* NAi Uitgevers, Rotterdam.

De Hoog, M. (2013). *The Dutch Metropolis; Designing Quality Interaction Environments.* THOTH, Bussum.

Feddes, F. (2012). *A Millennium of Amsterdam; Spatial History of a Marvellous City.* THOTH, Bussum.

Gottmann, J. (1957). 'Megalopolis, or the Urbanization of the Northeastern Seaboard', *Economic Geography*, 33(3), 189–200.

Hall, P. (1997). *Megacities, World Cities and Global Cities*, Megacities Lecture No. 1. Stichting Megacities 2000, Haarlem.

Hall, P. and Pain, K. (2006). *The Polycentric Metropolis: Learning from Mega-City Regions in Europe.* Earthscan, London.

Hemel, Z. (2016). *De toekomst van de stad: een pleidooi voor de metropool [The Future of the City: A Plea for the Metropolis].* Amsterdam University Press, Amsterdam.

Majoor, S. (2007). 'Amsterdam Zuidas: The Dream of 'new urbanity''. In: Salet, W. and Gualini, E. (Eds) *Framing Strategic Urban Projects; Learning from Current Experiences in European Urban Regions.* Routledge, London, 53–83.

Meijers, E. and Burger, M.J. (2015). 'Stretching the Concept of "borrowed size"', *Urban Studies*, 54(1), 269–291.

Meijers, E., Hoogerbrugge, M., Louw, E., Priemus, H. and Spaans, M. (2014). 'City Profile: The Hague', *Cities*, 41, 92–100.

Meyer, H. (1999). *City and Port; Transformation of Port Cities London, Barcelona, New York, Rotterdam.* International Books, Utrecht

North, D.C. (1990). *Institutions, Institutional Change and Economic Performance.* Cambridge University Press, Cambridge.

Ram, M., Gerretsen, P., Jaffri, S., Chorus, P. and Witteman, B. (2013). *Maak plaats!: Werken aan knooppuntontwikkeling in Noord-Holland [Making Places!: Working towards the Development of Nodes in North-Holland].* Provincie Noord-Holland/Vereniging Deltametropool, Haarlem/Rotterdam.

REOS (2017). *Ruimtelijk-Economische Ontwikkelstrategie Noordelijke Randstad, Zuidelijke Randstad en Brainport Eindhoven [Spatial-Economic Development Strategy Northern Randstad, Southern Randstad and Brainport Eindhoven]; Uitvoeringsprogramma 2017–2018.* [REOS Cooperation Network], s.l.

Ritsema van Eck, J., Van Oort, F., Raspe, O., Daalhuizen, F. and Van Brussel, J. (2006). *Vele steden maken nog geen Randstad [Many Cities Do Not Make a Single Randstad].* Ruimtelijk Planbureau/ NAi Uitgevers, The Hague/Rotterdam.

Salet, W. (2006). 'Rescaling Territorial Governance in the Randstad Holland: The Responsiveness of Spatial and Institutional Strategies to Changing Socio-economic Interactions', *European Planning Studies*, 14(7), 959–978.

Toonen, T. (1987). 'The Netherlands: A Decentralised Unitary State in a Welfare Society', *West European Politics*, 10(4), 108–129.

Tordoir, P. (2006). 'Sporen naar een dubbelstad Amsterdam-Almere' [Trajectories towards a Twin City Amsterdam-Almere], *Rooilijn*, 39(7), 342–347.

Trip J.J. (2008). 'What Makes a City: Urban Quality in Euralille, Amsterdam South Axis and Rotterdam Central'. In: Bruinsma, F., Pels, E., Rietveld, P., Priemus, H. and Van Wee, B. (Eds) *Railway Development; Impacts on Urban Dynamics.* Physica-Verlag HD, Heidelberg, 79–99.

Part V

Conclusion and outlook

16 Conclusion and outlook

Wil Zonneveld and Vincent Nadin

In this final chapter we briefly review the evidence to address the questions posed in the introduction: in summary, did the Randstad come about through deliberate intervention, has spatial planning influenced the spatial configuration of the region to help meet social and economic goals, what are the advantages and disadvantages of the spatial configuration of the Randstad, and what is the outlook for the future Randstad?

Did the Randstad come about through deliberate intervention?

"God created the earth, but the Dutch created the Netherlands" is a well-known saying about the country. It emphasises that the outlook of the country is not just influenced by its inhabitants but they also have moulded and shaped the territory. Is the Randstad indeed a creation? Is the Randstad human-made? The concept as such, a genuine metaphor emphasising its ring-shaped morphology, certainly is an invention as discussed in Chapters 6 and 11. But what about the urban structure itself? According to Meyer (Chapter 3) history is not as straightforward as the above proverb suggests. The first people settling in the Randstad area thousands of years ago did not have much choice about where to live. Subtle height differences of a few meters in an otherwise flat and flood prone country determined where people could build their home. However, through agriculture and drainage of wet peat soil they almost immediately started to shape their surroundings in a seemingly endless game of subsidence through oxidation of peat and getting rid of water which causes this oxidation. A wide range of hydrological inventions and interventions throughout the centuries (dams, dikes, sluices, windmills and diesel pumps) created a canvas for the development of the Randstad and its cities and towns.

Recent history shows that the capriciousness of the Dutch delta is becoming increasingly visible and tangible and the vulnerability of the territory is becoming ever more urgent in a context of climate change, sea level rise and volatile weather conditions. For instance, the Rhine river basin is nearly six times bigger than the land surface of the entire country, meaning that heavy precipitation in this gigantic hinterland can lead to serious flood risk downstream. The rather technical approach towards delta management developed over the course of decades and even centuries, and directed towards, water containment comes up against its limits. 'Room for the River' is currently the leading principle which is also gaining a foothold abroad, further upstream in the river basins of Rhine (and Meuse). Accommodating and working with the natural water system is also taking root in how Randstad cities are currently planned, as shown by the example of Rotterdam (Chapter 4).

From a historical perspective the question of whether the Randstad is the result of deliberate interventions can be addressed by investigating how 'rulers' over the course of time contributed to the (economic) fortunes of the individual cities of the Randstad. Brand (Chapter 2) shows how specific advantages given to cities, for instance trading and taxation rights in medieval times, had a clear influence on the economy of cities and through that, on population growth. This resulted in a constantly changing hierarchy between cities although the pattern becomes more stabilised in the modern age, from about 1800 onwards.

In the twentieth century not monarchs but the state through spatial planning becomes important, especially after WWII when the limited role of the state concerning mainly infrastructure development expanded quickly into many other fields of spatial development, alongside social and economic life. There is ample ground to say that the welfare state created from the late 1940s onwards clearly included a territorial dimension. One can summarise the post-war strategy towards the Randstad as reviewed by Zonneveld (Chapter 11) as directed towards balanced development: avoiding the growth of massive cities and agglomerations and safeguarding the openness of rural spaces between the Randstad cities as a public good, just like the creation of parks and parkways was added as a principle of late nineteenth and early twentieth-century town planning. Spatial planning not only became a Randstad project but even a national project, aiming for a fair(er) distribution of economic opportunities and welfare across the country right up until the mid-1980s: territorial cohesion *avant la lettre* (Faludi, 2007). The Netherlands was not the only country to deploy such policies, but the connections between spatial planning and regional policy were probably much closer than anywhere else. Also, housing policy became part of the Dutch post-war territorial welfare project (Chapter 9), providing good quality housing for lower-income groups not only in the main (Randstad) cities but from the 1970s onwards in the *groeikernen* (growth centres). This is often referred to as the marriage of convenience between the two policy systems of housing and planning. This marriage lasted until the early 2000s and was ended not by a divorce but by a phasing out of both policy systems.

Urban containment and controlling urban sprawl as prime objectives of the Randstad strategy leads to the question: was this strategy effective? Did policy interventions have a clear influence on the map of the Randstad? Answers can be found in Chapter 7 and in particular in Chapter 13, although causality between planning ('input') and outcome ('output') is always rather difficult to establish. The answer in short is that (national) planning had an influence. It was possibly more decisively through 'positive' policy tools like the support of the development of growth centres in the 1970s and 1980s, and compact city locations during the following two decades, than through negative instruments like curbing the growth of smaller towns and villages through directives from national government to provinces and municipalities prescribing the content of regional and local plans. The reason is that the Dutch spatial planning system has a rather decentralised orientation leaving room for discretion at provincial and municipal levels. It is for this reason that Van der Wouden (Chapter 13) concludes that the reputation of Dutch national spatial planning of being effective in containing urban sprawl is unwarranted, or at best only partly justified. Others, like Korthals Altes (2006) would say (in paraphrase), count your blessings, as during a period of several decades massive housing production took place on locations selected, stamped and approved by the planning system, and thus the possibility of much more dispersed urban development was avoided.

Looking at the effectiveness of spatial planning in the Randstad from this perspective is instructive. One of the prime ambitions of early national spatial planning was to prevent the Randstad becoming one single contiguous *megalopolis* (the noun is a nice example of framing) invading the quintessential Dutch *polderscape*. This certainly did not happen, although the Rotterdam-The Hague area comes close to it if one includes greenhouse complexes and the giant Rotterdam port area in the picture, as is clearly shown in Figure 1.1. But even there, government decided to invest in the preservation and restructuring of a green space to serve as a leisure area for the surrounding cities and towns: *Midden-Delfland*, nowadays a *Bijzonder Provinciaal Landschap* (Special Provincial Landscape).

Being effective to prevent the forming of a megalopolis has an important side effect, at least according to some observers: genuine *metropolitan* environments are rather scarce in the Randstad. We came across these environments in Chapters 10 and 11. The makers of the 1966 Second National Report on Spatial Planning regarded the Netherlands as a whole as well as individual (Randstad) cities as too small for 'top class' environments which can be found in large, concentrated mononuclear cities. Later on, opinions changed, for instance under the early 2000s concept of the Randstad as an integrated Deltametropolis (Chapter 11). De Hoog in Chapter 10 shows how so-called interaction environments, places for personal encounters and for the exchange of persons, goods (including cultural 'goods' like music, theatre or museological productions), capital and information, are today scattered over the Randstad (together forming the Holland Cluster), while at the same time concentrated in the main cities, spilling over in ever larger areas, in particular in Amsterdam.

The answer to the overall question above is unsurprisingly rather mixed and varied. Yes, deliberate interventions played a role, but these interventions show an enormous variety over time, from specific trade and taxation rights given to individual cities in the Middle Ages to 'Delta interventions' in their broadest sense across an entire millennium. State interventions under the banner of *spatial planning* are typical for the post-WWII period and include the support of rather massive housing programmes at locations selected according to explicit planning principles and classic zoning tools to curb development at other locations. It goes too far to conclude that the present structure of the Randstad is primarily the result of spatial planning. Nevertheless, the morphology of the present Randstad is quite 'ordered', specifically as one keeps in mind the enormous extension of built-up areas in the Randstad areas during the last three quarters of a century. Without planning a far more spread out development would most certainly have taken place.

Assessing the value of the management of the Randstad's spatial configuration, its polycentricity, for its economic, environmental and social performance is a complex task. The balance of opinion is that whilst significant challenges remain, planning has steered the Randstad towards a more sustainable pattern than might otherwise have been the case, and provided a structure that offers opportunities to create more resilience in the 2020s and beyond. Some years ago the Dutch government published a small booklet called '35 Icons of Dutch Spatial Planning' (Ministerie van Infrastructuur en Milieu/Ministry of Infrastructure and the Environment, 2012). One of these icons, in fact the very first one in the list, is called 'Randstad and Green Heart'. In the light of what we have concluded we believe this was a very appropriate choice.

The Randstad: just an idea or also a reality?

The second main question this book seeks to answer is whether the Randstad is fiction or truth. Is the Randstad a metropolis of a specific nature, namely with numerous centres located in different cities but together forming an integrated whole with a clearly recognisable morphology? For Peter Hall (1966, 1977, 1984) the answer was simply 'yes' as he included the Randstad in his three consecutive editions of 'World Cities', highly impressed by the fact that the country was clearly pursuing a spatial planning strategy for the most urbanised part of the country. Nevertheless, he had some worries about the implementation of this strategy, at least in the final 1984 edition.

To be effective, continuity in policy is needed. In terms of *urban form* there has been such continuity. The Randstad model was politically accepted as it served many goals, including goals outside spatial planning, such as promoting more self-sufficiency in food production as rural areas would be protected against urban sprawl, whilst enough space is allowed for industrial ports to expand contributing to the economic modernisation of the country. It is this continuity which inspired Faludi and Van der Valk (1994) to use the term 'planning doctrine', emphasising not so much the rigidity of Dutch planning (in fact Dutch planning is an example of a largely indicative system) but the durability. The 2012 National Spatial Strategy however dropped the 50-year old ambition to maintain the Green Heart and the buffer zones such as Midden-Delfland mentioned above. In planning terms these planning spaces were handed over to the provinces. Golden jubilee festivities to mark the fiftieth birthday of the Randstad-Green Heart 'doctrine' in 2010 (if one considers the 1960 first national report on spatial planning as the birth) never took place as national government was right in the middle of shaking off what was considered a redundant policy domain.

Parallel to half a century of consistency about the (desired) morphology of the Randstad there was inconsistency in planning how to perceive functional *relationships* between the cities forming the Randstad. Over the course of years, a rich vocabulary has formed: agglomerations, city regions, conurbations, wings, Western Wing, (national) urban network and Deltametropolis to name the most important ones (see Chapter 11). The conclusion which seems to hold up to the present day is that the Randstad is formed by two wings, one in the north, centred on Amsterdam, and one in the south, centred on Rotterdam and The Hague. So, not one single 'World City' but two metropolitan regions as both areas are called.

Empirical research on the exact nature of the Randstad over the course of years has not been very consistent either, as Meijers, Burger and Van Oort show in Chapter 6. Obviously, there is substantial relational complexity in the Randstad. This brings with it the conclusion that any answer to the question of functional coherence is very much dependent on the conceptual and methodological approach adopted by the researcher(s), as well as the data being considered which, of course, depends on availability. Whether there is a Randstad is in the eye of the beholder, so to speak.

Next to spatial and relational complexity there is governance complexity. Spaans, Zonneveld and Stead show quite an interesting picture of how Dutch government (and parliament!) has struggled with the question of whether and how to adapt the administrative structure of the country to deal more effectively with spatial integration in the Randstad and in some urban regions elsewhere in the country. Observers with a heart for spatial planning will possibly feel quite happy knowing that spatial issues have always dominated discussions about the best sort of regional governance. However, they could be dissatisfied as well as so many options were considered and eventually put aside. In the end, around 2015 the Dutch government opted for the softest form of regional governance: voluntary municipal governance through so-called metropolitan regions, a terminology developed bottom-up, first of all in the Amsterdam region. For the Amsterdam municipality this was obviously an effort to claim World City status at the level of the city and the surrounding region as Zonneveld suggests in Chapter 11. A nice example of framing, not so much with images (Faludi, 1996) but through language.

All-important in the first decades of this century is the gradual phasing out of national spatial planning, which we have already touched upon. In this new context, interventions in the development of the Randstad become much more dependent on the creation of governance capacity at the local and regional levels. Whether 'soft' cooperation bodies are effective is open for debate though. As discussed in Chapter 12, the OECD is not very optimistic. However, this conclusion might be based on perceptions of governance based on hierarchical relations between administrative layers, while the 'soft' power of metropolitan regions is closely related to the consensus seeking nature of Dutch politics in general (Hendriks and Toonen, 2001).

What are the advantages and disadvantages of a Randstad spatial structure?

One of the reasons why Peter Hall included the Randstad in all three editions of his 'World Cities' book was related to what he called the 'moral of the Randstad'. For him this moral was intrinsically connected to 'polycentric quality' as opposed to world city regions taking the shape of 'urban giants' like London, Paris or New York (Hall, 1966: 121). Hall admired the Dutch solution for planning for growth: along radial corridors stretching in outward direction while keeping all the advantages of open country between the 'lines'.

> There seems little doubt that for most of the rapidly growing world cities of the present time, the Dutch solution is the right model.
>
> (Hall, 1966: 121)

Since Peter Hall wrote down these words many more urban giants have developed across the globe, many of them without the advantage which the Randstad obviously had according to Hall, thanks to its history. Dutch planners themselves called their growth model *gebundelde deconcentratie* (concentrated deconcentration). There is no overall consensus about whether the Dutch planning system has effectively dealt with deconcentration or 'urban sprawl'. Some deplore that urban growth has been transferred to overspill centres as this has led to a loss of potential metropolitan qualities (for instance: Frieling, 1983, 1997). However, others like Ritsema van Eck and Van der Wouden in this volume (Chapter 7) conclude that possibly the greatest asset of the Randstad being polycentric is its diversity of small and medium-sized cities. Diversity is also emphasised by De Hoog (Chapter 10). The lens through which he looks at the Randstad is the concept of interaction environments, which is quite novel in the literature about the Randstad. For him the Randstad looks like the assembly of big and small tents at large music festivals, each offering different types of music, art and artists. There is an abundance of interaction environments, mostly in inner city cores which together form one giant 'Holland cluster'. So diversity holds sway, again.

A big challenge for polycentric urban regions is the supply of integrated, high quality public transport. According to Schrijnen (Chapter 15), such a system at the Randstad level does not exist. Even if one goes down one level of scale, the wing level, such systems are absent he concludes, although the Rotterdam-The Hague region some years ago acquired a new system with the somewhat misleading name Randstad Rail. Schrijnen's vision might be a bit too harsh as the network of the *Nederlandse Spoorwegen* (*NS*, the state-owned national railway company) in the Randstad area is gradually becoming a kind of proxy of a metropolitan rail system through the frequency of services (also through the night on some lines) and because main stations (the central stations in all four main Randstad cities, plus the national airport and Amsterdam South) have become hubs connecting the NS networks with regional and local public transport systems. Possibly the biggest policy failure, to use this grand term, is the lack of integration between spatial planning and (public) transport planning throughout the years.

Does the Randstad as a polycentric urban region face economic disadvantages as agglomeration economies seem to be less strong compared with concentrated urban regions? A concept which is getting a foothold in this discussion is 'borrowed size', originally coined by the planner and economist William Alonso (Alonso, 1973). According to Meijers and Burger (2017) borrowed size occurs when a city possesses urban functions and/or performance levels normally associated with larger cities. According to them, this is made possible through interactions in networks of cities across multiple spatial scales. These networks serve as a substitute for the benefits of agglomeration. The final verdict whether borrowed size holds for the Randstad or its constituent parts varies. An OECD study (OECD, 2016) suggests that the borrowed size effect does seem to occur in smaller urban regions but not at higher levels of scale such as the Rotterdam-The Hague region, let alone at the level of the Randstad.

If one summarises the above discussion, which of course cannot be complete as there are many dimensions at stake, then possibly the biggest advantage of the Randstad and its wings as polycentric urban regions is that they create 'liveability': a large diversity of living and working environments and access to open spaces outside cities, ranging from polder areas to a largely unspoiled coast with urbanisation right up to the seafront in only a few places, mainly Scheveningen, Noordwijk and Zandvoort. It is exactly this that the 1950s inventors of the Randstad as a planning concept had in mind: recognisable cities and towns of limited size with clear perimeters and accessible open space for 'recreation' around and in the centre of the Randstad. This legacy will be valued in the post-pandemic Netherlands. Nevertheless, cities have become much larger than they had in mind and also suburbanisation has gone further. A 'sea of houses' did not emerge, but for truly empty horizons and dark skies (plus higher than average sunshine) one has to visit the Wadden islands in the north of the country.

Outlook: future challenges and the role of spatial planning

At present, inhabitants of the Randstad do not worry a lot about their geographical situation, although apart from a rather narrow coastal zone the Randstad is located in areas below sea level, sometimes even several metres the famous Dutch polders. Nevertheless, this poses risks, even now. In the case of river dikes or the dune ridge breaking large areas will be inundated quickly (PBL, 2009). A major part of the Randstad is vulnerable as protection comes from one single dike which surrounds roughly all the areas south of the North Sea Canal, north of the Nieuwe Waterweg and Hollandsche IJssel and west of Utrecht (about this so-called Dike Ring 14 see for instance: Oost and Hoekstra, 2007). So, if there is one major challenge for the Randstad, in particular in the long run it is sea level rise in combination with an increasing seepage of saltwater. The situation is not helped by the fact that the soil of large parts of the country, particularly in the west and north, is subsiding at a speed faster than the rise of the sea level thanks to the withdrawal of groundwater (Koster *et al.*, 2018), a problem shared with many other delta areas across the globe. So far measures taken have a time horizon of 2050. Cautiously possible scenarios with a time horizon of 2100 and beyond are discussed. In particular engineers come up with technical solutions like the closure of the port of Rotterdam through a large sluice complex and the installation of very large pumps as a free fall of river water into the North Sea and Wadden Sea becomes difficult, especially at high tide. For some the prospect of a 'move' of the Randstad to higher ground in the long run comes in sight, a possibility mentioned in Al Gore's film 'An Inconvenient Truth'. This scenario is known as 'Amersfoort at Sea', as the city of Amersfoort is the only Randstad city situated on higher ground at a distance of about 65 kilometres from the coast.

Others are less pessimistic. For example, a group of researchers from Wageningen University developed an interesting scenario of how the country could look in 2120. Interestingly the shape of the country is still there while also the basic configuration of the Randstad has not changed either. However, all major urban agglomerations in the Randstad are to become interspersed with so-called green-blue arteries. Also, all new urban areas will be built on higher ground, in the east and south of the country and immediately east of Utrecht (see Figure 1.1 for the location of this city). This would lead to a shift of the centre of gravity of the Randstad to the east, the only critical change in its shape. Another major change is a complete overhaul of how rural areas are used. The only sort of agriculture to be found is circular while there is much more room for water. The Netherlands would no longer be the second food exporting country on the globe. Finally, another major intervention is how the country should be protected against floods: much more room for the rivers and a soft, forward type of sea defence. There are no vast dikes in this scenario.

Coming from Wageningen University (the former *Landbouwuniversiteit*: University of Agriculture) there is a particular sort of emphasis on rural areas, water and nature which this scenario combines with a soft engineering approach. There is for instance limited attention to the energy transition: this takes largely place on the North Sea through floating 'sun fields'. Whether this would be sufficient remains to be seen as the energy transition is another major challenge which the Randstad and the country as a whole is facing and which will remain critical in the coming decades. Scenario studies point out that the energy transition is rather space consuming, leading to (vast) 'energy landscapes' irrespective of whatever sort of non-fossil-based energy production takes place (Sijmons *et al.*, 2014).

Onshore energy landscapes are already taking shape but in a highly uncoordinated fashion. Targets for wind energy are formulated for each of the 12 provinces but there is not very much coordination between the provinces in the absence of overall principles for the location of wind turbines. On top of that, the environmental gains of wind energy are leaking away through the arrival of very large data centres of global technology firms. They are highly interested in a location in the Netherlands, either within the Randstad or in areas nearby the Amsterdam Internet Exchange node – one of the largest globally – as they can 'green' themselves through the ample availability of wind energy (which is partly paid for through taxation of energy use by households!). The biggest of these data centres use as much energy as the entire city of Amsterdam, which presents another reason for more coordination and guidance.

Another major challenge the country faces, that particularly affects the Randstad, is the availability of housing, both in number as well as price. The four main Randstad cities are struggling, Amsterdam in particular is a very attractive residential location, while the housing stock is under pressure thanks to tourism and Airbnb (Nieuwland and Van Melik, 2020). Lower and middle-income groups find it increasingly difficult to find a home for a decent price. Annual production volumes cannot keep up with demand. Major reasons have to do with high quality requirements imposed by (local) policies (including energy consumption) and the desire to build within the present perimeters of cities to avoid out of town greenfield development. However, inner city locations are often more difficult to develop and also are more expensive. This in turn leads to a heavy emphasis on the building of apartment blocks which given the present housing culture within the Netherlands, is not everybody's choice. The problem is known as 'one million homes', based on a rough calculation of present and future shortages but also as it communicates so well. Looking back, every decade since the 1950s had a one million homes issue. The terminology has been used over and over again so has become a kind of metaphor for public intervention.

What these challenges have in common is *interscalarity* as they do not manifest themselves on one spatial scale only. Take the example of energy transition. The level of an individual building is relevant here: insulation, new cooling and heating techniques as well as 'responsible' behaviour of homeowners. The scale of neighbourhoods, districts and the city at large is important, for instance through the realisation of heating networks. Zooming out one eventually arrives at the level of north-west Europe, by looking at the North Sea as a potential area for transnational wind energy production. This is only possible through the creation of integrated networks at a larger scale (OMA, 2008). For water management, one can tell a highly similar story: from the individual building plot (less hard surfaces – roofs, gardens and streets – to make infiltration of water possible in periods of heavy precipitation) to very large water systems: sea, coasts and estuaries and large river basins.

It is this interscalarity which makes spatial planning challenging. We have seen in Chapter 11 that from the early 2000s national government gradually handed over spatial planning responsibilities to provinces and municipalities and, while doing that, reducing the concept of the Randstad to a sort of place name, so no longer having a vision on its development, let alone a strategy. In 2014 government announced another drastic step: an overhaul of all laws related to the environment, including the planning law. The 33 existing laws will be partially or entirely integrated into one single act: the Environment and Planning Act. Main objectives are simplification, deregulation and decentralisation. The act is expected to take effect in 2022.

A new (planning) act means a novel type of a national policy document. Around mid-2019 a draft of the 'National Strategy on Spatial Planning and the Environment' was published (in Dutch: *Nationale Omgevingsvisie*; see: Ministry of the Interior and Kingdom Relations, 2019). The publication of this draft was delayed for several years, largely due to a great deal of uncertainty about its content and sometimes fierce discussions between government departments as the strategy is supposed to become far more integrative than any other previous national strategy or policy report.

The strategy is based on four key objectives called priorities. However, how these priorities come together on the ground in specific territories like the Randstad is not made clear. Indeed, the document is carefully stripped of any spatial concepts which could work in this way, in stark contrast to all post-war national spatial planning reports. There is one map called 'economic core areas and links' which shows the Randstad in its classic shape made up of two 'wings' (see Figure 16.1). The map is entirely indicative though. On the other hand, one can also draw the conclusion that certain key ideas, like the very existence of the Randstad as a relevant spatial scale, have become an intrinsic part of thinking about the spatial structure of the country.

Although the 2019 (draft) strategy is admirably comprehensive in its analysis of key planning and environment issues and possible objectives of transitions and interventions, the lack of any sort of spatial concept does not give it a lot of strategic authority. We do not plead for a return to the directive planning reports of the latter part of the previous century which included planning concepts and guidelines for about every square metre of the country (the sea was not yet included). What we would like to see is more of a scenario approach using spatial design to imagine possible futures across different spatial scales and the unavoidable trade-offs between priorities and objectives. This comes close to what John Friedmann has formulated as "the role of strategic planning for the longer range":

> [...] in-depth exploration of strategic issues of urban development under different sets of assumptions or 'scenarios' as a way to assess potential

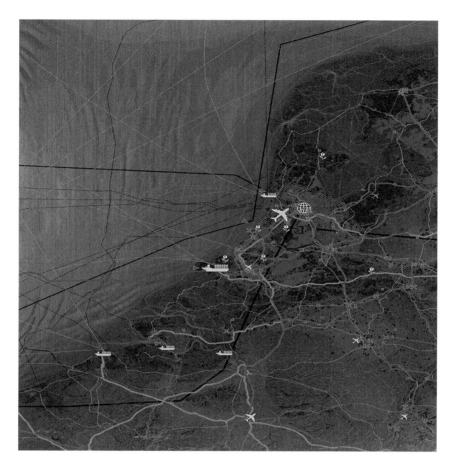

Figure 16.1 Economic core areas and international connections.
Source: Ministry of the Interior and Kingdom Relations, 2019.

outcomes and their effect on local populations, the economy and the ecology of cities. It is a way of probing the future in order to make more intelligent and informed decisions in the present. The object [...] would be not to produce 'plans' (not even strategic plans), but insights into prospective change to encourage and promote public debates about them.

(Friedmann, 2004: 56)

As the largest concentration of population, economic activity, real estate, as well as architectural and cultural heritage in the country, such 'probing the future' is highly needed for the Randstad. Apart from national government we do not think there is any other actor capable of having the capacity nor the authoritative position to organise this sort of strategic endeavour.

Epilogue

Writing the above took place in an extraordinary period, namely the weeks that the COVID-19 crisis took hold across the world. The crisis had enormous spatial consequences. The concept of social distancing alone is quintessentially spatial! There are many important planning questions, for example, related to good quality housing (think about people living in – tiny – houses with no external space whatsoever), easy access to green space and recreation, vulnerability and resilience of the urban economy including its cultural sector. The concept of interaction environment, introduced and analysed in Chapter 10, acquired quite a different meaning as suddenly interaction meant risk and danger. In our view, the spatial implications of the 2020 COVID-19 crisis are also characterised by interscalarity as even the large Randstad scale is relevant here. Spatial planning undeniably has contributed to diversity; a dispersed *world city* where cities and towns still have their own distinctive identities and where people are not locked-in in an endless 'sea of houses', the greatest fear of the 1950s makers of the Randstad concept.

We speculate that the Randstad idea – the value of a polycentric metropolis – will become more not less important in the post-pandemic future, as we see the value of avoiding damaging congestion caused by a sprawling metropolis. We will see new strategies for economic development that emphasise self-sufficiency and resilience of smaller cities and towns, more effective re-use of existing commercial urban areas, and much more attention to the natural systems that created the delta and the Randstad, as advocated by Hooijmeijer in Chapter 4. Meyer in Chapter 3 makes the radical proposition that in the long term this may inevitably involve managed decline of the Randstad cities and a move to higher ground in the east. Above all, the levels of government intervention required in the response to the COVID-19 crisis are unlikely to be undone quickly. There will be an appetite for stronger government action on managing the spatial development of the territory in the 2020s, in pursuit of the secure and healthy environments lauded in policy.

References

Alonso, W. (1973). 'Urban Zero Population Growth', *Daedalus*, 102(4), 191–206.

Faludi, A. (1996). 'Framing with Images', *Environment and Planning B: Planning and Design*, 23(1), 93–108.

Faludi, A. (Ed.) (2007). *Territorial Cohesion and the European Model of Society*. Lincoln Institute of Land Policy, Cambridge MA.

Faludi, A. and Van der Valk, A. (1994). *Rule and Order: Dutch Planning Doctrine in the Twentieth Century*. Kluwer Academic Publishers, Dordrecht/Boston/London.

Friedmann, J. (2004). 'Strategic Spatial Planning and the Longer Range (with comments by John Bryson, John Hyslop, Alessandro Balducci, Wim Wiewel & Louis Albrechts, and a brief introduction by Patsy Healey)', *Planning Theory & Practice*, 5(1), 49–67.

Frieling, D.H. (1983). 'Concepties en hun gevolgen' [Conceptions and their Consequences], *Stedebouw & Volkshuisvesting*, 64(6), 258–269.

Frieling, D.H. (1997). 'Verstedelijking als politieke opgave' [Urbanization as a Political Challenge], *Stedebouw en Ruimtelijke Ordening*, 78(5), 4–8.

Hall, P. (1966). *The World Cities*. London: Weidenfeld and Nicolson.

Hall, P. (1977). *The World Cities*; Second Edition. London: Weidenfeld and Nicolson

Hall, P. (1984). *The World Cities*; Third Edition. London: Weidenfeld and Nicolson.

Hendriks, F. and Toonen, T. (Eds) (2001). *Polder Politics: The Re-Invention of Consensus Democracy in the Netherlands*. Farnham: Ashgate [Reissued in 2018 by Routledge].

Korthals Altes, W.K. (2006). 'Stagnation in Housing Production: Another Success in the Dutch "planner's paradise?"' *Environment and Planning B: Urban Analytics and City Science*, 33(1), 97–114.

Koster, K., Stafleu, J. and Stouthamer, E. (2018). 'Differential Subsidence in the Urbanised Coastal-deltaic Plain of the Netherlands', *Netherlands Journal of Geosciences*, (97)4, 215–227.

Meijers, E. and Burger, M. (2017) 'Stretching the Concept of "borrowed size"', *Urban Studies*, 54(1), 269–291.

Ministerie van Infrastructuur en Milieu/Ministry of Infrastructure and the Environment (2012). *35 Iconen van Ruimtelijke Ordening in Nederland/35 Icons of Dutch Spatial Planning*. Ministerie van Infrastructuur en Milieu/Ministry of Infrastructure and the Environment, The Hague.

Ministry of the Interior and Kingdom Relations (2019). *Draft National Strategy on Spatial Planning and the Environment; A Sustainable Perspective for Our Living Environment*. Ministry of the Interior and Kingdom Relations, The Hague.

Nieuwland, S. and Van Melik, R. (2020). 'Regulating Airbnb: How Cities Deal with Perceived Negative Externalities of Short-term Rentals', *Current Issues in Tourism*, 23(7), 811–825.

OECD (2016). *OECD Territorial Reviews: The Metropolitan Region of Rotterdam The Hague, Netherlands*. OECD Publishing, Paris.

OMA (2008) *Zeekracht [Sea Power] – A Strategy for Masterplanning the North Sea*. OMA, Rotterdam, https://oma.eu/publications/zeekracht-a-strategy-for-masterplanning-the-north-sea.

Oost, J. and Hoekstra, A.Y. (2007). 'Flood Damage Reduction by Compartmentalization of a Dike Ring: Comparing the Effectiveness of Three Strategies', *Journal of Flood Risk Management*, 2(4), 315–321.

PBL, Planbureau voor de Leefomgeving (2009). *Overstromingsrisicozonering in Nederland: Hoe in de ruimtelijke ordening met overstromingsrisico's kan worden omgegaan [The Zoning of Flood Risks: How Spatial Planning Could Manage Flood Risks]*. PBL, The Hague.

Sijmons, D., Hugtenburg, J., Feddes, F. and Van Hoorn, A. (2014). *Landscape and Energy; Designing Transition*. nai010 Publishers, Rotterdam.

Index